THE POLYPHONIC MACHINE

D1300391

ILLUMINATIONS: Cultural Formations of the Americas

John Beverley and Sara Castro-Klarén, Editors

THE

CAPITALISM, POLITICAL VIOLENCE, & RESISTANCE IN CONTEMPORARY ARGENTINE LITERATURE

POLYPHONIC

MACHINE

NIALL H. D. GERAGHTY

University of Pittsburgh Press

An earlier version of chapter 1 was previously published as Niall Geraghty, "Ema Is by Nature a Political Animal: Politics and Capitalism in César Aira's *Ema, la cautiva*," *Journal of Latin American Cultural Studies* 23, no. 1 (2014).

Those elements in chapters 3 and 4 pertaining to Cohen's short story "La ilusión monarca" were previously published as Niall Geraghty, "Power in Transition in Marcelo Cohen's 'La ilusión monarca,'" *Bulletin of Latin American Research* 35, no. 4 (2016).

Published by the University of Pittsburgh Press, Pittsburgh, Pa., 15260
Copyright © 2018, University of Pittsburgh Press
All rights reserved
Manufactured in the United States of America
Printed on acid-free paper
10 9 8 7 6 5 4 3 2 1

Cataloging-in-Publication is available from the Library of Congress

ISBN 13: 978-0-8229-6553-4
ISBN 10: 0-8229-6553-4

Cover art: *Boy Pool Rhizome* by Mark Ingham, www.markingham.org
Cover design: Joel W. Coggins

FOR BRIAN AND BRENDAN

And we leave what is ours and all men's and God's to them that will enjoy and use it best.

After George Mackay Brown

CONTENTS

ACKNOWLEDGMENTS

IT IS PERHAPS INEVITABLE THAT WHEN YOU PUBLISH YOUR FIRST BOOK, there are more people to thank than there may ever be again. Your first book has, in a sense, taken your entire lifetime to write, and the number of people who have contributed in some almost imperceptible, seemingly inconsequential, yet fundamental way to the development of your thought and your work is incalculable. At least, that is how I feel. There are more people to whom I owe a considerable debt of gratitude for contributing in this way than I can possibly name individually. The project itself developed from my doctoral research which I completed at the Centre of Latin American Studies (CLAS), University of Cambridge, and the manuscript was revised while based at the Institute of Latin American Studies (ILAS), University of London. I've thoroughly enjoyed my time at both institutions and they have provided incredibly enriching environments within which to conduct academic research. With this in mind, I wish to thank the Arts and Humanities Research Council for funding the initial research, John Beverley and Sara Castro-Klarén, the series editors, and Josh Shanholtzer at the University of Pittsburgh Press for working with me to produce this book, which is its final result.

While numerous colleagues at CLAS and ILAS have provided me with significant encouragement and assistance, there are several in particular who warrant a specific vote of thanks. As regards CLAS, first and foremost I wish to thank Joanna Page for her guidance and support throughout my doctoral studies. I could not have asked for more from a supervisor at the time, and I still count on her advice now that she has become a friend. Geoffrey Kantaris provided insightful comments and feedback on my PhD and considerable assistance beyond the remit of his official role as my advisor. I am also grateful to Rory O'Bryen for his counsel and his friendship during this period. As with all students and academics who pass through CLAS, I also owe a very special thank you to Julie Coimbra. Officially, Julie is the center's librarian, but she is much more than this, and I'm privileged to count her as a very dear friend. I also wish to thank the center's then-administrator, Sam Mather, for his support throughout my studies and his continued friendship. Within my present role at ILAS, I must also thank Linda Newson for her mentorship and support. Similarly, I am grateful to Olga Jiménez, Chloe Pieters, and Penelope Elvy. Moving further back in time, I am particularly grateful to Karen Benavente (University of Texas Rio Grande Valley) for encouraging me to pursue further academic research and to Steven Boldy (University of Cambridge) and Karl Posso (University of Manchester) for their advice and guidance when I first conceived of the present project. While I was writing the manuscript, chapter 1 appeared in the *Journal of Latin American Cultural Studies* and elements of chapters 3 and 4 were published by the *Bulletin of Latin American Research*. I am grateful to both journals for permission to reproduce these texts in the present book. I am also particularly indebted to Bernard McGuirk (University of Nottingham) and Edward King (University of Bristol) for their incisive comments on an earlier draft of the book. Their astute observations were invaluable as I reworked the manuscript for publication.

There are several groups of friends, colleagues, and family to whom I am also especially grateful for their continued advice and encouragement. From Glasgow, Jacqueline, Aileen, Sam, Scott, Fraser and Minna; from Cambridge, Guy, Catriona, Chandra, Geoff, Cherie, Rebecca, Paul, Rachel, Emily, and Mara; and from London, William, Ainhoa, Elena, and Grace all deserve an individual mention. I only hope that I can, in some way, contribute to your lives as you have to mine. My first significant experience of Latin America came not in Argentina but rather when I lived for over two years in Chimbote, Peru. Hay demasiada gente importante de esta época de mi vida para nombrarlos a todos individualmente. Sin embargo, tengo que reconocer a las familias Villar Reyes y Arias Díaz, a Adita y Corina, y a Jorge y María en particular. Gracias por todo. Conocerles ha sido un don de verdad. Y, con respecto a Buenos Aires, a mis amigos zamudianos—Gisela, Mariana, Martín y Caro—tengo que decir gracias por darme la bienvenida a Argentina y por hacerme conocer el barrio y la ciudad. Siempre me dijeron "no somos cultos" (todavía no lo creo), pero me enseñaron mucho y estoy muy agradecido.

To Adriana, for reading so many drafts of the book, for your support, and for your love, thank you. The past three years may have been difficult at times, but they have been wonderful and I cannot (nor would I want to) imagine having lived them without you. To my parents, Maureen and Edmund; my siblings, Maureen, Alistair, and Timothy; their partners, Bobby, Ximena, and Eilidh; my Grandma, aunts, uncles, and cousins, I owe the greatest thanks of all. Without your love over the course of my life this book would simply not exist. You have all been such a constant in my life that I can honestly say that whatever achievements may be ascribed to me rightfully belong to you. I wish to extend my final and most sincere thanks to Sharon Jones for first introducing me to the study of literature and for instilling a belief in me that perhaps one day I could contribute something to the field. I fondly remember your classes and am eternally grateful for everything you did for us.

THE POLYPHONIC MACHINE

INTRODUCTION

CAPITALISM, POLITICAL VIOLENCE, AND RESISTANCE IN CONTEMPORARY ARGENTINE LITERATURE

IN 1969 IN HIS SHORT TEXT "WHAT IS AN AUTHOR?" MICHEL FOUCAULT applied his investigations into the nature of power relations to literary history.[1] Some six years later, Ricardo Piglia published the short story "Homenaje a Roberto Arlt" (1975) and created a literary experiment that synthesized his previous critical work in literary form and posed the question he perceived to be fundamental to all literary criticism: "¿cómo funciona la ficción en la sociedad?" (how does fiction function in society?).[2] A brief discussion of Piglia's text from the perspective provided by Foucault's will serve to illuminate the motivations and objectives of the present study. This is not, however, meant to suggest that Piglia consciously conceived of his literary text as a meditation on Foucault's critical work. While the publication of Piglia's diary does demonstrate that the Argentine author was familiar with Foucault's writing, it is equally clear that Piglia drew on vastly different sources to create this particular text.[3] Indeed, as we shall later see, the very fact that Piglia was not directly influenced by Foucault but that the two authors consistently demonstrate parallel concerns is of particular importance in and of itself.

In Foucault's celebrated essay, he argues that "an author's name is not simply an element of speech" but is in fact "functional in that it serves as a means of classification."[4] Thus he argues that "the 'author function' is not universal or constant in all discourse."[5] Instead, each written text exists within a network of power relations in any given society, and the "author function" is a mutable concept that is shaped through their application. As Foucault traces the genealogy of the "author function," he writes that:

> First, they are objects of appropriation; the form of property they have become is of a particular type whose legal codification was accomplished some years ago. It is important to notice, as well, that its status as property is historically secondary to the penal code controlling its appropriation. Speeches and books were assigned real authors, other than mythical or important religious figures, only when the author became subject to punishment and to the extent that his discourse was considered transgressive. In our culture—undoubtedly in others as well—discourse was not originally a thing, a product, or a possession, but an action situated in a bipolar field of sacred and profane, lawful and unlawful, religious and blasphemous. It was a gesture charged with risks long before it became a possession caught in a circuit of property values.[6]

Thus, as in all his work, Foucault's analytical technique "consists of taking the forms of resistance against different forms of power as a starting point" and "of using this resistance as a chemical catalyst so as to bring to light power relations, locate their position, and find out their point of application and the methods used."[7] For Foucault it is only when discourse expressed its "transgressive" qualities that the author function came into being. A further salient point for the present discussion is that, although the function of the author's name was once to assign judgment, to decry, and to punish, following the advent of capitalism, discourse became little more than "a possession caught in a circuit of property values."

In "Homenaje a Roberto Arlt," Piglia claims to have discovered "el único relato de Arlt que ha permanecido inédito después de su muerte" (the only Arlt story that has remained unpublished after his death), and the text contains the "Arlt" story and a critical prologue and explanatory notes written by Emilio Renzi, Piglia's literary alter ego.[8] By now Piglia's literary subterfuge is well established: the text apparently composed by Arlt is in fact a plagiarized copy of a Spanish translation of a text (*Las tinieblas*) by Russian author Leonid Andreyev.[9] The Andreyev text in question was an apposite selection as it demonstrates many key features of Arlt's work, and as Ellen McCracken notes, for a time the story was catalogued as Arlt's in libraries, and certain critics "analyzed it as if it were indeed his."[10] Moreover, the conception of plagiarism as a creative endeavor creates a strong link to such stories as "Pierre Menard, autor del *Quijote*" by Argentine writer Jorge Luis Borges. Indeed, many critics note that the text effectively synthesizes the literary projects of Borges and Arlt, and several have even argued that the text could equally be titled "Homenaje a Borges."[11] Investigations in this direction have frequently led to what Bruno Bosteels characterizes as a "fairly common reading, restricted to the intertextual effects of plagiarism."[12] For the present purposes, however, rather more important are those interpretations that note that the "crime of plagiarism is not a moral or literary problem but an economic one because it violates the laws of private property," and those which follow Piglia's own reformulation of Argentine literary history in which "los mecanismos de falsificación, la tentación del robo, [y] la traducción como plagio" (the mechanisms of falsification, the temptation of theft, [and] translation as plagiarism) are the essential components of "la tradición argentina" (the Argentine tradition).[13] In the first instance, economic interpretations of Piglia's story serve to demonstrate that it resists the "circuit of property values" inscribed in the contemporary author function.[14] In the latter case, it would appear that for Piglia the fundamental feature of Argentine literary history is that it transgresses the dominant relations of power at any given moment due to its insistent contravention of the norms dictated by the author function. When it is noted that Piglia's conception of Argentine literary tradition can be traced to Domingo Faustino Sarmiento's *Facundo: Civilización y Barbarie* (1845), a text written in a vastly different political context that opens with a falsely attributed quotation,[15] it becomes apparent not only that this transgression of the author-function is intimately connected with Argentine politics, but also that the function of this transgression has changed over time in accordance with developments in the nature of power relations. Each of these features reemerges with particular force when it is remembered that in Piglia's later novel *Respiración artificial* (1980), Renzi again appears as a character and returns to the foundational text of Argentine literature (*Facundo*) in order to account for the importance of falsification in Argentine literary history.[16]

Respiración artificial shares many of the same literary preoccupations as "Homenaje a Roberto Arlt." The figures of Arlt and Borges and the connection between false attribution, plagiarism and Argentine literary history are as important to *Respiración artificial* as they are to Piglia's earlier story. However, between the publication dates of each text, the historical circumstances had significantly changed, and with them the function of literary transgression altered accordingly. I refer, of course, to the advent of Argentina's most recent and most brutal military dictatorship of 1976–1983. With regard to Foucault's analysis, it would appear that rather than simply infringing the basic tenets of capitalist circulation, Piglia's later text demonstrates that the author's name once more served to denounce and to punish and as has been consistently argued in the existent criticism, illuminates the advent of political disappearance as a technique of power. And this is precisely the point. In the first instance, the purpose of the present book is to analyze the ways in which literary texts bring to light the forms of power instigated by the military coup of 1976 through their very ability to transgress and resist the same power relations that transpierce them.

Nonetheless, recent developments in theoretical discussions of the effects of the dictatorship somewhat complicate the matter. For example, a considerable body of scholarship examining cultural texts written in the postdictatorship period has come to question the validity of the democratic transitions in the Southern Cone, arguing that the economic and political transformation from national state to transnational market was both the most significant development within these countries and the triumph of the dictatorships.[17] Moreover, within this body of work, critics such as Idelber Avelar note that the Argentine case is unique in the Southern Cone insofar as this major transformation was only partially achieved by the dictatorship itself and fully implemented by the Peronist government of Carlos Saúl Menem some six years after the return to democracy.[18] As Argentine philosopher and psychoanalyst León Rozitchner argues, precisely because transitional Argentine democracy developed "against the background of a previous dictatorship, which can always return to re-impose its violence," a "disguised terror" remained "within Menem's political democracy."[19] As Rozitchner explains, this threat was exploited to persuade the Argentine people to "submit to the law of the Market and the State."[20] Thus the dictatorship itself, the transition to democracy, and the economic transformation of the country are inseparably and deeply interconnected. Moreover, as Avelar attests, "the Argentine transition to the global market was far more unstable than that of its neighbours" primarily because "the Argentine generals confronted a working class whose degree of organization and unionization was unparalleled in the continent" and because in Argentina "the phenomenon of armed urban guerrilla emerge *before* the coup."[21] As discussions of these phenomena have largely been articulated through the theoretical conceptions of mourning, melancholy, and trauma, they have concurrently focused on the postdictatorship period.[22] However, as the conceptual focus of the present book shifts to themes of power and resistance, it stands to reason that to account fully for the radical alterations of power relations in Argentina instigated by the most recent dictatorship of 1976–1983, it is necessary to take a long historical view and consider the dictatorship together with its antecedents and its aftereffects. Moreover, as the existing scholarship makes clear, the exercise of power in Argentina throughout this long historical period is inseparably connected both with the emergence of a neoliberal state in the early 1990s and with the consistent use of political violence (ranging from the pre-dictatorship guerrilla to the dictatorship's horrendous physical violence and to Rozitchner's "disguised terror") to achieve this goal.

For the reasons outlined above, the present study does not focus on the work of one sole author but rather engages in the detailed analysis of select literary texts by the important Argentine authors César Aira, Marcelo Cohen, and Ricardo Piglia written between 1979 and 1998. Conscious of "the proliferation of allegorical structures in the literature written under dictatorship" and during the postdictatorship period but nonetheless eschewing the well-established critical focus on trauma and memory, the book traces the allusive fragments of Argentine political history woven through the texts selected.[23] Hence, the book follows the development of Argentine politics from the period of revolutionary fervor epitomized by the civil uprising of students and workers known as the Cordobazo in 1969 through the period of military rule from 1976 to 1983, the transition to democracy begun in 1983, and ultimately to the structural adjustment program implemented by Menem in the early 1990s. In developing this historical narrative, the book delineates the complex intertwining of capitalism and political violence prevalent in late twentieth-century Argentine history, examines the changing nature of power relations throughout the period, and explores the potential of literature to precipitate resistance to these political developments. Thus I contend that certain Aira novels can be considered examinations of the development of capitalism in nineteenth-century Argentina and of the revolutionary fervor of the 1960s and 1970s; that Piglia's work contains an exploration of the philosophical origin, nature, and consequences of the most recent military government; and that Cohen's early novels are a critical reflection on the sociophilosophical nature of the transition to democracy begun in 1983 and on the late capitalist society engendered by the structural adjustment program of the early 1990s.

In the introduction to his study of allegory and mourning in postdictatorship literature, Avelar prefaces the justification for his own examination of the nature of resistance in the period by stating that "if 'resistance' was once the banner under which a certain Latin American literature was written, the advent of allegory in postdictatorship certifies that resistance has become a rather modest agenda. If resistance was the axis that connected individual and collective experiences under dictatorship, now this connection must be established otherwise."[24] In my own study, the attempt to trace the development of resistance as counterpoint to the alterations in power relations from the years preceding the dictatorship to the advent of neoliberal capitalism in the early 1990s also necessitates that the connections between these periods and theoretical conceptions must be established "otherwise." To demonstrate that across the work of Aira, Cohen, and Piglia political and structural violence is deeply interconnected and entangled with the development of neoliberal capitalism in Argentina, it has been necessary, as in the work of Foucault, to focus first on resistance. Nonetheless, as Avelar intimates, traditional theoretical conceptions of resistance sustained in the years preceding the military coup were decimated during the subsequent military government and their systematic program of state terrorism that they euphemistically referred to as the "Dirty War." For this reason I contend that each author conducts philosophical explorations to explain the connections between capitalism and political violence and that each attempts to invent new ways of being that are inherently opposed to the philosophical systems they discover. In order to create the new categories necessary to describe resistance across the period, the present study engages extensively with such theorists as Alain Badiou, Jean Baudrillard, Michel Foucault, and Félix Guattari and Gilles Deleuze (both individually and in their co-authored works). In adopting this approach, however, the danger remains that the book could reinforce a particular form of scholarly colonialism within which critical theory is largely developed in the Global North, while primary material is produced in the Global South. I would suggest, however, that the book resists this particular form of intellectual hierarchization. In the first instance, I have consistently read each author's work in line with Piglia's argument that literature represents "un modo de *significar* (y no de reflejar) de *iluminar la realidad* a través de una praxis específica, que tiene estructuras propias, [y] que no tolera intervención exterior" (a method of *signifying* [and not of reflecting], of *illuminating reality* through a specific praxis that has its own structures [and] that does not tolerate exterior intervention).[25] This is to say that each literary work analyzed in the present volume is understood as a form of praxis within which theory is produced through the very act of writing. Thus the present book is neither a study of history nor of philosophy but dwells in the borders between these disciplines as they are explored, contested, challenged, and rewritten through literature. Nonetheless, as in the previous discussion of "Homenaje a Roberto Arlt" in the light of Foucault's "What Is an Author?," it is inescapable that European theory provides me with a vocabulary and conceptual framework that can illuminate and describe the specific functions of each of the Argentine texts I examine. Returning briefly to my discussion of Piglia's story, therefore, will also elucidate further attempts to resist scholarly subordination.

Of those critical reflections on "Homenaje a Roberto Arlt," which closely follow Piglia's assertion that "todos los grandes textos son políticos" (all great texts are political), two of the most important are those written by Bruno Bosteels and Graciela Speranza. In the latter, Speranza notes that the text introduces a Marxist and Brechtian conception of plagiarism as a political literary practice, while Bosteels draws on Piglia's early critical writing to uncover the "the invisible lineage of Brecht–Mao" that underpins the story.[26] This is to say that, in both instances, these texts delineate those theorists who did influence Piglia and demonstrate how he deployed their work in order to unify the literature of the seemingly irreconcilable figures of Arlt and Borges in an explicitly political manner.[27] While repeating these arguments at length is unnecessary, a brief overview of Piglia's appropriations of Borges and Arlt will serve to highlight the key political features of "Homenaje a Roberto Arlt." In a diary entry from 1970, Piglia succinctly summarizes those elements of Borges's literature that he finds particularly engaging. As he writes:

> Tomé a Borges como ejemplo de la doble enunciación, o mejor, del texto doble. La cita, el plagio y la traducción, ejemplos de una escritura dentro de otra, que está implícita. Se lee por escrito un texto ajeno y la apropiación puede ser legal (cita), ilegal (plagio), o neutra (traducción). Borges usa su modo personal de traducir para apropiarse de todos los textos que cita o a los que plagia: su estilo "inconfundible" vuelve todo lo que escribe de su propiedad. Usa con gran destreza también las atribuciones erróneas, delirantes y múltiples: habitualmente le atribuye a otros sus propias frases pero también toma como propias formulaciones ajenas.[28]

> (I took Borges as an example of a double enunciation, or better still, of a double text. Citation, plagiarism and translation: examples of one form of writing implicit within another. One reads someone else's text through the act of writing, and the appropriation can be legal (citation), illegal (plagiarism), or neutral (translation). Borges uses his personal manner of translation in order to appropriate all of the texts which he cites or that he plagiarizes: his "unmistakable" style ensures that everything he writes becomes his property. He also uses outrageous and multiple erroneous attribution with great skill: he habitually attributes his own phrases to others but he also takes other people's formulations as his own.)

Piglia's indebtedness to Borges in the creation of "Homenaje a Roberto Arlt" is immediately apparent: both plagiarism and false attribution are literary practices that Piglia acquires from his literary forebear.[29] Nonetheless, it is essential for Piglia to fuse this practice with elements of Arlt's literature in order to transform it into an overtly political strategy. In his critical writing on the work of Arlt, Piglia argues that "el dinero . . . aparece como garantía que hace posible la apropiación y el acceso a la literatura" (money . . . appears as the guarantee that makes the appropriation and access to literature possible) and thus that Arlt "desmiente las ilusiones de una ideología que enmascara y sublima en el mito de la riqueza espiritual la lógica implacable de la producción capitalista" (refutes the illusions of an ideology that masks and sublimates the implacable logic of capitalist production as spiritual wealth).[30] This is to say that, for Piglia, Arlt exposes the structural functioning of the capitalist economic system that his own use of plagiarism (borrowed from Borges) ultimately transgresses. As Speranza and Bosteels suggest, a review of Piglia's laudatory praise of the work of Bertolt Brecht reveals a further political transgression implicit in the work of Arlt that can also be encountered in Piglia's homage.[31] In an article published in the important journal *Los Libros* in 1975, Piglia asserts that "para Brecht los valores y gustos dominantes no son otra cosa que la expresión ideal (en este caso: estética) de las relaciones sociales dominantes" (for Brecht dominant values and tastes are nothing other than the ideal [in this case, aesthetic] expression of dominant social relations) and that "el modo de producción capitalista transforma todas las relaciones 'espirituales' . . . en lazos económicos" (the capitalist mode of production transforms all "spiritual" relations . . . into economic ties).[32] In sharp contrast, as María Antonieta Pereira notes, "Arlt produjo una escritura perversa, fuera de la ley literaria instituida y, en ese sentido, inauguró otro estilo, que sería también la narrativa de las traducciones populares que él leía" (Arlt produced a perverse literature, outside the instituted literary laws and, in this way, inaugurated another style, which would also be that of the popular translations that he read).[33] Thus, Piglia argues, Arlt's literary style is inherently outwith the bounds of the dominant perception of good taste, and by attributing a plagiarized translation to Arlt in his "Homenaje," Piglia appropriates this style in order to expose the economic relations masked by aesthetic common sense, as in his interpretation of Brecht. As in Piglia's interpretation of the work of Mao, then, in "Homenaje a Roberto Arlt," "el efecto estético, la significación ideológica, el modo de producción, las formas de distribución y de consumo, los materiales y los instrumentos de trabajo, es decir el sistema literario en su conjunto, está determinado por los intereses de clase" (the aesthetic effect, the ideological meaning, the mode of production, the forms of distribution and consumption, the materials and instruments of work, which is to say the entire literary system, are determined by class interests), such that it contains both "una lucha 'democrática' contra el manejo de la oposición legible/ilegible manipulado por la burguesía y una lucha 'socialista' contra las relaciones de producción capitalistas que hacen del 'autor' el propietario privado del 'sentido'" (a "democratic" struggle against the management of the opposition legible/illegible manipulated by the bourgeoisie, and a "socialist" struggle against the capitalist means of production that make the "author" the private owner of all "meaning").[34] That in this instance Piglia recognizes the importance of the author within the capitalist mode of literary production while simultaneously undermining the privilege afforded to them also serves as a further connection to Foucault's "What Is an Author?" and reveals the coextensive nature of their respective analysis.

That Piglia and Foucault share parallel concerns is demonstrated in several instances in Piglia's critical work. For example, in his essay on Mao, Piglia seeks to address "el problema de la nueva función del arte" (the problem of the new function of art), while in his work on Brecht he reflects on "la función social del escritor" (the social function of the writer).[35] In an even more striking example found in another edition of *Los Libros*, Piglia paraphrases Gramsci and specifically states that "todos los que saben escribir son 'escritores,' ya que alguna vez en su vida han practicado la escritura. Lo que no hacen es cumplir en la sociedad la *función* de escritores" (everyone who knows how to write is a "writer," insofar as they have practiced writing at some point in their lives. What they do not do is fulfill the *function* of writers in society). Thereafter, Piglia proposes to "analizar los distintos 'contratos sociales' que se interponen entre un texto y su lectura" (to analyze the distinct "social contracts" that are interjected between a text and the act of reading it).[36] That the terminology and the analytical framework deployed by Piglia closely resemble those found in Foucault's essay is not entirely surprising given Piglia's involvement in *Los Libros*, a journal that was fundamental in introducing various strands of European critical thought (including structuralism) to Argentina.[37] Nonetheless, the parallels between the two authors are particularly notable. For example, each author has commented (though in disagreement) on the nature of the author function in the medieval period.[38] In addition, Foucault reflects that "even within our own civilization, the same types of texts have not always required authors; there was a time when those texts which we now call 'literary' (stories, folk tales, epics, and tragedies) were accepted, circulated, and valorized without any question about the identity of their author."[39] From this basis, Foucault goes on to envision a future culture within which "discourse would circulate without any need for an author" and "would unfold in a pervasive anonymity."[40] In a similar manner, Piglia has shown a persistent preoccupation with anonymous literary texts. For example, in an important essay from 1970, Piglia analyzes North American literature (an important influence on his own writing, as he frequently asserts) and argues that the texts produced by writers associated with the Black Panthers "vienen de la experiencia colectiva y tienden hacia el anonimato" (are derived from collective experience and tend toward anonymity).[41] Similarly, in diary entries in 1972, Piglia both asserts that North American writers of detective fiction are "artensanos anónimos" (anonymous artisans) and ruminates on creating "un grupo literario anónimo" (an anonymous literary group) to "publicar un panfleto contra los canales de distribución de la literatura" (publish a pamphlet contrary to the channels of literary distribution).[42] Once more, the proposal is not that Piglia was influenced by Foucault in establishing this position. Indeed, it is far more likely that Piglia's primary influence in exploring the nature of anonymous texts was, in fact, Borges. For example, in Borges's story "Tlön, Uqbar, Orbis Tertius," the discovery of an anonymous and supplementary addition to a plagiarized copy of the *Encyclopaedia Britannica* leads to the creation of an entirely new world ensconced within our present reality. Moreover, within this new world "es raro que los libros estén firmados" (it is unusual for books to be signed), as "no existe el concepto del plagio" (the concept of plagiarism does not exist), and "se ha establecido que todas las obras son obra de un solo autor, que es intemporal y es anónimo" (it has been established that all works are the creation of one author, who is atemporal and anonymous).[43] Given these features of Borges's story, it appears almost as if "Tlön, Uqbar, Orbis Tertius" serves as something of an ur-text for Piglia's "Homenaje a Roberto Arlt." Nonetheless, as we shall now see, it seems likely that the story also draws inspiration from the work of another Argentine author: Macedonio Fernández.

In a series of diary excerpts related to Fernández, Piglia records that on various occasions he "insinuó que estaba escribiendo un libro del que nadie iba a conocer nunca una página" (insinuated that he was writing a book of which no one would ever recognize a single page). As Piglia relates, Fernández planned to publish the book in secret such that no one would ever know it was his. While "en principio había pensado que se publicara como un libro anónimo" (in the beginning he had thought of publishing it as an anonymous book), he later thought "que debía publicarse con el nombre de un escritor conocido. Atribuir su libro a otro: el plagio al revés" (that he should publish it under the name of a known author. Attribute his book to another: plagiarism in reverse).[44] This is, of course, largely the same practice that Piglia deploys in "Homenaje a Roberto Arlt," and the incorporation of Fernández's work into Piglia's literary experiment also serves to highlight another means by which the present text evades the risk of intellectual hierarchization. In a diary entry from 1968, Piglia asserts that "desde el principio la literatura [argentina] se sentía en falta frente a las literaturas europeas" (from the outset [Argentine] literature considered itself to be lacking in comparison with European literatures). Nonetheless, he also proposes that "a partir de Macedonio y de Borges nuestra literatura—en nuestra generación—está en el mismo plano que las literaturas extranjeras" (from Macedonio and Borges onwards, our literature—in our generation—is found on the same plane as foreign literatures).[45] This is a claim reiterated several times in Piglia's diaries and one that he repeated again in an interview in 1996 stating that "estamos, usando un término de la música, mucho más 'en sincro.' Por fin somos contemporáneos de nuestros contemporáneos europeos y norteamericanos. Porque antes no lo éramos . . . tanto" (we are, using a term from music, much more "in sync." Finally we are contemporaries with our European and North American contemporaries. Because before, we were not . . . so much).[46] While Piglia certainly refers to international authors of fiction, the salient point is that by following the example of Borges, Fernández, Arlt, and others, Piglia has also become contemporary with European critical theorists and philosophers. I would also suggest that while their literary forebears may not be the same, this holds equally true for Aira and Cohen. Moreover, in line with the central thesis of the present book, I would suggest that this is particularly the case because each of the authors under discussion examines the colonizing forces of contemporary neoliberal globalization, as do each of the theorists whose work I draw on. Indeed, it is these same forces that ultimately imbue their texts with contemporaneity and negate any form of intellectual hierarchization.

This contemporaneity between Latin American authors and European theorists can perhaps be illuminated further by reflecting upon Doreen Massey's reformulation of the distinction between "space" and "place." For Massey, space should be understood both as a continual process and "as the product of interrelations" ranging "from the immensity of the global to the intimately tiny." Thus Massey posits that space is necessarily formed of a multiplicity understood "as a simultaneity of stories-so-far."[47] Having reconceptualized space in this manner, Massey goes on to propose that places thus become "collections of those stories," and she proposes "an understanding of place . . . as woven together out of ongoing stories, as a moment within power-geometries, as a particular constellation within the wider topographies of space, and as in process, as unfinished business."[48] For Massey, places are "spatio-temporal events."[49] Similarly, throughout the present study it is the specific place, Argentina, that emerges as a preeminent site for the localized application of globalized forces such that theoretical critiques of contemporary capitalism are illuminated in a particularly visceral manner. The idea of the nation endures as a useful concept, therefore, precisely because it localizes the power-geometries of increasingly globalizing forces that are then examined and contested through the ongoing stories recounted by the Argentine literature under examination. Nonetheless, as in Massey's conception of place, the resultant nation becomes "a constellation of processes rather than a thing," one that is understood "as open and as internally multiple," and crucially "one in which the elements of that multiplicity are themselves imbued with temporality."[50] This temporal element is especially pertinent given that the present study, at first sight, appears to contain two contradictory impulses. On the one hand, a chronological argument similar to that described by Foucault in "What Is an Author?" has been developed across the work of Aira, Cohen, and Piglia tracing the historical development of power relations and resistance in Argentina in the latter half of the twentieth century. On the other, however, the philosophical analysis of the three authors' work generates a series of connections between their texts that initially appear to undermine this same historical analysis. I would suggest that the problem both originates and is resolved in the fact that the Deleuzian conception of becoming, understood as "the very dynamism of change" in which "only difference returns and never sameness," is the central philosophical theme that I perceive in each author's work and that underpins the historical development of literary resistance in late twentieth-century Argentina.[51]

As Ronald Bogue explains, within Deleuze's philosophy of time, "history belongs to the world of Chronos, the time of measure and sequence," while becoming "partakes of the time of Aion, a convulsive, adifferentiated temporal flux."[52] While Deleuze's conception of Aion and Chronos will be examined in greater detail in chapter 6, I would suggest that, with regard to the arguments described above, the linear development of power relations and resistance corresponds to the historical time of Chronos, while the philosophical conceptions of resistance described in each text more properly belong to the time of Aion. This is particularly pertinent given that where "history is a memory that fixes time in discrete points[,] becoming unfixes those points and generates free-floating lines."[53] Thus it would appear that the apparent contradiction between the two lines of analysis is both inherent to and resolved within Deleuze's ontology and philosophy of time. For this reason, I have attempted to resolve this problem by incorporating a Deleuzian approach (suggested by the texts themselves) into the structure of the book. Indeed, the literary correlate of Deleuze's philosophical system has been the fundamental principle guiding the construction of the text.

In *A Thousand Plateaus*, Deleuze and Guattari explain their approach to literature by stating: "We will never ask what a book means, as signified or signifier; we will not look for anything to understand in it. We will ask what it functions with, in connection with what other things it does or does not transmit intensities, in which other multiplicities its own are inserted and metamorphosed, and with what bodies without organs it makes its own converge."[54] The essential point is that Deleuze and Guattari advocate a creative approach to literature that entails the connection of disparate elements in pursuance of new interpretations and new ways of being. To explicate this process, Deleuze and Guattari argue that a "book is an assemblage" that can be linked to other assemblages by "machinic" connections.[55] Joanna Page provides a succinct definition of each of these terms. As she explains. "For Deleuze and Guattari, both living organisms and technological apparatuses can function as machines if they engage in processes of becoming through being connected with other machines in ever-evolving assemblages. Those connections produce further connections, none of which are organized by any transcendent figure."[56] In his critical work *Fricciones*, Tomás Abraham suggests that within his book, Piglia and Aira appear as "dos zonas intensas" (two intense zones) liberated from their actuality.[57] To communicate the philosophical connections between Aira, Cohen, and Piglia in the present study, I too consider the three authors not so much as historical figures but as intensive zones of philosophical potentialities. Moreover, the structure of the book itself reflects the historical and philosophical arguments it contains by fusing two different critical approaches: that articulated by Aira in his book *Las tres fechas* and that delineated by Deleuze and Guattari in *A Thousand Plateaus* and *Kafka: Toward a Minor Literature*.

As Abraham notes, the subject that preoccupies Aira in *Las tres fechas* is "el tema de la experiencia" (the theme of experience). In this book Aira argues that "la experiencia se sedimenta en la psique y, cuando se la relata, necesariamente se desdibuja" (experience is deposited in the psyche and, when one narrates it, it is necessarily blurred).[58] In order to recover this original experience, every individual literary text can be interpreted through the relationship established between three different dates: "la de escritura, la de publicación, y la de los sucesos que cuenta" (that of writing, that of publication, and that of the relevant events).[59] As Aira makes clear:

> Cada fecha en uno de esos triángulos evoca un aspecto distinto de la vida del autor, y el lector necesariamente debe reaccionar de modo diferente a cada una de ellas, dentro de la unidad del libro. Y a su vez la ecuación inestable de las tres resuena en las ecuaciones de los otros triángulos y modifica la reacción individual a ellos.[60]
>
> (Each date in one of these triangles invokes a different aspect of the life of the author, and the reader should necessarily react in a different way to each one of them, within the unity of the book. And at the same time, the unstable equation of the three is echoed in the equations of other triangles and modifies the individual reaction to each of them.)

I retain the idea that individual works crystallize personal experience but also consider them to be imbued with the historical circumstances in which they were composed. Furthermore, this model is applied across the work of three authors, reflecting the machinic unity I perceive between their texts. This leads to the second of my structural models, the Deleuzian plateau. Deleuze and Guattari acquire the term "plateau" from Gregory Bateson's investigations into certain Balinese cultures, and it is described as "a continuous, self-vibrating region of intensities whose development avoids any orientation toward a culmination point or external end."[61] In *A Thousand Plateaus* each plateau is "precisely dated," yet Deleuze and Guattari argue that each one "can be read starting anywhere and can be related to any other plateau" as they "are not subjected to an external plan of organisation."[62] The book thus creates "a fabric of intensive states between which any number of connecting routes could exist."[63] Deleuze and Guattari name this fabric the "plane of immanence." The present work is divided into three plateaus, named after each author and dated in accordance with Aira's "tres fechas" (three dates). The first zone of intensity is "César Aira" and is subtitled "29 de Mayo de 1969, La fecha de los sucesos que cuenta" (29th May 1969, The Date of the Relevant Events). The date is that of the mass student and worker uprising against the military dictatorship of General Juan Carlos Onganía, known as the Cordobazo. The second zone is "Marcelo Cohen: 27 de Marzo de 1991, La fecha de escritura" (27th March 1991, The Date of Writing). The date is that in which the Ley de Convertibilidad Monetaria (Convertibility Law) was approved by congress.[64] This marks an important moment in the implementation of President Carlos Menem's Structural Adjustment Program and the opening to the world economy. It receives its title because "la [fecha] de escritura corresponde al presente" (the [date] of writing corresponds to the present).[65] In sociophilosophical terms Cohen occupies the most recent time frame in our chronological sequence, and the structural adjustment program arguably establishes the paradigm for this period. The third zone is "Ricardo Piglia" and receives the inscription "2100, La fecha de publicación" (2100, The Date of Publication). The justification is that, in Aira's system, this third date represents "el futuro remoto" (the remote future).[66] The date is drawn from a short critical essay by Piglia in which he channels Borges once more and eagerly anticipates "el año 2100, cuando el nombre de todos los autores se haya perdido y la literatura sea intemporal y sea anónima" (the year 2100, when the names of all authors have been lost and literature is atemporal and anonymous).[67]

In *A Thousand Plateaus* Deleuze and Guattari make the claim that "all we know are assemblages. And the only assemblages are machinic assemblages of desire and collective assemblages of enunciation."[68] Where it appears that Aira, Cohen, and Piglia are bound together in a continuous historical progression, I would argue that they are in fact held together in a different manner. Each author describes specific phenomena and presents distinct philosophical arguments that nonetheless appear in the work of the other two. In order to describe the machinic assemblages that emerge from such connections, each plateau concludes with a philosophical reflection on the individual author's work through the interpretive framework provided by *Kafka: Toward a Minor Literature*. I propose that each author's work corresponds to a single component of the literary machine that Deleuze and Guattari perceive in the work of Kafka. Thus the analysis of each author's work is connected as in Deleuze's analysis of Kafka, where three "different diabolical machines—letters, novellas, and so-called unfinished novels"—constitute the different elements of a single literary machine.[69] This connection is not at all arbitrary, as each Argentine author demonstrates a particular preoccupation with Kafka's work. This is evidenced for Piglia by the prominence of Kafka in *Respiración artificial* and his suggestion that he would have liked to author Kafka's diary.[70] For his part, Aira has categorically stated that, having reread Kafka continuously throughout his life, "en realidad nunca se sale de él" (in reality, I never leave him).[71] Finally, as Cohen recounts in the autobiographical text "Pequeñas batallas por la propiedad de la lengua," when Osvaldo Lamborghini came to visit him in Spain in the seventies, he demanded that Cohen "leyera *Kafka, por una literatura menor*, el libro de Deleuze" (read Deleuze's book, *Kafka: Toward a Minor Literature*).[72] This anecdote is particularly relevant as my own argument is that Deleuze's analysis of Kafka proffers a model for understanding the distinct forms of resistance encountered in the work of Aira, Cohen, and Piglia. As this analysis develops, it also becomes clear that Piglia's work, rather than serving as a historical connection between Aira and Cohen, can be considered the twist in the Möbius strip that returns all the authors to a single plane of immanence.

In *Las vueltas de César Aira* Sandra Contreras contends that Aira's "vuelta al relato" (return to the story) signals a return to narrative literature following the various formal experiments of the artistic vanguards of the 1960s and 1970s and those of Piglia and Juan José Saer in the 1980s.[73] Somewhat contradictorily, however, my own historical argument commences with Aira. Indeed, this opening chapter lays the foundation for the historical argument contained within the book as a whole. Moreover, while Aira's novel *La liebre* is the most important in his "ciclo pampeano" (pampas cycle) for the construction of Contreras's central argument, it is rather *Ema, la cautiva* that is of singular significance in delineating a political interpretation of Aira's work.[74] In chapter 1 I propose that Aira responds to the dual experience of state terrorism and the early development of a neoliberal capitalist economy under the most recent military dictatorship by returning to and reimagining nineteenth-century Argentine history. It is my contention that Aira allusively presents General Julio Argentino Roca's Conquest of the Desert as the foundational moment not only of the national state and a capitalist economy but of the systematic use of genocide as a political tool to achieve the first two objectives. Furthermore, I suggest that Aira advances this analysis in order to explore the philosophical and historical repercussions of the relationship between capitalism and political violence throughout twentieth-century Argentina.

Chapter 2 proposes that in *La prueba* Aira responds to the opening of the Argentine economy under Menem in the early 1990s by once more returning to the past. This time, however, I argue that Aira transposes the revolutionary impetus epitomized by the Cordobazo in 1969 to this contemporary moment. In facilitating this historical transference, I argue, Aira describes the process of obtaining a revolutionary subjectivity by engaging a truth-procedure as defined by Alain Badiou. This process in turn unleashes a schizophrenic process of becoming-other as defined by Deleuze, which is itself both product and limit of the neoliberal capitalist model implemented by Menem. Subsequently, I demonstrate that *La prueba* can be read as a strange philosophical and literary bildungsroman that describes the truth-procedure that Aira engages in the field of art through his unique literary process known as the "huida hacia adelante" (flight forward), a term derived from Aira's critical assessment of Alejandra Pizarnik that accounts both for his refusal to correct his own work and his prolific publication.[75] I propose that *La prueba* is paradigmatic of the process of continual metamorphosis, where incredible transmutation and transformation are the norm that underpins the majority of Aira's work and that demonstrates considerable correspondence with Deleuze and Guattari's interpretation of Kafka's stories. Indeed, it is my argument that *La prueba* accounts for the innumerable schizophrenic becomings-other that permeate Aira's work and that are inherently political and anticapitalist. In this way, I argue that Aira's literature is in perpetual resistance to the evolving structures of capitalist power.

In chapter 3 I establish that in the texts *Insomnio* and "La ilusión monarca" Cohen examines the transition to democracy and delineates the new forms of power, control, and resistance that emerge in its wake. Ironically, Cohen situates these texts, written in the aftermath of state-sponsored terrorism and strict control and set in the near future, in enclosed spaces subject to severe repression. These Cohen texts are punctuated by uncanny fragments and remnants of the dictatorship's systematic repression, manipulated by the author to expose the limits of the apparent freedoms gained through the transition. In this way I argue that Cohen reveals the continuation of corruption and violence beyond the conclusion of the period of state-sponsored terrorism and subjects the transition to a philosophical examination that gives it a rather different inflection. I therefore contend that Cohen reflects back on the processes at work during the so-called Dirty War to expose the fact that the last military government exercised both disciplinary and sovereign power, as described by Foucault, to control Argentine society. The chapter then discusses representations of resistance in the two texts that correspond to the transformational model of becoming as defined by Deleuze.

Chapter 4 opens with a brief discussion of "La ilusión monarca" that suggests that within the text Cohen begins to articulate the redundancy of disciplinary enclosures in contemporary society and to describe the emergent forms of power that replace them. In this way Cohen reveals the Argentine case to be paradigmatic of the transition from disciplinary to control society as described by Deleuze. The main body of the chapter then examines the novel *El oído absoluto* while also making reference to the later text *Variedades*. The chapter proposes that in these texts control has been generalized and dispersed throughout the worlds they describe and that the society of control has been fully realized. In the absence of overt state-sponsored terrorism, I argue, Cohen suggests that the mass media has assumed the position previously occupied by the military and that a proliferation of hyperreal images and a process of perpetual simulation, as described by Jean Baudrillard, are manipulated to consolidate the neoliberal capitalist state and coerce and control the population. Additionally, I demonstrate that Cohen continually attempts to discover strategies to counteract the new forms of power he describes. Much as Deleuze and Guattari argue that Kafka's novels are the logical extension of the strategies deployed in his stories, so too do I show that Aira's literature reaches an impasse that condenses into the sociopolitical description of the mechanisms of the society of control found in the work of Cohen. It is demonstrated that in this new reality a seemingly absolute yet closed set of hyperreal images, modeled on the Deleuzian simulacrum, masks the anarchic freedoms Aira espoused. The possibility of transmutation, metamorphosis, and transformation, heralded as a powerful force of resistance, has been assimilated within the matrix of control. Yet in the midst of this system of ostensibly total control, Cohen discovers the power of Baudrillardian seduction, of the anonymous text, and of rumor to proffer resistance as they become accessible to insurgency and present a challenge that forces power to reveal itself as such. Ultimately, however, I argue that Cohen's texts contract into an undecidable point where resistance and acquiescence become almost indistinguishable.

Regarding Piglia, I first contend that he is the writer par excellence of the 1976–1983 dictatorship and that his work serves as the literary connection between the other authors. In chapter 5, detailed analysis of *Respiración artificial* demonstrates that Piglia employs a remarkably similar strategy to that which Aira utilized in *Ema, la cautiva*: he decries the crimes of the military dictatorship not only by conflating historical periods but by dissecting the philosophical roots that rationally justified the military's actions. This investigation suggests that Piglia's novel reveals Immanuel Kant's conception of the cogito and the law to be at the center of the rational capitalist state and finds them culpable in justifying and sustaining the horrendous state violence of the time.

In response, I argue that Piglia attempts to define an alternative understanding of time that would liberate the individual from these logical underpinnings of the most recent military dictatorship.

Chapter 6 focuses on Piglia's novel *La ciudad ausente*, and my proposal is that it essentially anticipates Cohen's critique of contemporary neoliberal capitalism and realizes that which could only be hypothesized in *Respiración artificial*. In the new situation of the transition to democracy and Argentina's opening to the global economy, I suggest, Piglia begins to describe the limited freedoms gained through these processes, to sketch the outline of the control society, and to emphasize the importance of the mass media as a new technology of power. All of these features are more fully developed by Cohen. Additionally, the text suggests that this seemingly new situation is but a continuation of the logic underpinning the previous dictatorship and that Piglia counteracts it through the complex structure of the novel that defines a metastable form of time (Aion) that engages the eternal return in order to produce the new and absolutely different. I thus propose that in *La ciudad ausente* Piglia wills and unleashes the Deleuzian event masked by the military government's systematic repression and that the text itself becomes a timeless resistance machine opposed to political violence and neoliberal capitalism. The chapter also delineates the connections between Piglia's epistolary novel *Respiración artificial*, the story-producing machine described in *La ciudad ausente*, and Deleuze and Guattari's description of Kafka's letters. Through this analysis I demonstrate that while Cohen's literary project is predominantly related to *La ciudad ausente*, an incipient version can be found in *Respiración artificial*. Similarly, it is shown that while Aira's literary project is predominantly related to *Respiración artificial*, it can also be encountered in miniature in *La ciudad ausente*. Through further discussion of the three authors' work, I demonstrate that from a certain point of view each author appears to precede the others and that the processes they describe are co-implicated and complementary. In the conclusion, I argue that the three authors occupy a "plane of immanence" as described by Deleuze, that they reconfigure the Argentine nation in line with Félix Guattari's description of Integrated World Capitalism, and that their work perpetually generates resistance to this same capitalist system within Argentina.

It is important to note that my reading of the work of Aira, Cohen, and Piglia is deliberately provocative. For example, Contreras argues that Aira's engagement with twentieth-century vanguard artists is opposed to the theoretical connection between "vanguardia y revolución" (avant-garde and revolution) prevalent in 1960s Argentina, to the political and aesthetic vanguards of the 1970s, and to the aesthetics of "negatividad" (negativity) proposed in the

1980s.[76] My own argument is that elements of each of these intellectual trends are instrumental to Aira's literary process, and I present a new political reading of Aira's work of a type more commonly associated with the work of Piglia and Cohen. Similarly, I argue that the specific Argentine historical and literary context surrounding Cohen's early novels is particularly important, an argument that is more often made with regard to Aira and Piglia. Finally, I provide an original, highly theoretical (and Deleuzian) reading of the work of Piglia, despite the fact that he does not use such concepts in his own critical writing and has questioned their overt use in literary criticism.[77]

Arguably more controversial, however, is that, despite the fact that Aira and Piglia have become "dos imanes" (two idols) of Argentine literary culture, an apparent antagonism between them has solidified into something of a critical commonplace such that they are frequently considered to be irreconcilable poles of contemporary Argentine literature.[78] These arguments are not without foundation. In an early critical essay published in the 1980s, Aira claimed that *Respiración artificial* was "una de las peores novelas de su generación" (one of the worst novels of his generation) and that Piglia was paradigmatic of "una falta de auténtica pasión por la literatura en la narrativa argentina contemporánea" (a lack of authentic passion for literature in contemporary Argentine fiction).[79] It appears that this initial antipathy has endured, as years later Aira stated that he had no interest in Piglia's work.[80] It initially appeared that Piglia shared this cool indifference. Abraham relates in *Fricciones* that shortly after the publication of Aira's article, he met Piglia and asked if he had read it. Piglia did not reply.[81] In the intervening years these antagonisms condensed into an interpretive framework typified by Contreras, who presents Aira, in part, as the "anti-Piglia."[82] With the publication of the final volume of Piglia's diaries, we now know that the attacks emanating from Aira and his literary associates *did* preoccupy Piglia and his friends for several months in 1981. First Piglia claims that the journal that would publish Aira's (in)famous article *Vigencia* "hace la política cultural de la dictadura" (carries out the cultural policy of the dictatorship).[83] Later he makes an oblique reference to Aira's article, refusing to name the author and stating only that it was "escrito por un sirviente de O. L. [Osvaldo Lamborghini]" (written by a servant of O.L. [Osvaldo Lamborghini]), before again accusing the journal of working "para el nuevo consenso del general Viola" (for General Viola's new consensus).[84] A day later, Piglia makes his only direct reference to Aira, noting that "en una entrevista César A. dijo que yo tenía cara de policía" (in an interview César A. said that I had the face of a policeman), and he later laments that Aira's group have constructed him as their "enemigo ideal" (ideal enemy) and states that "no tengo nada que ver con la invención de rivalidades que no propongo ni me interesa" (I have nothing to do with the invention of rivalries that I do not propose and that do not interest me).[85] Despite these acute differences it is my intention ultimately to reject Aira's assertion that Piglia and Saer belonged to a different literary generation.[86] In the first instance, such a move could be defended through Piglia's early writings, where he both entirely rejects the compulsion to organize time in discrete decades and proposes that "si algo define a una generación—más allá de las exterioridades biológicas—es una problemática común, históricamente situada" (if something defines a generation—beyond any external biological appearances—it is a common problem, historically situated).[87] As I have explained above, this is precisely how I view the literature of Aira, Piglia, and Cohen. Yet this is not to suggest that there is a totalizing concordance between each of the authors, and I do not wish to overlook the important differences in their work. Rather, I consider a generation, defined in the manner above, to be akin to Massey's description of places, which, "rather than being locations of coherence, become the foci of the meeting and the nonmeeting of the previously unrelated and thus integral to the generation of novelty."[88] With this in mind, it is useful to consider some of the primary critical disjunctures that separate the work of Aira from that of Piglia.

Within the introduction to *Las vueltas de César Aira*, Contreras defines Aira's unique literary output in contradistinction to various recent trends in Argentine literature. A key component of this discussion is to define Aira's process in contrast to Piglia's literary project. In so doing Contreras summarizes Piglia's literary enterprise, suggesting that in the tradition of Macedonio Fernández he advocates the "poética de la novela como utopía negativa" (poetics of the novel as a negative utopia), a literary ethics and praxis that works with "lo que todavía no es" (that which is not yet) and is opposed to the "mecanismos abstractos del poder" (abstract mechanisms of power) and "las presiones del mercado" (the pressures of the market). Contreras then proposes that Aira specifically rejects Piglian negativity.[89] For Piglia the "poética de la negatividad" (poetics of negativity) is a literary strategy that entails the "rechazo a lo que podrían ser los lenguajes estereotipados que circulan en la cultura de masas" (rejection of what could be the stereotyped speech that circulate in mass culture) and the refusal to "entrar en esa especie de manipulación que supone la industria cultural" (enter in this kind of manipulation that the cultural industry proposes).[90] Thus Piglian negativity is an essential component of what he considers the purpose of literature: it resists the power of the state by creating fragmentary counternarratives that oppose the narratives and stereotypical language utilized by the powerful to maintain control.[91] Contreras and others interpret this Piglian strategy in such a way as to suggest that it is the "paradigma de negatividad . . . el que la literatura de Aira viene a transmutar" (paradigm of negativity . . . that Aira's literature comes to transmute).[92] Evelyn Galiazo is a particularly committed exponent of this critical approach. For her, Aira's "huida hacia adelante" (flight forward) is directly opposed to the "poética de la negatividad" (poetics of negativity), and she argues that in order to construct his own literary theory, Aira "necesita descargar toda su artillería contra Piglia" (needs to discharge all his artillery against Piglia).[93] Thus Galiazo proposes that Aira completely rejects "la negación" (negation) and finds its key exponents, Piglia and Saer, "responsables de una doble culpa: la de instalar al impulso negativo en primer plano y la de comprender a la praxis narrativa como un mero ejercicio de oposición" (responsible for a double offense: that of installing the negative impulse in the foreground, and that of understanding fictional praxis as a mere exercise in opposition).[94] Galiazo contends that Aira's affirmation of innovation, creation, and process (which is to say, the "flight forward") completely undermines Piglian negativity, and she passionately argues that the lesson Aira teaches us is that in literature, "no es cuestión de apropiarse del material mítico que aportó la dictadura para asegurarse unos cuantos lectores. La causa es la literatura misma y hay que inmolarse por ella; hay que sacrificar el éxito, e incluso la obra, para que triunfe el proceso, siempre" (it is not a question of appropriating the mythical material that the dictatorship produced in order to secure a few readers. The cause is literature itself and one must sacrifice oneself for it; one must sacrifice success, and even the work itself, so that the process will triumph, always).[95] Contreras is subtler in her approach yet still contends that Aira's "*afirmación inmediata de la potencia absoluta y autónoma de la invención*" (*immediate affirmation of the absolute and autonomous power of invention*) transforms Piglian negativity and completely changes "el elemento del que se deriva el sentido y el valor de la ficción" (the element from which the meaning and value of fiction is derived).[96] Importantly, several critics consider Piglian negativity to be more creative and innovative than Contreras and Galiazo acknowledge. For example, Joanna Page discusses Piglia's engagement with scientific discourse to demonstrate the creativity of his literary experimentation.[97] As will become clear, I share the perception of Piglia's work as inherently creative and question the dichotomous model proposed by Contreras and Galiazo.

Edgardo Berg has persuasively argued that the construction of literary genealogies is of central importance to Argentine literary criticism.[98] I would suggest that this tendency is the principal source for many antithetical readings of Aira and Piglia and has been exacerbated by the authors' adherence to the same trend. As we have already seen with regard to "Homenaje a Roberto Arlt," Piglia consciously constructs a literary genealogy that unites Arlt, Borges, and Macedonio Fernández, and his insistence on this specific literary genealogy has guided much criticism of his work. This leads to assertions such as that made by Pampa Olga Arán that "resulta poco menos que imposible hablar de la obra de Piglia sin hablar 'con' Piglia" (it seems a little less than impossible to speak about Piglia's work without speaking "with" Piglia) because he reduces "la distancia entre el proceso creativo y el interpretativo" (the distance between the creative and interpretive processes) to a minimum.[99] The same process is equally evident in criticism on Aira. For his part, Aira selects a different artistic lineage, suggesting that Manuel Puig, Alejandra Pizarnik, and Osvaldo Lamborghini are his "trío tutelar" (guardian trio), and I would suggest that a large body of criticism consistently reads Aira's literature through the framework of his own critical interventions.[100] Such strict and separate genealogies are, of course, too precise and are easily challenged. Thus Jorge Fornet (at least in part) reads Piglia in conjunction with both Lamborghini and Puig, and Ariel Schettini notes that Piglia composed a particularly influential essay on the latter author.[101] Similarly, Aira has called Arlt "el mayor novelista argentino" (the greatest Argentine novelist) and, despite suggesting that he has had his "altibajos en relación con Borges" (ups and downs in relation to Borges), has stated that "mi verdadero maestro de lectura fue Borges" (in truth, it was Borges who taught me how to read).[102] Indeed, he has even stated that "Arlt para mí es un grande. Bueno, habría que decir uno de los dos grandes: el otro, claro, es Borges. Tan distintos y tan parecidos, ¿no?" (Arlt, for me, is a [literary] great. Well, it should be said, one of the two greats: the other, of course, is Borges. So different and yet so similar, no?)[103] Thus it seems that it would be more appropriate to suggest that the work of both Aira and Piglia contains strong centripetal forces that draw the reader back to their own interpretations of their self-selected literary genealogies as well as equally powerful centrifugal forces that generate new lines of flight away from those same lineages. For example, as we have seen in "Homenaje a Roberto Arlt," Piglia creates a literary text that incorporates his critical work on Arlt, Borges, and Macedonio Fernández. However, when Piglia repeats the story of an author seeking first to create an anonymous text before choosing to falsely attribute it to another famous writer in his diaries, Piglia accredits the proposal (using several of the exact same phrases) not to Macedonio Fernández but to the author Ezequiel Martínez Estrada, claiming that Estrada described the project to him in 1959.[104] Thus even in a text that appears to synthesize perfectly his literary lineage, Piglia surreptitiously introduces an alternative frame of reference that constitutes a creative line of flight away from that same heritage. So too in the present work could other avenues of investigation, incorporating the work of other authors, have been explored.

As we have seen, Piglia has argued that to "cruzar a Arlt con Borges" (to cross Arlt with Borges) was "una de las grandes utopías de la literatura argentina" (one of the greatest utopias in Argentine literature).[105] It appears that at present to cross Aira with Piglia represents a similarly utopic goal. Nonetheless, due to the themes under discussion in the present book and the strong centrifugal forces encountered in the work of each Argentine author, it is clear that several other, equally important writers could have been readily included within the study. For example, where Galiazo contends that Aira's literature is opposed to that of Saer due to his literary relationship with Piglia, Nancy Fernández has demonstrated that their work can be constructively read together.[106] With this in mind, an exploration of "negativity" as developed in Saer's literary output could also have been incorporated within the present study. As mentioned above, Manuel Puig is included within Aira's self-selected literary genealogy, and Piglia was an early defender of his work. For this reason, Puig's work could also have provided another avenue of investigation. Indeed, his explorations of popular culture could provide an interesting counterpoint and historical antecedent to my analysis of the contemporary mass media society in the work of Cohen. Similarly, there are a series of other authors who examine the relationships between literature, psychoanalysis, politics, violence, and capitalism throughout their work who could have been productively integrated into the present analysis. Arguably most important in this regard is Osvaldo Lamborghini.

Not only did Aira compile and edit Lamborghini's complete works after his untimely death, but the blending of obscenity, pornography, and politics in texts such as *El fiord* is echoed in the more grotesque transformations found in Aira's fiction. Moreover, just as I argue that the spectacular metamorphoses found in Aira's literature are inherently political, so too Daniel Link has argued that *El fiord* "anticipated all political literature of the seventies."[107] In addition, as Lamborghini's conflation of politics and perversion is coupled with an excoriating reexamination of Argentine political history, it could provide an important addition to my analysis of the rewriting of history found in works by Aira and Piglia.[108] Similarly, Lamborghini's literature could provide a decisive corollary to my exploration of the sexual nature of contemporary capitalism in the work of Cohen, and of the anticapitalist and schizophrenic pursuit of desire in the work of Aira. As we have seen, it is also the case that it was Lamborghini who gave Cohen Deleuze and Guattari's book on Kafka.

My historical argument too could have been augmented through incorporation of such authors as Rodolfo Enrique Fogwill and Sergio Chejfec. As regards the former writer, Link has argued that the 1970s in Argentina represents a "long" decade, opening with the Cordobazo in 1969 and extending until the end of the most recent dictatorship in 1983. In making this argument, he proposes that it is Fogwill's 1983 novel *Los pichiciegos* that "marks the end-point of the seventies in Argentine literature."[109] Nonetheless, Martín Kohan argues that in his story "La larga risa de todos estos años," Fogwill comes to "cuestionar la ruptura bienpensante dictadura/democracia" (question the self-righteous rupture dictatorship/democracy).[110] This contradictory fusion of closure and continuance following the return to democracy could provide a further perspective on my analysis of similar tendencies in the work of Cohen and Piglia. Moreover, this would also necessarily include consideration of the Falklands-Malvinas conflict. With regards to Chejfec, his explorations of time and subjectivity in the postdictatorship period under neoliberalism in novels such as *Lenta biografía* and *Los planetas* could supplement my analysis of the same philosophical themes in the work of Aira, Cohen, and Piglia.[111] More-over, Chejfec's more recent novels such as *Los incompletos* and *La experiencia dramática* could be deployed to extend my analysis of capitalism in Argentine literature beyond the economic crash of 2001–2002 and explore how this event reconfigured conceptions of capitalism and the nation.[112] It appears, then, that much work remains to be done. Nonetheless, I chose to focus on the work of Aira, Cohen, and Piglia because their work coalesced around a shared set of philosophical ideas, historical problems and literary practices.

In *Fuera de campo: literatura y arte argentinos después de Duchamp*, Speranza conducts a highly original reading of Piglia's fiction and argues that it corresponds to the model of the Duchampian ready-made and the idea of "el *détournement*" (misappropriation), understood as the aspiration to over-come bourgeois conceptions of originality and private property through art.[113] During this examination Speranza cites Lautréamont's maxim that "el plagio es necesario, el progreso lo implica" (plagiarism is necessary, it is implied in prog-ress).[114] It is important to remember that Aira has claimed that Lautréamont "es en definitiva mi escritor favorito" (is, in the end, my favorite writer), and he consistently refers to the model of the ready-made in his criticism.[115] As Speranza continues her argument, she describes Borges as the "gran plagia-rio del Río de la Plata" (the great plagiarist of the River Plate) and notes the importance of his work to Piglia.[116] It is essential to note that in the preface to *Difference and Repetition*, Deleuze references Borges's "Pierre Menard, au-tor del *Quijote*," "as a supreme justification to his philosophy of difference and repetition," in which "the most exact, the most strict repetition has as its cor-relate the maximum of difference."[117] Such a model is equally evident in the Du-champian ready-made, as it is in William Burroughs's cut-up method, praised by both Piglia and Aira.[118] This latter connection is especially important given that, as Page notes, Cohen too "understands his own work to engage to a signif-icant extent with the 1960s and 1970s novels and stories published by Thomas

Pynchon, William Burroughs, and J. G. Ballard."[119] Where Abraham notes that "es evidente que [Aira] ha leído la obra de Deleuze" (it is evident that [Aira] has read the work of Deleuze)—and this holds equally true for Cohen—with the publication of his diaries, we now know that Piglia also read Deleuze (singling out his book on Leopold von Sacher-Masoch for particular praise) and taught his philosophy to a class of psychoanalysts.[120] Thus the theoretical framework that unites the three authors in the present study is the method utilized to justify my provocative reading. Moreover, that the three Argentine authors coalesce around the work of Burroughs's experimental method of composition provides me with my final stylistic cue for the present book.

In his diaries, Piglia describes writing an early article on North American literature by stating that "usé en cierto sentido el método del cut-up de Burroughs e intercalé en el ensayo frases y dichos de distintos escritores y busqué, por primera vez, usar la forma del collage" (I used, in a certain sense, Burroughs's cut-up method and inserted phrases and sayings from different authors into the essay and sought, for the first time, to use the collage form).[121] While the requirements of academic writing prevent me from appropriating the words of others in the same manner as Piglia, I have nevertheless sought to "cut up" and incorporate copious citations into my own prose. Indeed, I approached writing the book in a similar manner to the way György Ligeti composed music. As Ligeti makes clear, he would "divide up the score into a large number of individual parts," regardless of the fact that "as far as hearing them was concerned, these individual parts were completely submerged in the overall texture," a compositional technique he would name "micropolyphony."[122] While my own strategy is not a direct appropriation from the work of Ligeti, I have nonetheless tried to incorporate numerous other voices into my own prose such that "polyphony is written, but harmony is heard," as he summarized the function of micropolyphony.[123] In this way, it is my hope that the present text carries the trace of the "single and same voice for the whole thousand-voice multiple" that raises the "clamour of Being for all beings" in Deleuze's univocal ontology.[124] In a small way, I hope the present book reflects the polyphony inherent in the univocity of being that is manifest in the plane of immanence with which I conclude.

In "Homenaje a Roberto Arlt," Piglia makes the claim that "el crítico literario es siempre de algún modo un detective" (the literary critic is always, in a certain way, a detective).[125] Given that in the present study I have attempted to follow clues scattered throughout the novels and critical texts written by Aira, Cohen, and Piglia to uncover a deep philosophical connection between them, this statement has a certain resonance. Equally, I have employed a methodology that implies that reading is a creative endeavor. As such there is the risk that the specific role of detective I have assumed is that of Erik Lönnrot from Borges's "La muerte y la brújula," who follows clues entirely of his own conception.[126] If this is the case, I can only hope that some future reader will assume the role of Red Scharlach and infuse my arguments with a truth value that they presently lack. Given these qualms, I draw great comfort (and perhaps the ultimate justification for the book itself) from the work of Aira. As he categorically states, "el malentendido es una parte importante de la literatura" (misunderstanding is an important part of literature), and "nunca hay que subestimarlo" (it must never be underestimated) because, ultimately, it is "la fuerza interior de la metamorfosis" (the interior force of metamorphosis).[127] I can but hope that the present volume has contributed to this transformative process.

CÉSAR AIRA: 29 DE MAYO DE 1969, LA FECHA DE LOS SUCESOS QUE CUENTA

(29 MAY 1969: THE DATE OF THE RELEVANT EVENTS)

El malentendido es la fuerza interior de la metamorfosis.

Misunderstanding is the interior force of metamorphosis.

César Aira, *Diario de la hepatitis,* 35–36

CHAPTER 1

EMA IS BY NATURE A POLITICAL ANIMAL

IN *NARRACIONES VIAJERAS: CÉSAR AIRA Y JUAN JOSÉ SAER*, NANCY Fernández comments that "fisgón, entrometido e irreverente, Aira juega, destrozos y deleites mediante, con las reliquias de la cultura nacional, convirtiéndolas en materia de curiosidad, ensoñación, entretenimiento o despojo" (nosy, meddling and irreverent, Aira plays, with delight and destruction, with the relics of national culture, converting them into objects of curiosity, fantasy, entertainment or plunder).[1] As noted in the introduction, other critics (notably Speranza and Contreras) focus on Aira's overt engagement with twentieth-century avant-garde artists in his literature and criticism in order to elaborate the internal dynamics of Aira's literary process and his relation to Argentine literary tradition. Aira's novel *Ema, la cautiva*, written in a comic mode, undoubtedly exhibits the traits Fernández perceives in Aira's literature. Indeed, Leo Pollmann notes that in this text, "el mundo indio . . . pasa a ser una especie de modelo lúdico" (the indian world . . . becomes a kind of ludic model) and Aira's own author's note stresses its playfully inventive aspects.[2] Aira states that he intended to write "una 'gótica' simplificada" (a simplified "gothic" novel), and that while writing he envisioned himself as "Sei Shonagon" and "Scherazada"; he also playfully states that during the writing process, for "varias semanas me distraje. Sudé un poco. Me reí" (several weeks I was distracted. I sweated a little. I laughed).[3] For Contreras it is Aira's novel *La liebre*—like *Ema, la cautiva*, set in nineteenth-century Argentina during a period of expansion into the pampas and featuring a journey through this space—that "mejor cristaliza la operación" (best crystallizes the operation) of aspects of Aira's literary process.[4] Contreras argues that "*La liebre* de César Aira reescribe una fábula de identidad nacional—el cuento clásico del viaje de la civilización a la barbarie—en la *forma* de una novela inglesa" (César Aira's *La liebre* rewrites the fable of national identity—the classic tale of the journey from civilization to barbarism—in the *form* of an English novel) and therefore that Aira's engagement with such discourse is primarily related to literary forms.[5] It appears that these positions converge throughout *Ema, la cautiva* and that the interpretive key to the novel is Aira's comic engagement with canonical texts from Argentine literary history. However, these approaches overlook the possible political connotations of Aira's considered engagement with these canonical texts and the historical setting of his novel. As Aira's novels are steeped in irony and his use of historical information problematic, such political undertones are tangential, elusive, and ambiguous, yet they undoubtedly permeate his work. Thus a careful consideration of *Ema, la cautiva* is of paramount importance in constructing a political reading of Aira's work that has received little emphasis in critical approaches to date. Furthermore, this critical examination of Aira's early novel lays the foundation for the politico-philosophical consideration of Aira's literary process contained within chapter 2.

Ema, la cautiva consists of two distinct sections, the first differing significantly from the main body of the text. The protagonist, Ema, is only alluded to and remains anonymous. This first section instead follows a French engineer, Duval, as he accompanies a brutal forced march to the pampas lead by an Argentine officer, Lavalle. The march passes through the fort of Azul, controlled by Colonel Leal, before arriving at its destination, the fort of Pringles, controlled by Colonel Espina. At this stage Ema emerges as the novel's protagonist, and subsequently the action follows her as she is kidnapped during an indigenous raid and travels throughout the indigenous territories becoming wife, lover, or concubine to various members of the indigenous community before returning to Pringles and employing indigenous labor to establish a pheasant farm.

From the outset, Aira's novel is clearly in dialogue with several important texts from Argentine literary history.[6] The opening section of the novel evokes the writings of Alfred Ébélot for the magazine *Les Revue de Deux Mondes*, as Aira's Duval, like Ébélot himself, is a French "ingeniero contratado por el gobierno central para hacer trabajos especializados en la frontera" (engineer, contracted by the central government to carry out specialized works at the frontier).[7] Similarly, the novel is undoubtedly in dialogue with Lucio V. Mansilla's 1870 text *Una excursión a los indios ranqueles*, which recounts his journey through the indigenous territory in an attempt to negotiate a peace treaty with the Ranquel Indians. While I will discuss important connections between Aira's and Mansilla's texts later, other incidental associations abound. For example, where Mansilla notes that "los indios aman tanto el tabaco como el aguardiente" (the Indians love tobacco as much as liquor), Aira notes that "sus pasatiempos eran el tabaco, la bebida y la pintura [del cuerpo]" (their hobbies were tobacco, drinking, and painting [their bodies]).[8] Significantly, both Ébélot and Mansilla's texts are now important historical sources; the former provides crucial insight into "la perspectiva del viajero europeo del siglo XIX que se interna en el desierto" (the perspective of the European traveler of the nineteenth century who advances into the desert), as Contreras points out, and due to his very detailed description of indigenous life, Mansilla's text is also an important sociological document.[9] In addition, as Ema assumes the role of protagonist and ventures through the indigenous territories, the novel returns to one of the foundational genres of Argentine literature: that of the female captive narrative, of which Esteban Echeverría's *La cautiva* is the principal example. Although this is a fictional genre, it is important to note that early examples, such as that written in 1612 by Ruy Díaz de Guzmán, a Spanish soldier, were not written as fiction.[10] Finally, Aira's novel unquestionably engages with *Facundo: Civilización y Barbarie*, the 1845 text by the writer-statesman and president of Argentina, Domingo Faustino Sarmiento. As with Mansilla, I will discuss important connections between Sarmiento's text and Aira's novel later, yet other connections proliferate. For example, many commentators note that as Sarmiento had never visited the pampas at the time of writing *Facundo*, his descriptions of the landscape frequently rely upon stereotypical "Orientalist" images.[11] These elements are comically present in *Ema, la cautiva*. Aira describes fantastical creatures such as "un tapir, grande como un rinoceronte" (a tapir as large as a rhinoceros) and compares Espina to the "caudillos de la Mesopotamia" (leaders of Mesopotamia) and the fort of Azul to the "torre de Babel" (tower of Babel).[12] Indeed, following a particularly grandiloquent description of the splendor of the natural scene, Sarmiento asks: "¿Creéis por ventura, que esta descripción es plagiada de *Las Mil y una Noches*, u otros cuentos de hadas a la oriental?" (Do you by chance think this description is copied from *A Thousand and One Nights* or other Oriental fairy tales?)[13] At that point it seems almost as if Aira's description of himself as "Sei Shonagon" and "Scherazada" in his author's note directly responds to Sarmiento's question. Importantly, Sarmiento's central discourse of "Civilization and Barbarism," which espoused the theory that within Argentina there are "dos sociedades distintas, rivales e incompatibles; dos civilizaciones diversas; la una española, europea, culta, [y situada en Buenos Aires] y la otra bárbara, americana, casi indígena [y situada en el interior]" (two distinct, rival, and incompatible societies, two diverse civilizations: one Spanish, European, cultured [and situated in Buenos Aires], and the other barbarous, American, almost indigenous [and situated in the interior]), underpins all the other historical texts mentioned.[14] Indeed, as Roberto González Echevarría points out, "few men have had a greater impact on their country's founding"; in *Facundo* Sarmiento established "a national discourse, a set of ideas and figures through which the country could think itself."[15] Despite his efforts to undermine this dichotomous formulation and promote a policy of engagement toward the indigenous population of Argentina, even Mansilla engages with the same ideas in his premeditated response to Sarmiento's theory.[16] The crucial point is that in addition to the fictional referents contained in *Ema, la cautiva*, several texts that Aira engages in his novel are important historical sources, and Echevarría's comments not only stress their importance in the development of Argentine society but also the potential, and vast, political scope of *Ema, la cautiva*.

The potential political importance of Aira's text is strengthened by the fact that the novel is set at a critical juncture in Argentine history, immediately before the culminating episode of the Conquest of the Desert, the term applied to the numerous military excursions led against the indigenous peoples of Argentina from General Juan Manuel de Rosas's initial campaign of 1833–1834, to General Julio Argentino Roca's campaign conducted throughout 1878 and 1879.[17] Early in the novel, Colonel Leal references the "disposición de las dos líneas de fortines, que le debemos a las elucubraciones del inepto Alsina" (arrangement of the two lines of forts, which we owe to the far-fetched ideas of the inept Alsina).[18] The reference is to Adolfo Alsina, minister of war from 1874 until his death (while still fighting the indigenous population) in 1877.[19] During his tenure as minister of war and following a failed attempt to negotiate a treaty with certain indigenous leaders, Alsina adopted a containment strategy toward the indigenous population.[20] His idea was to conduct a military campaign against the indigenous people to push them further south, construct a line of forts along the frontier, and link these with a massive trench to try and prevent the indigenous people raiding the frontier settlements. Leal's scathing comments about Alsina certainly contain an element of truth: "in the short term, Alsina's approach . . . failed. The Indians merely bypassed the forts and traversed the ditches," as David Rock comments.[21] Regardless, the implication of Leal's comment is that Pringles is one of the forts founded by Alsina following his expedition against the indigenous communities of the pampas begun in March 1876.[22] It is subsequently revealed that Pringles is ten years old and, following her return to the fort, that "Ema pasó dos años entre los indios" (Ema spent two years among the Indians).[23] This evidence appears to situate the novel historically. Absent from Aira's text, however, is the fact that, following Alsina's death, General Julio Argentino Roca became minister of war, abandoned Alsina's plan, and conducted a far more aggressive campaign against the indigenous population. Indeed, Roca ostensibly executed the final campaign of the Conquest of the Desert.

Attitudes to Roca's campaign have significantly altered over time. In 1935 Alfred Hasbrouck conducted a careful examination of the cost of Roca's campaign and concluded that "on the whole the conquest of the desert, from the financial and business point of view, was an excellent investment" and that Roca's campaign "may be considered fully as important as any event in the history of that country since it became an independent nation."[24] In 1992, however, Carlos Martínez Sarasola described Roca's campaign as an act of genocide and stated that Roca was "el arquetipo de la 'solución final' en el 'problema' indígena, defensor de la tesis de la guerra ofensiva sin concesiones" (the archetype of the "final solution" to the indigenous "problem," the defender of the thesis of an uncompromising war).[25] Similarly, David Viñas comments that "para la Argentina oficial 1879 significa el cierre de la conquista de la Patagonia y el decisivo sometimiento de los indios" (for official Argentine history, 1879 marks the end of the conquest of Patagonia and the final subjugation of the indians).[26] In sharp contrast, the indigenous communities within Aira's novel are independent and thriving. However, at the novel's conclusion, historical veracity returns and Aira refers to the "masacre" of the "indios" (massacre of the indians).[27] Of paramount importance is that Aira sets his novel immediately prior to the culminating episode of the Conquest of the Desert that, as Sarasola emphasizes, resulted in "the political-administrative unification of the nation-state," "the establishment of an economic model . . . based on the large scale estate or *latifundio* and the agroexportation model," and "the consolidation of national military power."[28] As we shall see, that Aira sets his novel at this moment of fundamental political importance in Argentine history is particularly pertinent given that his novel was also published at another moment of significant political upheaval.

Published in 1981, Aira's novel was, of course, written under the military government brought to power in the coup of 1976, another period of internal division and repression. If tracing an analogy between these two historical moments might seem rather crude, we should remember that the military dictatorship itself employed references to the Conquest of the Desert to justify its intervention in Argentine politics. As Michael Goebel states, "The phrase 'process of national reorganisation' arguably invoked a rerun of the period of 'national organisation'" and, as has been noted, "Argentine historians have generally defined 1880 as the year when the process of national organization was consummated."[29] The military regime's dedication to this historical moment is striking. It engaged in public demonstrations of praise for Roca and the Conquest of the Desert, and numerous commentators note that Aira's novel was published shortly after the centenary celebrations of the conquest led by the military government throughout 1979.[30]

It seems particularly relevant that Aira's novel appeared at the precise moment when the military dictatorship sought to celebrate the military's role in the unification of Argentina and establish their own self-styled "Dirty War" as a continuation of "las acciones militares contra los indios" (the military actions against the Indians).[31] Indeed, the then–minister of internal affairs, General Albano Eduardo Harguindeguy, opened a conference celebrating the Conquest of the Desert and "seized the opportunity to support the 'tradition' of the National Army as guardian and promoter of order in opposition to 'the barbarism' of the past—the aborigines—and that of the present—the 'stateless subversive.'"[32] This argument was consistently repeated: for example, "en 1979 una reedición de algunos textos sobre la Campaña al Desierto, con un prólogo firmado por el entonces Jefe de la Policía Federal, Juan Bautista Sasiaiñ" (in 1979 a reissue of some texts about the Campaign of the Desert, with a prologue signed by the then-chief of the federal police, Juan Bautista Sasiaiñ) described "los indios como 'subversivos'" (the Indians as "subversives").[33] Care should be taken not to infer too much from the precise date of the novel's publication, however: although Aira's text was published in 1981, he himself dates it 21 October 1978. Nonetheless, as Goebel indicates, "already in mid-1976, an army official had portrayed the 'Dirty War' as a latter-day repetition of the ideals of 1880, depicting 'subversives' as the descendants of 'Indians and foreigners.'"[34]

Equally important is that left-wing militants of the seventies also revisited nineteenth-century history to justify their actions. For example, the very name of the armed Peronist group the Montoneros "indicated, with its allusions to the nineteenth-century montoneras, [that] their self-understanding, . . . was first and foremost grounded in a revisionist understanding of national history and identity."[35] Given the persistent emphasis on Roca's Conquest of the Desert in the military government's discourse and the pervasive political use of nineteenth-century Argentine history by left-wing militants of the 1970s, it seems that focusing exclusively on comic elements within *Ema, la cautiva* overlooks the political relevance of Aira's novel. Equally, an approach such as that taken by Contreras, focusing on the literary forms of Aira's work, limits the possible sociopolitical importance of his text by reducing it to its literary tropes. In contrast, I argue that *Ema, la cautiva* is a text of particular political importance.

The conflation of the historical moment in which Aira sets his novel (the culmination of the Conquest of the Desert) and that in which he wrote the novel (the military dictatorship of 1976 to 1983) is one that David Viñas makes in *Indios, ejército y frontera*. Viñas argues that the indigenous people of Argentina were "los primeros 'desaparecidos'" (the first "disappeared") and "han cumplido el rol histórico de los esclavos en la dialéctica fundamental de la dominación" (have fulfilled the historical role of slaves in the fundamental dialectic of domination).[36] This parallel between the disappeared of the 1970s and the indigenous population in 1879 offers a possible political interpretation of Aira's text, as has been noted by other critics, for whom the novel's opening section is particularly important. As Colonel Leal states early in the novel: "Los cargamentos de presos a Pringles son incesantes, hemos contado uno por año en los diez que lleva el fuerte, cada uno con más de mil convictos, ¡y la población de Pringles, hoy, no pasa de 300 blancos!" (The shipments of prisoners to Pringles are incessant, we have counted one per year in the ten years that the fort has existed, each one with more than a thousand convicts, and the population of Pringles today, doesn't count more than three hundred whites!)[37] Given this evidence and the publication date of Aira's novel, Pollmann equates the brutal march, which results in the death of countless prisoners, with the fate of the "desaparecidos" (disappeared) during military rule.[38] Similarly, Pollmann considers Colonel Espina's desire to produce ever greater quantities of money to fill the "vacío" (emptiness) of the pampa and suggests that "es una sátira del estado económico de la Argentina contemporánea con su dinero inflacionario" (it is a satire of the economic state of contemporary Argentina with its inflationary money).[39] Having made these connections, however, Pollmann immediately recants these positions. Regarding the march, he considers other evidence and states that "significaría, pues, caer en la trampa de una perspectiva demasiado fácil—mimética, naturalista—considerar este viaje desde el punto de vista político" (to consider this journey from the political point of view would mean falling into the trap of an overly easy, mimetic and naturalist perspective).[40] Similarly, he qualifies his economic argument by stating in a footnote that Aira's satire is "posiblemente también de la Argentina histórica" (also possibly of Argentine history).[41]

Although Pollmann's impulse to limit the scope of his political argument is correct, he is too expeditious in dismissing it entirely. Despite rejecting his political interpretation of the forced march, considerable evidence in the text remains that strengthens the argument he briefly elaborates. First, there is the brutality of the march itself. From the outset, Aira stresses the prisoners' mistreatment, making it clear they are denied food and barely surviving. Additionally, Lavalle has a cruel delectation for sexual violence, first revealed when he comments on the female prisoners, stating that "por su voluntad o contra ella, cumplen una función; satisfacen a los hombres" (by their will or against it, they fulfill a function; they satisfy the men).[42] Indeed, Lavalle allows his soldiers to rape female prisoners repeatedly, and after arranging for Duval to develop a relationship with one of them, he forces her to have sex with him in plain view of Duval and his subordinates. In an abhorrent development, when Duval leaves and attempts to sleep, her screams keep him awake. The sexual violence experienced by the female prisoners in Aira's novel could be interpreted as an allusion to that suffered by those women disappeared during the military dictatorship. As Rock wrote in 1977: "There can be no doubt about the veracity of reports of torture and the sexual abuse of female prisoners among the many hundreds of detainees held in different parts of the country."[43]

Another ambiguous yet possible comparison can be drawn when Ema's "husband," Gombo, remarks that in Pringles "la vida es imposible, y la muerte también" (life is impossible, and death as well), an oblique reference, perhaps, to the condition of the disappeared; perpetually defined by their absence, they are condemned to be categorized as neither alive nor dead.[44] Considered in this way, there is dark irony in Gombo's subsequent comment that "quizás las cosas cambien en el futuro. Quizás dentro de cien años la vida sea posible . . . pero afortunadamente no voy a vivir para verlo" (perhaps things will change in the future. Maybe within a hundred years life will be possible . . . but luckily I'm not going to live to see it), as almost exactly one century from the period in which Aira's novel is set, disappearances perpetrated by the Argentine military resumed.[45]

Regarding economics, it is possible to interpret aspects of Aira's novel as another indirect allusion to the period immediately before the coup of 1976. Following Perón's return to Argentina and the presidency in 1973, the Peronists attempted to implement a "social pact" between labor and businessmen to curb inflation. Although initially successful, the pact later disintegrated (due in part to the oil crisis in the same year).[46] It is this crisis that is possibly reflected in Espina's obsession with printing excessive amounts of paper money. Paul H. Lewis notes that in Argentina "between the end of 1972 and the end of 1973 the money supply doubled from 28.8 billion to 56.2 billion pesos, with most of the increase occurring during the latter half of 1973" under Perón.[47] Lewis adds that "to continue fueling the economy, money was churned out at a dizzying rate. . . . Inflation, which had been brought down from around 100 percent at the time Cámpora took office to just over 30 percent when Perón was inaugurated, climbed again to over 74 percent by May 1974. In the next two years it was to reach 954 percent."[48]

This economic reality seems to be reflected in *Ema, la cautiva*, where an indigenous person from Pringles comments that "no sabemos qué valor nominal tienen los billetes" (we don't know what nominal value the banknotes have) and where Aira comments that "la aldea se inundó de dinero. La paga de los soldados había sido centuplicada" (the town was flooded with money. The soldiers' pay had been increased a hundredfold).[49] The connection with economic crisis is enhanced when Espina rhetorically asks: "¿Cómo no habría de ser un cataclismo el papel moneda, en el que la cantidad es todo y siempre está a punto de multiplicarse?" (How could paper money not be a cataclysm, in that in it, quantity is everything and it's always at the point of multiplying?)[50] Although the strongest connection appears to be between Espina's actions and the Peronist government's policy of printing ever increasing quantities of money, it is also important to note that following the military coup of 1976, and despite the efforts of economic minister José A. Martínez de Hoz, inflation continued to be a significant problem.[51] Furthermore, during the military government's tenure there would also be a severe banking crisis in 1980, which further serves to connect this period with the sense of impending economic chaos suggested by Espina's comments.[52]

As Pollmann intuits, however, these economic parallels are problematic. Considering the comparison of Espina's compulsion to print money and the hyperinflation experienced during the Peronist government of 1973–1976, it is inescapable that throughout the twentieth century in Argentina many governments resorted to printing increasing quantities of money to resolve fiscal deficits, and this frequently resulted in high rates of inflation.[53] Indeed, as Gerardo Della Paolera, Maria Alejandra Irigoin, and Carlos G. Bózzoli noted in 2003, in Argentina "positive rates of inflation persisted in every year from 1940."[54] Regarding the conflation of the "Dirty War" and Aira's novel, the forced march that Aira describes is not in itself sufficient evidence to equate his novel with the actions of the military dictatorship of 1976. For example, Aira's march could equally be related to the massacre of striking workers in Patagonia in the 1920s where many supporters were tortured and "over 2,000 strikers were killed."[55] Or indeed, the actions of Aira's soldiers could perhaps echo General Uriburu's creation in the 1930s of "a Special Section within the federal police for dealing with labor organizers, left-wing propagandists, and Radical party plotters" that would "beat up and torture the government's opponents" or those of General Aramburu during the "Liberating Revolution" from 1955, which sent "some 200 . . . high union officials . . . to a prison camp in Tierra del Fuego" and "summarily" executed twenty-seven leaders of an uprising of workers and Peronist members of the military on 9 June 1956.[56]

Another problem with direct comparisons is that in twentieth-century Argentina "political instability and sociocultural fragmentation" were consistently underpinned in political discourse with recourse to nineteenth-century history.[57] As Goebel notes, "elements of *nacionalismo* . . . fueled military coups ideologically (in 1930, 1943, 1955, 1966 and 1976)," and "historical revisionism" was mobilized as an oppositional discourse "at times of heightened political conflict, economic crisis and deficient legitimacy of the holders of power (as in the 1930s, between 1955 and 1976 and in 2001–2003)."[58] Crucially, reinterpretation of nineteenth-century history was an essential part of *nacionalismo* and historical revisionism. Both movements based their historical analysis on a dichotomous model opposing "the 'real' nation [that] could be found in the untainted interior of the country, where Hispanic and Catholic traditions had merged into a Creole identity embodied in the archetype of the gaucho and their militias" with "a conspiracy between British imperialism, the 'oligarchy' and the intelligentsia of Buenos Aires [that] had subjugated Argentina's national consciousness."[59] These arguments clearly evoke Sarmiento's discourse of "Civilization and Barbarism" but with a simple inversion of the positive term. The crucial point is that during the twentieth century such theories were mobilized to justify political positions ranging from right-wing, if not fascist, trends emerging in the 1930s (*nacionalismo*) to left-leaning and populist currents emerging in the 1960s (through the work of such historical revisionists as Arturo Jauretche).[60] Ultimately, due to the "constant drawing of analogies between the nineteenth-century past and contemporary politics and culture," the period in which Aira sets his novel suffers from an excess of signification.[61] Although this makes the development of parallels between historical periods fraught with difficulty, contrary to Pollmann's dismissal of political interpretations of Aira's novel, I contend that this very excess of signification, inversely and paradoxically, emphasizes the singular political importance of the text.

Scattered throughout Aira's novel are teasing echoes of the present that are deliberately not given the clear-cut status of allegories or analogies. However, cumulatively they do suggest a latent criticism of the military government, their systematic repression, and Peronist economic policies of the 1970s. The salient feature of these echoes, however, is that they could easily be applied to other periods of Argentine history. Thus the surplus of signification inherent to the period in which Aira sets his novel (due to the consistent political use of nineteenth-century Argentine history) suggests a cyclical conception of history. Certainly, the novel conveys a sense that violent episodes have consistently replayed throughout Argentine history. This idea is strengthened at the novel's conclusion when Ema and a group of indigenous companions travel to "Las cuevas de Nueva Roma." The colony of Nueva Roma was founded in 1856 by Silvano Olivieri, an Italian immigrant who served in the Argentine army and whose ghost is mentioned in the text. The colony failed due to the excessive severity of the militaristic regime Olivieri implemented: there was an uprising among the colonizers, and they assassinated him.[62] The episode serves to highlight the recurrent instances of militaristic repression and violent reaction throughout Argentine history. Indeed, the comic elements contained within *Ema, la cautiva* seem to invoke Marx's famous assertion in *The Eighteenth Brumaire of Louis Bonaparte* that "Hegel observes somewhere that all the great events and characters of world history occur twice, so to speak. He forgot to add: the first time as high tragedy, the second time as low farce."[63] The connection seems especially relevant given that Lavalle mentions that he lived in France before the "advenimiento del tirano" (accession of the tyrant), who Duval identifies as "Bonaparte."[64] Given this connection, the military government's desire to emulate previous military actions against the indigenous population cannot but recall Marx's argument that in any given situation, historical agents "summon up the spirits of the past, borrowing from them their names, marching orders, uniforms, in order to enact new scenes in world history, but in this time-honoured guise and with this borrowed language."[65]

The connection with Marx and Hegel has further significance that can be clearly seen by considering Aira's essay "La ciudad y el campo." In this essay, Aira contends that authors frequently select "escenarios ya sistematizados en parejas, cuyo contraste va dictando los rasgos pertinentes: ciudad/campo, ricos/pobres, pasado/presente, Europa/América, liberales/conservadores, etc." (settings already systematized in pairs whose contrast dictates the pertinent characteristics: city/countryside, rich/poor, past/present, Europe/America, liberal/conservative, etc.)[66] Aira then argues that in "el Río de la Plata el contraste campo/ciudad se dio más marcado que en cualquier otro país del continente" (the Río de la Plata area the country/city distinction was more noticeable than in any other country in the continent), that the rural/urban dichotomy represented "dos civilizaciones distintas, con culturas autónomas" (two distinct civilizations, with independent cultures) and that "hacia las décadas 1870–1880 el dispositivo ciudad/campo ocupó toda la literatura rioplatense" (around the decades 1870–1880 the city/country dichotomy was found in all the literature of the Río de la Plata area), to the point that it became "la cara literaria del proceso de creación de la nacionalidad" (the literary face of the process of creating nationality).[67] Aira's binary opposition between the city and the countryside indubitably evokes Sarmiento's theory of "Civilization and Barbarism," and as his comments suggest, the literary manifestation of the dichotomy has an important political correlate. I contend that Aira's novel is written in such a way as to emphasize that the "politics of history" (understood as "the ways in which history was written and mobilized in order to affect the distribution of political power in a society") employed in Argentina during the twentieth century relies on Sarmiento's dichotomous model, which in turn is undoubtedly influenced by Hegel.[68]

As previously discussed, Sarmiento's model provided the theoretical underpinning for various episodes of military and guerrilla violence throughout the twentieth century in Argentina. However, as opposed to the Hegelian dialectic, the oversignification inherent in the period in which Aira sets his novel suggests that this model periodically materializes in cyclical repetitions without ever reaching a transcendent unity. An alternative paradigm for interpreting Aira's novel can be discerned, however, when one considers Aira's enigmatic comment that in composing *Ema, la cautiva*, "el Eterno Retorno fue mi recurso" (the eternal return was my resource).[69] This elusive reference suggests that Aira's text can be considered in a Nietzschean (rather than a Hegelian) sense, concerned with the repetitions of history. In this, Aira seems to utilize a similar philosophical approach to Deleuze, who constructed "a critique of Hegelian dialectics, where a principle of negation itself becomes that which transcends" by engaging "Nietzsche's idea of affirmation [that] emerges out of processes of negation but frees itself from them."[70] With this in mind and conscious of Pollmann's doubts concerning a direct political interpretation of Aira's novel, I would suggest that *Ema, la cautiva* contains a latent political critique of a different order. This critique (which closely parallels Deleuze and Guattari's development of aspects of Marx's theories) relates to the underlying impulse that has (arguably) driven the violent repetitions of Argentine history, namely, the development of capitalism. In this way, the present analysis follows a similar structure to that developed by Aira himself in his essay "Exotismo." In this piece, Aira traces the development of the "género exótico" (exotic genre), arguing that its first manifestation took the form of the "extranjero en nuestro mundo cotidiano" (foreigner in our daily world) and that this "se hizo ciencia, y salió del campo de la literatura" (became science, and exited the field of literature). Aira then contends that the exotic genre came to be understood "como moda, como frivolidad y tontería" (as fashion, frivolity, and nonsense). Finally, Aira argues that "el exotismo se hace comercial" (exoticism becomes commercial) and that "el género va a la zaga de la expansión capitalista" (the genre follows capitalist expansion).[71] So too in my analysis, I note that the "exotic" texts of Argentine literary history that Aira engages have become important historical and sociological documents, that Aira's novel has frequently been understood as frivolity and nonsense, and, ultimately, that it contains a powerful critique of capitalist expansion.

As numerous critics note, Roca's Conquest of the Desert was an essential element in the development of capitalism in Argentina, and this is echoed throughout Aira's novel.[72] Reflections on capitalism permeate his text, and he definitively describes the development of the Argentine state as the development of a capitalist economy. Significantly, women in Aira's text have a central role in facilitating this development. This is evident in an early discussion between Lavalle and Duval. When the latter asks what will become of the female prisoners on arrival at Pringles, Lavalle's response is highly significant:

> —Quién sabe. De cualquier modo, tampoco es eso lo que importa. Son musas. . . . Los indios, por alguna razón que ellos conocerán mejor que nosotros, aprecian a las mujeres blancas como elemento de intercambio, de modo que no bien llegan a la frontera empiezan a "circular" en toda clase de tratos . . .
>
> —¿Quiere decir—exclamó el francés—que se las *venderán* a los salvajes?[73]
>
> (—Who knows. Anyway, that isn't the important thing. They're muses. . . . The Indians, for some reason they know better than us, value white women as an element of exchange, so, as soon as they arrive at the frontier, they begin to "circulate" in all kinds of deals . . .
>
> —Do you mean to say—exclaimed the Frenchman—that *you'll sell them* to the savages?)

Lavalle's comments reveal the purpose of bringing so many women to the frontier as prisoners: to facilitate exchanges between colonizers and indigenous people. Furthermore, Duval immediately conceives of these exchanges in capitalist terms, suggesting that the women will be sold into bondage. However, when Lavalle later states that "eso basta para introducirlas al mundo del que serán una de las monedas" (this is sufficient to introduce them to the world in which they will be a form of currency), he reveals a further use of women in the colonizers' capitalist project.[74] When Lavalle anachronistically comments that "el famoso intercambio de mujeres es un lugar común de la etnología" (the well-known exchange of women is commonplace in ethnology), the particular use that women are put to becomes apparent.[75] For Claude Lévi-Strauss, "marriage regulations" function primarily as a language and method of communication between tribal groups where "the mediating factor . . . should be the *women of the group*, who are *circulated* between clans, lineages, or families, in place of the *words of the group* which are *circulated* between individuals."[76] In Aira's text the colonizers essentially exploit this mode of communication in indigenous culture but account for it in capitalist terms, replacing the original significance of the exchanges (communication) with that of a material transaction. Hence, by utilizing women as currency in exchanges with the indigenous people, the colonizers familiarize them with the vocabulary and concept of the general equivalence of money in material exchanges. Thus the exchanges constitute a cunning colonial project as they prepare indigenous communities for introduction to the capitalist system the colonizers are attempting to impose. This will by extension also bring them within the control of the nascent state.

Equally important, it is Espina who facilitates these exchanges, and his principal activity is the printing and distribution of money. This too can be considered another strategy utilized to control the indigenous population: when a native army arrives near the fort and intends to attack, Espina simply pays their representatives with his money to avert it. Although the "raid" is later revealed to be a hoax arranged by Espina, one of the indigenous witnesses to the payoff comments that "la historia no es más que una sucesión de pagos, cuanto más exorbitantes mejor. Lo único que ha variado ha sido la forma y el crédito" (history is nothing more than a succession of payments, the more exorbitant, the better. The only thing that has changed has been the form and [the introduction of] credit).[77] Thus in Aira's novel the indigenous population already seems aware of the basis of contemporary capitalism, "crédito" (credit), and it becomes an integral part of the colonization of the pampa. When two other indigenous people discuss this payoff, the significance of the distribution of money is reinforced:

> —Por ahora ese dinero va a ir a las manos de uno o dos caciques, quizás de Caful solo . . .
> —Es lo mismo. A Caful, o a quien sea, no le servirá de nada si no logra distribuirlo. Al menos distribuir lo suficiente como para crear un "clima" de dinero.[78]
>
> (—For now the money will go into the hands of one or two chiefs, maybe only to Caful . . .
> —It's all the same. It won't be of any use to Caful or anyone else if he doesn't manage to distribute it. Or at least, distribute enough of it to create an "atmosphere" of money.)

Placing emphasis on creating "un clima de dinero" (an atmosphere of money) reinforces the idea that Aira's colonizers are attempting to create an environment in which even traditional exchanges and communication are understood in capitalist terms. Again, the creation of a culture of monetary exchange appears as a colonial strategy to absorb traditional practices within the capitalist system. Espina deliberately manipulates existing practices (this time, indigenous raids) with the goal of distributing his money and establishing a system whereby *interactions* will be increasingly understood as *transactions*. The full extent of Espina's project is betrayed when he reflects that "los resultados de la maniobra fueron subjetivos. De pronto, aquellos indios remotos y casi míticos, los súbditos de Catriel, de Cafulcurá, los tributarios del emperador Pincén, entraban al campo de la imaginación cotidiana de la gente, ya que los billetes circulaban (al menos eso creían) uniéndolos" (the results of the ploy were subjective. Suddenly, those remote and almost mythical indians, Catriel and Cafulcurá's subjects and Emperor Pincén's taxpayers, entered into the people's daily imagination, since the banknotes circulated [or at least that's what they believed], uniting them).[79] This remark suggests that the staged attack and payoff works in three distinct ways. First, it demystifies the perception of the indigenous communities within the "white" population. Second, perceived differences between different tribes and the white population are eliminated. Finally, all the people are united under the system of monetary circulation. Thus Aira makes the purpose of establishing a capitalist system plain to the reader.

These two elements (the exchange of women as a commodity and Espina's payments to the indigenous "raiders") have implications that suggest Aira's novel contains a latent critique of capitalism. In *The Passions and the Interests: Political Arguments for Capitalism before Its Triumph* (1997), Albert O. Hirschman attempts to answer the question: "How did commercial, banking, and similar money-making pursuits become honorable at some point in the modern age after having stood condemned or despised as greed, love of lucre, and avarice for centuries past?"[80] Reviewing the work of philosophers from the eighteenth century and before, Hirschman demonstrates that there was a widely held belief that *"one set of passions, hitherto known variously as greed, avarice, or love of lucre, could be usefully employed to oppose and bridle such other passions as ambition, lust for power, or sexual lust."*[81] This passion for "lucre" hence came to be defended as an "interest" (as opposed to a dangerous passion), and arguments in favor of capitalism thus defined came to triumph. These arguments have important correlations with Aira's text. In Hirschman's terms Espina effectively utilizes the indigenous people's "love of lucre" to oppose their "lust for power" in that he (at least symbolically) wards off an attack by paying the leaders of the revolt. In another development that goes further than Hirschman, Espina and other colonizers attempt to encourage the indigenous people's "love of lucre" to bring their "sexual lust" within the relations of material exchange by utilizing women as a form of currency. This is a particularly apposite strategy in that Aira states that in the indigenous society "todo era sexualidad y amor" (everything was sexuality and love).[82]

It is in this way that Aira first appears to critique the development of capitalism itself. Whereas such thinkers as Jean-François Melon claimed in 1734 that "the spirit of conquest and the spirit of commerce are mutually exclusive in a nation" and Sir James Steuart in 1767 would state emphatically that a "modern economy . . . is the most effective bridle ever was invented against the folly of despotism," in Aira's narrative, the forced march emphasizes that the expansion of capitalism itself is a despotic and cruel conquest. Thus Aira constructs a similar argument to that made by Marx, who stressed "some of the more violent episodes in the history of European commercial expansion," in order to mock the idea that capitalism would prevent conquest or despotism.[83] Indeed, through his depiction of the role of capital in the conquest of an indigenous population, one is also reminded of Deleuze and Guattari's tripartite description of societal development. In *Ema, la cautiva* it initially appears that the indigenous population derives all meaning from the "immanent unity of the earth," which is to say, from the natural world.[84] Nonetheless, when this "primitive territorial machine" (as Deleuze and Guattari name such societal configurations) comes into contact with Espina's fort, a new arrangement is forged. In Aira's novel the development of the Argentine state relies on its fundamental opposition to the indigenous communities that surround their forts, and Espina strives to control and centralize the production of money. As in Deleuze and Guattari's analysis of the second stage of societal development, the "role of money in commerce hinges less on commerce itself than on its control by the State," and this new "despotic barbarian formation has to be conceived of in terms of an opposition between it and the primitive territorial machine: the birth of an empire."[85] However, although Lavalle, Leal, and other colonizers describe the indigenous people as "salvajes" (savages) and Espina as "semisalvaje" (half-savage), "apasionado por el terror y tiránico al grado máximo" (impassioned by terror and tyrannical to the maximum extent), once Ema reaches Pringles and throughout her journey through the indigenous territory, her life is idyllic and ludic (the exception being the indigenous raid in which she is captured).[86] This suggests that Aira's novel contains a particularly nuanced critique of capitalism. Indeed, it would appear that as Espina attempts to create a "clima de dinero" (atmosphere of money), within which women function as currency and sexual relations are understood in capitalist terms, that a "civilized capitalist machine" is being constructed within which flows of desire are decoded and subordinated to capital, as in the third stage of societal development for Deleuze and Guattari.[87]

In developing their analysis of capitalism, Deleuze and Guattari argue that "nature itself, the Whole of existence, is at once a matter of flows, and that any society must structure these flows in order to subsist."[88] Thus all previous social formations "coded" and contained flows within certain parameters to control the population and centralize power. As they state, "to code desire . . . is the business of the socius."[89] However, they also argue that "capitalism is the only social machine that is constructed on the basis of decoded flows" and that it functions by breaking the rules and norms previously exercised to maintain power.[90] Instead capitalism subjugates flows to "a law of general equivalence in the form of monetary value."[91] As Jonathan Roffe demonstrates, this includes the "decoding" of sexual relationships, stripping them of their significance and "making possible new kinds of relations that were excluded by the coding regimes in question."[92] This process is evident in Aira's text. The "decoding" of sexual relationships allows indigenous people to forge them with "mujeres blancas" (white women), including Ema.[93] Although these relationships are not expressly forbidden, their significance definitively changes. When Ema establishes a relationship with the indigenous leader, Hual, he acts "en contra de la opinión de su padre" (against his father's opinion) by taking her to the island of Carhué, a "refugio sagrado que no debía mancillar la presencia ambigua del blanco" (sacred refuge that shouldn't be besmirched with the ambiguous presence of the white man).[94] It seems that the mere presence of white women contributes to the island "perdiendo su carácter divino" (losing its divine character), and the indigenous leaders no longer travel there seeking "protección mágica alguna sino por la mera absorción de lujo y ocio por contacto" (any kind of magical protection except that gained through a proximity, as if by osmosis, to luxury and leisure).[95] As in Deleuze and Guattari, a new type of relationship is made possible, and the original significance of previous formations is stripped away. These new relationships also contribute to a general loss of significance in indigenous life. The island's magical nature is lost, at least partly due to the relationship between Hual and Ema, a point proven when Hual takes "una bestial cantidad de somníferos" (a beastly quantity of sleeping pills), "láudano y morfina" (laudanum and morphine), and spends most of his time on the island in a drug-induced stupor.[96] As the colonizers deliberately introduce the women to the indigenous communities as a form of currency, Aira's novel also demonstrates the incorporation of sexual relations under the "law of general equivalence in the form of monetary value."[97]

Considered in this way and attentive to the ludic qualities of Ema's life on the frontier, it appears that Aira employs her characterization to investigate the apparent freedoms that capitalism has afforded women. It has been argued that Lévi-Strauss's "way of reading kinship systems excludes women from the role of cultural *agents*, treating them only as cultural *objects*."[98] Regarding Aira's text, Ema remains captive during her journey and dependent on men, yet she is granted degrees of agency unheard of at that time. She travels further than any soldier, further even than the soldiers manage to spread their money. This permits her paradoxically to function as both cultural object and agent simultaneously. As discussed, the circulation of women as currency in Aira's novel forms an integral part of the colonization of indigenous communities and their introduction to capitalist society. Thus Ema is again both cultural object and agent simultaneously: she is manipulated by Espina and others to bring the indigenous population within the capitalist system and their control, yet this allows Ema freedom to travel and affords her a degree of agency. That this freedom is illusory is, however, made clear several times in the novel. Following her travels, Ema decides to return to Pringles, and her then-partner, Evaristo Hugo, allows her to choose her own destiny and bestows on her certain gifts. These gifts are significant for understanding the limitations of Ema's newfound freedom. Before leaving the outmost indigenous city, Hugo presents Ema with maps that delineate indigenous territory (and the land occupied by the colonial forts), allows her to visit a pheasant farm, and gives her two pheasants.[99] Hugo's gifts represent the knowledge of Aira's indigenous society with which Ema returns, knowledge she immediately utilizes to create her own pheasant farm. Through this process Ema appears to gain complete autonomy: she moves of her own volition and does not subordinate her decisions to any sexual partner. Furthermore, as Ema's plan is to generate vast wealth from her farm, she wins this freedom by entering the capitalist system. By allowing Ema to become a commercial farmer and thus liberate herself from her dependence on men, Aira recognizes that capitalism liberated women from traditional family roles and granted them autonomy to enter the labor market.

Ema's transition to entrepreneur, however, contains another latent criticism of capitalism. To facilitate her plan, Ema borrows money from Espina to purchase land and livestock. Ema frees herself from her traditional role, but by accepting Espina's loan she enters into a new type of bondage. Her subjection is simply financial rather than reproductive. Furthermore, Espina's motivation for granting the loan is highly significant. As Aira states, "cualquier negocio que emprendiera, por fallido que resultara, serviría a sus propósitos de extender el alcance del dinero que imprimía" (whatever business she undertook, however unsuccessful it turned out to be, would serve his intention of extending the reach of the money he printed) among the indigenous population.[100] Ema is clearly still manipulated by Espina to integrate the indigenous people into the capitalist system and bring them under the control of the state. Where previously Espina had used Ema's sexual and reproductive properties in order to begin the dual processes of colonization and capitalization, he now holds her in financial servitude and manipulates her similarly. Due to the knowledge Ema returns with, she is especially suited for this task. She takes Espina's money to a pheasant fair where she trades with the indigenous people, causing Espina to reflect that "ninguno de mis espías lo hubiese logrado" (none of my spies had managed it).[101] With this in mind, Ema's ability to convince the indigenous people, who "despreciaban el trabajo" (despised work), to work on her farm assumes a rather different inflection.[102] Ema's return to the fort and transition to capitalist farmer makes it clear that the apparent freedoms she gains are chimerical. In Ema's case, as in Deleuze and Guattari's critique, "while imitating the decoding that makes possible the freeing up of flows and new ways of existing, capitalist society only produces a different, more insidious, kind of unfreedom."[103]

Another parallel between Aira's novel and Deleuze and Guattari's analysis of the capitalist system emerges when one returns to the historical and literary context in which Aira situates his novel. Unsurprisingly, following Roca's campaign against the indigenous people of the pampas, they become somewhat absent from political discourse. Indeed, as Sarasola indicates, during the dictatorship their very existence was denied by decree in one province.[104] This explains why Mansilla's *Una excursión a los indios ranqueles* is an important sociological document. Mansilla not only sought to write the indigenous populations of Argentina into official history, but the text provides one of the few records of the indigenous people's own words. However, in attempting to counteract Sarmiento's discourse of "Civilization and Barbarism," Mansilla repeatedly strives to elevate the reader's perception of the indigenous population by drawing parallels between their society and western democracy. Thus he talks of an indigenous "plebiscito" (plebiscite), states that indigenous meetings are "una cosa muy parecida al parlamento de un pueblo libre, a nuestro congreso, por ejemplo" (something very similar to the parliament of a free people—our own congress, for example), and concludes that "la máquina constitucional llamada por la libertad Poder Legislativo, no es una invención moderna extraordinaria; que en algo nos parecemos a los indios" (the constitutional machine that liberty knows under the name of legislative power is no extraordinary modern invention, that in some things we resemble the Indians).[105] Furthermore, Mansilla describes in great detail the system of "crédito" (credit) he perceives in indigenous society.[106] Both these elements are present in *Ema, la cautiva*.

By including the indigenous population in his novel, setting the majority of the text in their land and by describing their customs, Aira attempts to redress their absence from Argentine history. Moreover, like Mansilla, Aira compares his indigenous society to Western models, but such parallels are exaggerated to the point of absurdity. Thus the outermost indigenous territory is organized around a summer "ciudad" (city), referred to as "la capital" (the capital), containing numerous "mansiones" (mansions), "suburbios" (suburbs) and even a "palacio real" (royal palace).[107] Needless to say, this description bears little resemblance to the actual structures of indigenous *toldos*.[108] Aira strays further from historical reality when Ema discovers that the community is in fact an "imperio indígena" (indigenous empire) subject to an unusual form of capitalism.[109] As Hugo states: "Lo real, le dijo el ministro, era el Estado. Su prueba suprema consistía en delegar en los particulares su única facultad inalienable, la emisión de dinero. Cada ciudadano tenía derecho a la libertad, siempre que ésta fuera tan completa que excluyese al pensamiento" (Reality, said the minister, was the state. Its supreme test consisted of delegating to the individual their only inalienable right, the issue of money. Each citizen had the right to freedom, provided it was so complete that it excluded thought).[110] It appears that the production and distribution of money is the very basis of this fictionalized indigenous society. I contend that this comic incongruity highlights a particular problem discussed at length by Dipesh Chakrabarty in *Provincializing Europe: Postcolonial Thought and Historical Difference.*

In this book, Chakrabarty directly challenges the teleological view of "universal history" espoused by Kant, Hegel, Marx, and many others. In "Idea of a Universal History from a Cosmopolitan Point of View," Kant presents a "philosophical interpretation of history" that "is, in effect, a variation of the common eighteenth-century theory of progress," whereby history "would make sense if it could be seen as a continuous, though not perhaps straightforward, progression towards a better state of affairs," as W. H. Walsh explains.[111] Similarly, Hegel proposes "to 'make sense' of history by means of the notion of progress" by introducing the dialectic into his theory of historical development.[112] Marx, in turn, applies Hegel's theory to economic problems in an attempt to uncover the universal material forces that propel history forward. In each case, teleological historical development is presumed to be universal, regardless of variations in historical and cultural context. In contrast, Chakrabarty addresses the problems that arise when such theories are applied to nations beyond Europe (which is to say, in the "third world"), while ignoring both the European roots of these theories and the specific and divergent histories of these other countries. As he states, "so-called universal ideas that European thinkers produced in the period from the Renaissance to the Enlightenment . . . could never be completely universal and pure concepts" and "must have imported into them intimations of pre-existing histories that were singular and unique."[113] Thus Chakrabarty argues that "philosophers and thinkers who shape the nature of social sciences have produced theories that embrace the entirety of humanity" but also recognizes that "these statements have been produced in relative, and sometimes absolute, ignorance of the majority of humankind—that is, those living in non-Western cultures."

It seems that Aira's novel highlights what Chakrabarty denominates the "everyday paradox of third-world social science," which is that despite the European focus of such concepts, postcolonial social scientists and historians find these categories "eminently useful."[114] By exaggerating the types of descriptions found in Mansilla's text, Aira demonstrates that applying seemingly "universal," European political categories to indigenous societies, even when the goal is to defend such societies, is inherently colonial. And this is precisely the point. Aira's descriptions of indigenous society comically suggest that "capitalism has haunted all forms of society" and that if "the rules formulated by Marx are followed exactly," "it is correct to *retrospectively* understand all history in the light of capitalism."[115] This is to say that Aira's text responds to the problem that Chakrabarty perceives by demonstrating that *capitalism colonizes the past* by determining the very "conditions and the possibility of a universal history," as Deleuze and Guattari argue.[116] It should be noted that through its use of European theory to discuss Argentine texts, Chakrabarty's paradox also appears to underpin the present study. Nonetheless, as in Aira's novel, in the present book it is the expansion of *capitalism* that has created the possibility of universal history and that makes the European theory deployed applicable to the Argentine case.

Reverberations of this colonizing process can be observed elsewhere in Aira's novel. For example, within the strange capitalist society Aira describes, the indigenous "state" does not produce money itself, nor set its value, nor provide any regulatory control for the financial system. Thus it inverts the typical state function and is arguably closer to the neoliberalism of the 1970s and 1980s whereby the state would ensure that the conditions for market freedom are maintained and little else. This idea is strengthened when Hugo stresses the minimal role of the state, pondering, "¿qué es la política? Su ciencia, el laissez-faire. Su técnica, la nariz de una reina" (what is politics? Its science; laissez-faire. Its technique; the nose of a queen).[117] In this regard, it is interesting to note that in 1989 Francis Fukuyama declared the "unabashed victory of economic and political liberalism" and argued that they constituted "the end point of mankind's ideological evolution" within the teleological view of universal history.[118] I contend, however, that the process is in fact inverted in Aira's description of indigenous society. As in the work of Deleuze and Guattari, it is rather that capitalism "is inserted into the interstices of the pre-existing social body," which is to say the state, and that under capitalism it is "up to the State to recode as best it can, by means of regular or exceptional operations, the product of the decoded flows."[119] Moreover, Aira's indigenous "state" grants its citizens complete freedom, yet when confronted with this freedom, thought itself becomes impossible such that it is "money and the market" that must act as "capitalism's true police."[120] Within Aira's depiction of various competing "capitalisms," there are remnants of institutions that never seem truly to hold power. Even regarding Espina, Aira suggests that he might be sending his money to Great Britain, and he includes a portrait of Queen Victoria besides his own on his banknotes. This certainly implicates Espina in the neocolonial subjugation of Argentina to British interests and again serves to displace power and locate it perpetually "elsewhere." In Aira's novel, as in Deleuze and Guattari's analysis, capitalism in and of itself is a colonizing discourse.

Aira has stated that he became disillusioned with politics in his youth and that "hubo un momento, antes del golpe del '76 en que me había apartado mucho de toda ilusión política, en realidad no la recuperé nunca" (there was a moment, before the coup of '76 in which I had strayed far from all political excitement, in reality I never recovered it).[121] Indeed, he has also stated that this disillusionment occurred "hacia el año '71–'72 cuando estuve preso y terminé en el '75, por completo" (around the year '71–'72 when I was in prison, and it ended completely in '75).[122] In the same interview, Aira stresses that literature became his "consuelo" (consolation), his "alegría" (happiness) and his "vida" (life). These comments, coupled with his statement that "quise escribir sobre cuestiones políticas, sobre situaciones sufridas de la vida general, pero al final me parece oportunismo" (I wanted to write about political questions, about the long-suffering situations of life in general, but in the end it seemed like opportunism), seem to suggest that, as Contreras argues, Aira is principally concerned with literature in and of itself.[123] Nonetheless, when one considers the period that Aira selects as the historical setting for *Ema, la cautiva*, the situation in Argentina at the time he wrote his novel, and especially the parallels the military government drew between the two in its own political discourse, it seems almost impossible to ignore the possible political implications of his work. Although Aira's method of incorporating political references demands a considerable degree of caution in emphasizing any single political argument, it equally seems that *Ema, la cautiva* contains a latent critique of the military government and a more abstract critique of the development of capitalism in Argentina. Indeed, although Aira may have become disillusioned with the existent state of Argentine politics at the time of writing *Ema, la cautiva*, it seems that he remained intimately concerned with the development of capitalism, which in the novel appears as the hidden motor of political history. Aira's ironic mode of writing does not permit us to equate his work with unequivocally Marxist perspectives, but in this regard *Ema, la cautiva* (as is the case with Deleuze and Guattari) can be seen to deploy a Marxist framework.

Aira's appraisal of the capitalist system is, however, nuanced and carefully considered. He is judicious in demonstrating the freedoms afforded by capitalism as he simultaneously critiques the same system. With this in mind, there is one final irony that emerges from Aira's author's note to his text. Aira begins his note by describing "una linda mañana de primavera, en el Pumper Nic de Flores, donde suelo venir a pensar" (a beautiful spring morning, in the Pumper Nic in Flores, where I usually come to think).[124] Thus Aira precedes his novel with an idyllic scene set in an Argentine copy of a North American business (Burger King), one of the most visible manifestations of the type of neoliberal policies the military government attempted to implement and which Aira critiques in the very same novel. Furthermore, just over ten years later in 1992, at a very different moment of crisis in Argentina, Pumper Nic (and the supermarket Disco) provide the setting for Aira's novel *La prueba* that describes a far more direct and visceral assault on the development of neoliberal capitalism in Argentina, as we shall see in chapter 2.[125]

CHAPTER 2

ACCESSING THE REAL

HAVING ESTABLISHED THAT *EMA, LA CAUTIVA* CAN BE READ AS A CRIT-
ique of the development of capitalism, both in Argentina and as a discursive
formation, the foundation has been laid to consider the wider political importance of Aira's literary oeuvre and to reconcile this element with his literary process, the perpetual "huida hacia adelante" (flight forward) outlined
in the introduction. Dierdra Reber has suggested that "a close-reading foray
into Aira's present reveals a sustained—if euphemistic, elliptical, or indirect—
commentary on neoliberal commodity culture."[1] I argue that Aira's novel *La
prueba* (not discussed by Reber) is not only paradigmatic of this "commentary"
but that it can be read as a bildungsroman that facilitates the unification of
Aira's political and artistic projects. In this text, two punk lesbians (denom-
inations they vociferously deny), Mao and Lenin, attempt to seduce a third
teenage girl, Marcia, in a fast food restaurant and then set out to prove their
love for her by rampaging through a supermarket in a murderous frenzy of cinematic violence. For Josefina Ludmer, the novel can be considered "el cuento
de la última globalización" (the story of late globalization), and she argues that
"Mao y Lenin, las guerrilleras anteriores, ahora punk-lesbianas, atacan de raíz
. . . cierta 'modernización' latinoamericana" (Mao and Lenin, those previous

guerrillas turned punk-lesbians, attack from the roots . . . a certain Latin American modernization).[2] Cognizant of César Barros's suggestion that Ludmer's notion of modernization is "un poco vago" (a little vague), I situate the novel in the precise historical context of the early 1990s in Argentina, namely, "the structural adjustment program [that] included: an extreme privatization program; deregulations of all kinds, in particular with regard to the 'flexibilization' of labor markets; and a new 'opening' to the world economy."[3] By reading the text in this way, I contend that Aira responds to this precise political context by reimagining and transposing a certain revolutionary impetus specific to the events of the late 1960s in Argentina to this contemporary moment. Whereas in *Ema, la cautiva* Aira critiqued the use of historical precedents to justify current violence, I will argue that in *La prueba* the transposition highlights the crucial differences between these two historical moments and allows the text to be read in conjunction with the work of Alain Badiou, Gilles Deleuze, and Félix Guattari to reveal both the nature of the event Aira describes and the synchronicity between Aira's political and literary projects. Where it is generally held that the philosophies of Badiou and Deleuze are ontologically incompatible, that "one has to choose" between them and that this choice "in the end . . . would seem to come down to a matter of taste, as Deleuze wrote to Badiou," I will proffer a reading of *La prueba* that to a certain degree overcomes this obstacle.[4] This is to say that I will propose that certain Badiouian and Deleuzian concepts can be deployed simultaneously to illuminate Aira's unique conception of literary praxis that reciprocally illuminates some of the limitations of political action as conceived by Badiou and Deleuze.

As in the case of *Ema, la cautiva*, Aira's novel *La prueba* is set at a pivotal moment of twentieth-century Argentine history: specifically, one of financial crisis and economic reform. Indeed, one commentator writing at the time stated that "the Argentinian crisis is probably the most serious in Latin America" and that "the country is an extreme example of fiscal crisis."[5] Following the return to democracy in 1983, the economic crisis initiated under the previous military government had only worsened under new President Raúl Alfonsín and the country suffered from hyperinflation.[6] After this difficult period, the Peronist presidential candidate Carlos Menem ran a populist campaign and was elected in 1989.[7] However, the Menem government immediately "surprised the world and particularly Washington by its immediate and full compliance with the neoliberal approach"; "liberalization and privatization were given absolute priority."[8] This was perhaps due to the fact that the World Bank and the International Monetary Fund "insisted on orthodox stabilization and free-market economic reforms as a condition for their economic support."[9] These reforms undoubtedly stabilized the economy and growth resumed; however, unemployment, informal employment, and poverty concurrently rose due to these same measures.[10]

Although Aira's novel precedes the most visible and trenchant effects of Menem's neoliberal reforms, the fact that in *La prueba* the seduction takes place in a fast food restaurant and the assault in a supermarket precisely locates the text within the context of consumer capitalism. The selection of the burger chain Pumper Nic and the supermarket Disco as the novel's settings are also particularly interesting. While Ludmer describes Pumper Nic as "el McDonald's argentino" (the Argentine McDonald's), and the restaurant chain was undoubtedly an Argentine copy of this model of North American business, its logo was copied directly from Burger King, which forced Pumper Nic to change its branding after the U.S. chain arrived in Argentina in 1989, shortly before Aira published his novel.[11] For its part Disco, originally an Argentine business, had been at least partly owned by a Uruguayan company since 1967 and had recently been taken over by a different Uruguayan concern that had significant interests in banking and finance.[12] That the action in the text takes place in two of the most important and visible loci of the early development of neoliberal globalized capitalism in Argentina certainly stresses Aira's acute awareness of the beginnings of rapid economic and societal change.

Although Aira's political target is undoubtedly suggested by the settings for his novel, from the outset, Mao and Lenin consistently insist that their action is a proof of love, not a statement of political conviction or commitment. Very early in their exchange with Marcia, Mao asks her, "¿No creés en el amor?" (Don't you believe in love?) and insists that she has fallen in love with Marcia.[13] As she explicitly states: "Escuchame, Marcia, lo que te dije es cierto. Fue verte y quererte. Es *completamente cierto*" (Listen to me, Marcia, what I told you is true. As soon as I saw you, I loved you. It's *completely true*).[14] This unusual conception of love, and particularly the suggestion that the extremely violent assault is a loving action, is incompatible with any normal definition of the term. Mao's pronouncement as the supermarket assault begins makes this explicitly clear:

> —Este supermercado ha sido tomado por el Comando del Amor. Si colaboran, no habrá muchos heridos o muertos. Algunos sí habrá, porque el Amor es exigente. La cantidad depende de ustedes. Nos llevaremos todo el dinero que haya en las cajas y nos iremos. Dentro de un cuarto de hora los sobrevivientes estarán en su casa mirando la televisión. Nada más. Recuerden que todo lo que suceda aquí, será *por amor*.[15]
>
> (—This supermarket has been taken over by the Commandos of Love. If you all cooperate, there won't be many injured or dead. There will be some, because Love

is demanding. The number depends on you. We'll take all the money there is in the cash registers and we'll leave. Within a quarter of an hour the survivors will be in their houses watching the television. That's all. And remember: everything that will happen here will be *because of love*.)

The strange combination of militancy and passion, of violence and traditional clichés concerning love ("Love is demanding"), again suggest a corruption of the concept of love that is entirely incongruous with any traditional understanding of the term. Indeed, framing the violent assault on the supermarket in *La prueba* as a militant action dedicated to a higher ideal (in this instance, "love") could easily be considered a cynical parody of the total political commitment of armed militant groups in the 1970s. This interpretation would seem to be borne out when Mao threatens another young girl working in the Pumper Nic, where the majority of the initial conversation takes place. Following the altercation Mao reflects on the fact that the poor waitress works to help her family and to support herself during her studies and reacts with violence, stating that "a esa clase de gente hay que destruirla . . . para que no sufra más" (this class of people must be destroyed . . . so they don't suffer any more).[16] Any political action directed against the globalized system of consumerist capitalism would presumably have as its goal the liberation of the working classes, exploited in the continued pursuit of ever-increasing profit margins. However, although Mao proclaims that her actions are always directed by love, she remains certain of the fact that this entire class of people (those that work within the current system in an attempt to improve their lives) must be destroyed. Considered in this way, the novel appears to offer a subtle criticism of the callous disregard for the individual and the very people militant action is supposed to liberate. However, the simple fact that the "heroines" of the text are those conducting the violent action suggests a certain nostalgia for the militant commitment of previous generations in Aira's work that somewhat complicates this position. Certainly, the very names Mao and Lenin and the adoption of the moniker "el Comando del Amor" (the Commandos of Love) are reminiscent of politically militant groups of the 1960s and 1970s.

In discussing Albertina Carri's seminal filmic exploration of postdictatorship memory and subjectivity, *Los rubios*, Joanna Page observes that "our perspective on militant violence in the 1970s is colored by a contemporary nostalgia for an all-consuming political commitment that, it is imagined, remains untouched by the egotism and individualism of today's society."[17] In addition, Page highlights that *Los rubios* addresses "a growing sense of the chasm that separates the contemporary generation's configuration (actual or imagined) of the relationship between the personal and the political from that of the previous generation."[18] Following Page's thought, it appears that *La prueba* is not only critical of total political commitment but simultaneously reflects a certain fondness for a particular trend of Argentine intellectual thought prevalent during the 1960s. As Silvia Sigal argues in her study of the role of intellectuals in Argentina in the 1960s, following the fall of Perón in 1955 and the subsequent proscription of Peronism, in "1960 el marxismo comienza a convertirse en la *lingua franca* de anchas franjas de la intelectualidad progresista" (1960 Marxism began to be transformed into the *lingua franca* of broad groups of progressive intellectuals).[19] This strand of intellectual thought would seem to be reflected in the very names Mao and Lenin, suggesting that the novel is far from a cynical parody of militancy. However, although Mao and Lenin's assault on the supermarket may seem reminiscent of the violence of leftist militant groups of the 1960s and 1970s in Argentina, beyond the names that the girls adopt, the intellectual underpinnings of these militant groups are entirely absent from the novel. Aira selects as his central characters two young punk lesbians who reveal no knowledge of Marxism (or any other political system) and could in no way be considered intellectuals. However, the centrality of Marxism in intellectual discussion was only one strand of the complex cultural milieu of the 1960s in Argentina. There is another historical precedent in Argentina that not only conflated the areas of love, sex, and politics but that also better reflects the nature of Mao and Lenin's revolt.

In addition to traditional Marxist thought, other theories and positions also freely circulated in the 1960s in Argentina. In intellectual spheres, particularly through journals of the time, international theorists such as Louis Althusser, Jacques Lacan, Frantz Fanon, and many others were notably influential.[20] The proponents of these theorists, closely associated with artistic vanguards in Argentina, constituted a new left somewhat distanced from traditional Marxist parties and intellectuals.[21] This vanguard, committed to "neomarxismo" (neo-Marxism), at times came into confrontation with the traditional leftist groups: the communist party would ban the use of psychoanalysis to its members and other leftist groups would denounce new artistic productions for their supposed homosexuality.[22] These "neo-Marxist" positions were of particular importance for youth movements that, inspired by international and domestic events, were committed to societal change. As Oscar Terán recounts in his essay "Ideas e intelectuales en la Argentina, 1880–1980," a group of young people even disrupted an academic conference to deliver a statement proclaiming that the life of Che Guevara and the action of French students in 1968 were more important artworks than all those gathered in the world's museums.[23] Terán also articulates that the intellectual milieu of 1960s Argentina was multifaceted: "He aquí entonces las al menos cuatro almas que habitarían el periodo: el alma Beckett del sinsentido, el alma Kennedy de la Alianza para el Progreso, el alma Lennon del *flower power*, el alma Che Guevara de la rebeldía revolucionaria" (Here are, therefore, the at least four souls that would inhabit the period: the Beckett soul of nonsense, the Kennedy soul of the Alliance for Progress, the Lennon soul of flower power, and the Che Guevara soul of revolutionary rebellion).[24] As Terán makes clear, in Argentina as elsewhere in the world, revolutionary fervor (the Che Guevara soul) coexisted with hippy idealism (the Lennon soul, which would include liberal sexual attitudes among other aspects) and enthusiasm for U.S. models of development (the Kennedy soul).

Aira, who was twenty years old in 1969, has stated that "yo me formé en los años sesenta, con toda la provocación que existía en el aire" (I was educated in the sixties, with all of the provocation that there was in the air) and that "seguía muy vivo ese sentimiento de ir hacia delante, de crear algo nuevo y de crear valores nuevos" (this feeling of moving forward, of creating something new and creating new values, was still very much alive).[25] Such ideas are explored in greater detail in Aira's text "La nueva escritura." In this essay, Aira argues for the return to principles espoused by twentieth-century vanguard artists and demonstrates a sympathy for international influences in the form of "constructivismo, escritura automática, ready-made, dodecafonismo, cut-up, azar, indeterminación" (constructivism, automatic writing, the ready-made, the twelve-tone system, the cut-up, randomness, uncertainty) and the work of John Cage.[26] Thus the text suggests his affinity for cultural developments prevalent in the sixties in Argentina. Aira's friendship with the sexually rebellious writers Alejandra Pizarnik, Copi, and Osvaldo Lamborghini further strengthens this association with the artistic vanguard. In this essay Aira makes no political statements, and his affiliation seems only with the aesthetic avant-garde. However, throughout the 1960s attempts were made to unite political and artistic vanguards, and I argue that in *La prueba*, Aira attempts to recreate the intermingling of the projects of artistic vanguards and political radicals.

In some journals in the 1960s, attempts were made to forge alliances between "la izquierda y zonas importantes de la vanguardia estética" (the Left and important areas of the aesthetic avant-garde), but this task required a moment of specific action.[27] This moment came following the coup d'état that brought Juan Carlos Onganía to power in 1966. Laura Kalmanowiecki notes that before Onganía came to power (and especially during the Peronist era) "'deviant behavior' was increasingly defined in political terms as subversive of the social order," and "city police persecuted those who seemed to pose a danger to the lives of 'decent' people, ranging from political subversives to those who defied the cultural, moral, and legal order."[28] Continuing this trend it was Onganía and his "authoritarian, ultra-Catholic" government, "violently opposed to 'subversives' of whatever political tint," that inadvertently brought artistic vanguards, youth movements and traditional leftist groups together by conflating their different theoretical underpinnings and branding them all subversives.[29] As the military government was "determined to stamp out immorality" as well as supposed subversion, it initiated campaigns against "el pelo largo, los músicos de rock" (long hair, rock musicians), and "el uso de la minifalda" (the use of the mini-skirt).[30] The government confiscated books, censored and banned popular foreign films, and raided publishing houses and hotels used for amorous encounters.[31] As Terán makes clear, the Onganía government, "imbuido de una mirada autoritaria incapaz de discriminar entre el modernismo experimentalista y las actitudes políticas expresamente orientadas al cambio revolucionario, . . . terminó por unificar las almas Lennon y Guevara de los sesenta" (infused with an authoritarian outlook incapable of distinguishing between experimental modernism and those political attitudes expressly oriented towards revolutionary change, . . . ultimately united the Lennon and Guevara souls of the sixties).[32] However, uniting revolutionary ideals and struggles for sexual liberation against those of conservative forces hoping to implement U.S. models of development required a specific event. I contend that this event, the Cordobazo, has a particular resonance with Aira's novel and that the conflation of love and politics in *La prueba* is a reimagining of this episode of Argentine history.

Where in Europe and other parts of the world, May 1968 marks a point of revolutionary student uprising, it is in fact May 1969 that marked a high point of revolutionary fervor in Argentina.[33] Onganía may have been the first to presume a correspondence between artistic and sexual vanguards and militant leftist groups, but as Jill Hedges explains, in Córdoba such disparate groups were united in a moment of action: "In the case of the *Cordobazo*, student and trade union militancy came together (despite the traditional distrust between the two sectors) to produce the largest civil uprising against the military government and the security forces until that time."[34] The Cordobazo left at least fourteen people dead and marked not only the beginning of the end of Onganía's government but also the beginning of increasing violence perpetrated by divergent leftist groups. It is also particularly pertinent for Aira's novel. Onganía's government not only sought to repress "subversive" groups but also implemented a strict economic plan "aimed at controlling prices and wages in order to reduce inflation, and at stimulating industry through devaluations and import promotion aimed at bringing in foreign investment."[35] That is to say, the government implemented an economic plan that held much in common with Menem's in the early 1990s at a different moment of crisis in Argentina. In fact, throughout the 1970s and 1980s consecutive military governments attempted to implement neoliberal economic reforms, further strengthening this link between the crisis that precipitated the Cordobazo and that which precipitates Aira's *La prueba*. Indeed, Pablo Pozzi suggests that the economic "policies implemented by the Menem government bear a remarkable resemblance to those of the 1976 dictatorship."[36] Moreover, immediately following the Cordobazo, "on 2 June, a series of supermarkets linked to the Rockefeller family were bombed, marking an upsurge in violence which would continue to climb for a decade," and as the economic crisis worsened following the return to democracy, supermarkets in Buenos Aires would be attacked during riots in 1989.[37] Given that participants in these riots "termed them azos" in direct reference to previous uprisings such as the Cordobazo, it seems that Aira's supermarket assault is also a further echo of this event.[38]

My argument is that the historical crisis that precipitated the *Cordobazo* is linked to that depicted in *La prueba* by painful economic reform, by attacks on supermarkets and by an impending sense of chaos. I argue that Aira utilizes the text to reimagine the circumstances that led to revolt in the late 1960s in Argentina to construct an attack on contemporary globalized capitalism. Aira reimagines the circumstances that led to one insurrectionary response to a political and economic crisis in order to transpose them onto characters faced with a new crisis. Nonetheless, the textual echoes of the late 1960s in *La prueba* also highlight several important cultural developments of the intervening years. Thus the names Mao and Lenin reflect the total political commitment derived from Marxism that inspired the revolutionary fervor of the "alma Che Guevara." However, drained of their intellectual content they now stand as empty signifiers, suggesting that contemporary actions have been liberated from the grand narratives that had not survived the history of twentieth-century Argentina. As Pozzi notes, unlike the Cordobazo the riots of 1989 were indeed more an expression of anger than of organized struggle as the traditional left-wing parties had been decimated by the dictatorship of 1976–1983, demoralized by the collapse of the Soviet Union, and the traditional Peronist defenders of the working class were now implementing the neoliberal reforms.[39] Returning to Aira's novel, the hippy soul of sexual freedom represented by the "alma Lennon" is reflected in Mao and Lenin's lesbianism yet is rewritten as a nihilistic punk ethos, a point borne out by their extended anecdote about Sergio Vicio, a direct reference to Sid Vicious of the Sex Pistols. This coincidence also stresses the importance in Argentina of international influences, in this instance, the influence of alternative artistic movements. Finally, the importance of international theorists remains, but Althusser, Lacan, and Fanon are supplanted in Aira's text by the post-Marxist theorists Badiou and Deleuze. As we shall now see, it is through this engagement that Aira creates a fictional event that has "retroactive effects that accomplishes the temporal synthesis between two moments of which the event is an interval," the two moments being the crisis-ridden Argentina of the late 1960s and that of the late 1980s.[40]

The initial point of contact between Aira's novel and Badiou's conception of political philosophy can be discerned by considering that the names Mao and Lenin have been separated from their intellectual foundation. Simon Critchley summarizes the principle behind Badiou's conception of political commitment in the following manner: "Now, perhaps the epoch of great politics, like the epoch of great art for Heidegger and Hegel, is over. Perhaps. And perhaps that is a good thing. Perhaps we have had enough of the virile, Promethean politics of the will, the empty longing for total revolution. . . . Perhaps we just have to content ourselves with smaller actions and smaller victories, and everyday and heroically antiheroic militancy. That is, we have to expect much more from much less."[41] Critchley's comments make clear that Badiou's philosophical conception of political commitment can be understood as an attempt to revive certain aspects of that militancy, while redeeming it from the "Promethean politics" of the past. It is this project that I contend Aira shares in *La prueba*. In introducing his discussion of Aira's novel, Barros writes that

> La novela de Aira es una crítica al consumo como formación de sujeto
> y comunidad. Al entrar y destruir el supermercado las protagonistas de
> *La prueba* no sólo escenifican el rompimiento de una de sus más típicas
> topologías, sino que también construyen un espacio en el cual se puede
> conceptualizar un sujeto, o como diría Aira, un *procedimiento* de sujeto.[42]

> (Aira's novel is a criticism of consumption as the formation of the subject and the
> community. On entering and destroying the supermarket, the protagonists of *La
> prueba* not only stage the destruction of one of the most typical topologies of con-
> sumption, but they also construct a space in which a subject or, as Aira would say,
> a subject *procedure* can be conceptualized.)

This statement could also be considered a summary of my own approach to Aira's novel. However, where Barros reads the text in conjunction with the work of Lacan and stops short of reading the text as one of political commitment, I analyze the text through the framework of Badiou's theory of the "truth-procedure" that "aims to link what exceeds the means of rational presentation, the *event*, to what is singular par excellence, the *subject*, and therefore to articulate the *generic procedures* through which universal *truths* are produced."[43] I will discuss each of these terms in close relation to Aira's text in due course in order to argue that the novel's narrative arc conveys Marcia's transition (in Badiou's terminology) from a nonsubjective adherence to the situation, to that of a militant subject of the truth presented to her by Mao and Lenin. Essentially, I will demonstrate that Aira's text, like Badiou's philosophy, is principally concerned with "the production of the new by means of subjective struggle."[44]

Throughout the novel's initial stages, Aira is at pains to stress Marcia's rational nature and to contrast it with Mao and Lenin's irrational and illogical nature. Indeed, Aira specifically states that "Marcia no era histérica, ni siquiera nerviosa, ni impresionable, ni paranoica, era bastante tranquila y racional" (Marcia was not hysterical, not even anxious, nor impressionable, nor paranoid, she was quite calm and rational), and as Marcia attempts to engage Mao in conversation, Aira again notes that for Marcia, "era imposible hablar racionalmente con ella" (it was impossible to talk rationally with her).[45] Nevertheless, Marcia continually attempts to follow a line of interrogation that is "muy lógico" (very logical) and "muy racional" (very rational) and that would allow her, in Aira's terminology, to "'marcizar' toda la situación" ("Marcia-cize" the entire situation), which is to say, to fully control the conversation.[46] This proves impossible. Marcia desperately attempts to find a vocabulary that will situate the girls' position and allow her to translate the events that are occurring into a language that she can understand. However, Mao and Lenin frustrate each of these attempts. Mao and Lenin declare that "somos amantes" (we are lovers) but "no somos una pareja" (we are not a couple), leading Marcia to define the girls as lesbians, a classification that they subsequently refute.[47] Thereafter, Marcia tries to define the girls as punks but is very abruptly told that "nosotras no somos 'punks'" (we are not "punks"),[48] and she receives a similar rebuttal when she attempts to describe them as nihilists. Mao and Lenin simply reject outright any attempt to classify them. Patrick O'Connor stresses that neither "names and labels" nor "political names" have any importance to the girls and thus argues that "what looked at first as if it would be a showdown between two cultures is suddenly presented as a showdown between culture and anti-culture."[49] An alternative framework for reading this dynamic is, however, provided by Badiou. Read in this way, Marcia's continual attempts to define the other girls' position reveal her to be an adherent to the "situation." Similarly, Mao and Lenin's refutation of every classification reveal them to be "militants" of a "truth-procedure."

For Badiou, seemingly everything is named and classified within the construction of any given situation, and language is used to fix people within a particular social order to maintain control and exercise power, a process that is "effectively absolute."[50] Nonetheless, developing his theory from Cantorian set theory (with its principle that no set is complete and that another set is always possible), Badiou argues that the "real" is constituted by those elements that cannot be named in the situation, and the militants' task is to "extract [the real] from the surrounding reality" by naming it and thus to precipitate an "event" that will irrevocably alter the situation by effectively destroying it. This inherently "violent process," which Badiou denominates "a truth-procedure," also produces a subject who co-emerges with the event itself.[51] Thus I propose that Mao and Lenin's refusal of the vocabulary of the situation indicates the first stage in the development of an emergent truth-procedure. This seemingly innocuous action is in fact the preliminary stage that will lead to a coming event that will also produce a new truth and a named subject. That the Badiouian event necessarily constitutes "a site of contradiction and violent break"[52] is encapsulated in Aira's statement that Mao and Lenin "eran la violencia. Eso era inescapable" (were violence. That was inescapable), yet where Badiou primarily refers to the violent breaking of societal norms, rules, and codes of practice, Aira transliterates this violence into the physical assault on the supermarket.[53] Moreover, the necessary naming of the emergent subject in Badiou's "truth-procedure" is reflected in Mao's assertion that:

> — Lo que no quiere decir que no podamos cambiar de nombre tantas veces como se nos dé la gana. Más te digo, Marcia, a partir de mañana nosotras dos, Lenin y yo, vamos a llamarnos "Marcia." ¿Qué te parece?
> —¿Por qué a partir de mañana?—preguntó Marcia.
> —Porque mañana va a ser una fecha importante en nuestras vidas—le respondió, críptica.[54]
>
> (—That doesn't mean that we can't change name as many times as it occurs to us. More than that, Marcia, from tomorrow on the two of us, Lenin and I, we're going to call ourselves "Marcia." What do you think?
> —Why from tomorrow on?—asked Marcia.
> —Because tomorrow is going to be an important date in our lives—she responded, cryptically.)

Thus it would appear that the names Mao and Lenin reflect that the girls are already militant adherents to the truth that has yet to come, and they immediately grasp that they will be named anew when the coming event precipitates the real. Indeed, there is a certain irony in that the name that will be bestowed upon Mao and Lenin will be "Marcia." In her attempts to "situate" both Mao and Lenin, Aira suggested that Marcia sought to "marcizar" (Marcia-cize) the situation. By selecting the name "Marcia," Mao and Lenin will indeed "marcizar" (Marcia-cize) the situation, but this word will signify their revolt against it rather than their submission to it.

That Mao and Lenin are representatives of the mysterious and uncertain "real" of the situation first becomes apparent through the effect meeting them has on Marcia. Following her first exchange with the girls, Marcia reflects that "ahora la música había cambiado de sentido. Era como si se hubiera vuelto real, cosa que nunca sucedía con la música. Esa realidad le impedía oírla. . . . Era como si el pensamiento se hubiera hecho real" (now the music had changed its meaning. It was as if it had become real, something that never happened with music. This reality prevented her from hearing it. . . . It was as if thought itself had become real). She then quickly states that "en efecto, todo había cambiado" (in effect, everything had changed).[55] As Mao and Lenin present the unnameable real to Marcia, the absolute certainty of her situation has been fundamentally challenged, and she experiences a transformative potential in the world. This is echoed again when Marcia reflects later that "desde que las dos chicas se habían dirigido a ella en la esquina de enfrente, menos de un cuarto de hora antes: el mundo se había transformado una y otra vez" (ever since the two girls had approached her in the corner opposite, less than a quarter of an hour earlier, the world had transformed itself over and over again).[56] Indeed, when their initial conversation concludes and the girls leave the fast food restaurant to re-join the people outside, Marcia cannot escape the sensation that "el lugar se había vuelto irreal" (the place had become unreal) as the certainties she had previously felt have been called into question.[57] For Marcia the world repeatedly transforms and appears both more real and unreal simultaneously, a sensation echoed again when Marcia enters the supermarket with Mao and Lenin. As the girls set out to prove their love for her in the most violent way, Marcia perceives the process as both the beginning of a dream and, paradoxically, the beginning of reality. The disconcerting oscillation between reality and unreality not only suggests that Marcia has encountered the transformative potential of the real for the first time but also that the "event is both *situated*—it is the event of this or that situation—and *supplementary*; thus absolutely detached from, or unrelated to, all the rules of the situation."[58]

Once the brutal supermarket robbery begins, it appears as a radical break from the novel's opening section yet is contingent with it. This too reflects the fact that the event is "a fragment of being" immanent to the very situation that it will disrupt and forever alter.[59] Indeed, throughout the initial stages of the novel, Aira carefully suggests correlations between the girls' conversation and the coming event. This interpretation, however, functions retroactively, only becoming apparent once Mao and Lenin have offered their proof of love, that is, conducted the supermarket massacre. During the long extended conversation, Mao and Lenin are described as "pura violencia" (pure violence) and intimidate those around them.[60] Most notably, Mao violently threatens the fast food worker as previously mentioned. Her complete lack of compassion for the girl and assertion that people like her must be destroyed is of course a dark precursor of the atrocity in the supermarket. This link, however, can only be understood a posteriori. The supermarket takeover still appears as a radical break to the reader. Furthermore, the girls' declaration that "el amor también admite un rodeo, y sólo uno: la acción. Porque el amor, que no tiene explicaciones, tiene de todos modos *pruebas*" (love accepts one route, and only one: action. Because love, which has no explanations, does have *proofs*) again reflects the necessity of an *action*, an "event" to bring the truth-procedure to effect.[61] This is reiterated in Mao's statement that "nosotras sí podríamos hacer del mundo un relámpago, un parpadeo. . . . Hay un súbito, un instante, en que todo el mundo se hace real, sufre la más radical de las transformaciones: el mundo se vuelve mundo" (us, yes, we could transform the world into a lightning strike, a blink. . . . There is a sudden unexpected moment, an instant, in which the entire world becomes real, it undergoes the most radical of all transformations: the world becomes world).[62] Again, this statement reflects the nature of the event as an "instant" or a "lightning strike" in which the entire world, or "situation," can be transformed. Nonetheless, the girls still present their truth as imminent and continuous with the present situation. Not only will the world become world through the girls' actions, but Mao also declares that "ese mundo tuyo está dentro del mundo real, Marcia. Voy a condescender a explicarte un par de cosas, pero tené en cuenta que me refiero al mundo real, no al de las explicaciones" (this world of yours is inside the real world, Marcia. I'm going to condescend to explain a couple of things to you, but keep in mind that I'm talking about the real world, not the world of explanations).[63] The "real" world that Mao and Lenin will expose already contains the present world within it. In its pretensions of being absolute, they recognize it as false and thus they will reveal the real world to Marcia. The world will be transformed, but it will remain continuous with the present situation.

As the supermarket assault approaches, Aira relates that Marcia "sentía que se acercaba el momento, en realidad se precipitaba, de tomar una decisión" (felt that the moment for making a decision was drawing near, in reality it was accelerating toward her). Although Marcia initially perceives that this decision will be "encontrar un modo de despedirse" (to find a way of saying goodbye), it is clear that she is being called to make a decision to join Mao and Lenin before knowing what that decision may entail.[64] Ultimately Mao simply challenges Marcia to decide, instructing her to: "Pensá que es muy poco lo que te separa de tu destino. Sólo tenés que decir que sí" (Think that there is very little separating you from your destiny. All you have to do is say yes).[65] Marcia accepts the challenge by accompanying the girls to the supermarket, the location where the "event" will transpire. As Marcia makes this decision, she reflects that "la prueba que todavía no estaba en un cierto lapso del futuro tenía abierto el crédito de la existencia" (the proof that did not yet exist in a certain period of time in the future had opened a belief in its existence).[66] As Jean-Jacques

Lecercle argues, "the temporality of the [Badiouian] event" is "in the *future anterior*" precisely because the "prospective subject" must make a "decision that what she is being faithful to will turn out to have been an event."[67] As Marcia's comments make clear, she too must make a decision to be faithful to the event that is in the process of coming into being.

Within Badiou's philosophy an event can only take place within one of the four fields that constitute the conditions for philosophy: art, science, love, and politics. I contend that when the previously outlined historical context of *La prueba* is considered, Aira's novel makes it clear that the specific situation to which Marcia belongs is that of the seemingly absolute and inescapable realm of globalized capitalism. Despite the fact that the assault on the supermarket closely corresponds to the characteristics of the Badiouian event, however, insofar as it takes place within a novel, it is of course not a real event at all. This seems to confirm Lecercle's argument that, although art remains one of Badiou's four conditions of philosophy, "as a general rule, a work is not an event" but rather "stages an event that occurs in one of the three other fields."[68] Certainly I agree that Aira's novel effectively stages an event that could occur in the field of politics. Aira frames his novel within the context of globalized capitalism, describes Mao and Lenin as an "elemental force in society," and articulates the general characteristics of both the truth-procedure before the event's occurrence and its actual eruption.[69] However, Lecercle is too quick in dismissing the potential for a Badiouian event to occur in the field of art in its own right. Indeed, as I shall go on to argue, the process involved in *La prueba* is the inverse of that which Lecercle describes: the novel represents an event in the field of politics that describes the truth-procedure that Aira engages in the field of art.

In setting out the preoccupations of his literary process, Aira has stated that "para mí siempre fue más importante lo nuevo que lo bueno" (for me, the *new* was always more important than the *good*).[70] It is this topic that Aira explores in detail in the essay "La innovación" and that can be seen to describe a truth-procedure in the field of art. In the first instance, Aira elaborates on his search for "the new," affirming that he has been "militando desde hace años a favor de lo que he llamado, . . . 'literatura mala'" (actively promoting, for many years, what I have called . . . "bad literature") and arguing that "al fondo de la literatura mala" (at the heart of bad literature) one can discover "la buena, o la nueva, o la buena nueva" (the good, or the new, or the good news).[71] I want to propose that one can consider Aira's advocacy of "bad literature" as an attempt to discover the real that has been excluded from the current situation. This idea is strengthened when one considers Aira's comment that in literature "la cosa es inventar algo nuevo, inventar un valor nuevo a partir del cual se pueda juzgar lo bueno de acuerdo con los nuevos paradigmas que ha establecido un determinado creador" (the thing is to invent something new, invent a new value from which one can judge the good according to the new paradigms that have been established by a given creator).[72] As in the Badiouian truth-procedure, Aira espouses the discovery of the new as a method of revolutionizing the artistic landscape. When one considers Aira's short text *El infinito*, the suitability of the Badiouian framework is reinforced. In this text Aira elaborates a childhood "juego matemático, o seudomatemático, que se jugaba de a dos, y consistía simplemente en decir un número mayor que el contrincante" (mathematical, or pseudomathematical, game that was played in twos, and that simply consisted of saying a number higher than that declared by your opponent).[73] Aira then relates that he and his friend continued playing until they discovered the word "infinito" (infinity).[74] It is of particular importance that the two friends then come to the realization that "dos infinitos fueran mayores que un infinito solo" (two infinities were greater than a single infinity), that even the conceptualization of an "infinito de infinitos" (infinity of infinities) only leads to the creation of "series como la anterior" (series like the previous one) and thus the awareness that "la serie de infinitos podía prolongarse indefinidamente" (the series of infinities could be extended indefinitely).[75] All this is to say that within this seemingly simple game, Aira discovers the rudimentary Cantorian principle that underpins Badiouian philosophy: there is no complete set, and another set is always possible. With this principle established, Aira becomes Badiou's contemporary. Indeed, the resemblance between Aira's conception of "the new" and Badiou's truth-procedure is remarkable. First, as in Badiou's conception, Aira elaborates that "lo nuevo no está adelante, ni arriba, ni abajo, ni atrás, *sino en otra dimensión*, en lo que nosotros . . . podemos llamar lo Desconocido" (the new is neither in front, nor above, nor below, nor behind, *it is rather in another dimension*, in what we may call the Unknown).[76] Similarly, Aira stipulates that "lo nuevo es el gran ready-made" (the new is the great ready-made), stressing that it is simultaneously situated within the given situation, yet supplementary to it.[77] Furthermore, where Badiou argues that the "real" of the situation generates the singular truth-procedure, Aira proclaims that "lo nuevo es lo real" (the new is the real) and that it precipitates "un realismo en *proceso*, contiguo a la realidad" (a realism in *process*, contiguous with reality).[78] Additionally, Silvio Mattoni's argument that according to Aira "las vanguardias . . . , antes que cierto acontecimiento datable, sería la ruptura contra la autoperpetuación de las formas y la especialización que éstas requieren" (the vanguards . . . , before any event that can be dated, would be the break with the self-perpetuation of artistic forms and the specialization that these require), is suggestive of a certain future-anterior fealty to the event that will come to pass.[79] Finally, Galiazo's suggestion that within Aira's literature "las ideas que valen la pena . . . irrumpen como los relámpagos" (the ideas that matter . . . burst in like lightning strikes) is testimony to their eventual nature. All this suggests that the artistic process that Contreras and Speranza have described in such detail can be considered as a Badiouian truth-procedure.[80] This realization takes on further importance when one considers that, with regard to the series of infinities that he uncovers as a child, Aira reflects that such a series "no podía ser más que dinero" (could be nothing else but money) and that, when he returns to the theme of "la buena nueva" in *La trompeta de mimbre*, he postulates that "la Buena Nueva en sí sería el triunfo del arte sobre la mezquindad mercantil de la obra de arte" (the Good News in itself would be the triumph of art over the mercantile meanness of the work of art).[81] Given these simple yet overt connections with finance and the market, it seems particularly suitable to suggest that *La prueba* describes the political manifestation of the truth-procedure that Aira engages in the field of art.

Nonetheless, I do not wish to suggest that Badiou's theory provides a perfect template for understanding the entirety of Aira's oeuvre. Indeed, considering the ethics at play within *La prueba* clearly demonstrates that Badiou's philosophy is insufficient to account for all of the action that takes place in Aira's novel. For Badiou, ethics "should concern the destiny of *truths*, in the plural," and as the "event" constitutes the specific moment when a certain truth comes into being, a truth-procedure necessarily constitutes an ethical action.[82] With regard to Aira's novel, insofar as the supermarket assault is considered a truth-procedure, it must also be considered an ethical action. This is suggested by Mao herself when she states, "ese mundo de explicaciones en el que vivís, es el error. El amor es la salida del error" (this world of explanations in which you live, is the error. Love is the way out of this error); it is through the proof of Mao's love (the assault) that Marcia can free herself from "error," and thus the event is an ethical truth-procedure.[83] Nonetheless, by describing the horrendous violence and brutality of Mao and Lenin's assault in great detail, Aira's novel can also be read as a *critique* of the ethical component of Badiou's theory. Within Badiou's description of ethics, "evil can take one of three main forms: the form of *betrayal* (the abandonment of fidelity to the event), the form of the *simulacrum* (the replacement, through naming, of the void in the fullness of the community), and the form of a dogmatic *totalization* of a truth."[84] Mao and Lenin could never be considered as lacking "fidelity to the event" or as having tried to totalize their particular truth and assume absolute power, but the visceral and abhorrent violence of the assault cannot but suggest that the action described is morally wrong or, indeed, evil. Thus Aira's novel raises a similar point to Ernesto Laclau in his essay on Badiouian ethics, "An Ethics of Militant Engagement," when he states that "all that the subjects engaged in a truth procedure can do, *once they accept the event as a true one*, is to be clear about what perverting an event would consist of—but this by itself does not establish a criterion for distinguishing truth from simulacrum."[85] Laclau's point is that there is no way to distinguish between a true event and its simulacrum, a point that Aira's novel also makes in a particularly visceral manner. From Badiou's perspective, there is no way of discerning whether Mao and Lenin's assault is a legitimate action or simply a series of brutal murders with a mere semblance of political justification. However, the conflation of love and politics in the novel, or more accurately of *desire* and politics, does suggest another possible reading of their actions.

Although Mao certainly suggests that her pursuit of Marcia derives from her love for her, it cannot be ignored that the opening line of her dialogue with Marcia, of the very novel itself, is, "¿Querés coger?" (Do you want to fuck?)[86] Mao and Lenin consistently obey their desires instinctively, regardless of consequences. Their decision to seduce Marcia having seen her for only a few seconds and their decision to conduct their violent assault on the supermarket make this clear. In considering characters from Aira's *El congreso de literatura*, Reber notes that: "From an interpretative point of view informed by the work of Deleuze and Guattari (e.g., *Anti-Oedipus*, *A Thousand Plateaus*) such a representation of subjectivity may be readily understood as an expression of resistance to the programmatically rational model of selfhood demanded by capitalist logic."[87] This description is equally suitable for Mao and Lenin. The girls' refusal of every attempt to define their existence coupled with their continued pursuit of Marcia, which is to say, their uninhibited pursuit of the satisfaction of their desire, means their very being can be interpreted as "a model of anti-teleological subjectivity best embodied in the figure of the schizophrenic who obeys desire without aim or purpose."[88] As previously discussed, Deleuze and Guattari argue that capitalism is unique in the history of social formations in that "the decoding of flows and the deterritorialization of the socius" are "the most characteristic and the most important tendency of capitalism."[89] As they continue their discussion, they argue that this decoding (the removal of rules and norms in order better to integrate flows of desire under relations of exchange to promote the pursuit of capital) can generate "a spontaneous or unpredictable form of desire freed from social coding."[90] They argue that this desire resists and disrupts the very capitalist system that produced it and name it schizophrenia.[91] Again, as Aira frames *La prueba* in the context of the expanding neoliberal and capitalist Argentina of the early 1990s, Mao and Lenin's completely uninhibited, wild, and savage pursuit of their desire can be understood as both the product and limit of the capitalist system, as in Deleuze and Guattari's conception of schizophrenia.[92] This is to say that the setting of Aira's novel suggests that Mao and Lenin's unbridled desire and extreme violence is immanent to the capitalist system, while its schizophrenic expression fundamentally opposes that same system.

Toward the conclusion of the supermarket assault in *La prueba*, the narrator states that "si todo está permitido . . . todo se transforma" (if everything is permitted . . . everything transforms).[93] This suggestion of the transformational potential of the event effectuated by Mao and Lenin is further developed when the narrator continues:

> El incidente había alumbrado, aunque en las sombras, el fantástico potencial de transformación que tiene todo. Una mujer por ejemplo, un ama de casa del barrio que había ido a hacer las compras para la cena, se fundía en su lugar a la vista de sus congéneres que no le prestaban atención. . . . Se hacía animal, pero todos los animales al mismo tiempo, animal espectáculo con los barrotes de la jaula saliéndole como espinas de cada repliegue del cuerpo, animal selva cargado de orquídeas.[94]

> (The incident had illuminated, although in the shadows, the fantastic potential for transformation which everything contains. A woman, for example, a housewife from the neighborhood that had gone to do the shopping for dinner, was melting in plain sight of the others in the supermarket who did not pay her any attention. . . . She was becoming an animal, but all animals simultaneously, an animal spectacle with the iron bars of the cage projecting out of her like thorns from every fold in her body, a jungle animal loaded with orchids.)

Mao and Lenin's violent assault engenders a no less violent transformation among the occupants of the supermarket. As Contreras argues, the "elemento genético del relato, 'la fuerza del amor' es también su potencia de variación, su elemento diferencial. El relato empieza y ya todo había sido transformado por la brutalidad del amor" (the genetic element of the story, "the power of love," is also its potential for variation, its differential element. The story begins and everything has already been transformed by the brutality of love).[95] Mao and Lenin's actions precipitate a process of metamorphosis and transformation that continues spontaneously and sporadically, radically altering the witnesses to the event and the entire situation.

As noted in the introduction, Tomás Abraham has argued that "es evidente que [Aira] ha leído la obra de Deleuze" (it is evident that [Aira] has read the work of Deleuze).[96] In addition, he has proposed that Aira is especially interested in Deleuze's "idea de las metamorfosis" (concept of metamorphoses).[97] Certainly, the climax to the supermarket assault unleashes a metamorphic process that demonstrates a close correspondence to the concept of becoming-other, described at length by Deleuze and Guattari in *A Thousand Plateaus*.[98] In brief, Deleuze and Guattari describe becoming-other by first establishing key binary oppositions such as woman/man, adult/child and human/animal and then arguing that becoming-other entails a metamorphic transition from the dominant to the minoritarian position. Thus becoming-other can be further subdivided into such categories as becoming-woman, becoming-child, and becoming-animal (though there are many others). As is evident in the quotation above, *La prueba* concludes in an instance of frenetic becoming-animal. Moreover, as the narrator reflects, "es cierto que la transformación es una pregunta; en esta ocasión no obstante se afirmaba, momentánea y cambiante; no importaba que siguiera siendo pregunta, era respuesta también" (it is certain that transformation is a question; in this occasion, however, it affirmed itself, momentary and volatile; it didn't matter that it remained a question, it was the answer as well).[99] This suggests that the event is both the product of becoming and begets further becoming, which is to say, it is part of a continuing and immanent process. That Mao and Lenin's assault can be understood as an instance of becoming-other is further strengthened when the narrator describes the event as "el nacimiento del universo" (the birth of the universe) and reflects that "era como si todo lo conocido estuviera alejándose, a la velocidad de la luz, a fundar a lo lejos, en el negro del universo, nuevas civilizaciones basadas en otras premisas" (it was as if everything known was moving away, at the speed of light, to found far away in the distance, in the blackness of the universe, new civilizations based on other premises).[100] For Deleuze and Guattari, in all cases, becoming-other tends toward becoming-imperceptible, which would be to commune with the very process of becoming itself, lose all sense of subjectivity, and become nothing more than a confluence of forces subject to continual transformation. As they explain, becoming-imperceptible "is to world (*faire monde*), to make a world (*faire un monde*)" and "to be present at the dawn of the world."[101] As the primary function of becoming-other is to "set in disequilibrium the binary oppositions that are formulated and enforced by power" and thus "has the potential of transforming social and environmental relations in unpredictable ways," Deleuze and Guattari contend that all "such becomings . . . are political in nature."[102] So too in *La prueba* Mao and Lenin's schizophrenic action induces a gradual becoming-other that sets in disequilibrium innumerable power structures and sets off a chain reaction that effectively creates a new world.

As implied in Abraham's critical reflections on Aira's literature, such becomings-other are a central trope of Aira's wider literary oeuvre. There are innumerable examples of such animalistic becomings-monstrous throughout Aira's corpus that lead to further reflections on the nature of his artistic process. In a particularly precise example, in the opening paragraphs of Aira's novel *Dante y Reina*, Dante is "asombrado de su definitiva mutación" (astonished by his definitive mutation) and realizes that "ahora soy un perro" (now I am a dog). In typical and paradoxical fashion, Aira then recants this position, suggesting that "antes también había sido perro" (I had also been a dog before) and that true transformation is to "volverse lo que se había sido siempre" (to become what one had always been). Nonetheless, the novel then claims that "todo se convierte en humano" (everything became human) and the novel relates the fantastic tale of the anthropomorphic marriage between a fly and a dog.[103] More frequently, however, the becomings-other that permeate Aira's oeuvre tend toward becoming-monstrous. To cite but a few examples (such is Aira's consistency in this regard that others abound), in *El congreso de literatura* an attempt to clone Carlos Fuentes results in the duplication and terrible amplification of a silk worm that threatens to destroy the city hosting the titular conference, while in *Yo era una chica moderna*, the female narrator and her friend brutally murder a pregnant girl in a public bathroom, and this abhorrent violence leads to the grotesque transformation of the girl's unborn fetus into a monster that rampages through the city. Similarly, in *La abeja* a failed attempt by the military to create a weapon to destroy all tax records in Argentina leads to the resurrection and metamorphosis of a cemetery full of dead queen bees. The resuscitated bees immediately kill all the central characters with one exception: a female character forms a mutant hybrid with the "esencia real de la abeja" (royal essence of the bee) and Aira concludes his novel with the cryptic words "nada volverá a ser como antes" (nothing will ever be as it was before).[104]

The proliferation of Deleuzian becomings-other in Aira's oeuvre suggests that the wider Deleuzian conception of becoming, understood as "the very dynamism of change, situated between heterogeneous terms and tending towards no particular goal or end state," could be usefully deployed to illuminate Aira's advocacy for the production of "el procedimiento para hacer obras, sin la obra" (the procedure to make works of art, without the works themselves).[105] Certainly, when one considers that Aira's essay "La nueva escritura" is centered on an extended consideration of John Cage's "Music of Changes," one is reminded of Deleuze and Guattari's description of Cage's work as "a process against all structures and genesis" and as "experimentation against any kind of interpretation."[106] This Deleuzian interpretation is further reinforced when one considers Aira's novel *Cómo me hice monja*. In this text Aira appears as the first-person narrator, self-identifies as a young girl, and narrates her own death. Thus Aira establishes a series of binary oppositions (male/female, adult/child, and alive/dead) and simultaneously undermines each of them. The connection with Deleuzian becoming-other is immediately apparent and, as Francine Masiello notes, Aira thus "exposes the fallacies of logic underlying the process of binary thought" and "explores (and mocks) the structures of apprehension that are central to all interpretive experience."[107]

As we have seen, then, elements of the philosophies of Badiou and Deleuze can be deployed both to illuminate the internal dynamics of *La prueba* and to elucidate Aira's wider conception of literary process. Within the novel, Mao and Lenin can be considered simultaneously as adherents of a truth-procedure (as delineated by Badiou) or as schizophrenic subjectivities (as delineated by Deleuze and Guattari). Similarly, Aira's literary process can be understood as a Badiouian truth-procedure that instigates the continual movement of Deleuzian becoming. Framed somewhat differently, it could be suggested that elements of the philosophical systems of both Badiou and Deleuze essentially co-function within Aira's unique conception of literary praxis, a startling revelation given that the work of Badiou and Deleuze is generally held to be incompatible both ontologically and at the level of the subject. While both philosophers aim to reject the notion of the transcendental and "to think immanence not as immanent to something else, but as immanent only to itself," each broaches this task in a unique way that ultimately leads to an ontological incompatibility between their projects.[108] For Badiou the rejection of the transcendental is achieved by assigning ontology to the field of mathematics and utilizing set theory as the guarantor of a multiplicity that refutes the transcendental. He argues that the four conditions of philosophy (science, art, love, and politics) are "immanent to their situations" and "do not harbour any transcendent elements" and from this basis constructs his theory of the "truth-procedure," where he "aims to link what exceeds the means of rational presentation, the *event*, to what is singular par excellence, the *subject*, and therefore to articulate the *generic procedures* through which universal *truths* are produced."[109] In contrast Deleuze revisits the work of philosophers such as Duns Scotus, Spinoza, and Nietzsche in order to develop their work and reject the transcendental by constructing a "doctrine of the eternal return of pure differences" that "allows for a full immanent ontology" in which "all things, whether identifiable or not, are posited as complete only through their relation to an immanent transcendental field of pure differences (Deleuze's 'virtual')."[110] Thus he constructs an ontology divided between the virtual and the actual where "the virtual and the actual are two mutually exclusive, yet jointly sufficient, characterisations of the real." In this division, "the actual/real are states of affairs, bodies, bodily mixtures and individuals," and the virtual is the field of all the unique potentialities that each thing could become.[111] Crucially, Deleuze argues that the virtual is not transcendental as the entire virtual field is always present and every bit as real as the actual. Moreover, he names the unceasing movement between the two domains "becoming" that, as previously stated, is an entirely asubjective process.[112]

In discussing the disparity between Badiou and Deleuze, Lecercle makes specific reference to each philosopher's ontological conception of the "event." As he notes, events can either be considered "as the rare and instantaneous supplements to the situation, introducing the radically new and originating procedures of truth," as in Badiou's philosophy, or "as actualisations of the one virtual Event" through the unending process of becoming, as in the work of Deleuze.[113] Despite this seeming ontological discordance, Aira's conception of the event in *La prueba* effectively synthesizes Deleuze and Badiou's philosophies in its functioning. Similarly, the very process that Aira engages in generating his prodigious literary output contains both Badiouian and Deleuzian elements concurrently: Aira is the militant subject of a Badiouian truth-procedure in the field of art, yet the event that he unleashes through this process results in the unending transformation of Deleuzian becoming-other. In this regard, Aira's literature is arguably closer to the Deleuzian rather than the Badiouian philosophical system. While Badiou argues that Deleuze privileges the virtual over the actual and that it is therefore transcendental, Deleuze rejects Badiou's argument that sets are multiplicities precisely because he denies that these sets contain a virtual element.[114] For Deleuze this means that Badiou's ontology only ever refers to the "actual" state of affairs and thus "fails to hold thought firmly within immanence."[115] It could be argued that within Aira's conception of literary production, the "actual" element of Aira's literary process can be understood as a Badiouian truth-procedure that in its functioning begets a process of becoming-other that represents its virtual component.

This interpretation of Aira's literary process has important political consequences. For Badiou a truly political action is only ever a truth-procedure that occurs in the field of politics. With this in mind, it can be argued that it is *La prueba* that most clearly articulates the actual political correlate of Aira's artistic truth-procedure. However, for Deleuze, politics is principally concerned with the possibility of transformation and metamorphosis and "the combat within individuals, as becoming, is the precondition of . . . resistance" or political action.[116] It is for this reason that Deleuze and Guattari assert that all becomings-other "are political in nature."[117] Thus Aira's numerous becomings-other can be understood as the virtual element of his political project. Given this claim, the centrality of capitalism in *Ema, la cautiva*, and the scattered references to finance, the market, and capitalism throughout Aira's wider body of work, it seems that the subjectivity that we name "Aira"—which he refers to elsewhere as the "mito personal" (personal myth)—obtained through his particular literary process is schizophrenic in nature: it incorporates an unruly and liberated form of desire generated by contemporary capitalism yet ultimately directed toward its destruction.[118] Moreover, considering this destructive element in Aira's wider body of work also demonstrates how his conception of literary process circumvents the seemingly incontrovertible contradiction between Badiou's subjective and Deleuze's asubjective conception of the event.

Each case of becoming-other highlighted above is concomitant with a strong element of violence. Even in *Dante y Reina*, Dante saves Reina from an attempted rape only for it to be later revealed that the attack was in fact simulated by Dante, who is thus both the perpetrator of and savior from the assault. In general terms, however, the pervasive violence is typified by the production of monsters and tends toward total destruction, epitomized by the virtual reality game in *El juego de los mundos* that is played remotely and involves the actual destruction of entire civilizations, species, and planets. However, throughout Aira's short novels, such radical becomings-other are also preemptively condemned to defeat. As the stories develop, accelerating through series of increasingly fantastic and monstrous becomings-other, they arrive at an impasse. Having unleashed a transformative potential capable of total destruction, the situation is invariably abandoned and resolved in a few brief pages. As Reinaldo Laddaga laments:

> los finales de Aira nunca se preparan; advienen súbitamente. De ello se deriva un comentario que no es infrecuente entre sus lectores: que sus libros acaban, en general, de un modo insatisfactorio, innatural, forzado; que traicionan el contrato narrativo dilapidando el capital narrativo acumulado, incendiando, simplemente, el edificio narrativo que han erigido.[119]
>
> (Aira's endings are never prepared; they arrive unexpectedly. A comment which is not infrequently made among his readers originates from this fact: that his books end, in general, in an unsatisfactory, unnatural and forced manner; that they betray the narrative contract squandering the narrative capital previously accumulated, quite simply burning down the narrative edifices that the novels have erected.)

Contreras offers us two particular models for understanding this impasse. First, she suggests that it arguably "se deriva del relato como experiencia de supervivencia" (originates in the story as an experience of survival), reflecting Aira's own critical assertion that "un cuento sólo puede contarlo un sobreviviente" (a story can only be told by a survivor).[120] Second, and most important, Contreras contends that Aira's narrative impasses reflect

> [el] doble impulso que es índice de la instauración de una relación transfigurada con el tiempo y que la literatura de Aira traduce, formalmente,

en sus dos figuras centrales y constitutivas: la figuración del Final—la catástrofe, el Fin del Mundo—y la figuración del Comienzo—los nacimientos, la génesis.[121]

([the] double impulse which indicates the establishment of a transfigured relation with time and which Aira's literature translates, formally, in his two central and constitutive figures: the figuration of the End—the catastrophe, the End of the World—and the figuration of the Beginning—births, genesis.)

This double impulse is made manifest in Aira's novel *Yo era una mujer casada* when the eponymous wife discovers a statue that she considers to represent "el Fin y el Comienzo" (the End and the Beginning).[122] At the level of Aira's literary process, however, this double impulse is represented by the tendency toward destruction, the rapid resolution of the disastrous situation, and the repetition of the process through the commencement of a new novel in Aira's prolific publication. Importantly, the double impulse of the impasse reached and the "imperativo . . . de empezar de nuevo" (the imperative . . . to begin again) leads to an important commentary on Aira's literary production.[123] The concurrent tendency toward destruction and genesis, toward "el Fin y el Comienzo," arguably reflects what Badiou has called the "terrorist commandment" for the militant of a truth-procedure who "finds himself in the situation of the character of Beckett's *The Unnamable*, [and] whose situation is summed up in the famous last words of the text: 'You must go on, I can't go on, I'll go on.'"[124] This is to say that, Aira's "huida hacia adelante" (flight forward) could also be understood within the model of the Badiouian truth-procedure. Furthermore, by relentlessly pursuing this same "huida hacia adelante" (flight forward), Aira has emerged as a central figure within the canon of contemporary Argentine literature, which is to say that he has become a revolutionary subject in the field of art. Nonetheless, it is important to note that Aira himself assumes a central role in manifold texts such as *El infinito*, *El cerebro musical*, *La costurera y el viento*, *La trompeta de mimbre*, and *El congreso de literatura*. Throughout his literary output, then, the subject we call Aira continues to rewrite, undermine, and destroy his own subjectivity. This is to say that the Aira subject produced by the event is inherently unstable precisely because it is continually susceptible to further Deleuzian transformations, a process that arguably reaches its zenith in *Cómo me hice monja* when Aira appears as a female character and narrates her own death. In this instance, the subject completely undermines itself through its simultaneous affirmation and denial and Aira appears to construct a paradoxical zone of *asubjective* subjectivity. In this, Aira's bizarre conception of subjectivity resonates with Deleuze's evolution of Foucault's thought, within which the "struggle for subjectivity is a battle to win the right to have access to difference, variation and metamorphosis."[125]

While I have proposed thus far that the work of Badiou and Deleuze can be utilized simultaneously to explicate Aira's conception of literary process, I now want to suggest that the particular impasse reached in *La prueba* reveals one last irony that highlights the very limitation of the political aspect of Aira's work. In a reciprocal fashion, this will also uncover the limits of political action within the framework of the Badiouian and Deleuzian event. Aira names his would-be revolutionaries Mao and Lenin: two names of truly revolutionary personages from the twentieth century. However, within the novel, Mao and Lenin's actions are ultimately restricted and stilted. Their violent "revolutionary" action engenders a wild transformation, but it lacks the potential to assume control or suggest any kind of alternative societal organization. Their action can only ever be oppositional to the dominant system. As in the case of Badiou's political philosophy, "politics is not a programme aimed at a blueprint for society, but a movement that seeks to abolish or dislocate the dominant state of affairs; politics is the emancipatory insurrection of a subject that the situation and its statist representation treat as politically non-existent."[126] The same description could equally be applied to Deleuze's conception of the political role of the schizophrenic. Neither conception can ever proffer an alternative; it can only seek to "abolish or dislocate the dominant state of affairs." In summarizing the problem with regard to Badiou, Slavoj Žižek writes, "it is Badiou who is unable to expand the encounter of the Real into a *discourse*," and thus "one continues to rely on state power as that against which one defines one's own position."[127] Again, this criticism holds equally true for Deleuze as it does for Badiou, and it is made manifest throughout Aira's literary project. It is by naming his characters after those political figures who did strive (rightly or wrongly) for a political subjectivity in their own right and to assume power to create it that Aira's text ironically delineates the limit of the political element of his own literary process, as it also suggests the limited transformative abilities of Badiouian and Deleuzian politics.

The analysis of Aira's novels now complete, it is possible to articulate the connection between his literary oeuvre and Deleuze and Guattari's *Kafka: Toward a Minor Literature*. In this text, Deleuze and Guattari divide Kafka's work into three constituent parts (the stories, the unfinished novels, and the letters) and explore the political and philosophical potential of each. They argue that the first of these, the stories, are epitomized by metamorphosis in the form of becoming-animal.[128] The connection with the work of Aira is immediately apparent. As explained above, Aira's novels feature innumerable violent examples of becoming-monstrous that tend toward the total destruction exemplified by the annihilation of entire planets in *El juego de los mundos*. Furthermore, Aira "deliberately kills all metaphor, all symbolism, all signification, no less than all designation" and emphasizes a process of continual metamorphosis where incredible transmutation and transformation are the norm, in keeping with Deleuze and Guattari's analysis of Kafka's stories.[129] While Aira's becomings-monstrous are far more violent than those found in Kafka, they nonetheless demonstrate considerable correspondence with Deleuze and Guattari's interpretation of the Czech writer's work. Where Deleuze and Guattari argue that Kafka's becomings-animal "stake out the path of escape," so too Aira's novels violently escape the strictures of reality. Moreover, Aira's novels develop in an unpredictable "continuum of intensities" where the incredible and the unpredictable invariably occur, echoing Deleuze and Guattari's assessment of Kafka's stories.[130] Deleuze and Guattari's argument that "the becoming-animal is an immobile voyage that stays in one place; it only lives and is comprehensible as an intensity" is equally applicable to Aira's novels.[131] These texts are predominantly set in recognizable places and time frames described with an uncanny resemblance to reality, yet within them the everyday and commonplace are transgressed by pure metamorphic intensity.

Deleuze and Guattari also suggest that Kafka describes "a world of pure intensities where all forms come undone, as do all the significations, signifiers, and signifieds."[132] It seems that in Aira's oeuvre, even proper names lose their signifying function. Such real personages as Cafulcurá, Rosas, and his daughter Manuelita appear in *La liebre*, and even Aira himself appears as protagonist throughout his work. In each case these real figures are subject to comic exaggeration and transformation. Again, this process ultimately reaches fruition in *Cómo me hice monja* as Aira constructs a narrative that undermines all logical comprehension of reality and in which "all forms come undone." The parallel with *Cómo me hice monja*, however, also allows us to develop an important difference between Aira and Deleuze and Guattari's Kafka. Where the latter theorists argue that for Kafka "the animal is the object *par excellence* of the story: to try to find a way out, to trace a line of escape," Aira's becomings-other ultimately tend toward total destruction.[133] It seems that in the work of Aira, even Kafka's the becoming-animal is subject to spectacular transformation and becomes the unhindered desire to destroy. This significant difference, however, leads paradoxically to both an important correlation and divergence between the work of Aira and Kafka. In the political sphere, Deleuze and Guattari argue that Kafka directly opposes the "becoming-animal" to the "diabolical powers" of the totalitarian state.[134] As we have seen, in *La prueba* the monstrous nature of Aira's becomings-other assumes a political inflection and the text names their target as the system of neoliberal capitalism. In this text, Mao and Lenin can be understood as the embodiment of a schizophrenic subjectivity as described by Deleuze and Guattari in the two volumes of *Capitalism and Schizophrenia*. Where Kafka's stories trace lines of escape from the machinic assemblages of "Fascism, Stalinism, Americanism, *diabolical powers that are knocking at the door*," Aira directs his destructive transformations (especially in *Ema, la cautiva* and *La prueba*) against the power of neoliberal capitalism.[135] However, where Kafka imagines creative lines of escape from the diabolical bureaucratic machines of the future, Aira imagines the immanent potential of schizophrenia, understood as both product and limit of capitalism itself, to lead to the destruction of the entire system and of the world itself. I would suggest, however, that Aira's total destruction is also liberatory in that it implies the possibility of starting anew, unencumbered with the constraints of the capitalist system. Surprisingly, this also leads to a further connection between the two authors.

Within their analysis of Kafka's stories, Deleuze and Guattari also define the limitations of the model of resistance that he describes. As they explain, despite the "literary splendor" of Kafka's stories, they "bump up against a no-way out of the animal way out, an impasse of the line of escape," and "for this reason . . . they end when they erect this impasse."[136] Despite the liberatory potential implied by Aira's tendency toward total destruction, it is never realized as the radical becomings-other he describes are also preemptively condemned to defeat. As the stories develop, accelerating through series of increasingly fantastic and monstrous becomings-other, they too arrive at an impasse. Having unleashed a transformative potential capable of total destruction, the situation is invariably abandoned and resolved in a few brief pages. When Deleuze and Guattari later comment that the "becoming-animal effectively . . . traces a line of escape, but is incapable of following it," it becomes particularly clear that this aspect of Aira's literature represents a further connection between the Argentine and Czech authors' work.[137] As we have seen in *Ema, la cautiva*, in the novel's concluding section reality returns and the massacre of the indigenous population is named in the text. In this instance, reality is inescapable due to the continuing existence of the military regime and their abuses of history and the population. Aira simply cannot follow his imagined line of escape. In *La prueba* the failure is somewhat different. As previously discussed, by naming his central characters Mao and Lenin Aira ironically suggests a similar argument to that made by Slavoj Žižek, who contends that as the concepts of the Badiouian truth-procedure and Deleuzian becoming-other are defined in opposition to state power, they are unable to create a political subjectivity capable of assuming a position of power. *La prueba* reaches much the same impasse, and this also explains Aira's inability to realize the liberatory freedom implied by his tendency toward destruction: having destroyed the previous model, the strategy he employs cannot construct an alternative politics. However, as Deleuze and Guattari note, while Kafka's stories "show a way out that the becomings-animal are themselves incapable of following," they simultaneously contain "something different" that acts "inside them" and that can only be expressed "in the novels."[138] So too in my own analysis, having defined Aira's act of resistance and reached its limit, I can only augment my argument by considering another part of the literary machine I am attempting to describe. To explore further the conditions that lead to this political impasse and indeed, the possibility of moving beyond it, I must consider the work of another Argentine writer: Marcelo Cohen. Moreover, this discussion will reveal that Cohen's novels are intimately connected with Deleuze and Guattari's analysis of Kafka's novels, as we shall now see.

MARCELO COHEN: 27 DE MARZO DE 1991, LA FECHA DE ESCRITURA

(27 MARCH 1991: THE DATE OF WRITING)

El insomnio es la gran enfermedad de la nación.

Insomnia is the great illness of the nation.

Piglia, *La ciudad ausente,* **118**

CHAPTER 3

"IS THERE ANY THING WHEREOF IT MAY BE SAID, SEE, THIS IS NEW?"

HAVING ESTABLISHED THE CENTRAL IMPORTANCE OF CAPITALISM WITH-in Aira's literature in chapter 1, I have also shown how Aira responds to the realignment of the Argentine economy with the neoliberal model in my second chapter: he reimagines the revolutionary impetus of the 1960s, transforms it within a Deleuzian and Badiouian framework, and transposes it to the neoliberal reform of the early 1990s. I have also described Aira's artistic process as the correlate of this politico-philosophical mechanism. Finally, I have argued that Aira effectively acknowledges and defines the limitations of this type of political action. In discussing Marcelo Cohen's novel *El oído absoluto*, Patrick Dove makes the observation that "in Argentina . . . the term 'transition' in fact applies to two historical events: the transition from dictatorship to democracy coincides with the substitution of state economy by market economy."[1] Additionally, Jimena Néspolo has argued that "el gran tema de Cohen es el Poder . . . , el modo en que el poder se perpetúa a través de sus relatos, el modo en que los sujetos colaboran o se resisten en esa perpetuación" (Cohen's great theme is power . . . , the way in which power is perpetuated throughout his stories, the way in which the characters collaborate or resist this perpetuation).[2] It is my contention that certain of Cohen's early novels (those written during the period 1986–1998) can be read as an exploration of the changing nature of power relations and resistance engendered by the dual nature of the Argentine "transition" that Dove describes. Broadly speaking, this chapter will explore the sociopolitical aspect of the transition, while chapter 4 will more directly address the implications of the opening to the market economy.

Dove also makes the assertion that "the triumphant arrival of neoliberalism is not easy to separate—chronologically or ontologically—from recent histories of military dictatorship."[3] In this way, Dove situates Cohen's novel within a body of scholarship that questions the validity of the democratic transitions in the Southern Cone, arguing that the economic and political transformation from national state to transnational market was in fact the triumph of the dictatorships.[4] With these arguments in mind, I propose that within the dystopian visions of the future described in the short story "La ilusión monarca" and the novel *Insomnio*, Cohen includes salient contextual information that reflects the development of power relations initiated during the most recent military dictatorship, carried through the political transition to democracy, and beginning to take full effect after the structural adjustment program of the Menem presidency in the early 1990s. The short story "La ilusión monarca" in particular has received important critical attention. Annelies Oeyen follows Idelber Avelar's Benjaminian analysis of postdictatorship literature centered on allegory and mourning and argues that Cohen's story should be read as "una alegoría de la Argentina" (an allegory for Argentina) containing "un espacio histórico y políticamente cargado" (a historic and politically charged space).[5] In contrast, Joanna Page considers the story as exemplifying the process of "entropy," which she argues "emerges in Cohen's work as a privileged metaphor for literary creativity."[6] Uniquely, Page argues that within Cohen's work, entropy should be understood as "the notion of the creativity and energy available in dissipative structures, which make use of chaotic processes and flows across their borders to produce new kinds of order."[7] Additionally, she directly rejects Oeyen's allegorical interpretation of Cohen's story, arguing that such "readings are all too consciously *invited* by the text" and that "the process of metamorphorization" that she perceives in the text "undermines the validity of proposing any one reading, including those suggested in the text itself."[8] My own argument occupies a space somewhere between these two positions; by considering the story in conjunction with the novel *Insomnio*, I argue that the contextual markers throughout each text are demonstrative of changing social relations begun during the military dictatorship (in line with Oeyen's argument) and that both texts, albeit in distinct ways, "stage an encounter with difference" (in line with Page's argument).[9] While cognizant of the limitations of direct allegorical readings that Page highlights, I nonetheless argue that the historical contextual information contained in these two works is of central importance and that through it Cohen problematizes Michel Foucault's conception of the "disciplinary society" in order to reflect the changing nature of power relations during the transition period. In this, my argument is close to that made by Miguel Dalmaroni, who has argued that "la ficción de Cohen se construye . . . como pasaje entre fantástico e hipótesis de anticipación sociológica" (Cohen's fiction is constructed . . . like a passage between the fantastic and an anticipatory sociological hypothesis).[10]

Both "La ilusión monarca" and *Insomnio* proffer dystopian visions of the near future. In the former text the action is confined within a strange prison built on a beach, its cells both facing and permanently open to the seafront. The prison is guarded by robots, and significantly the prisoners' freedom seems tantalizingly obtainable: despite the fact the prison walls stretch some two hundred meters out into the water, they are not connected and the prison remains open to the sea. The story follows the protagonist and antihero, Sergio, as he gradually becomes accustomed to life in the prison until he makes his own bid for freedom and swims out far beyond the prison walls, only then to elect to return to the prison. His final enigmatic words (indeed, the final words of the story), spoken to another prisoner, are: "sabés, Frankie, me pasó una cosa" (you know, Frankie, something happened to me).[11]

Similarly, *Insomnio* is set entirely within the Patagonian city of Bardas de Krámer.[12] The city has experienced a recent petrol boom, corresponding mass immigration and exponential growth. However, at some unspecified point before the opening of the novel, the wells have dried out and the city's economy has collapsed. As a result, those countries near the city, concerned that they will be inundated with impoverished economic migrants, have instructed the "Fuerza Interamericana" (Inter-American Forces) to besiege the city, and no one is allowed to travel beyond its boundaries. The city itself has essentially become a prison as the citizens of Bardas de Krámer (like the prisoners in "La ilusión monarca") are kept under constant supervision. There are spies everywhere in the city, and there is a permanent military presence in the industrial wasteland. Furthermore, as in the case of "La ilusión monarca," *Insomnio* features a solitary male protagonist, Ezequiel Adad, a scribe and one of only two people able to write in a city that has become almost entirely illiterate. Additionally, freedom again appears to be tantalizingly obtainable as the city's mayor has organized the "Parte de Salidas" (Exit Register), a secret lottery that grants permission to leave the city to just a few people each time it is drawn. In a final point of direct comparison, when Ezequiel's name is drawn in the Parte de Salidas at the culminating point in the novel, he elects to remain in Krámer, much as Sergio decides to return to the prison.

Despite each text's setting in the near future, there are contextual markers that serve to highlight their focus on the transition to democracy. First, in "La ilusión monarca" there is Cohen's frequent mention of the "mundo inflacionario" (inflationary world), a direct reference to the increasing rates of inflation that had begun during the military regime and persisted until the implementation of Menem's structural adjustment program. Similarly, although Sergio has been imprisoned because "se había metido en el tráfico de glándulas, . . . pituitarias, suprarrenales que . . . importaba de Rusia o Armenia" (he had got involved in the trafficking of glands, . . . pituitaries, adrenals that . . . he imported from Russia or Armenia), very quickly it becomes clear that Sergio is the victim of a corrupt and failing justice system.[13] His clients and superiors in the illicit trade have remained free, and the judge in his case has been paid off with the organs in question. Certain political developments are crucial for understanding the importance of these actions. For example, following the return to democracy, Argentines had witnessed early advances in the search for justice for the victims of the systematic plan of state terrorism implemented by the military government. The first democratically elected president in the transition period, Raúl Alfonsín, played a key role in creating the Comisión Nacional sobre la Desaparición de Personas (CONADEP, National Commission on the Disappearance of Persons), which published its final report, *Nunca más*, in 1984. Moreover, Alfonsín oversaw the trial of the Argentine Junta in 1985. Despite these advances, however, Alfonsín yielded to rising pressure from certain sections of the military and the Ley de Punto Final (Full Stop Law) was passed in 1986. This legislation prevented further trials being prosecuted beyond a fixed date, and it was soon followed by the Ley de Obediencia Debida (Law of Due Obedience) in 1987, which prevented the prosecution of subordinate military personnel if they were following the orders of their superiors. Shortly before the publication of Cohen's story, Alfonsín's successor to the presidency, Menem, would complete this process by pardoning those already convicted in response to further pressure from members of the military. Given this context, an immediate connection can be drawn between the actions of the corrupt judge within Cohen's story and the pardons granted to the military junta by Menem. This comparison is further strengthened when one notes that, as Luis Alberto Romero has argued, corruption in Argentina "creció espectacularmente en dos momentos: durante la última dictadura militar y en los diez años de gobierno de Menem" (increased spectacularly in two moments: during the last military dictatorship and in the ten years of Menem's government).[14] Arguably most important, however, is that because the prison remains open to the sea, the possibility of escape becomes the prisoners' perpetual obsession. As the story progresses, various prisoners enter the sea and attempt to swim for their freedom. While some simply disappear, the bloated and dismembered bodies of various others wash back up on the prison beach. Neither the characters within the story nor the reader learns anything concerning their fate. As Oeyen argues, the "cadáveres arrastrados en la playa recuerdan las víctimas del Proceso" (corpses dragged on the beach recall the victims of the Process).[15] Certainly, Cohen's horrific descriptions of these mutilated bodies washing up on the shore and the complete lack of information concerning their fate cannot but constitute an echo of the victims of the "vuelos de la muerte" (death flights), whose bodies, naked, bound, and disfigured, washed up on various beaches during the last military dictatorship, as related in the pages of the newspaper *Clarín* at the time.[16] Importantly, although there were suspicions that such death flights had taken place when Cohen published his story, these were not confirmed until Adolfo Scilingo made his confession in 1995, three years after Cohen published "La ilusión monarca."[17]

Similar echoes of the transition to democracy can also be found throughout *Insomnio*. As in the case of the prisoners in "La ilusión monarca," many of the poor, desperate, and mainly immigrant population of Bardas de Krámer are engaged in some form of petty "criminality." This behavior ranges from theft and robbery to illicit drug-dealing and taking and to the trafficking of antibiotics. Furthermore, as in Cohen's later story, this petty criminality of the lower classes simply masks that of the dominant groups. In *Insomnio* the spies that constantly observe the citizens of Krámer also engage in assault, theft, and many other forms of criminality. However, in a similar way to the judge in "La ilusión monarca," these authority figures remain immune from any punishment and can hide their own corruption in plain sight. This again echoes the failing and corrupt justice system of the time. Additionally, that graffiti slogans painted by the enigmatic "Empecinado" (Stubborn One) begin to appear throughout the city fomenting unease and disquiet is another possible echo of the transition period. As Claudia Kozak argues, such graffiti not only echoes the situationist slogans found in Paris in 1968 but is reminiscent of the political graffiti created by groups such as "Los Sujetos" (the Subjects) during the 1980s in Buenos Aires.[18] I would suggest that the anxiety and disturbance generated by the graffiti also prefigures that aroused by a form of political demonstration prominent during the 1990s in Buenos Aires known as *los escraches*. Initially conceived by the group Hijos por la Identidad y la Justicia Contra el Olvido y el Silencio (HIJOS, Sons and Daughters for Identity and Justice against Forgetting and Silence), the *escrache* was a form of performative protest that involved publicly denouncing those people implicated in the crimes of the military dictatorship who had not been brought to justice.[19] Of particular relevance to Cohen's story is that the *escrache* could include the marking of "the doors of torturers' homes in order to remind the public of the cruelty of their neighbors."[20] Indeed, the social and political setting of Cohen's novel itself demonstrates a certain uncanny yet inverted prescience. Where Cohen's Patagonian city suffers mass unemployment and deprivation due to the exhaustion of the oil wells, in reality it would be the privatization policies of the Menem government that would lead to similar problems throughout Patagonia. For example, the privatization of the national petroleum company resulted in some 80 percent of its employees being made redundant and had catastrophic effects on several Patagonian communities. As Pablo Pozzi notes, the significant rises in unemployment and poverty caused by such privatization resulted in civil unrest in several cases and the security forces even besieged the inhabitants of such Patagonian townships as Cultural Có and Plaza Huincal.[21] In a similar inversion of the reality that would transpire after Menem's neoliberal reforms, where Cohen's inhabitants are isolated from wider society yet unable to leave their environs, "the elimination of 'inefficient' rail lines and the reduction of airline flights" following neoliberal reforms would leave "areas of the country full of ghost towns."[22]

Given that both Cohen texts feature spaces of enclosure in which people are subjected to strict control and constant observation, it is not surprising that each text demonstrates a strong element of panopticism, designed first by Bentham and theorized by Michel Foucault in *Discipline and Punish*. Indeed, both texts would seem to encourage such an interpretation: Cohen describes a hotel in *Insomnio* as "un panóptico inabarcable" (a vast panopticon) and it is mentioned that the prison in the city is "un edificio bajo, pulido y cilíndrico de granito blanco diseñado para Krámer por un sociólogo francés" (a low, smooth and cylindrical building of white granite, designed for Krámer by a French sociologist), which could easily be interpreted as an oblique reference to Foucault himself.[23] With regard to "La ilusión monarca," Oeyen notes the centrality of "la idea del panóptico, tal como la formuló Michel Foucault" (the idea of the panopticon, as formulated by Michel Foucault), and Miriam Chiani has even gone so far as to suggest that Cohen's work in general "tiene su paradigma en la imagen de una cárcel que recuerda el Panóptico programado por Bentham" (finds its paradigm in the image of a prison that reminds one of the Panopticon planned by Bentham).[24] Undoubtedly, in each Cohen text discussed as in Foucault's work, "it is the fact of being constantly seen, of being always able to be seen, that maintains the disciplined individual in his subjection," and the constant observation and surveillance certainly has a profound effect on the prisoners and the inhabitants of Bardas de Krámer.[25] Several other parallels with Foucault's description of panoptic disciplinary society are readily identifiable in the texts. For example, Foucault argues that within panoptic societies, "arms trafficking, the illegal sale of alcohol in prohibition countries, or more recently drug trafficking" demonstrate that "the existence of a legal prohibition creates around it a field of illegal practices" that dominant groups can "supervise, while extracting from it an illicit profit through elements, themselves illegal, but rendered manipulable by their organisation in delinquency."[26] So too in "La ilusión monarca": Sergio's involvement with the illegal trafficking of human organs allows the judge to profit from the self-same practice, to mask his own criminality, and to punish Sergio for their shared crimes. Similarly, in *Insomnio* the petty criminality of the inhabitants of Bardas de Krámer allows the spies scattered throughout the city to engage in illegal activity of their own while masking it as justice. Thus in both texts as in Foucault's analysis, "delinquency, solidified by a penal system centred upon the prison, thus represents a diversion of illegality for the illicit circuits of profit and power of the dominant class."[27]

This close correspondence with Foucault's analysis also connects these Cohen texts to the most recent Argentine dictatorship. As Pilar Calveiro notes in her particularly Foucauldian study of the Argentine Clandestine Centers for Detention, Torture and Extermination, these spaces resembled "un pequeño panóptico" (a small panopticon), and she notes various instances in which the security forces engaged in the theft of property belonging to those disappeared due to their "subversive" activities.[28] Indeed, Calveiro explicitly states that "las Fuerzas Armadas asumieron el disciplinamiento de la sociedad" (the Armed Forces undertook the disciplining of society).[29] Moreover, just as Foucault contends that the prison provides the model for the exercise of power in society that creates a "carceral system," so too Calveiro contends that "la desaparición y el campo de concentración-exterminio dejaron de ser una de las formas de la represión para convertirse en *la* modalidad represiva del poder" (disappearance and the concentration-extermination camp ceased to be one of the forms of repression in order to become *the* repressive method of power) that created the "política concentracionaria" (concentrationary politics) that governed Argentina during the dictatorship.[30]

It is important to note, however, that Cohen's texts do not correspond exactly to the Foucauldian model of the disciplinary society. Where Foucault asserts that "time-tables, compulsory movements, regular activities, solitary meditation, work in common, silence, application, respect, [and] good habits" are fundamental to panoptic disciplinary institutions, as "the individual's body as a social instrument . . . must be rendered a docile and pliable tool of economic productivity," these are completely lacking from each Cohen text.[31] In "La ilusión monarca" the prisoners' day is simply not structured, and as Page notes, beyond a futile attempt to feed the prisoners at regular intervals, no effort is made to discipline the prisoners.[32] The prisoners barely acknowledge the delivery of food to their cells, preferring to fish from the sea and trade among themselves, and they simply ignore the command to use the showers. Similarly, Oeyen observes that there are "referencias a objetos que sirven para medir el tiempo, pero no lo hacen" (references to objects that serve to measure time, but they do not do so).[33] At the beginning of the story, the reader is informed that a "tablero digital que indica la hora y la temperatura" (a digital board that indicates the time and the temperature) stands in plain sight of all the prisoners; however, it is never used to structure their day in a regulated way, and when it breaks it is never fixed.[34] The prisoners simply reject the few vain attempts at imposing some kind of structure that would govern and control their activity.

Although examples are not as precise and easily identifiable in *Insomnio*, it is nonetheless absolutely crucial that the inhabitants of Krámer are not subject to any form of regulated activity or discipline. Within Cohen's dystopian city no character enters an institution that could instill order, and there is no attempt to transform the inhabitants of Krámer into obedient workers in the larger economic system as Foucault prescribes. The citizens of Krámer have certainly been enclosed within the city, and they are undoubtedly subject to permanent supervision, yet they have essentially been abandoned and left to organize their own informal economy. They are not subject to the influence or control of any other institution that would regulate their activities and even the authorities (represented by the spies) in this seemingly lawless society only act sporadically and arbitrarily to exploit the population. It would thus seem that each text does not reflect Foucault's perfectly realized "despotic discipline" but rather depicts something of a perfectly realized and despotic *in*discipline.[35]

Indeed, within these Cohen texts (and especially within "La ilusión monarca") it would actually seem that the despotic society of indiscipline demonstrates a greater correspondence with the historically previous "sovereign society," which Foucault defines in contradistinction to the emergent form of "disciplinary society." Within this formation, the sovereign power of the monarch was absolute and his power was maintained through the use of "punishment as a spectacle," which served the juridico-political function of reasserting the absolute authority of the monarch "by manifesting it at its most spectacular."[36] Indeed, according to Foucault's analysis, within sovereign societies "public torture and execution must be spectacular, it must be seen by all almost as its triumph."[37] This process can be clearly seen in "La ilusión monarca" through the fate of Sergio's fellow inmate Jolxen. This character is particularly interesting in that he is a prisoner who serves as something of a spiritual guide to Sergio, yet he also confesses to him that he helped design the prison and entered it in order to observe his experiment at close quarters. Critically, when Jolxen enters the sea and swims for freedom, he neither disappears nor washes back up on the shore. His body does, however, return to the prison: a gate is opened and a horse carrying his horribly mutilated body enters the beach.[38] As with comparisons with the disciplinary model of social organization, however, the return of Jolxen's horrifically tortured body is not a perfect reflection of sovereign power as described by Foucault. For Foucault "the function of the public torture and execution was to reveal the truth; and in this respect it continued, in the public eye, the work of the judicial torture conducted in private."[39] Jolxen's mutilated body certainly completes the second part of this dual function; it undoubtedly makes his private torture and suffering public. However, what it does not—indeed cannot—do is "reveal the truth." Jolxen's symbolic torture and execution doubtless signifies a great deal, yet it is impossible to intuit exactly what this significance might be. Neither the reader nor the prisoners can be certain *why* it is only Jolxen who has suffered this unique fate. It is impossible to ascertain with any certainty if he was responsible for the creation of the prison, the only unique factor in his life of which the reader is made aware. As Page notes, "it is at least as likely that he is deluded or deceitful," and "this interpretation is neither confirmed nor dismissed."[40] Although it may be impossible to intuit exactly what Jolxen's death *means*, it is nonetheless possible in a practical sense to perceive what his death *does*: it unquestionably demonstrates the "dissymmetry [and] the irreversible imbalance of forces [that] were an essential element in the public execution" and the absolute "arbitrariness of monarchical power," which Foucault argues were essential components of public torture in sovereign societies.[41] Thus, where the aperture to the sea seems to suggest to the prisoners that "la cárcel es una prueba de selección: un tamiz . . . ideado para recompensar a los más aptos y los que tienen más huevos" (the prison is a test of selection: a screen . . . invented in order to reward the most competent and the bravest), and that by swimming beyond the walls of the prison, they can expedite a migration of sovereignty from the invisible sovereign power to themselves, Jolxen's death actually confirms that the sea is merely "la *ilusión* monarca" (the monarchical *illusion*) affirming only the arbitrary, cruel and absolute sovereign power that governs the prison.[42]

Although the correlations between Foucault's sovereign society and *Insomnio* are not quite as precise and succinct as they are in "La ilusión monarca," they nonetheless permeate the text. For example, in a subplot in *Insomnio*, the owner of several "pornoshops" and massage parlors, the cocaine addict and dealer Chalukián, attempts to organize a plot to overthrow the mayor and seize control in Krámer. As the novel draws to a conclusion, the authorities and military intervene, violently subdue the potential uprising, and execute the organizers of the would-be revolt. Martial authority is restored and reasserted across the city and a new mayor installed. The leaders of the potential revolt may not be subjected to a public display of torture as in the case of Jolxen in "La ilusión monarca," but the preemptive defeat of the uprising is no less spectacular. Military forces flood the city and act with tremendous violence to crush the prospective insurrection. Moreover, their arrival is accompanied by the blaring of Mahler's eighth symphony from loudspeakers throughout the city. As before, such a tremendous show of force cannot but reaffirm the essential and total "imbalance of forces" utilized to maintain order in sovereign societies.[43] Furthermore, that the prime responsibility of the authorities in Krámer is to organize the Parte de Salidas cannot but affirm the absolute "arbitrariness of monarchical power" in sovereign societies.[44] In place of regimented power based on the law and exercised to control and manipulate bodies in disciplinary societies, the authorities in Krámer ultimately utilize chance to create the illusion of freedom while manipulating and exercising absolute and arbitrary control over the population. Indeed, following the defeat of the failed revolt, Ezequiel (who had been courted by the plotters to act as their spokesman and who is the only other literate person in the city beside the new mayor) is drawn in the Parte de Salidas. This suggests that the lottery is not as subject to chance as it would at first appear, reaffirming the absolute and arbitrary nature of the authorities' power.

Clearly, Cohen's depiction in "La ilusión monarca" of an authoritarian power that acts arbitrarily yet with impunity and indulges in spectacular torture while concealing rather than revealing any truth other than their own absolute power serves as another particularly clear link to the most recent military government, which "operaba de noche y aparentaba normalidad de día" (operated at night and feigned normality by day)and utilized the "secretos a voces" (open secrets) of torture and disappearance to hide their horrendous crimes in plain sight and "diseminar el terror" (disseminate terror) among the Argentine population.[45] Indeed, even in her subtle development of Foucauldian disciplinary society, Calveiro recognizes "la *arbitrariedad* del sistema" (the *arbitrariness* of the system) implemented by the military government and "su verdadera *omnipotencia*" (its true *omnipotence*).[46] Moreover, although she never states that it belongs to the sovereign mode of societal organization, Calveiro specifically references Foucault's analysis of "el suplicio de la Edad Media" (medieval torture) to describe the "modalidad inquisitorial" (inquisitorial modality) of power exercised by the dictatorship.[47] The complete lack of Foucauldian discipline in both texts also serves as another link back to this period of Argentine history. As Romero argues, the military government's economic policy had a detrimental effect on the very institutions that would normally apply discipline, and "de acuerdo con la nueva doctrina neoliberal" (in accordance with the new neoliberal doctrine), it was decided that "el mercado debía disciplinar la sociedad" (the market should discipline society).[48] So too in Cohen's texts: neither the prisoners nor the residents are subject to discipline, and they both establish their own unregulated economy.

These connections, however, are not merely a mournful remnant of the military regime's brutal plan of systematic torture and disappearance. Rather, they connect Cohen's texts to processes that persisted through and beyond the transition to democracy. As Argentine philosopher and psychoanalyst León Rozitchner argues, precisely because transitional Argentine democracy developed "against the background of a previous dictatorship, which can always return to re-impose its violence," a "disguised terror" remained "within Menem's political democracy."[49] Moreover, Rozitchner contends that this threat was exploited to persuade the Argentine people to "submit to the law of the Market and the State."[50] The various military uprisings of the late 1980s would ensure that this "disguised terror" was palpable at the time Cohen published these texts. Moreover, reports in subsequent years of disappearance,[51] the use of the cattle prod as an instrument of torture, and the charge that "torture and abuse" remained "standard practice among contemporary Argentine police forces" suggest that the prisoner's bodies that wash back up on the shore in Cohen's story serve not only as a visceral link to the unresolved crimes of the dictatorship's plan of state terrorism or to the threat of the return of terror articulated by Rozitchner but to the continual abuses committed by the Argentine state.[52] In a similar way, Romero also explains that beyond the transition to democracy, capitalist logic affected and altered the behavior of the armed forces, the security services, the judiciary, and the civil service, which all learned to tolerate, conceal, and participate in corrupt exchanges while simultaneously increasing the "arbitrariedad" (arbitrariness) of the legal system itself, making their offices "el instrumento de negocios privados" (the instruments of private enterprise) and "preparándose para el proceso de privatización posterior a 1989" (preparing themselves for the process of privatization begun after 1989).[53] Thus the judge's actions in "La ilusión monarca" and those of bribed "funcionarios" (public servants) in *Insomnio* serve to highlight that the military government "dejó una herencia de funcionarios, policías y jueces corruptos y acostumbrados a vivir en la corrupción, y una pobre idea del respeto a la ley" (left a legacy of corrupt public servants, policemen, and judges who were accustomed to living in corruption, and a poor idea of respect for the law).[54] Finally, it is equally important that at the time Cohen published "La ilusión monarca," the Menem government utilized the economic crisis affecting the country significantly to augment its own power while also realigning the Argentine economy with the neoliberal model to its detriment. As Jorge Mayer argues, the Menem government's "forma de procesar las crisis sirvieron de justificación a una ampliación creciente de las atribuciones de los presidentes" (method of processing the crises served as justification for an increasing extension of the powers of the presidency).⁵⁵ Thus economic developments begun during the military government and continued throughout the transition to democracy were accompanied by significant alterations in structures of power.

With this in mind, the resurgence of sovereign methods of spectacular punishment in Cohen's texts can be considered as reflecting the changing nature of power relations in Argentina during the transition period. Other deviations from the Foucauldian model of panoptic disciplinary society, however, lead to revelations that are rather more philosophical in nature. For example, within Foucault's analysis of panoptic institutions, "to punish is to exercise," and "disciplinary systems favour punishments that are exercise—intensified, multiplied forms of training, several times repeated."⁵⁶ As previously suggested, such regimented, regulated, and repetitive exercise is entirely absent from Cohen's prison in "La ilusión monarca." Importantly, however, life within the prison is structured on the basis of repetitive cycles; it is simply that these are natural in origin. As Oeyen makes clear, the extraordinary architectural nature of the prison creates the impression of "un islote monótono y continuo que se caracteriza por la eterna repetición de lo mismo" (a monotonous and continuous islet characterized by the eternal repetition of the same) where the "mar representa una dinámica que . . . ofrece la seguridad de una vida carcelaria que siempre sigue igual" (sea represents a dynamic that . . . proffers the security of a prison life that always continues the same).⁵⁷ Certainly the natural cycles of tide and time represented by the sea essentially come to replace the repetition of exercise that is indispensable to Foucauldian disciplinary institutions. The prisoners' lives are structured around the natural rhythms of the sea and the sun instead of the regular movements of the digital clock and the ineffectual and apathetic attempts by the guards to establish a regimented routine. Furthermore, Cohen opens each chapter with an intricate, elegiac, and beautiful description of the sea and the natural surroundings of the prison. The reader, like the prisoners, is consistently confronted with the natural cycles of the sea, a process that only ends when Sergio finally swims away from the beach in the story's concluding section.

Oeyen's suggestion that the repetitions of the sea "siempre sigue igual" (always continue the same) is, however, somewhat undermined by the structure and form of Cohen's story itself. As Page notes, "the sea, the subject of 'La ilusión monarca,' does not simply refer to a mass of water but to the history of its representation in art and literature, Romantic and modern."[58] No two of Cohen's descriptions of the sea are the same, and he describes each seascape in intricate detail. In contrast to Oeyen's suggestion, Cohen's strict repetition of descriptions of the sea do not represent the monotony of "lo mismo" (the same) but in fact represent "a serious, committed attempt to stage an encounter with difference," as Page argues.[59] Through Cohen's increasingly detailed descriptions of the natural seascape, the reader essentially becomes aware that "even in nature, isochronic rotations are only the outward appearance of a more profound movement, the revolving cycles are only abstractions: placed together, they reveal evolutionary cycles or spirals whose principle is a variable curve," which is to say that they come to represent difference as defined by Gilles Deleuze.[60] Just as Deleuze rejects that tradition of thought in western metaphysics that subordinates difference to the same and proceeds by comparison and the construction of hierarchies, so too in Cohen's text there is no original or ideal description of the sea, and each depiction presents only a profusion of difference. Moreover, the series of seascapes created by Cohen ultimately uncover a "concept of repetition in which physical, mechanical or bare repetitions (repetitions of the Same) would find their *raison d'être* in the more profound structures of a hidden repetition in which a 'differential' is disguised and displaced," as in the work of Deleuze.[61] I would suggest that Cohen's story is in fact constructed from *"these concepts of a pure difference and a complex repetition"* that "connect and coalesce" in his repetitive descriptions of the natural world that in turn structures the prisoners' lives.[62] This philosophical functioning of Cohen's prison represents an easily overlooked deviation from Foucauldian panoptic disciplinary institutions. For Foucault, concurrently with repetitive exercise, the disciplinary institution is founded on the principle of "normalisation" where "the power of normalisation imposes homogeneity" by measuring individuals against an artificial norm. Thus the disciplinary institution "compares, differentiates, hierarchises, homogenises, excludes," and *"normalises"* through a model of representation where difference is subordinate to sameness.[63]

I would argue that *Insomnio* too is intimately concerned with Deleuzian difference and repetition. As in "La ilusión monarca" this novel also appears to be constructed from numerous repetitions: Ezequiel's office is contained in a building that is a copy of the "Chrysler Building de Nueva York" (Chrysler Building in New York), and the central station in Krámer is described as "una copia triunfal de la Gare de Lyon" (a triumphant copy of the Gare de Lyon).[64] Far more important, however, are the numerous literary referents found in *Insomnio*. For example, Chalukián's plot to seize control of Krámer is somewhat reminiscent of that devised by the "Astrólogo" in Roberto Arlt's *Los siete locos*.

Particularly significant, however, are the frequent references and allusions to James Joyce's *Ulysses* throughout the text. For example, the novel opens and closes with a description of human advertising boards as they cross the city, a scene reminiscent of that described in the "Lestrygonians" episode of Joyce's novel where the protagonist, Leopold Bloom, also pays particular attention to the human advertising board for Wisdom Hely's establishment.[65] Undoubtedly ambiguous, this connection nonetheless sets the scene for a series of other striking correspondences between the two novels. Both Ezequiel and Bloom are Jewish within predominantly Catholic countries, the action of each novel remains strictly within the confines of single city, and at the end of each novel both protagonists decide to remain where they are: Bloom returns to his wife Molly, and Ezequiel refuses the opportunity to leave Krámer. Similarly, both Ezequiel and Bloom work with words and language but in a lowly and commercial capacity; Bloom works in local advertising, and Ezequiel is a scribe for the popular classes. This strong correspondence is reinforced when Ezequiel's close friend and confidant, Tadeo, ponders the fate of Ezequiel's wife, rhetorically asking: "¿Ofelia va a ser, la pobre? ¿*Penélope*? ¿Porcia?" (Will the poor woman be Ophelia? *Penelope*? Portia?)[66] In the structural correspondence between Joyce's *Ulysses* and Homer's *Odyssey*, Molly Bloom, of course, fulfills the role of Penelope. Thus *Insomnio* is something of a repetition of a novel that is itself already a repetition of a previous text.

Links between *Insomnio* and *Ulysses*, however, are only ever partial. Despite clear connections between the texts, differences also emerge. This can be seen particularly clearly at each novel's conclusion. In *Ulysses* Bloom returns home to his wife, yet in *Insomnio*, in order to remain in Krámer, Ezequiel abandons his wife (who left Krámer some seven years before the commencement of the novel) and begins a new life with his lover, Selva. Bloom the faithful cuckold becomes Ezequiel, the adulterer. Admittedly, in this regard, Cohen demonstrates a certain faithfulness to Joyce's text. In Joyce's transposition of the classical text, faithful Penelope is reincarnated in Molly the adulteress. In Cohen's transposition, faithful Leopold is reincarnated in Ezequiel the adulterer. In a further deviation from *Ulysses*, however, the man Ezequiel usurps when he begins a relationship with Selva is named Leopoldo, a Latinized version of Bloom's given name, Leopold. Arguably the most important aspect of these Joycean references, however, is that they provide a framework through which one can interpret the numerous literary references contained within *Insomnio*. This can be most clearly perceived by considering Ricardo Piglia's interpretation of Joyce's novel. For Piglia, in *Ulysses* "el sistema de las referencias homéricas fue una etapa necesaria en la construcción de la obra" (the system of Homeric references was a necessary stage in the construction of the work) and as such can be considered "como el molde de hierro de una escultura que desaparece, retirado o escondido por el material" (like the iron mold of a sculpture that disappears, withdrawn or hidden by the material).[67] Piglia thus argues that *Ulysses* creates the impression that it contains "una historia 'olvidada,' secreta, [que] circula bajo la superficie y define los hechos" (a "forgotten," secret story [that] circulates under the surface and defines the events) within the novel.[68] It is my contention that *Insomnio* also features a secret history below the surface of the text that defines the events that transpire. However, where Piglia suggests that for *Ulysses* "la *Odisea* es una referencia importante para el que escribe el libro, pero no para el que lo lee" (the *Odyssey* is an important reference for he who writes the book, but not for he who reads it), I contend that for the reader the referential model contained in *Ulysses* provides a method by which one can interpret other important *biblical* repetitions contained within *Insomnio*.[69]

When Ezequiel first encounters Selva in his office, she brings him a Bible that has been underlined by her previous lover. Selva believes that Ezequiel can analyze the underlined phrases and explain why her lover abandoned her. The underlined sections pertain to two different books from the Old Testament; the first of these is the Song of Songs (Cantar de los cantares). As Ezequiel astutely observes, this biblical text is particularly ambiguous and can be understood "como un alma que se casa con Dios, o como la descripción de un matrimonio pagano" (as a soul who marries God, or as the description of a pagan wedding).[70] Ezequiel, however, eventually concludes that Selva's lover had simply used this text to seduce her. Most important, however, is that Ezequiel's encounter with the Cantar invokes powerful memories of his own childhood, memories both of being taught to read the Talmud by an uncle and of his sexual awakening, and he immediately begins to think about Selva with reference to the Cantar. For example, Ezequiel notes that "la primera frase subrayada en el Cantar era *Como aceite que se derrama es tu nombre*" (the first underlined phrase in the Song of Songs was *Thy name is as ointment poured forth*), and the narrator then immediately informs the reader that "él no sabía si Selva era de verdad un nombre como aceite derramado" (he did not know if Selva was really a name like ointment poured forth).[71] By conceiving of his own relationship with Selva in this way and like Leopoldo before him, Ezequiel essentially begins to use the book to seduce Selva and establish a relationship with her. In a certain sense, Selva's previous relationship is reactivated in her burgeoning relationship with Ezequiel through the use of the Cantar, a point further suggested when Tadeo comments that "después de él [Leopoldo] viene el otro hombre de sus [Selva's] desvelos, que sos vos" (after him [Leopoldo] comes the other man that has captivated her: you).[72]

In a similar way, the book of Ezekiel is also partially repeated in *Insomnio*. Within this biblical text Ezekiel, an exiled prophet, is shown the destruction of Israel by God and founds and builds a new city.[73] Indeed, Cohen appears to encourage the reader to think that this biblical text will provide a direct template for *Insomnio* in much the same way Homer's *Odyssey* does for *Ulysses*. As with the *Cantar*, Ezequiel experiences powerful recollections when he thinks of this text, and he even recalls that "*hace mucho decidieron llamarme Ezequiel y el nombre escondía la esperanza de una revelación*" (*a long time ago they decided to call me Ezequiel and the name concealed the hope of a revelation*).[74] Such recollections lead Ezequiel to look for symbols from the biblical prophet's visions in his own life in Krámer. Crucially, Ezequiel later remembers that it was expected that he would "*reencarnar al que el Espíritu había elegido para transmitirle un libro con endechas y gemir y plañir*" (*reincarnate he whom the Spirit had chosen to give a book with lamentations, moaning, and wailing*) and become the new embodiment of the prophet Ezekiel.[75] Although Ezequiel immediately laments that he does not share any prophetic vision, this is directly contradicted in the narrative. During one of the frequent dream sequences that permeate the novel, Ezequiel has a vision that is immediately realized when he wakes. During the novel, a couple who has adopted a young girl, Alina, who cannot speak any intelligible language, employs Ezequiel in the hope that he can learn to communicate with the girl. Shortly after this encounter, Ezequiel dreams that the girl arrives in his office with a letter explaining that her parents are leaving Krámer in the Parte de Salidas, that they are abandoning Alina, and that they hope that Ezequiel will adopt her. Ezequiel awakes and discovers that Alina is indeed in his office and has arrived with a tape-recorded message largely describing the situation that he had envisioned. This certainly suggests that Ezequiel has inherited a prophetic ability and has thus in a certain sense come to reincarnate his biblical namesake as was predicted when his name was chosen. This textual example demonstrates that there has been a transmigration of the gift of prophecy from the biblical precursor Ezekiel to Cohen's character Ezequiel.

Given that Ezequiel can be understood as the reincarnation of his biblical forebear, one is immediately reminded that the term "metempsychosis," which Molly Bloom asks Leopold to explain to her in Joyce's *Ulysses*, is of particular importance to that text. As Piglia notes, "metempsicosis, transmigración, reencarnación: podemos ver allí el núcleo del relato. Ulises reencarnado en un judío de Dublín que no recuerda nada de su vida anterior y Penélope reencarnada en Molly, la mujer infiel" (metempsychosis, transmigration, reincarnation: we can observe here the nucleus of the tale. Ulysses reincarnated in a Jew from Dublin who does not remember anything of his previous life and Penelope reincarnated in Molly, the unfaithful wife).[76] Indeed, the connection is made especially palpable when Piglia comments that in *Ulysses* "la metempsicosis funciona como un nudo entre el sueño y la realidad" (metempsychosis functions as a connection between dream and reality).[77] It is during Ezequiel's insomnious visions, which fuse both dream and reality, that he essentially effects the transmigration of Ezekiel's prophetic ability by envisioning future events. The text also seems to encourage the reader's belief that Ezequiel will more completely reenact the life of his biblical antecessor. For example, in the book of Ezekiel one of the reasons for the destruction of Israel is the practice of idolatry. So too in *Insomnio* many of the citizens of Krámer believe that they have been abducted by aliens and revere "el Monumento al OVNI" (the Monument to the UFO), and Ezequiel recalls that it was his uncle's hope that he would "*redimir a mis paisanos de la idolatría*" (*redeem his countrymen from idolatry*).[78] Furthermore, the novel advances with a deep sense of foreboding and the ominous sensation that something terrible is about to occur. This is particularly encouraged by the inclusion of such symbols as an hourglass that Tadeo always carries and later gives to Ezequiel and, most important of all, by the frequent repetition of the phrase "Veni creator spiritus" (Come Holy Spirit), which Ezequiel hears repeatedly throughout the city. Given the overt references to the book of Ezekiel throughout the novel, the expectation that Krámer will suffer a moment of divine destruction is entirely plausible. Of course, as previously intimated, when the novel reaches its culmination, the approaching threat is revealed to be far worldlier in nature: it assumes the form of the military intervention to crush Chalukián's revolt accompanied by Mahler's eighth symphony, which features "Veni creator spiritus" as its central refrain. Although Ezequiel shares his namesake's prophetic vision, these other aspects of the book of Ezekiel are absent from Cohen's text. Yet this is precisely the point. With regard to *Ulysses*, Piglia continues his analysis, commenting that "la metempsicosis es una metáfora de los efectos de la lectura, las vidas posibles, las vidas deseadas, las vidas leídas. El tema del libro que se lee se autonomiza, como una vida paralela. La lectura produce una escisión, un desdoblamiento" (metempsychosis is a metaphor for the effects of reading, the possible lives, the desired lives, the lives read. The subject of the book that one reads becomes autonomous, like a parallel life. Reading produces a split, a division).[79] As in Piglia's analysis, I would contend that in *Insomnio* too "la metempsicosis es una metáfora de los efectos de la lectura" (metempsychosis is a metaphor for the effects of reading) that produces "un desdoblamiento" (a division). The crucial difference between *Ulysses* and *Insomnio*, however, is that rather than reincarnating a solitary Homeric referent, the process of metempsychosis in Cohen's text tends toward proliferation, and Ezequiel partially reincarnates a series of literary and biblical predecessors as the wider novel repeats features from several literary sources.

The tendency toward proliferation has important repercussions for the nature of reading engendered by this same process. The conscious incorporation of numerous literary referents throughout *Insomnio* suggests "a way of thinking about multiplicity that does not posit relations of 'influence' in literature and the rest of the world as one of reference," as Page suggests in a somewhat different context, but rather reflects a conception of literature that has intertextuality as its fundamental condition.[80] While it may at first appear that the Bible functions as a primary source for *Insomnio*, it is important to note that no single book from the Bible constitutes a foundational source for the novel. I have already described the importance of both the Song of Songs and the book of Ezekiel to Cohen's novel, and I shall go on to argue that the book of Ecclesiastes is another essential referent for *Insomnio*. Similarly, I have demonstrated that Cohen's novel repeats and reimagines various elements from *Ulysses* that, by extension, creates an intertextual link between *Insomnio* and Homer's *Odyssey*. As opposed to a linear chronology of literary influences, *Insomnio* instead includes a multiplicity of literary referents, none of which are privileged or given primacy, thus eroding the significance of originality. In turn, this undermines the conception of literature as a series of models and copies governed by influence. In Cohen's novel as in Deleuze's philosophy, the proliferation of literary referents reflects "the infinite movement of degraded likeness from copy to copy," through which "we reach a point at which everything changes nature, at which copies themselves flip over into simulacra and at which, finally, resemblance or spiritual imitation gives way to repetition."[81] Thus, as in the case of "La ilusión monarca," the structure of *Insomnio* essentially performs the continual process of difference and repetition that Deleuze names "becoming." As Cliff Stagoll notes, following difference, becoming is the second cornerstone of Deleuze's ontology and can be understood as "the eternal, productive return of difference."[82] This conception of ontology leads Deleuze to argue that "rather than theorizing how individuals might be grouped, it is more important to explore the specific and unique development or 'becoming' of each individual."[83] This process can also be observed in the development of each of the protagonists of the Cohen texts discussed, and in each case it also has important political implications.

In *Insomnio* the process of becoming that Ezequiel experiences as an individual is, once again, biblical in nature. As previously noted, when Selva entrusts her Bible to Ezequiel, sections of two books have been underlined. The second of these, the book of Ecclesiastes, is especially important to the present discussion. Where Cohen encourages the reader to suspect that Ezekiel will provide the hidden structure for *Insomnio*, only then to confound these expectations, the novel in fact maintains a very close (if highly unusual) relationship with Ecclesiastes. Furthermore, it is through this relationship that Cohen mediates Ezequiel's personal process of becoming. Importantly, Ecclesiastes is intimately concerned with repetition, and as in the case of "La ilusión monarca," many of the most pertinent passages of the biblical text also concern the repetitive cycles of nature. For example, in the opening chapter of Ecclesiastes, the narrator comments that "one generation passeth away, and another generation cometh: but the earth abideth for ever" and that the "sun also ariseth, and the sun goeth down, and hasteth to his place where he arose."[84] The narrator then describes a further series of natural cycles before stating that "the thing that hath been, it is that which shall be; and that which is done is that which shall be done: and there is no new thing under the sun."[85] Ecclesiastes (as in the case of the Song of Songs) is particularly ambiguous, and these lines have been "interpreted in a variety of ways, some of these in direct opposition to others."[86] For some "the poem praises the cosmos as glorious and eternal in this image of cyclic return," and Ecclesiastes is a text of wonder and hope, while for others "this poem characterizes nature as an endless round of pointless movement, a rhythm that engulfs generations as well," and Ecclesiastes is a lamentation for the futility of human existence.[87] Within *Insomnio* Ezequiel appears to share the latter position, as he believes that Leopoldo underlined sections of Ecclesiastes as he "estaba a punto para matarse" (was ready to kill himself).[88] I argue, however, that it is the very existence of the repetitions in and of themselves that are important and that through a process of metempsychosis and becoming, Ezequiel comes to commune with and inhabit the biblical text.

As with the other books of the bible previously discussed, Ecclesiastes gradually repeats itself within *Insomnio*. Indeed, there is a closer correspondence between these two texts than in any other previous case. Furthermore, these repetitions far more closely correspond to Piglia's model of "el molde de hierro de una escultura que desaparece, retirado o escondido por el material" (the iron mold of a sculpture that disappears, withdrawn or hidden by the material), and they more precisely reproduce the process of metempsychosis.[89] Surprisingly, it is not the phrases that are underlined in Ecclesiastes (and thus incorporated into the text of *Insomnio*) that are repeated; rather, other phrases and statements, absent from Cohen's novel, provide an almost exact template for the decisions Ezequiel makes, as if his actions were preordained. For example, at the novel's conclusion, and despite the trauma of the military intervention in Krámer, Ezequiel and Selva elect to return to work immediately, thus fulfilling the fatalistic command in Ecclesiastes that "whatsoever thy hand findeth to do," one must "do it with thy might; for there is no work, nor device, nor knowledge, nor wisdom, in the grave, whither thou goest."[90] As in the biblical text, confronted with their own mortality, Ezequiel and Selva simply return to work. Similarly, when one considers Ezequiel's decision neither to join Chalukián's revolt nor to leave Krámer, one is reminded of the passage from Ecclesiastes that reads: "If the spirit of the ruler rise up against thee, leave not thy place; for yielding pacifieth great offences."[91] Moreover, this connection highlights that the mechanism of biblical repetition invoked in this instance involves not only Joycean metempsychosis and Deleuzian repetition (in that Cohen's characters effect the reincarnation of the biblical text by fulfilling the commands it contains) but also incorporates Foucauldian statements.

At this point it is important to note that there is a considerable degree of debate as to who exactly is speaking throughout Ecclesiastes, a discussion that Doug Ingram explores at length in *Ambiguity in Ecclesiastes*. As Ingram makes clear, the fundamental question is whether the words of the text belong to the "preacher" or the "frame narrator." Additionally, there are debates as to who the preacher is: it has been suggested that the preacher is Qoheleth and equally Solomon (literally the son of David as claimed in the opening of the book). Ingram suggests that the same opening phrase could also be understood as referring to a different king in Jerusalem and discusses each possibility in detail. Ultimately, Ingram concludes "that Ecclesiastes is fundamentally ambiguous *by design.*"[92] I would suggest that this uncertainty surrounding the speaking subject in Ecclesiastes allows us to read the text (as it appears in *Insomnio*) as a collection of Foucauldian statements, which is to say those elements of discourse that circulate freely and can be repeated by different subjects in different times and contexts, generating new meanings. As Foucault makes clear, the statement is the basic unit of discourse that "is unique, yet subject to *repetition, transformation, and reactivation*" as it creates "a particular, vacant place that may in fact be filled by different individuals."[93] This is to say that "the position of the subject can be assigned" for any given statement, and it can therefore be repeated by different speakers uninhibited by the subjective context of its creation.[94] So too in *Insomnio* the subject position of the statements found in Ecclesiastes is assigned to Ezequiel through a process of Joycean metempsychosis. Furthermore, I would contend that this process facilitates the Deleuzian repetition of pure difference, a process of becoming. Importantly, in Deleuze's interpretation of Foucault's early structuralist work, he argues that as "the statement does not refer back to any *Cogito* or transcendental subject that might render it possible," and as there "are many places from which any subject can produce the same statement," the repetition of statements generates pure difference.[95] Within *Insomnio* as in Deleuze's conception of difference and repetition, "the most exact, the most strict repetition has as its correlate the maximum of difference."[96] It is by repeating the statements in Ecclesiastes in his own life that the word is made flesh and Ezequiel essentially comes into being as an individual subjectivity. Or rather, it is by incarnating the words of the biblical text that Ezequiel reveals his own individual becoming. This process of becoming also appears to lead to Ezequiel's only political action in the novel. Late in the text of Ecclesiastes, the narrator relates: "There was a little city, and few men within it; and there came a great king against it, and besieged it, and built great bulwarks against it: Now there was found in it a poor wise man, and he by his wisdom delivered the city; yet no man remembered that same poor man."[97] The image of a city besieged by "a great king" and containing "a poor wise man" cannot but call to mind Cohen's Patagonian city and Ezequiel, one of only two literate inhabitants in the city. Indeed, Ezequiel arguably "delivered the city" from the danger of the invading army by wisely refusing to join Chalukián's revolt. Furthermore, his passivity and refusal to leave Krámer, despite being drawn in the Parte de Salidas, arguably contains an element of civil disobedience that challenges and resists the very power structure of the perfectly despotic society of indiscipline. This too potentially reflects the words of the narrator in Ecclesiastes that "wisdom is better than strength," that the "words of wise men are heard in quiet more than the cry of him that ruleth among fools," and ultimately that "wisdom is better than weapons of war."[98]

"La ilusión monarca" can also be seen to describe an individual and personal process of becoming; in this instance, however, it takes the recognizable form of "becoming-other" discussed at length in relation to Aira's La prueba in chapter 2. Where Oeyen argues that Sergio's journey into the sea should be considered "una catarsis" (a catharsis), and Page argues that Cohen's description of this almost spiritual journey "strongly evokes the effect of Dionysian art for Nietzsche," I propose a complementary Deleuzian interpretation more in keeping with the present argument.[99] Specifically, I contend that when Sergio finally enters the sea to make his escape, he undergoes a process of becoming-other. Indeed, as Sergio swims further and further out, he passes through various recognizable stages of becoming-other: he becomes-sea, becomes-landscape, and eventually becomes-imperceptible. As Sergio begins to sense the permeability of his own body and its fusion with the sea, Cohen's description is reminiscent of Deleuze's assertion that "the movement of the swimmer does not resemble that of the wave. . . . When a body combines some of its own distinctive points with those of a wave it espouses the principle of a repetition which is no longer that of the Same, but involves the Other—involves difference, from one wave and one gesture to another, and carries that difference through the repetitive space thereby constituted."[100] As Sergio continues to swim, he gradually experiences the disintegration of his own body and its communion with the entire landscape. As Cohen writes, Sergio "era trizas, era diez mil, era joven, era viejo, lo mojado y lo seco, el plancton y el platino, no había nacido, estaba muerto, era la ceniza de las olas, era el crepúsculo, sólo aliento, sólo claroscuro" (was fragments, was ten thousand, was young, was old, the wet and the dry, the plankton and the platinum, he had not been born, he was dead, he was the foam of the waves, he was the twilight, only breath, only chiaroscuro).[101]

Indeed, as Page argues, "when Sergio in 'La ilusión monarca' finally swims out to sea, the intensely sensorial experience of his body's immersion in water teeming with life initially leads him to lose a sense of his self."[102] Sergio gradually loses all sense of himself as an individual with a history or as an independent subjectivity with memory at all, an experience perfectly encapsulated in Deleuze's assertion that "things and beings which are distinguished in the different suffer a corresponding radical destruction of their *identity*."[103] That the experience can be understood as a process of becoming-landscape is further suggested when Cohen comments that Sergio moves through the water "como un pedazo de mar con forma" (like a piece of the sea with form).[104] Such descriptions are also readily identifiable with the Deleuzian conception of the Body without Organs, which "is not a dead body but a living body all the more alive and teeming once it has blown apart the organism and its organisation."[105] Deleuze derives this concept from the work of Antonin Artaud and explains that it "is opposed less to organs than to that organisation of organs we call an organism" and that it represents "an intense and intensive body."[106] This is to say that the Body without Organs represents a state of becoming whereby the self is destroyed and an individual's body is disarticulated and only experiences forces acting upon it as it is fused with "the absolute Outside that knows no Selves because interior and exterior are equally a part of the immanence in which they have fused."[107] The Deleuzian parallels continue when one notes that becoming-other in the form of becoming-imperceptible is "to world (*faire monde*), to make a world (*faire un monde*)" and thus "to be present at the dawn of the world."[108] So too in "La ilusión monarca" Sergio focuses on his breathing and argues that "el globo de saliva" (the globe of saliva) that forms on his lips "es el mundo" (is the world) and also makes the pronouncement that "Sergio es el mundo" (Sergio is the world).[109] Each phrase further emphasizes the process of becoming-landscape that Sergio undergoes while also subtly suggesting the creation of a new world. Through this, the definitive moment of action in the story, it would appear that something fundamental has changed in the order of the world and Sergio then returns to the prison arguing that from then on, "sólo se preguntará cómo sumergirse mejor en el mundo . . . , cómo estar de veras donde esté" (he will only ask how better to submerge himself in the world . . . , how to be truly where he was) and "cómo seguir estando" (how to continue being).[110] It appears that in order to create a *new* world, Sergio realizes that all he can alter is his own relationship *with* the world. In a curious development, Sergio inverts the power structure of the perfectly despotic society of *indiscipline* by becoming *disciplined* and returning to the prison. Furthermore, as Oeyen and Page note, Sergio now "decide no participar en la degradación general" (decides not to participate in the general degradation)and "seeks out community to communicate what has happened to him" by engaging Frankie in conversation.[111]

Undoubtedly, through his encounter with the sea, Sergio experiences a certain revelation of his oneness with the universe that leads him to return to the prison and seek out communication and some form of comradeship or solidarity with his fellow prisoners. At first this may appear to constitute a very minor revolution, yet returning to specific comparisons with the conditions of those detained during the most recent dictatorship emphasizes that it is highly significant. As recounted in *Nunca más*, the scarcity and poor quality of food provided to the detainees constituted another part of their torment and torture. Furthermore, any captive who attempted to share their food with a less fortunate cellmate was severely punished, as "la solidaridad estaba prohibida" (solidarity was prohibited).[112] In Cohen's text Sergio's encounter with the sea leads him to overcome the prohibition of solidarity and to seek some common experience with his fellow prisoners. Given this context it would seem that Sergio's decision to return to the prison and his submission to his confinement may reflect Deleuze's assertion that "one can't really tell if submission doesn't finally conceal the greatest sort of revolt and if combat doesn't imply the worst of acceptances."[113]

Considering Irma Antognazzi's study of life inside the Villa Devoto women's prison for the dictatorship's legalized inmates, however, highlights the limits of this particular form of resistance. As Antognazzi makes clear when the women in the prison discovered that they were "rehenes" (hostages)—where "hostage" is understood as "un objeto político a merced de la arbitrariedad del poder" (a political object at the mercy of the arbitrariness of power)—they, like Sergio, realized the "necesidad de la lucha colectiva y no aislada o meramente individual" (necessity of collective and not merely isolated and individual struggle).[114] However, where Antognazzi stresses that the women's situation in Villa Devoto created "las bases materiales para la unidad en la acción" (the material bases for unity in action), Sergio's experience in the sea leads him toward an existential, rather than a collective and political, solution to the problems he confronts.[115] Indeed it is inescapable that following his experience in the sea, Sergio abandons the thoughts of revenge that had previously obsessed him, and he becomes completely pacified in his imprisonment. Similarly, in *Insomnio* Ezequiel refuses to join Chalukián's attempted revolt (however dubious the latter's motivations in attempting such an uprising may have been), and his final act of resistance entails refusing to leave the city in which he is imprisoned. As in "La ilusión monarca," Ezequiel undoubtedly seeks out companionship and solidarity by surrounding himself with a small group of survivors of the military intervention, yet any thought of political resistance is entirely abandoned. Arguably, Ezequiel's refusal to join the revolt and his focus on himself and his immediate circle of friends and acquaintances preempts any possibility of societal change in Krámer and ensures only the maintenance of the status quo. The same holds equally true for Sergio's quiet, existential revolution in "La ilusión monarca." Ultimately, both texts reach an undecidable point where submission and acquiescence become indistinguishable from resistance. This impasse is somewhat familiar.

In the later stages of his career, Foucault would contend that the purpose of his life's work had "not been to analyse the phenomena of power, nor to elaborate the foundations of such an analysis," but rather "to create a history of the different modes by which, in our culture, human beings are made subjects."[116] Foucault also makes clear that by "subjects" he means that individuals are both "subject to someone else by control and dependence; and tied to his own identity by a conscience or self-knowledge."[117] In his philosophical homage to Foucault's work, Deleuze focuses on these arguments to suggest that "Foucault's fundamental idea is that of a dimension of subjectivity derived from power and knowledge without being dependent on them."[118] Importantly, as noted in chapter 2, in Deleuze's development of Foucault's thought, this "struggle for subjectivity is a battle to win the right to have access to difference, variation and metamorphosis."[119] Certainly, my analysis of "La ilusión monarca" and *Insomnio* thus far corresponds to this model: Sergio and Ezequiel essentially gain their subjectivity through an experience of metamorphosis engendered by the ceaseless repetition of difference understood as becoming. Crucially, Deleuze and Foucault also remain radically opposed to a conception of the law and state power that would mean that "revolutionaries can only demand a different legality which comes from winning power and installing a new machinery of State" and argue instead that "against this global policy of power, we initiate localized counter-responses, skirmishes, active and occasionally preventative defenses" and ultimately that "we have no need to totalize that which is invariably totalized on the side of power."[120] However, as in the case of *La prueba*, the form of resistance precipitated by the experience of becoming in "La ilusión monarca" and *Insomnio* offers neither a program of political action nor any position from which power can be taken. Each Cohen text thus reaches an impasse that delineates the limitations of resistance proffered by the Deleuzian model. As we shall see in chapter 4, however, Cohen (unlike Aira) exceeds this impasse by exploring in great detail the shifts in power relations that have compounded the problem and restricted the potential forms that resistance may take. Furthermore, Cohen creatively imagines new forms of resistance appropriate to this new historical and sociological situation.

CHAPTER 4

THE TRANSITION TO CONTROL

As discussed in the previous chapter, the power relations in *Insomnio* and "La ilusión monarca" reflect the aftereffects of the military dictatorship and the transition to democracy and vacillate between disciplinary and sovereign modes of organization. Furthermore, within the texts resistance is a process of Deleuzian becoming that reaches a familiar impasse as it cannot offer an alternative mode of societal organization. Indeed, each text reaches an undecidable point where the protagonist's ultimate act of resistance cannot be distinguished from conformity. However, "La ilusión monarca" begins to reveal the development of a new form of societal organization that will form the basis of the discussion in the present chapter. Moreover, this development is intimately connected with the opening of the Argentine economy to the transnational market that, as many critics note, was of fundamental importance during the democratic transitions in the Southern Cone.[1]

That the logic of sovereign indiscipline that Cohen describes in "La ilusión monarca" has some commonality with both the military dictatorship and the Menem government suggests that the text reflects the changing nature of power relations that accompanies the "epochal transition from State to Market."[2] Indeed, I will go on to argue that "La ilusión monarca" describes a form of societal organization emerging in Argentina at the time, namely the movement from "disciplinary society" to the "society of control" as described by Deleuze. That this Deleuzian concept would be particularly relevant to the work of Cohen is not entirely surprising. As Page notes, Cohen was particularly influenced by the work of William Burroughs, and Deleuze draws both the title and elements of his theory from the work of the North American writer.[3] The concept of the control society was developed late in Deleuze's career in a few short essays, and as it is considered a historical development of state power, it is consistently described in contradistinction to Foucault's conception of disciplinary society. As opposed to disciplinary societies principally defined by Panoptic enclosures (such as the school or the prison), where people are subjected to (the possibility of) constant supervision and ceaseless repetitive exercise regulated by "time-tables, compulsory movements, [and] regular activities," Deleuze argues that within contemporary globalized capitalism, "structures of confinement" are no longer needed to exercise power.[4] For Deleuze late globalized capitalism is focused on services and metaproduction, which is to say that it is "no longer directed toward production but towards products, that is, toward sales or markets." As "markets are won by taking control rather than by establishing a discipline, by fixing rates rather than reducing costs, by transforming products rather than by specializing production," Deleuze argues that such societies "no longer operate by confining people but through continuous control and instant communication" and that within them the logic of the market is internalized and the population becomes subject to a capitalized form of self-control.[5]

Such structural developments can be readily observed in Argentina following the neoliberal economic reforms instigated by Menem. As Jorge Mayer notes, the indiscriminate opening of the Argentine economy and high interest rates necessary to stabilize the exchange rate led to a significant increase in the availability of financial capital, which in turn led to a sharp increase in speculation and a substantial rise in foreign imports. Concurrently, however, national companies were disadvantaged, and many factories and workshops that could not compete with the new foreign imports were forced to close.[6] Moreover, Pablo Pozzi noted at the time that "eight out of the ten major corporations in Argentina are subsidiaries of multinationals, as are nine of the ten major banks. Foreign corporations were involved in almost 60 percent of all goods bought and sold in Argentina in 1995. . . . If Argentina was always dependent on the world economy, because of its agricultural-export-oriented economy, now this dependency has increased through the transnationalization of its economy; it has literally become a subsidiary economic system."[7] This clearly reflects the movement from production to metaproduction that Deleuze describes.

Given this context, I would suggest that it becomes especially pertinent that Oeyen connects Cohen's story with Kafka's "In the Penal Colony."[8] While Oeyen does not comment further on this connection, it is notable that Kafka's story describes a society undergoing a profound alteration in its organization and its techniques of power. As the officer in Kafka's story explains, where the "Old Commandant's tradition" consisted of spectacular torture and execution carried out "before hundreds of spectators," the new commandant has all but abandoned these practices and developed an organizational system where administrative meetings "have turned . . . into public spectacles."[9] From these brief comments it is immediately apparent that the transition could be understood, in Foucauldian terms, as one from sovereign to disciplinary society. Thus it seems appropriate to suggest that Cohen's rewriting of the story reflects the later transition from disciplinary to control society. Indeed, as Cohen's prison in "La ilusión monarca" is literally open to the sea, it seems emblematic of the "the general breakdown of all sites of confinement" that Deleuze argues accompanies such economic developments.[10]

That the characters in "La ilusión monarca" have internalized the logic of control is first suggested by the fact that Sergio trades human organs. In Cohen's text bodies are not the "pliable tool[s] of economic productivity" demanded by disciplinary society but are dissected and integrated directly into the globalized market. Furthermore, this internalization of capitalist logic is reflected within the prison when the narrator states that "los presos están en la cárcel pero la cárcel está dentro de los presos" (the prisoners are inside the prison, but the prison is inside the prisoners).[11] In this regard, it must also be remembered that through the removal of disciplinary regulation in the prison, by allowing the prisoners to attempt to leave the penitentiary, they also become the executioners of their own punishment. Furthermore, while Deleuze argues that new socio-technologies will be developed to exercise power within control societies, he also makes the enigmatic suggestion that "it may be that older means of control, borrowed from the old sovereign societies, will come back into play" and coexist with these other new technologies.[12] Given that I have argued that "La ilusión monarca" reflects postdictatorship Argentine society insofar as it demonstrates the reactivation of spectacular sovereign torture as a method of control, it appears that Cohen's text in particular and Argentine society more generally are paradigmatic of the transition that Deleuze describes.

Given the strong correspondence between Deleuze's conception of the society of control and Cohen's short story, it would now appear that Sergio's own return to the prison could also be considered the ultimate expression of the type of internalized self-subjection demanded by the control society. And this is precisely the point. Within his description of the control society, Deleuze argues that disciplinary enclosures "are molds, different moldings" that rigidly shape those who pass through them. In contrast he argues that "controls are a modulation, like a self-transmuting molding continually changing from one moment to the next, or like a sieve whose mesh varies from one point to another."[13] It would now appear that in "La ilusión monarca" Cohen raises the possibility that these perpetually mutating controls conform to, or imitate, the very model of Deleuzian becoming. This is borne out by the fact that the Body without Organs that Sergio experiences in the sea as his body loses central organization and becomes a series of organs bisected by immanent forces finds its opposite in the organs without bodies that Sergio trades and inserts directly into the fluctuations of the market. In each case, a "wave with a variable amplitude flows through the body without organs" tracing "zones and levels on this body according to the variations of its amplitude."[14] Thus Cohen's story calls into question the validity of the Deleuzo-Guattarian conception of becoming-other as an act of resistance within the society of control. At best the story reaches an undecidable point where submission and acquiescence become indistinguishable from resistance. Sergio's return to the prison could be considered a metamorphic contestation of the controls to which he is subject, but as intimated, it could also be considered a perfect reflection of insidious self-control. Just as Calveiro has argued that the Argentine detention and torture centers sought to produce "un nuevo sujeto, completamente sumiso a los designios del campo" (a new subject, completely submissive to the designs of the camp), it also appears that Sergio's radical becoming-other arguably produces a new subjectivity completely submissive to the authorities that run Cohen's dystopian prison.[15] Moreover, the text suggests that the relationships of power instigated in the society of control mirror the "strategy of struggle" that Deleuze and Guattari name becoming-other.

To expand this analysis further still, it is now my contention that in his novel *El oído absoluto*, Cohen more thoroughly explores the nature of the emergent techniques of power and the resultant alterations they actuate in the nature of resistance within the Deleuzian control society. Of central importance to this discussion is the fact that significant alterations in the nature of mass media culture occurred concurrently with the development of the control society, yet as Mark Poster notes, "what is lacking in Deleuze's understanding of the move from discipline to control society is precisely an analysis of the media as technologies of power."[16] This omission is particularly important in the Argentine case because, concomitant with Menem's neoliberal reforms, politics became increasingly influenced by contemporary mass media. As Pozzi notes, during Menem's presidency elections "stopped being issue-oriented or program-oriented" and instead became "a question of polls, slogans, publicity, and marketing."[17] Conscious of this context, I contend that Cohen's text essentially resolves the shortcoming in Deleuze's work by considering the role of mass media culture simultaneously with the modulations of control. In his discussion of the control society, Michael Hardt tantalizingly suggests that within such societies "its assemblages or institutions are elaborated primarily through repetition and the production of simulacra."[18] As I will go on to argue, Cohen's texts are not only illuminated by Deleuze's description of the control society, but the use of the mass media in the society he describes can be concurrently understood in the light of Jean Baudrillard's theories concerning simulation, which actively consider the "media as technologies of power." Baudrillard, like Deleuze, was greatly concerned with the "redistribution of power out of (and away from) the body of the state back into a civil society that has itself been technologically internationalized and radically reconfigured," and Cohen's texts also serve to highlight the close correspondence and potential cofunctioning of work by these theorists.[19]

As is the case in *Insomnio* and "La ilusión monarca," *El oído absoluto* proffers a dystopian vision of the near future. In this case, however, the society Cohen describes is particularly apposite for exploring the nature of control societies and the use of the mass media within them. *El oído absoluto* is set in the islands of Lorelei and the broadly Latin American theme park of El Recinto that they contain. The reader learns that the singer Fulvio Silvio Campomanes, having sold millions of copies of a popular album worldwide, constructed El Recinto as an act of philanthropy: every citizen in the world has the right to visit the theme park, for free, once during their lifetime. As Gabriel Ignacio Barreneche notes, the "raison d'être of the Disney-style theme park and Cohen's Recinto is to create a fictitious world where the visitor can isolate himself or herself from the outside world," which is presented as dangerous, chaotic and subject to non-specific threats from nameless terrorist groups.[20] So severe is the supposed threat that the location of the islands is a well-kept secret maintained by supportive governments and organizations who supply counterinformation to prevent their location being discovered. However, as Barreneche also notes, "whereas every citizen of the world has the opportunity to vacation at the Paradise of Lorelei only once in his or her lifetime," those who work there have no choice but to "reside there until the authorities determine that they are fit for reintegration into society."[21] Thus the protagonist, Lino, his partner, Clarisa, and all other permanent residents are revealed to have been forcibly moved to Lorelei by the mysterious Oficina para la Indefinición Social (Office for Social Indeterminacy) due to their various transgressions, which range from heroin addiction and promiscuity to unspecified subversive activities.

As in "La ilusión monarca," the world of *El oído absoluto* presents an intermediary social order between disciplinary and control societies. Thus Lorelei and El Recinto appear to form traditional Foucauldian "enclosures" utilized to discipline "delinquents," yet the methods employed to exercise power in Cohen's text demonstrate the transition toward the control society. For example, visitors to the theme park are obliged to wear "una pulsera anticólera" (an anti-anger wristband), which monitors biological changes in the body and prevents visitors in the park from becoming angry, and when Lino attempts to cash a check, even this most basic of banking functions requires a complex corporeal analysis. While each of these examples suggests a certain connection with disciplinary regulation, they also reflect Saul Newman's argument that the "emergence of the control society is . . . coextensive with the paradigm of biopolitics."[22] Thus I would suggest that they are in fact demonstrative of "the *approaching* forms of ceaseless control in open sites" that will be fully realized with "the generalization of the logics that previously functioned within" Foucauldian enclosures "across the entire society."[23] This interpretation is strengthened by the fact that the department of Indefinición Social (Social Indeterminacy) operates globally and pervades all sectors of society, further diminishing the idea that Lorelei is a traditional enclosure utilized to instill discipline and suggesting that it is simply one more location where the modulations of control are continually exercised.

The close correspondence between Deleuze's description of the control society and Cohen's novel is further strengthened when it is recalled that although *El oído absoluto* simultaneously retains certain features of the disciplinary society (in that the central characters have their movements forcibly restricted within a defined enclosure), by coming to the park visitors nonetheless freely consent to manipulation and control. Moreover, despite the fact that in *El oído absoluto* Cohen makes reference to nation-states that still exercise some form of power (however reduced it may be), it is also suggested that large corporations are the principle and fundamental agents of control. As in Deleuze's description of the control society, then, "businesses take over from factories" and other traditional disciplinary enclosures.[24] It is, however, those elements relating to contemporary mass media culture that make it particularly pertinent and important to consider Cohen's text in relation to Deleuze's theory. As previously mentioned, absent from Deleuze's theory is "an analysis of the media as technologies of power," an analysis that is readily discernible in Cohen's novel.[25] For example, as Barreneche observes, in El Recinto the "first method of behavior control is music," as Campomanes's songs supply a constant and "soothing auditory opiate for the visitors."[26] As *El oído absoluto* explores the role of mass media culture simultaneously with the modulations of control, it goes beyond and essentially augments Deleuze's analysis. Moreover,

Baudrillard's conception of the production of simulacra can be usefully deployed to illuminate the role of mass media in the society Cohen describes.

As discussed, El Recinto exhibits the key features of the Deleuzian control society. However, it is also clear that elements of Baudrillard's theory can also be utilized in order to describe Cohen's dystopian theme park. In this regard it is important to note that a close analysis of the work of Baudrillard and Deleuze reveals a considerable degree of correspondence between their critical projects. For example, where Deleuze argues that in contemporary society we "are witnessing the end of perspectival and panoptic space," Baudrillard also proposes that Foucault's *"Discipline and Punish*, with its theory of discipline, [and] of the 'panoptic'" is "magisterial but obsolete."[27] Thus the redundancy of the enclosure in Cohen's novel is the first element that suggests that both theories could be deployed simultaneously to delineate the structure of power within Cohen's imagined future. With this in mind, it is particularly relevant that while Deleuze confronts the redundancy of disciplinary society by focusing on the obsolescence of the enclosure and the substitution of metaproduction for production, Baudrillard centers his analysis on the proliferation of images within contemporary mass media society. As he argues, "simulation is no longer that of a territory, a referential being, or a substance" but is in fact "the generation by models of a real without origin or reality: a hyperreal."[28] Thus the key feature of Baudrillardian hyperreality is simulation, understood as the proliferation of images, or simulacra, in mass media society that bear no connection with reality but are only ever connected to a seemingly endless series of further images.

Importantly, for Baudrillard "Disneyland is a perfect model of all the entangled orders of simulacra."[29] With its production of *Macbeth* in Quechua and its "robots stationed along the airport highway . . . dressed in regional, folkloric outfits," it is clear that this statement would be equally applicable to Cohen's theme park.[30] Moreover, given that the park extends its reach far beyond the confines of Lorelei through the open invitation to all citizens of the world to visit El Recinto, and the global nature of the department of Indefinición Social (Social Indeterminacy), which forcibly procures the theme park's employees, it appears that in these later texts, "the Disney enterprise" perceptible in *El oído absoluto* "goes further than the imagination" and "is currently taking over the whole of the real world to incorporate it into its synthetic world in the form of an immense 'reality show,' in which it is reality itself which presents itself as spectacle, in which the real itself becomes a theme park."[31] Crucial to my own argument is that the proliferation of Baudrillardian simulacra in *El oído asoluto* is manipulated as a deliberate form of Deleuzian control. For example, the park features public messages constantly projected into the sky over

Lorelei by a powerful laser from the enormous Columna Fraterna (Fraternal Column) that towers over the islands. As Barreneche notes, these "ethereal messages written on the sky juxtapose the idyllic space of vacation and leisure with the uncertainties of the conflictive and fragmented world outside the park's gates."[32] Thus visitors to the park are continually notified of current events such as: "Juzgan al violador del presidente de Irak" (The rapist of the president of Iraq is tried) and "Suicídanse en Ankara doce contrabandistas de residuos radioactivos" (Twelve smugglers of radioactive waste kill themselves in Ankara).[33]

However, as in Baudrillardian hyperreality, in Lorelei "there is more and more information, and less and less meaning."[34] No context is provided, and no attempt is made to explain the significance of such global events. Instead, the messages merely remind the visitors to (and inhabitants of) Lorelei that the outside world is a precarious, dangerous, and chaotic place. Certainly, Cohen's mention of "los heridos" (the wounded), the horribly disfigured ex-combatants of a chemical war visiting the park, suggests that there is a degree of truth in this idea.[35] However, the ideological manipulation of the news is equally clear. For example, Clarisa reveals that before coming to Lorelei, she witnessed fifty prisoners forced into a six-by-six-meter cell, missiles launched at a market, and gas sprayed over informal housing settlements by various authorities. Such news, however, is never projected on the skies over Lorelei. This manipulation of the news on the islands demonstrates that, as in Deleuze's analysis, "information is precisely the system of control."[36] This idea is reinforced by propaganda messages continually interlaced with the news stories that at times directly encourage the capitalist consumption that maintains the system. For example, the inhabitants of the park are exposed to such propagandistic statements as "Una nación, la del trabajo esperanzado. Una patria, la de la canción" (One nation, that of hopeful employment. One people, that of the song).[37] Yet they are also implored to spend money: "No guarde su dinero en la billetera. No cobre mañana el cheque que le entregan hoy. El monstruo de la inflación se alimenta de su pasividad. Federación iberoamericana del consumidor" (Don't keep your money in your wallet. Don't wait until tomorrow to cash the check you receive today. The monster of inflation feeds on your passivity. The Latin American consumer federation).[38] Thus in Lorelei as in Baudrillard's work, "propaganda and advertising fuse in the same marketing and merchandising of objects and ideologies."[39] Indeed, the calls for political unity through consumption and popular music would appear to demonstrate Brian Massumi's point that in the society of control, "the creation of a niche market through advertising is the creation of a niche power-object that is also a potential political constituency." Given that *El oído absoluto* features a unique cultural product (the traditional *bolero* that Campomanes sings) subjected to hyperreal simulation in order to create a "niche market" and a "niche power-object" over which control can be maintained, it can be concluded that in Cohen's text as in Massumi's work, *"the power to exist has been transformed into an internal variable of the capitalist supersystem."*[40]

Beyond this level of manipulation the messages projected onto the sky simultaneously and more insidiously function on a second level; they create an artificial distinction between the interior of the park and the external world. As in Baudrillard's analysis of Disneyland, where he argues that the park exists to mask the fact that America is "no longer real, but belongs to the hyperreal order and to the order of simulation," so too in Lorelei the messages written in the sky mask the fact that the theme park is not an escape from the unpleasant reality that exists outside the park but is rather an exemplary instance of the continual exercise of control over all global citizens.[41] Indeed, all the simulacra in El Recinto are employed to "mask the absence of a profound reality," namely, that there is a difference between the world inside the theme park and that found outside.[42] Thus in Cohen's novel the control that is only allusively referred to in Deleuze's description is shown to be exercised by the manipulation of Baudrillardian simulation.

Given the developments in the nature and exercise of power and control outlined above, I would suggest that the question of what becomes of the resistance strategies detailed in chapter 3 is of particular importance to Cohen's novel. Furthermore, I would suggest that considering the fate of such strategies in *El oído absoluto* reveals a further degree of detail concerning the interconnection between the theories of Deleuze and Baudrillard in Cohen's work. In *El oído absoluto* Cohen's discussion of resistance appears to be principally related through the action of Clarisa's father, Lotario Wald. Indeed, Cohen seems to emphasize the central importance of Lotario by structuring the novel around his visit to Lorelei. Notably, the key sections of the text relating to Lotario do not describe his actions but rather relate his philosophical musings on the nature of music. These reflections are broadly categorized into two groups: those deriding music of the type produced by Campomanes and those extolling the virtues of (European) classical music. Thus Lotario compares Campomanes's music to bacteria that spreads out and fills the air and calls it an "epidemia" (epidemic).[43] In sharp contrast, he later states that classical music is "lo *único* que me gusta" (the *only* thing that I enjoy) and suggests that this, true music, "existe en la cabeza de uno aunque nadie la esté tocando, aunque se pierda el papel donde la escribieron, aunque se quemen todos los instrumentos del mundo" (exists in one's head even if no one is playing it, even if the paper where it was written has been lost, even if all the instruments in the world have been burned) and declares that it exists as "un montón de fragmentos" (a heap of fragments) that are combined in each individual's memory.[44] Clearly, for Lotario, classical music constitutes a bridge to more philosophical musings. As Dove argues, he bases his discussion of music on "the old conviction that music has to do with presentation in its purest sense: the presentation of presentation itself," and thus that it "provides a model . . . for thinking the origin of sense."[45] Most importantly for our own discussion is that for Deleuze and Guattari music serves a similar function and the now familiar trope of "becoming is capable of proceeding through music."[46] Indeed, as Ronald Bogue reminds us, "Deleuze and Guattari . . . propose . . . a means of construing music as an open structure that permeates and is permeated by the world" and as we shall see, this conception of music shares much in common with that proposed by Lotario.[47]

When Lotario continues his discussion of the nature of music, he declares that "la verdadera organización de la música no la impone el compositor: viene de adentro, de un sonido fundamental que vence al ruido; lo que el compositor hace es manifestar este sonido a su manera" (the true organization of music is not imposed by the composer: it comes from inside, from a fundamental sound that overcomes noise; what the composer does is express this sound in their own way).[48] Lotario's argument that this organizational element comes from inside but that it does not originate within the composer is immediately reminiscent of the displaced center of the basic unit of Deleuzian music: the refrain.[49] In simple terms, Deleuze and Guattari argue that a refrain is not necessarily sonorous and is instead any repetitive pattern that when reproduced constructs a territory consisting of a "point of stability, a circle of property and an opening to the outside."[50] It is important to note, however, that for Deleuze and Guattari, while every "territory has a center of intensity where its forces come together," this same center "is at once within the territory and outside it, always at hand yet difficult to reach," just as is Lotario's conception of composition.[51] That Lotario's conception of music comes into being when it "overcomes noise" also demonstrates that it forms a "point of stability" in the midst of chaos. Furthermore, that it can be ascribed to a specific composer demonstrates that it forms "a circle of property." Additionally, when Lotario declares that each piece of music "cambi[a] con cada grupo que la interpreta, con cada persona que la escucha" (changes with every group that performs it, with every person who listens to it) and reflects that "siempre es la misma pieza, y siempre distinta" (it is always the same piece, and always different), he demonstrates that music retains "an opening to the outside," as it necessarily mutates with each and every performance as it does with every audience who listens.[52] This comment is also suggestive of the "deterritorialization" proper to the Deleuzian refrain, which can be understood as the potential for the refrain to be repeated in a new set of circumstances by a different agent to construct another new territory.[53] As Lotario intuits, each time a piece of music is performed, it becomes deterritorialized and forms new territories due to the unique interpretation of any given audience or performer. Ultimately, Lotario's comments reveal that "a refrain is something which is repeatable" and that while its repetitions or rhythm "may be very inexact," it continually forms new territories and difference every time it is performed or heard.[54]

Given the correlation between Lotario's conception of classical music and the Deleuzian refrain, when he argues that music emanates from "un sonido fundamental" (a fundamental sound) that pre-exists any composition, he arguably echoes Deleuze and Guattari's assertion that "music is not the privilege of human beings" but that "the universe, the cosmos, is made of refrains."[55] This idea is strengthened when Lotario suggests that music exists as eternal fragments that are reconfigured in the mind of every individual each time they hear a specific composition, as this is comparable with the form and function of the Deleuzian refrain. Thus when Lotario states that the "verdadero realismo es la música, lo demás son datos" (true realism is music, everything else is information), he reflects Deleuze and Guattari's belief that "the refrain is neither an accompaniment to life, nor even its crowning achievement, but an expression of life's basic force of production."[56] This is reinforced when Lotario compares the development of his own life to that of music, declaring that "también mi vida es distinta ahora que ayer, aunque sea la misma vida" (my life is also different today than it was yesterday, even though it is the same life), perfectly reflecting the fact that in Deleuze and Guattari's conception "human beings measure the movements of their lived existence with the refrains that mark the rhythm of the different moments they live."[57] That music in both conceptions exceeds human life yet provides a model for the development of individual lives also demonstrates that in each case music constitutes a process that is "essentially one of *becoming*, a becoming-woman, a becoming-child, a becoming-animal or a becoming-molecular."[58] We have already observed that Lotario grasps that difference emerges from strict repetition through each unique performance, and it now becomes clear that he also perceives that the true origin of music is variation in and of itself. Thus when Lotario muses that "la vida son treinta y dos compases que se repiten continuamente" (life is thirty-two meters that continuously repeat) and that "cuantas más maneras encuentres de tocarlos, más cerca vas a estar del fuelle ese" (the more ways you discover to play them, the closer you will be to the breath of it), he indicates that his objective is to merge with the very process of dynamism and change that is becoming.[59]

Importantly, however, in *El oído absoluto*, this process has become entirely blocked.

In *El oído absoluto* Lotario declares that the obstacle that prevents him from moving toward the "fuelle" (breath) of music and life is Campomanes. Indeed, Lotario explains that he spent ten years "ideando ejercicios para acercarme a la fuente de los sonidos" (conceiving exercises to bring me closer to the source of sounds) yet decries the fact that Campomanes "hacía dinero construyendo tapias, porque eso son sus canciones, paredes para no ver la verdadera música" (made money creating walls, because that's what his songs are, walls that prevent true music from being seen).[60] Lotario then condemns Campomanes's tendency to construct songs that announce their entire development and conclusion in their very first bar as "una máquina de crear complicidad" (a machine for creating complicity).[61] The problem is that Campomanes's songs obscure the true nature of music in their form and their ubiquity. Equally, they are an important component of the system of control within the physical territory of El Recinto and extend the modulations of control and complicity beyond the park. Thus Campomanes's music uncovers the "potential 'fascism'" contained within the Deleuzo-Guattarian conception of music.[62] Disconnected from the potential for creative escape characterized as the deterritorialization of the refrain, Campomanes's music blocks the continual process of becoming by consolidating individuals under a single totalizing refrain.[63] The fascistic function is made manifest when Lotario reflects on his mother's death in a Nazi concentration camp and compares it directly with Campomanes's music. Indeed, this is the ultimate justification Lotario provides for his repeated assertion that Campomanes must be killed. It would appear that Lotario's philosophical interpretation of music leads him toward a violent, revolutionary action, which contains an echo of Deleuze and Guattari's assertion that "sound invades us, impels us, drags us, [and] transpierces us" yet somewhat inverts their final declaration that sound "makes us want to die."[64] Although Campomanes's music can be readily understood as an example of the fascistic realization of Deleuzian music, it is equally clear that it could also be interpreted as a second-order Baudrillardian simulacrum that "masks and denatures a profound reality."[65] Regardless, Lotario's plan to remove the obstacle that obscures the potential becoming of music ultimately fails. When he comes to enact his revolutionary plan, he discovers that Campomanes has already been assassinated by the "Consejo Asesor" (Advisory Council) that manages the theme park, his death used further to extend their power and their control.

Following the assassination of Campomanes at the hands of the Consejo Asesor, these same people hide their crime and use Campomanes's death as an opportunity to renew and reinvigorate their control over the population. Moreover, they achieve this through the proliferation of a series of further simulacral images. Thus the Consejo emulates, idolizes, and exalts Campomanes's widow, Sarima, as "la viuda evangélica" (the evangelical widow), despite the fact that this depiction bears little or no connection with reality.[66] Similarly, the Consejo rapidly produces a film to explain Campomanes's death in a way that furthers its own objectives: the film reinforces the idea that "el mundo encierra mucha vileza todavía; y nunca descubriremos al asesino porque el mundo todavía encierra mucha vileza" (the world still contains a great deal of vileness; and we will never discover the identity of the assassin because the world still contains a great deal of vileness).[67] It also installs the film's star, Armando Divito, as a replacement for Campomanes. That this strategy is effective is confirmed when Clarisa's mother (who lives outside Lorelei) compares Campomanes after his death to Lincoln, Gandhi, and Kennedy in a letter to her daughter. Thus Campomanes's murder generates ever more Baudrillardian simulacra in order to maintain control, order, and the status quo, much as his music had been used previously. And therein lies the rub: in this novel, Baudrillardian simulacra have essentially been utilized to obscure the revolutionary potential of Deleuzian becoming.

The strategy deployed in the theme park is particularly apposite when one remembers that in Deleuze's "immanent-evolutionary conception of being," conceived as the ceaseless generation of difference through repetition known as becoming, "bodies are images; or rather, bodies are produced as images and images are produced as bodies."[68] This is to say that, within Deleuze's ontological conception of the world, "images do not serve to represent reality" but are in fact fully immanent and "comprise the whole of reality, a reality which changes and regenerates without ever ceasing to be itself."[69] What Cohen's text serves to highlight is that within the proliferation of simulacra in the Baudrillardian hyperreal world, there is also a "definitive *immanence* of the image, without any possible transcendent meaning."[70] In the case of Campomanes's pop-songs, which obscure the becoming-music of the Deleuzian refrain, the strategies of resistance previously depicted have become blocked. What Cohen's novel ultimately suggests is that in the transition from discipline to control, the strategies have changed. As described in the previous chapter, disciplinary society relied on exercise and normalization to reduce repetition to that of the same, but now it can be perceived that within the control society Cohen depicts, a seemingly absolute yet closed set of immanent images are disseminated through the mass media in order to block access to the process of becoming. It seems that the situation Cohen describes is almost hopeless. Indeed, in one crucial deviation from Baudrillard's work, where he argues that hyperreality "engenders catastrophe due to its incapacity to distil crisis and critique in homeopathic doses," in *El oído absoluto*, it appears that the Consejo Asesor is even able to dispense "homeopathic doses" of crisis (Campomanes's death) in order to further its influence.[71] However, as Deleuze argued, in the society of control, "it's not a question of worrying or of hoping for the best, but of finding new weapons."[72] As Saul Newman notes, Deleuze "does not tell us what these weapons might be," but I would suggest that in this novel, Cohen makes an important suggestion.[73]

In his discussion of *El oído absoluto*, Miguel Dalmaroni draws attention to the fact that before his untimely demise, the community in Lorelei are acutely aware that Campomanes has not appeared in public for some time. As Dalmaroni notes, Campomanes's absence stimulates the circulation of rumors among the population and leads them to speculate that he may be ill, or dead, or some kind of cybernetic machine.[74] It is this circulation of rumor that constitutes a possible form of resistance within the society that Cohen describes, a suggestion first made within the text by Lino's friend Tristán. It is revealed that Tristán is not only a heroin addict but that before arriving in Lorelei he had been, paradoxically, both a well-paid publicity agent and militant in the Movimiento Independentista Mediterráneo (Mediterranean Independence Movement).[75] From this unique position as both central to the implementation of control (through his work in advertising) and militant, it is Tristán who perceives the reality of the system the characters inhabit, reveals the peripheral nature of power in Lorelei, and establishes the possibility of resistance. Tristán articulates this revelation through his theory of paranoia, stating that "los paranoicas saben que la saturación del aire les pone en peligro, que les coarta la libertad" (the paranoid know that the saturation of the air puts them in danger, that it restricts their freedom).[76] What Tristán perceives in the anxieties of the paranoid is that the modulations of control are omnipresent and dangerous. That these fears may bear no relation to reality is the first indication that they may potentially foment resistance within Baudrillardian hyperreality. As Tristán argues, "si un paranoico se inventa un complot contra él, es para darle una forma a ese mogollón de agresividad que hay en el aire" (if a paranoiac concocts a plot against him, he does so in order to give form to all this heap of aggression that's in the air). This is to say that the machinations of paranoia give form to the (at times imperceptible) modulations of control. For this reason, "volviéndose paranoicos [la gente] serán más libres. Al menos tendrán adelante una realidad más real" (by becoming paranoiacs [the people] will be more free. At the very least they will have a reality in front of them that is more real).[77]

Hence Tristán perceives that to encourage resistance they should foment and encourage paranoia among the population. With this in mind, Tristán delights in the circulation of rumors concerning Campomanes's nonappearance as they increase both paranoia and suspicion among the populace. Crucially, this strategy merges two forms of resistance evident in the work of Baudrillard and Deleuze. In one of the few brief suggestions Deleuze makes for the possibility of resistance within the control society, he argues one should "consider information as the controlled system of order-words that are used in a given society," then elusively suggests "that there is counterinformation."[78] Similarly, in her analysis of popular resistance within contemporary capitalist hyperreality, Rosemary J. Coombe notes that "faced with only the signifier, people construct a signified; in a world of empty signification people may invest their own meanings."[79] From this observation, Coombe highlights that "rumor is elusive and transitive, anonymous, and without origin," that it "belongs to no one and is possessed by everyone," and thus that it is "accessible to insurgency."[80] As we shall now see, this is exactly what takes place within Lorelei: counterinformation circulates in the form of rumor "possessed by everyone" and "accessible to insurgency."

What Tristán effectively understands is that the fears of paranoiacs confirm that "social space has not been emptied of the disciplinary institutions but completely filled with the modulations of control."[81] Tristán argues that the paranoid simply give control a concrete form and thus that paranoia can be manipulated as a form of resistance, a strategy that Lino also appears to intuit. Thus he comments that to escape the pervasive hyperreality of El Recinto, "el único remedio era suministrar más irrealidad" (the only solution was to administer more unreality), and he frequently visits a Tarot reader to discuss the rumors that circulate.[82] Certainly, the rumors surrounding Campomanes's nonappearance, like the graffiti painted in *Insomnio*, are disconcerting and foment disquiet. However, as Lino conjectures, "estaba ocurriendo algo más grave que la desaparición de Campomanes" (there was something more serious than Campomanes's disappearance taking place), and the rumors created that extend beyond this limited sphere of significance reveal the truth of what is happening in Lorelei.[83] Specifically, rumors circulate that something is occurring at the compost plant and connected port in Lorelei that may involve either a shipment of valuable recyclable material, arms, or possibly diamonds and that this situation is connected with Campomanes's nonappearance. The rumors thus establish the location of the genuinely important occurrences in Lorelei. However, as Deleuze notes, "the act of resistance is neither information nor counterinformation," and "counterinformation is effective only when it becomes an act of resistance."[84] Ultimately, it is Lino who will act on the imperative dictated by these rumors and transform the counterinformation into an act of resistance by visiting the recycling plant to try to establish what is actually happening on the islands. When he does so, he is immediately stopped by an armed guard and violently assaulted; the guard even seems to insert an object around Lino's eye and into his head. Although it is never revealed exactly what has been done to Lino nor what is happening at the port, his actions represent a "challenge to power to be power, power of the sort that is total, irreversible, without scruple, and with no limit to its violence," which is precisely one of the possibilities for resistance within Baudrillard's analysis of hyperreality.[85] Lino's actions force those in control to reveal their true nature, their violence, and their total power, as they disprove the myths about Lorelei disseminated by the Consejo Asesor. Although Lino's actions cannot reveal exactly what is happening in Lorelei, they expose the fact that the messages incessantly disseminated are mere simulacra and reveal the underlying violence of the system of control.

Interestingly, as *El oído absoluto* draws to a conclusion, it is suggested to Lino that Campomanes's death is also directly linked to the occurrences at the port. The Tarot reader, who it is revealed also went to the recycling plant, explains that Campomanes was also present and was taken away by the authorities following an altercation concerning the containers stored there. Although the full meaning of this event is never explained, the rumors have nonetheless revealed something of the truth. Lino does intuit, however, that this lack of concrete information constitutes a fundamental problem with the conception of rumor as a strategy of resistance. As he states,

> Al fin y al cabo las respuestas que me faltaban nunca iban a concentrarse en un esquema útil. Como las noticias que el láser pintaba en el cielo, como las canciones que excedían al autor, la muerte de Campomanes pertenecía a una verdad que en relación a nuestra vida de este lado de la historia giraba muy lejos, como un artefacto en órbita.[86]
>
> (In the end, the answers that I lacked were never going to come together into a useful scheme. Like the news that the laser drew in the sky, like the songs that surpassed their author, Campomanes's death belonged to a truth which in relation to our lives, from this side of history, turned at a great distance, like a device in orbit.)

The problem is that, as Lino perceives, the rumors that circulate belong to the same order of reality as the messages projected in the sky and Campomanes's songs. Undoubtedly, this is their unique strength and explains their effectiveness as a resistance strategy in a control society saturated with hyperreal images. In Lorelei the laser and the proliferation of simulacra are employed to maintain control through the dissemination of information, while the power of rumor is that it introduces counterinformation into the system and reveals the true nature of the park. As Lino laments, however, the rumors cannot form "a useful scheme," and he grasps the difficulty of converting counterinformation into a true act of resistance that would alter society.

The formal equivalence between rumor as resistance and the hyperreal images and messages manipulated to maintain control in *El oído absoluto* provides an interpretive framework for understanding another of Cohen's novels, *Variedades*, which is equally concerned with the contemporary hyperreal society of control. Crucially, this later text—it was published in 1998—explores the sexual nature of contemporary mass media society while also extending Cohen's critique and delineating a form of resistance that bears a striking resemblance to that outlined by Baudrillard in his 1979 book *Seduction*. As is the case with *El oído absoluto*, *Variedades* is set in the near future and explores the interconnections between hyperreality and the society of control. In this text society has completely dispensed with the Foucauldian enclosures found in Cohen's earlier novels, and the characters are entirely controlled by a sinister, mysterious, and powerful corporation called CUALO. The corporation has diverse business interests including the production of fertilizer, the manufacture of fabric, and significant involvement in radio and television communication. The narrator in this first-person account is never named, is employed in the public relations arm of the corporation, and is subject to an irrevocable contract. In addition, the extension of biopower as a mechanism of control that is perceptible in *El oído absoluto* reaches its apogee in *Variedades*: CUALO exercises such complete control over the narrator that they are able physically to redesign his body through extensive surgery so that he can act as a living double for the Barón Ignazio de Marut at various publicity events. When this particular stage in the narrator's employment terminates, the company subjects him to yet more surgery and redesigns his body again. That this manipulation of the narrator's body constitutes a method of control is made particularly clear when the company insert "un chip detector" (a detector chip) in his abdomen.[87] As in Deleuze's description of the control society, then, in the world of *Variedades*, "marketing is now the instrument of social control and produces the arrogant breed who are our masters."[88] For example, CUALO organize publicity events where they control all in attendance. In another, more perverse account, a clinic founded by CUALO discards hazardous material that falls into the hands of a young girl who the local population believes can use it to cure various ailments. Not only does the company promote this practice despite the fact that the material inflicts serious harm, but it also manipulates and exploits the girl and her family as a public relations exercise when she develops numerous tumors due to her contact with the material. This callous disregard for the truth is echoed again when it is revealed that Marut is possibly a pedophile, and once more when it is divulged that he has killed his wife. The former case is never examined at all, and in the latter case the company decrees that it will resolve the problem itself, without the intervention of the press.

It is important to note that *Variedades* is also evocative of Baudrillard's theories concerning contemporary hyperreality. For example, as Kim Toffoletti reminds us, in Baudrillard's work, "plastic surgery procedures also enable the remodelling of the body as sign," and "Baudrillard argues that the body is being manufactured into a sign for consumption" in contemporary hyperreality.[89] This model of simulacral production is perfectly applicable to *Variedades*. Additionally, when Marut is forcibly disappeared after murdering his wife, both the narrator and his artificial partner (Mansi) literally become copies with "no relation to any reality whatsoever."[90] Finally, it is particularly pertinent that, as in *El oído absoluto*, the radical ideas suggested in previous chapters have ceased to be effective strategies of resistance. In one interview Baudrillard has commented that, with regard to the "possibility of transmutation: becoming-animal, becoming-woman," "what Gilles Deleuze says about it seemed to me to fit perfectly."[91] Nonetheless, in *Variedades*, the central concept for the novel can be read as revolving around a hyperreal perversion of becoming-other. Although the narrator reflects that "he visto que en nuestra era el cuerpo puede ser vehículo para una libertad fabulosa, esto es, la libertad personal de reinventarse" (I have seen that in our era the body can be a vehicle for a fantastic freedom, that is to say, the personal freedom to reinvent oneself), this particular "freedom" has always already failed as a method of resistance.[92] In *Variedades* the possibility of transmutation, metamorphosis, and transformation, heralded as a powerful force of resistance, has become the strategy of manipulation and control.

As the narrative of *Variedades* advances, it becomes especially clear that the iteration of the mass media control society it describes incorporates sexuality and love into the capitalist matrix. For example, when the narrator undergoes his second round of extensive plastic surgery, he is persuaded to have an operation that amplifies the size of his penis. Moreover, as the narrator states, he was primarily motivated to accept employment within CUALO due to his desire to live with Mansi, the employee who assumes the role of Marut's wife, Finita. Indeed, the narrator will later convince himself that he became Marut in order to fall in love. Mansi too demonstrates an awareness of this sexualized form of capitalism insofar as she utilizes a sexual encounter to manipulate the narrator's affection. Indeed, Mansi is clearly far more aware of the power of her sexuality in this new reality: displaying her genitals to the narrator in a sexual manner, she comments that "hay muchos que se vuelven locos por esto" (there are many people who become crazy for this).[93] While Baudrillard and Deleuze disagree on the function and role of "desire" in contemporary capitalism, they nonetheless agree that "political economy (Marx), on the one hand, and libidinal economy (Freud), on the other, are *one and the same economy*," as in Deleuze and Guattari's analysis of contemporary capitalism in *Anti-Oedipus*.[94] This conflation of the political and libidinal economies is clearly evident in *Variedades* and also highlights a potential form of resistance in Cohen's work.[95] In Baudrillard's formulation, while there is "but one sexuality" that is "masculine" and centered on "the phallus, castration, the Name-of-the Father, and repression," the "strength of the feminine is that of seduction," which also constitutes a potential form of resistance to the culture of hyperreality.[96] This statement is of course highly controversial and has been subject to significant critique among feminist authors.[97] However, Baudrillard's suggestion that "one calls the sovereignty of seduction feminine by convention, the same convention that claims sexuality to be fundamentally masculine," certainly suggests that he describes rather than advocates this particular form of capitalist patriarchy.[98] Insofar as Mansi utilizes her sexuality to manipulate the narrator in *Variedades*, she could undoubtedly be considered a seductress in the traditional sense of the word. Nonetheless, when one recalls that for Baudrillard, "seduction consists in letting the other believe himself to be the subject of his desire, without oneself being caught in this trap," the possibility emerges that Mansi could be considered a Baudrillardian seductress.[99] The relevance of these arguments to Cohen's novel is further strengthened by the comment that Mansi's face, "más que hermosa, . . . era una constelación de planos de caras" (more than beautiful, . . . was a constellation of diagrams of faces).[100] For Baudrillard seduction "consists of finery, it weaves and unweaves appearances," because within the contemporary situation of globalized capitalism, "it is appearances, and the mastery of appearances, that rule."[101]

Crucially, Mansi is also more able than the narrator to utilize her position within CUALO to her advantage. For example, the narrator follows advice given to him by a CUALO employee and uses his wages to buy shares in the company, only later to discover a protocol preventing him receiving anything but an insignificant interest from his investment. In sharp contrast, Mansi invests her money in underground water that will become more valuable than oil. Similarly, when the Barón de Marut murders Finita, Mansi's immediate reaction is that she can exploit the situation to earn more money. Indeed, Mansi labors exclusively for her own benefit and liberation. In another particularly clear example, where the narrator discovers that becoming a simulacral copy of another person has a deteriorating effect on his own subjectivity and this topic becomes his perpetual obsession, Mansi's comment that "no tenés idea de quiénes somos" (you have no idea who we are), certainly suggests that she is fully aware that they reside in a "deceptive world in which an entire culture labours assiduously at its counterfeit," but that this is "not at all a negative fate, so long as uncertainty itself becomes the new rule of the game."[102] This becomes clearer still when Mansi is "kidnapped" during one of her publicity appearances. The narrator's ensuing comment, that she subsequently appears in an interview that she paid for herself, suggests that she has manipulated the very simulation techniques that control her in order to win her freedom. So too within Baudrillard's conception of seduction "the very distinction between authenticity and artifice is without foundation," a feature that "also defines the space of simulation." Indeed, in both seduction and simulation, "one cannot distinguish between reality and its models," and seduction thus "provides radical evidence of simulation, and the only possibility of its overcoming—in seduction."[103] Ultimately, however, it is the effect that Mansi has on the narrator that most clearly demonstrates her power as a seductress. Following her departure, the narrator becomes obsessed with her face, perfectly reflecting Marcus A. Doel's assertion that "to be seduced is to be drawn towards something that constantly eludes us, like the inexhaustible face of the beloved, and to lose ourselves on its surface."[104]

Cohen's novel does, however, suggest several problems with this form of resistance. In the first instance, Mansi's manipulation of the narrator and the requests to which she herself consents arguably reflect Baudrillard's assertion that "the game of the seductress involves a certain mental cruelty, towards herself as well as others."[105] More important, however, is that the common root and the similar strategies of both simulation and seduction make it impossible to know which process is developing at any one time. Mansi could equally be the victim of simulation or a powerful seductress. It appears that Baudrillard's comment that "he who stakes his all on the spectacle will die by the spectacle" could also be applied to his theory of "seduction."[106] Certainly this is the case in *Variedades*: it is stated that Mansi dies from the effects of exposure to radiation during a publicity event. Later in the novel, however, the narrator encounters a girl who also works for the same corporation, and when he believes he recognizes her voice, he begins to equate this girl with Mansi. This certainly suggests that Mansi's death could have been yet another simulation and that she remains in the employ of CUALO. When the narrator begins a relationship with this girl and confesses that "yo he sido otra persona" (I have been another person), she responds that she has too.[107] Although the reader is never informed whether the girl's comments are as literal as the narrator's, the possibility is certainly raised that this girl and Mansi are one and the same. Another more fundamental problem in *Variedades* is that Mansi's "seduction" fulfills a key function of contemporary capitalism in both Deleuze and Baudrillard's analyses of the system. As Deleuze comments, the society of control introduces "an inexorable rivalry presented as healthy competition" that "sets individuals against one another and sets itself up in each of them, dividing each within himself."[108] Similarly, Baudrillard remarks that in contemporary hyperreality, "self-management will be universal," and "self-seduction will become the norm."[109] Both processes are easily observed in the narrator: not only does he become divided within himself but he convinces himself that his situation is his own responsibility and denies that anybody else is culpable. Similarly, Mansi's "seduction" is ultimately individualistic, selfish, and manipulative, and at a fundamental level her resistance delivers her to the same fate as the modulations of control.

As we have seen, in *El oído absoluto* the rumors that circulate in the text assume a similar form to the hyperreal images utilized by the authorities to maintain control. This suggests that they constitute another form of seduction within the control society that Cohen describes. Moreover, the text delineates the limited effectiveness of this strategy of resistance. In much the same way, in *Variedades* it is undecidable whether Mansi's seduction is a form of resistance to control or whether she has simply been reabsorbed into ever more simulation. Both *Variedades* and the concluding section of *El oído absoluto* thus demonstrate the limited effectiveness of Baudrillard's model of seduction as resistance. As Rex Butler notes, for Baudrillard "seduction is not a limit or an outside to power" but is rather "that reversibility between power and its other without which there would not be power in the first place."[110] Although this binds Baudrillardian seduction to power in a reciprocal relationship, it must be remembered that "reversibility is predicated on Baudrillard's belief . . . that systems have within them a kind of built-in ability to undermine themselves by their functioning."[111] Indeed, as Baudrillard himself states, "inject the slightest dose of reversibility into our economical, political, institutional, or sexual machinery (*dispositif*) and everything collapses at once."[112] Yet this is not the case in Cohen's novels.

As noted previously, in *Variedades*, Mansi's seduction is individualistic and impossible to separate from the process of simulation, which continues unabated. In *El oído absoluto*, the problem is presented with a greater degree of subtlety. Following the rumors, incomplete revelations, and violence subsequent to Campomanes's death, Clarisa and Lino initially decide to attempt to leave Lorelei, only to discover that this is now exactly what the authorities want them to do. Moreover, in something of an echo of the intertwining of libidinal and political economies found in *Variedades*, they realize that in order to leave they would first have to consent to having children. Thus leaving Lorelei will necessarily involve submitting their bodies to further control. As it becomes clear that the system of control extends throughout the world and is omnipresent and inescapable, it is equally apparent that relocating will not change their situation whatsoever. In this way, both of Cohen's novels describe a situation somewhat akin to A. Keith Goshorn's argument that it is the already powerful classes "who are successfully utilizing just such strategies" as seduction "in the postmodern political arena" and that it is "world power elites" who have "effectively learned the secrets of . . . seduction."[113] Again, it is undecidable whether Mansi is resisting control or has simply been reabsorbed into ever more simulation, and in *El oído absoluto*, despite Lino's defiant act of resistance, those in power remain in power and continue manipulating the characters as before: Lino and Clarisa remain entirely trapped. It appears that, as was the case in both "La ilusión monarca" and *Insomnio*, for Lino and Clarisa, acutely aware of this new desire to relocate them, the only way to manifest their resistance is to withdraw their consent by choosing to remain in Lorelei. This suggests that the narratives of *El oído absoluto* and *Variedades* condense into much the same undecidable point as *Insomnio* and "La ilusión monarca."

It now appears that in all of these texts, Cohen, like Foucault before him, essentially argues that analyses of power should take "the forms of resistance against different forms of power as a starting point" in order "to bring to light power relations, locate their position, and find out their point of application and the methods used."[114] Moreover, in contrast to the powerful force of "reversibility" described by Baudrillard, it seems that Cohen's texts ultimately demonstrate Foucault's argument that "every strategy of confrontation dreams of becoming a relationship of power, and every relationship of power leans toward the idea that . . . it may become the winning strategy," that "between a relationship of power and a strategy of struggle there is a reciprocal appeal, a perpetual linking and a perpetual reversal."[115] In Cohen's texts as in Foucault's analysis, the relationships of power used to maintain control and the strategy of struggle understood as Deleuzian becoming or Baudrillardian seduction hold a reciprocal appeal; they are perpetually linked and perpetually at the point of reversing one into the other. This leads now to the relationship between Cohen's fiction and Deleuze and Guattari's analysis of Kafka's novels.

A consideration of Cohen's sociological and philosophical project reveals the strong correlation between his work and the second component of Kafka's literary machine: the incomplete novels. For Deleuze and Guattari, Kafka's novels reveal him to be "the prophet of a future world," who anticipates fascism, Stalinism, and U.S. capitalism.[116] Additionally, in contrast to their interpretation of the short stories, Deleuze and Guattari argue that the key feature of

Kafka's novels is that they forego becoming-animal in favor of the "the machine and assemblages."[117] So too in the Cohen novels discussed, such becomings-other as proliferate in Aira's texts are essentially neutralized. For example, Sergio's becoming-landscape in "La ilusión monarca" leads to his return to the prison, and Lotario's attempt to derive a political action from the process of becoming-music is preemptively blocked in *El oído absoluto*. In addition, Deleuze and Guattari note (with particular reference to *The Castle*) that "the indistinction of inside and outside leads to the discovery of another dimension, a sort of adjacency marked by halts, sudden stops where parts, gears, and segments assemble themselves" in a complex state formation.[118] As previously intimated, the most important feature of Kafka's novels is the construction "of the machine and assemblages," and the continual construction of this evolving state formation (or *social assemblage*) is the antithesis of the potentially infinite and creative machinic connections of the Deleuzian assemblage. Once more the creative freedom espoused by Deleuze and Guattari finds its dark counterpart in a reciprocal form of power. It is also clearly identifiable in *Insomnio*, "La ilusión monarca," and *El oído absoluto*. As the texts reach their conclusion, the central characters in each case come to the realization that the inside and the outside of the enclosures are essentially indistinct; they are merely representative of a total system that is seemingly inescapable. Moreover, in each case contact with the mechanisms of control reveals the "parts, gears, and segments" of this total social assemblage.

As Deleuze and Guattari continue their discussion of Kafka's novels, they note that "the machine is no longer mechanical and reified" but is instead "incarnated in very complicated social assemblages that, through the employment of human personnel, through the use of human parts and cogs, realize effects of inhuman violence."[119] In the Cohen texts discussed, robots and machines proliferate, but they are of secondary importance, and it is the human characters who become embroiled in the mechanisms of capitalist control: they become consumers, products, victims, and agents of control simultaneously. Equally, Deleuze and Guattari note that "a text that includes an explicit machine will not develop unless it succeeds in plugging into a concrete sociopolitical assemblage."[120] This is also the case in Cohen's texts, which directly plug into the "sociopolitical assemblage" of contemporary Argentina. *Insomnio* and "La ilusión monarca" express a close correlation with the transition to democracy and reveal aspects of the sociopolitical changes initiated by the military government and furthered through the implementation of neoliberal economic policies. In a similar way, *El oído absoluto* explores the development of the contemporary mass media as a political tool and mechanism of power following the opening of the Argentine economy. In each case, the sociopolitical description of reality is exaggerated so as to become visible and to reveal the underlying violence that sustains the system, be it physical violence and corruption in the former texts or structural violence leading to physical violence in the latter.

The robotic and mechanized elements that permeate the texts discussed reveal another key correlation between the work of Cohen and Kafka's novels. As Deleuze and Guattari argue, "Kafka doesn't think only about the conditions of alienated, mechanized labor" but also "considers men and women to be a part of the machine . . . in their adjacent activities, in their leisure, in their loves, in their protestations, [and] in their indignations."[121] This statement could also be applied to Cohen's science fiction: he perceives the importance of the robotic and technological development of society and includes such elements in his texts but, more importantly, he uses them as a tool to highlight the ways in which humans are further assimilated into the system of late capitalist control. As in Kafka's novels, the capitalist social assemblage Cohen describes absorbs leisure through the theme park and even protestations and indignations, as in the case of Sergio, Ezequiel, Lino, and Clarisa, who all realize that their protests against and attempts to leave their respective enclosures always already form part of the machine in question.

As the characters in the Cohen novels discussed realize that complete escape from the systems they inhabit is unattainable, they inevitably look for alternative forms of philosophical liberation while remaining within these restrictive spaces. The central characters thus come to much the same realization as the characters in certain Kafka novels that, confronted with expanding and prohibitive state formations, "one can't really tell if submission doesn't finally conceal the greatest sort of revolt and if combat doesn't imply the worst of acceptances."[122] Where Cohen and Kafka diverge, however, is that within Deleuze and Guattari's analysis of Kafka's novels, "there is no longer a revolutionary desire that would be opposed to the machines of power."[123] This is definitively not the case in Cohen. In *Insomnio*, "La ilusión monarca," and *El oído absoluto*, there remains a strong revolutionary desire, however quiet its expression may be. In these three texts many important characters express a minor revolutionary desire, and in each case every "failure is a masterpiece, a branch of the rhizome."[124] The apparent failures in these novels are especially pertinent in that they all suggest a deeper functioning of reality: in *Insomnio* Ezequiel undergoes a process of becoming induced by metempsychosis that results in his refusal to leave Krámer; in "La ilusión monarca" Sergio communes with the sea and becomes-landscape, directly leading to his (albeit muted) revolutionary decision to remain in the prison; and in *El oído absoluto* Lotario Wald endeavors to realize the political manifestation of his lifelong commitment to becoming-music by planning to assassinate Fulvio Silvio Campomanes. Thus each failure indicates the potential to "engage in processes of becoming" that would generate an exponential growth in machinic connections "in ever-evolving assemblages" directly opposed to the oppressive state formations Cohen describes.[125] Thus Cohen's characters at least attempt to engage the process of becoming in order to initiate an analogous process of becoming-other. In *El oído absoluto*, however, it is apparent that a seemingly absolute yet closed set of hyperreal and immanent images mask the more profound process of becoming. Thus where previously I stated that the model of resistance described in the work of Aira (radical becomings-other) had become blocked in Cohen, it would perhaps be more appropriate to suggest that it has become almost completely obscured. Aira's impasse (the necessity of defining oneself in permanent opposition to capitalism and the inability to follow the line of escape and construct an alternative society) leads to the sociopolitical description of the mechanisms of the society of control in Cohen. As in the case of Aira, my analysis of Cohen has reached an impasse that I cannot surmount through an interpretation of his novels alone. Surprisingly, it is by now turning to Piglia's analysis of power and resistance during a previous historical period that I shall attempt to move beyond this particular obstacle.

RICARDO PIGLIA: 2100, LA FECHA DE PUBLICACIÓN

(2100: THE DATE OF PUBLICATION)

Cada uno es dueño de leer lo que quiere en un texto.

Everyone is in control of reading what they want to in a text.

Ricardo Piglia, *Crítica y ficción,* **13**

CHAPTER 5

THE ARTICULATION OF A PROBLEM

THUS FAR I HAVE ARGUED THAT AIRA RESPONDED TO THE OPENING OF the Argentine economy under the most recent dictatorship by returning to the development of a capitalist economy in nineteenth-century Argentina and criticizing its violence from the outset. Subsequently I suggested that Aira countered the neoliberal realignment of the economy during the Menem presidency by returning to the revolutionary impetus of the 1960s and 1970s in Argentina. Reading the transposition of this radical moment to a new set of historical circumstances in conjunction with the work of Badiou and Deleuze, I argued that Aira's artistic practice constitutes a truth-procedure that engenders resistance through a series of becomings-other. In contrast, I have proposed that Cohen explores the limited freedom afforded by the transition to democracy. I argued that Cohen examines the redundancy of Foucauldian disciplinary enclosures within contemporary globalized capitalism, creating a dystopian vision of the future that closely resembles Deleuze's description of the control society yet incorporates several elements of Baudrillard's analysis of the contemporary mass media as a technology of power. Importantly, in Cohen's texts the Deleuzian model of resistance articulated by Aira becomes obscured; it ceases to function, and his characters' only means of resistance is to withdraw their consent. As yet the most recent dictatorship and its so-called Dirty War have only appeared tangentially and fleetingly in certain texts by Aira and Cohen. I will now consider Ricardo Piglia's two most celebrated novels, *Respiración artificial* and *La ciudad ausente*, to explore his philosophical reflection on the nature of the military regime itself and to establish a further connection between the analyses propounded with regard to Aira and Cohen. As in the case of the other authors, references to the dictatorship's systematic plan of state terrorism appear in allusive fragments in these Piglia novels. However, the discursive structures that supported the military government and the relations of power that it established are subjected to a far more comprehensive critique in Piglia's novels than in any text previously discussed. Additionally, the present chapter will demonstrate the philosophical and critical connections between *Respiración artificial* and my reading of Aira and the following chapter will explore the theoretical relationship between *La ciudad ausente* and the work of Cohen, arguing that these three authors construct a common critique of capitalism and political violence in Argentina.

Respiración artificial is composed of two distinct sections: the first consists of an epistolary exchange between the protagonist (the failed author Emilio Renzi) and his uncle (the amateur historian Marcelo Maggi), which gradually reveals their family history; the second follows Renzi as he travels to Concordia to visit Maggi. Upon arrival, Maggi has disappeared, and Renzi converses at length with Maggi's friend, the Polish immigrant Tardewski (a character largely based on Witold Gombrowicz), first about the history of Argentine literature and then about Tardewski's theory concerning a possible encounter between Hitler and Kafka in Prague in 1909–1910.[1] During the novel's opening section it is revealed that Enrique Ossorio (grandfather to Luciano Ossorio who is, in turn, Maggi's father-in-law) served as secretary to General Juan Manuel de Rosas and as a spy for General Juan Lavalle, which is to say that he collaborated with both sides in the Argentine civil wars (1814–1880). Subsequently, Enrique was forced into exile in the United States, where he made a fortune during the gold rush before traveling to Chile to commit suicide. Enrique has left to his descendants a dual inheritance: a fortune and his personal papers. The former now belongs to Luciano; the latter to Maggi, who, believing Enrique's life to be paradigmatic of Argentine history in general, is attempting to write Enrique's personal history from these papers. It is also revealed that Enrique planned to write a utopic novel consisting of letters composed in the nineteenth century yet addressed to the future and dated 1979. These letters appear in the text and are variously received by Luciano and Arocena, a contemporary spy, who examines the documents looking for secret codes by which he can predict future events.[2]

In 1989 Piglia declared that "*Respiración artificial* es una novela política" (*Respiración artificial* is a political novel), and it has become a critical commonplace to suggest that "the novel's main theme [is] the denunciation of the Argentine military dictatorship of 1976–1979" and of their self-styled Dirty War.[3] The novel was written and is set in 1979 (coincidentally, the year of the centenary celebrations of the Conquest of the Desert of such importance to Aira's *Ema, la cautiva*) and was published during military rule despite its critique of the dictatorship, which is only indirectly implied in Piglia's novel. For example, Teresa Orecchia Havas notes that the very dedication to Piglia's novel "evoca a dos militantes conocidos de Piglia, y al hecho real-histórico de su desaparición" (recalls two activists known to Piglia, and the real historical event of their disappearance), and many critics note that the eventual disappearance of Emilio Renzi's uncle, Marcelo Maggi, is an indirect allusion to the victims of state violence and the disappeared.[4] Similarly, in the novel's second section, when Tardewski postulates "the probably apocryphal encounter between Hitler and Franz Kafka in Prague in 1909–1910," many critics note the correspondence between the Spanish title of Kafka's novel *The Trial*, *El proceso*, and the Proceso de Reorganización Nacional (Process of National Reorganization) and argue, in line with Havas, that "el relato entrecruza entonces los destinos de Hitler y Kafka, inventa el encuentro de ambos, y los combina en secuencias paródicas y alegóricas que presentan a la literatura como una experiencia visionaria, proyectándose sobre los crímenes del totalitarismo" (the story intertwines the destinies of Hitler and Kafka, invents an encounter between the two men, and combines them in parodic and allegoric sequences that present literature as a visionary experience, foreshadowing the crimes of totalitarianism).[5]

In general, Piglia's allusive references to the dictatorship and their extreme repression have been understood as a strategy to obtain censor approval or to reflect the impossibility of presenting the horror witnessed during the dictatorship in literary form.[6] While Daniel Balderston notes that Aira and Piglia share a common preoccupation with nineteenth-century Argentine history, it is also evident that the strategy Piglia employs in *Respiración artificial* to condemn the military government is remarkably similar to that which I argued Aira utilizes in *Ema, la cautiva*: neither author names the subject of his critique and both instead incorporate fragmentary allusions to the violence perpetrated during the dictatorship in their texts.[7] Furthermore, both authors reference other genocides (the Conquest of the Desert in Aira, the Nazi holocaust in Piglia) and conflate historical periods to expose contemporary crimes. Crucially, this shared strategy is linked at a deeper philosophical level. As discussed in the first two chapters, Aira decries the violence inherent to the Argentine version of the Hegelian dialectic established with the discourse of civilization and barbarism and attempts to undermine this discursive structure through his own literary practice. Ultimately, he reveals the history of capitalism to be inseparably linked to that of political violence and the target of his critique. As we shall now see, each of these elements is equally present in *Respiración artificial*.

In the novel's second section, Tardewski relates Maggi's theory that the archetypal model for Argentine intellectual tradition consists of intellectual pairs represented by one European and one Argentine thinker where the European invariably represents universal knowledge. Tardewski's statement that Maggi believed that they too, as an intellectual pair, belong to this tradition immediately highlights Chakrabarty's "everyday paradox of third world social science," discussed in chapter 1, whereby postcolonial scholars find "universal" concepts "eminently useful" despite their European origin.[8] Furthermore, Seymour Menton suggests that this dualism and the novel's structure itself represent further instances of the "conflict between the Europeanized 'civilization' of Buenos Aires and the *criollo* traditions of the 'barbaric' hinterland."[9] At first this argument appears to be supported by Piglia's own critical work. For example, Piglia perceives a series of binary oppositions in the work of Borges and argues that "estas oposiciones no hacen más que reproducir la fórmula básica con que esa tradición ideológica ha pensado la historia y la cultura argentina bajo la máscara dramática de la lucha entre civilización y barbarie" (these oppositions do nothing more than reproduce the basic formula that this ideological tradition has used to conceptualize the history and culture of Argentina under the dramatic mask of the struggle between civilization and barbarism).[10] What Menton overlooks, however, is Balderston's argument that

> El tío de Renzi, Maggi, es un historiador que trata de escribir una contra-historia de los conflictos de la Argentina del siglo XIX, centrándolo no en Rosas o Sarmiento sino en una figura imaginaria atrapada en el medio, un agente doble y finalmente un suicida, Enrique Ossorio, a quien Maggi considera como simbólico del país en su totalidad.[11]
>
> (Maggi, Renzi's uncle, is a historian who attempts to write a counterhistory of the nineteenth-century conflicts in Argentina, focusing not on Rosas or Sarmiento but rather on an imaginary character caught in the middle, a double agent, and in the end a victim of suicide, Enrique Ossorio, who Maggi considers symbolic of the country in its totality.)

Thus, despite Menton and Piglia's assertions, Maggi's historical project can be considered an attempt to overcome the foundational myth of the conflict between civilization (represented by Sarmiento) and barbarism (represented by Rosas) by focusing on a character (Ossorio) who has simultaneously represented and betrayed both sides in the conflict. Aira adopts a similar strategy in *Ema, la cautiva* by constructing a counterhistory with a female protagonist focused on Argentina's indigenous population. Furthermore, as Fernanda Elisa Brava Herrera notes, a key component of Piglia's critical work is a reappraisal of the Argentine literary canon and "la disolución de dicotomías y antagonismos" (the dissolution of dichotomies and antagonisms), a task undertaken in *Respiración artificial* by Piglia's literary alter ego, Emilio Renzi.[12] This trait is evident throughout Piglia's literary oeuvre. For example, as noted in the introduction, Piglia attempts to unite the literary projects of Borges and Arlt in his short story "Homenaje a Roberto Arlt." Thus it can be argued that Piglia attempts to undermine Hegelian dialectics through literature in a similar way to Aira in such texts as *Cómo me hice monja*. Ultimately, as Page notes, Piglia "retains a vision of the dialectical process of historical and literary change" in order to decry "the violence implicit in the Hegelian overthrow of each historical period by its successor, which appears in *Respiración artificial* to generate an endless series of massacres and civil wars," and simultaneously attempts to undermine these same structures.[13] Again, this is much the same task we have observed in *Ema, la cautiva*.

Further exploring the parallels between the work of Aira and Piglia also serves to reveal the centrality of capitalism to Piglia's literary critique. In this instance, considering Piglia's critical assessment of Roberto Arlt (conveyed by Renzi in *Respiración artificial* and largely comparable to Piglia's own critical work) demonstrates that the very elements that Piglia acclaims in Arlt's literature are equally discernible in the work of Aira. The first point that Piglia (speaking through Renzi) stresses is that Arlt "escribía mal . . . en el sentido moral de la palabra" (wrote badly . . . in the moral sense of the word).[14] As Piglia then states, at the time Arlt was writing, literature developed a new ideological function in Argentina: it was utilized to defend the purity of the national language from the corruptions of the new immigrant population. Piglia argues that the work of Leopoldo Lugones typifies this ideological function and that Arlt contested it by consciously writing in poor Spanish. Piglia's praise of Arlt's "mala escritura" (bad writing) in *Respiración artificial* is therefore redolent of Aira's exaltation of "literatura mala" (bad literature), discussed in chapter 2.[15] Piglia argues elsewhere that Arlt shuns this ideological style at its inception and eschews immediate political concerns in his literature yet paradoxically captures "el núcleo secreto de la política argentina" (the secret nucleus of Argentine politics) and composes "la verdadera literatura política" (the true political literature).[16] As we have seen, Aira does include specific historical facts and personages in his literature, yet he enthusiastically distorts their representation to absurdity in order to create a political literature that, like Arlt's work, resists the power of the state. Indeed, in *La prueba* the names Mao, Lenin, and el Comando del Amor (the Commandos of Love) are evocative of politically militant groups of the 1960s and 1970s. This suggests that Aira also consciously shuns the specifically political and ideological style of literature produced by the "intelectual comprometido" (engaged intellectual) throughout these decades and thus that his work contains a similar ideological transgression to that found in Arlt.[17] Moreover, as we have seen, it is through this transgression that Aira's work becomes truly political. In a similar way, Piglia argues that Arlt's fiction and style are inextricably connected, and as discussed previously, Aira's style, prolificacy, and philosophical project are also inseparably linked through the perpetual "huida hacia adelante" (flight forward). Piglia's argument that Arlt "trabaja sobre los mundos posibles: sobre la posibilidad que tiene la ficción de transmutar la realidad" (works with possible worlds: the possibility that fiction has to transform reality) and that "en Arlt la ficción se transforma y se metamorfosea" (in Arlt, fiction transforms and metamorphoses itself) reinforces the connection.[18] Aira too creates new worlds and transforms reality through the innumerable becomings-other in his fiction, and he places particular importance on both "la metamorfosis" (metamorphosis) and "la transformación" (transformation) in *Diario de la hepatitis*.[19] Moreover, throughout his work, Piglia stresses that Arlt's literature is fundamentally linked with capitalism. An early indication of this connection is discernible in a letter, purportedly sent to Arlt by a close confidant, that Piglia includes in "Homenaje a Roberto Arlt." The letter decries professional authors who "publican porquerías" (publish junk) and extols the virtues of literary amateurs, ultimately claiming that "todo el mundo es escritor" (everyone is a writer).[20] These assertions are similar to those made by Aira in "La nueva escritura," where he argues that the professionalization of art limits its potential and reduces its frame of reference. Aira instead advocates literary amateurism so that the author "quedará liberado de toda esa miseria psicológica que hemos llamado talento, estilo, misión, trabajo, y demás torturas" (will be released from all that psychological destitution that we have called talent, style, mission, work, and other tortures).[21] Each example denounces the capitalization of literary production, and the specific styles of Arlt (as Piglia understands it) and Aira are shown fundamentally to resist this process. This anticapitalist tendency is reciprocally present within each author's work. Thus Piglia emphasizes that Arlt's characters do not *earn* money but rather *make* money, a fundamentally important feature of *Ema, la cautiva* too.[22] Indeed, when Piglia states that in Arlt "hacer dinero es salvarse" (to make money is to save oneself) or that the action of falsifying money "se afirma en la ilusión de transformar el vacío en dinero" (establishes itself in the illusion of transforming the void into money), the parallel is striking.[23] In *Ema, la cautiva*

Espina intends to fill the void of the desert with his falsified money, just as Ema (albeit temporarily) saves the indigenous population through this same proliferation of counterfeit money. While the function of counterfeit money is unique in each case (for Arlt it creates alternative structures of exchange for those prevented from entering capitalist society, while for Aira it provides a means to criticize the nature of capitalist expansion), the denunciation of capitalism is common to both.

Thus Piglia's interpretation of Arlt (present in *Respiración artificial* as in his critical output) shares much in common with my analysis of Aira's oeuvre and locates capitalism at the center of its critique. A similar appraisal is discernible throughout Piglia's work: he frequently includes such anticapitalist aphorisms in his work as Bertolt Brecht's "¿Qué es robar un banco comparado con fund-arlo?" (What is robbing a bank compared to founding one?) and Pierre-Joseph Proudhon's "la propiedad es un robo" (property is theft).[24] Moreover, Piglia argues that capitalism is the central theme of both the work of Arlt and the North American fiction he frequently discusses.[25] Importantly, Arlt's anticapitalist tendencies have also influenced Piglia's own fiction, perhaps most clearly seen in "Homenaje a Roberto Arlt." As outlined in the introduction, this story has frequently been understood as paradigmatic of Piglia's intention to blend criticism and fiction and to unite the literary projects of Borges and Arlt. However, it has also been interpreted as a text that resists the basic tenets of capitalism. For example, Ellen McCracken notes that the "crime of plagiarism" of such importance to Piglia's story "is not a moral or literary problem but an economic one because it violates the laws of private property."[26] Similarly, John F. Deredita proposes that Piglia's story "dramatiza la diseminación en el sórdido contexto de la propiedad privada y el comercio, contexto que se imponía a Arlt y que se impone a Piglia cuarenta y cincuenta años más tarde en una Argentina todavía capitalista" (dramatizes distribution in the sordid context of private property and commerce, a context that prevailed upon Arlt and that prevails upon Piglia forty and fifty years later in a still capitalist Argentina).[27] Thus, due to Arlt's influence, Piglia's own literary project can be closely related to Aira's.

In *Respiración artificial*, Piglia, like Aira in *Ema, la cautiva*, also suggests that capitalism is both the hidden motor of history and the driving force for his narrative.[28] Piglia's exploration of capitalism in *Respiración artificial* diverges significantly from Aira's treatment of the same topic in *Ema, la cautiva*, however, and is closest to that expressed in his essay "Ideología y ficción en Borges." In this essay Piglia argues that, due to the different cultural inheritance Borges received from his father and mother, ideology is expressed in his literature through the tension between "la cultura y la clase [que] se vinculan con la herencia y el linaje" (culture and class, which are linked to inheritance and lineage).[29] Piglia also suggests that Borges resolves the fundamental contradictions engendered by this dual inheritance by applying the Marxist conception of dialectical materialism to his literature.[30] Inheritance also drives the plot in *Respiración artificial* and can be seen to contain an abstract philosophical connection with capitalism. Luciano Ossorio first highlights the possible connection between inheritance and capitalism when he states that "los lazos de sangre, o mejor la filiación ha sido siempre, antes que nada, económica, y la muerte un modo de hacer *fluir* la propiedad" (the bonds of blood, or better still, of filiation, have always been, before anything else, economic, and death a method of making property *flow*) and that "la muerte y el dinero están hechos . . . de la misma sustancia corruptora" (death and money are made . . . of the same corrupting substance).[31] In his own case, Luciano argues that as his father died while fighting a duel before his birth, he preemptively inherited his father's fortune and thus feels himself to be irredeemably indebted. As Luciano's father also inherited Enrique's fortune before his birth (due to Enrique's suicide), Luciano concludes that Enrique is the true hero, unencumbered with debt and to whom all the others are indebted. Maggi also shares this debt as he inherited Enrique's papers, which he in turn will pass to Renzi.

While neither inheritance nor debt is a uniquely capitalist mode of exchange, in *Respiración artificial*, they can be seen to contain a latent philosophical function that fundamentally links them to capitalism. In his discussion of the link between death, money, and inheritance, Luciano first suggests a philosophical interpretation of inheritance by emphasizing that, for the ancient Greeks, the concept "ousía" (οὐσία) signifies both the transcendental form of the object and "la riqueza, el dinero" (wealth, money).[32] Luciano also states that one truly owns something when one knows its origin. That Luciano's wealth derives from an origin that is preemptively absent (through Enrique's suicide) is also particularly important, as in this way the circulation of inheritance in *Respiración artificial* can be understood as the movement of the "impossible exchange" that Baudrillard argues is integral to capitalism. Baudrillard defines this concept by referencing Nietzsche's analysis of the Christian perception of God. In summarizing Nietzsche's argument, he explains that by sacrificing his own son to redeem humankind's sin, God "created a situation where the debt could never be redeemed by the debtor, since it has already been redeemed by the creditor." Baudrillard then argues that this strategy "is also the ruse of capital" that "plunges the world into ever greater debt" yet "works simultaneously to redeem that debt," thereby "creating a situation in which it will never be able to be cancelled or exchanged for anything" and can only circulate.[33] According to Luciano's analysis, due to Enrique's material legacy and his suicide, these two versions of the impossible exchange are united. Enrique assumes the position of Nietzsche's God by sacrificing himself through his suicide. Thus the creditor has preemptively redeemed his descendants' debt, preventing them from repaying it and forcing it to circulate. The movement of this debt is thus, metaphorically, the movement of capital and the hidden motor of the novel's narrative. Thus Aira and Piglia, albeit in very different ways, return to the origin of capitalism in nineteenth-century Argentina, highlight the philosophical indebtedness of contemporary capitalism to this moment, and propose that capitalism continues to propel history forward.

Piglia's engagement with Kafka in *Respiración artificial* is in itself demonstrative of a further significant similarity with Aira. At a simple level, the latter writer has publicly stated his enthusiasm for Kafka's literature, while his interest in both "la metamorfosis" (metamorphosis) and "la transformación" (transformation) invariably connects his own oeuvre to that of Kafka.[34] Indeed, as discussed at length in chapter 2, the work of Aira and Kafka is undoubtedly linked through the Deleuzian conception of becoming-other. Similarly, although I do not claim that Piglia was directly influenced by Deleuze in composing *Respiración artificial*, his use of Kafka in the novel shares much in common with the work of Deleuze and this connection establishes the foundation for the present analysis. Piglia's use of Kafka in *Respiración artificial*, however, also establishes an important difference between the two Argentine authors. When Tardewski (philosopher and former pupil of Wittgenstein) first discusses Kafka with Renzi, he pays particular attention to Kafka's unique situation as a German speaker in a Slavic culture and argues that he is thus displaced with regard to language. Additionally, Tardewski highlights that Kafka claimed to confront "la imposibilidad de no escribir, la de escribir en alemán, la de escribir en otra idioma, a lo cual se podría agregar casi una cuarta imposibilidad: la de escribir" (the impossibility of not writing, of writing in German, of writing in another language, to which one could add a fourth impossibility: that of writing).[35] In this, Tardewski's analysis of Kafka's work is analogous to that articulated by Deleuze and Guattari in *Kafka: Toward a Minor Literature*. Like Tardewski, Deleuze and Guattari also focus on Kafka's situation as a German-speaking Jew in Prague to develop their theory of minor literature, arguing that it "does not come from a minor language" but rather that it is "that which a minority constructs within a major language."[36] Additionally, Deleuze and Guattari reference exactly the same Kafka source to argue that "the impossibility of not writing, the impossibility of writing in German, the impossibility of writing otherwise," constitutes the first feature of minor literature.[37]

This correspondence also highlights the close parallels between the critical work of Piglia and Deleuze and Guattari. In their book on Kafka, Deleuze and Guattari describe three key features of minor literature. The first we have already seen: the minor use of a major language. Importantly, Deleuze and Guattari also comment that "this can be compared in another context to what blacks in America today are able to do with the English language."[38] As they proceed, they argue that the "second characteristic of minor literatures is that everything in them is political," and the third is that "everything takes on a collective value . . . precisely because talent isn't abundant in a minor literature, there are no possibilities for an individual enunciation that would belong to this or that 'master' and that could be separated from a collective enunciation."[39] What is remarkable is that in 1970, some five years before the publication of Deleuze and Guattari's book, Piglia perceives the exact same qualities in the literature of black authors in the United States. As he writes, "Los escritos de Malcolm X, de Eldridge Cleaver, de Ralph Brown se leen y se escriben *en* la práctica de los Black Panthers, rompen la escritura como actividad privada y se convierten en la palabra misma del pueblo negro: vienen de la experiencia colectiva y tienden hacia el anonimato" (The writings of Malcolm X, Eldridge Cleaver and Ralph Brown are read and written *in* the practices of the Black Panthers, they break the idea of writing as a private activity and they become the words of the black people themselves: they come from collective experience and tend toward anonymity).[40] In this instance, Piglia precisely prefigures the work of Deleuze and Guattari: it is in the black population of the United States that Piglia encounters a minor literature that is necessarily collective and inescapably political, precisely because they are understood through the actions of the Black Panther Party.

Such parallels are also found in *Respiración artificial*. For example, when Tardewski reveals his discovery of the (probably apocryphal) meeting between Hitler and Kafka, he argues that this allows Kafka's fiction to be considered a dark precursor to the future of Nazism. In this instance, the vocabulary Tardewski uses is reminiscent of that used by Deleuze and Guattari: Tardewski states several times that Kafka "sabe oír" (knows how to listen) or that "él es quien sabe oír" (he is the one that knows how to listen) while Deleuze and Guattari argue that "Kafka listens to . . . the sound of a contiguous future" and thus formulates a "creative line of escape" that absorbs "in its movement all politics, all economy, all bureaucracy, all judiciary . . . in order to make them render still unknown sounds that come from the near future—Fascism, Stalinism, Americanism, *diabolical powers that are knocking at the door.*"[41] Thus where Piglia imagines a meeting in which Kafka can literally hear Hitler's future plans and can render them in literary form before they have occurred, Deleuze and Guattari forgo such a necessity. However, the only significant difference that results from these two assessments of Kafka's work is that Deleuze and Guattari argue that Kafka also anticipates other forms of "totalitarianism," namely, Stalinism and U.S. capitalism. Given that Piglia utilizes Kafka's apparent critique of Nazism to condemn the Argentine dictatorship, it seems that he (if not Tardewski) shares this belief with Deleuze and Guattari. As will become clear, however, the most important correlation between Piglia's text and Deleuze and Guattari's assessment of Kafka is more philosophical in nature. It is revealed through close consideration of a further connection between Piglia and Aira and ultimately illuminates the philosophical underpinning of Piglia's novel as a whole.

In relating the story of his father's death to Renzi, Luciano argues that the aftermath of the duel had greater significance than was immediately apparent, as it was the first crime of honor to be tried in public before a jury in Argentina. Crucially, the duel took place in 1879, and as Luciano states, for the first time in Argentina, justice became independent from "una mitología literaria y moral del honor que había servido de norma y de verdad" (a literary and moral mythology of honor that had served as regulation and truth).[42] As Luciano develops his argument, he explains that at this historical moment the "gentlemen" who had previously killed one another for honor realized that by establishing the rule of law, they could act in unison to kill those that did not recognize their authority, namely, immigrants, gauchos, and "indios" (Indians).[43] Moreover, Luciano argues that these actions explain the developments that brought Julio Argentino Roca to power. Hence Piglia reveals an argument very close to that made by Aira in *Ema, la cautiva*. Piglia also recognizes 1879–1880 as a decisive period in Argentine history and, for Piglia as for Aira, the consolidation of the nation-state was facilitated by the repression of marginalized groups. However, where Aira's text follows Viñas in suggesting that the indigenous population were the first disappeared in Argentina and laments the violent reverberations that these actions have precipitated throughout the twentieth century, Piglia's text offers a more detailed critique of the logic that has underpinned these same violent episodes.

As suggested by Luciano's account of his father's death, a new conception of law and justice was established when Roca assumed power in 1880. In the Piglian version of Argentine history, this marks the point at which older moral codes based on honor were replaced by formalized, regimented, and codified laws and justice. This point is supported by Laura Kalmanowiecki's argument that the formalization of the nation-state in 1880 necessitated the formation of a modern police force.[44] However, as Kalmanowiecki argues, political policing designed to counteract civil unrest was prioritized by the police force from its inception and throughout the twentieth century.[45] This is especially relevant to Piglia's novel in that, as Roberto Echavarren notes, each of the central characters is in some way a traitor or a criminal.[46] Of particular importance in this regard is that Maggi has spent a considerable time in prison. Although this at first appears to be due to the theft of his wife's inheritance, he later proclaims that he was imprisoned for being a member of the Unión Cívica Radical and a supporter of Amadeo Sabattini. The connection is important as Sabattini was monitored throughout his career, and following the overthrow of his government in 1930, the police established a sophisticated surveillance network specifically to restrict the actions of Radical activists.[47] That this included installing an officer as head of the Bureau of Posts and Telegraphs is particularly pertinent, as *Respiración artificial* also features letters intercepted by agents of the state.[48]

Given this historical context and the fact that the "heroes" of Piglia's text are those who transgress the law, *Respiración artificial* seems to suggest that the national state founded in 1880 depended upon a conception of the law that, though organized and logical, was despotic and ultimately led to the military violence of 1976–1983. Edgardo Berg reinforces this idea when he stresses that Tardewski reads the *Discurso del método* as a police novel "centrada en la búsqueda azarosa de la ley y la evidencia" (centered on the random search for the law and evidence) and *Mi lucha* as its parody, and thus argues that Tardewski understands rationalism as a precursor to fascism.[49] The transition from rationalism to fascism, however, requires more careful elaboration, and as before it involves the work of both Deleuze and Kafka. For Deleuze and Guattari the short story "In the Penal Colony" is exemplary of the fact that within Kafka's oeuvre, "the law can be expressed only through a sentence, and the sentence can be learned only through a punishment."[50] Developing this point, Deleuze and Guattari argue that for Kafka the law is also permanently displaced.[51] In Piglia's novel too (as in Argentine society at the time), the law enforced by the dictatorship is expressed only through punishment, and it remains permanently displaced and hidden. In *Respiración artificial* this is evidenced by Maggi's eventual disappearance and in Argentine society more generally by such aftereffects of the operation of the law as bodies washing ashore following the "vuelos de la muerte" (death flights) or, indeed, disappearance. However, where Piglia names the second section of his novel "Descartes" and draws particular attention to *The Discourse on Method*, I argue that the philosophical core of this rational and fascist law lies elsewhere. Following Piglia's suggestion that "lo más importante de una historia nunca debe ser nombrado" (the most important element of a story must never be named), I contend that the logic of fundamental importance to Piglia's novel is in fact that developed by Kant.[52]

For Deleuze Kant represented a philosophical opponent, and he developed a sharp critique of Kant's method throughout his work.[53] I would suggest that

Piglia essentially shares this critique with Deleuze. Again, this connection is elaborated in the first instance through the work of Kafka, as Deleuze argues that in Kafka's literature as in Kant's philosophy, "the law no longer depends on a preexistent Good that would give it a materiality; it is a pure form on which the good such as it is depends. The good is that which the law expresses when it expresses itself."[54] It is this Kantian conception of the "law" and the "good" that Deleuze argues underpins the machinations of justice in "In the Penal Colony." In this case, Deleuze not only suggests that the law is discerned through punishment but he implies that for Kant the simple exercise of the law contains a self-fulfilling morality. Although Kant is only mentioned directly twice in *Respiración artificial*, once by Maggi to illustrate a minor point in a letter to Renzi and once by Tardewski in a direct comparison to Maggi (an example I shall discuss later), I would suggest that by using Kafka to criticize the military government, it can be argued that Piglia's novel also contains an indirect critique of Kant. Read in this way, *Respiración artificial* suggests that it is Kant who provides the perverse logic that justified the violence of the so-called Dirty War and arguably the continual political violence over the course of the twentieth century in Argentina. Moreover, this implicit critique of Kant can be extended further still. Piglia has suggested that "no eran los sectores que tradicionalmente impulsan los golpes de Estado y sostienen el poder militar los responsables de la situación, sino ¡todo el pueblo argentino!" (it was not the sectors of society who traditionally drive coups d'état and sustain military power that were responsible for the situation, but rather all of the Argentine people!)[55] As I will now discuss, this broad conception of inadvertent complicity with the military government is also present in *Respiración artificial* and is suggestive of Deleuze's argument that within the Kantian conception of "the moral law, it is reason by itself . . . which determines the will" and that the moral law thus teaches us "that it is we who are giving the orders."[56]

In interview, Piglia has postulated that "la sociedad [argentina] tenía que hacerse un examen de conciencia" ([Argentine] society had to carry out an examination of conscience) so that each individual could discover within themselves "las tendencias despóticas del hombre argentino; el enano fascista; el autoritarismo subjetivo" (the despotic tendencies of the Argentine man, the fascist dwarf, the subjective authoritarianism) that inadvertently sustained the terrorist state.[57] In his discussion of fascism, Deleuze advocates a similar examination of conscience. While Deleuze recognizes that "fascism invented the concept of the totalitarian State," he also argues that "there is no reason to define fascism by a concept of its own devising." Instead, Deleuze contends that "what makes fascism dangerous is its molecular or micropolitical power," which he names "microfascism."[58] As Deleuze laments, it is "too easy to be antifascist on the molar level, and not even see the fascist inside you, the fascist you yourself sustain and nourish and cherish," which in turn sustains the totalitarian state.[59] The similarity between Piglia's "enano fascista" (fascist dwarf) and Deleuzian microfascism is striking, and I argue that in *Respiración artificial* Piglia attempts both to describe the precise nature of the microfascism that functioned in Argentine society and to indicate a potential escape from it.

In discussing Hitler's *Mein Kampf*, Tardewski argues that it is "la inversión perfecta (y lógica) del punto de partida de René Descartes" (the perfect [and logical] inversion of René Descartes's starting point), as it is founded on the hypothesis that doubt must be expunged from thought rather than forming its necessary condition.[60] Thus Tardewski argues that *Mein Kampf* represents "la culminación del racionalismo europeo" (the culmination of European rationalism) and "la razón burguesa llevada a su límite más extremo y coherente" (bourgeois reason taken to its most extreme and coherent limit).[61] By extension, Piglia associates the Argentine dictatorship with apparently logical and rational thought. This echoes another aspect of Deleuze and Guattari's criticism of Kant and also suggests the nature of the microfascism at play in Piglia's novel. In this instance, the salient point is that Deleuze and Guattari contest Kant's idea that "moral philosophy is . . . based on the idea of autonomy," where autonomy "literally means giving the law to oneself."[62] Within Kant's moral philosophy, he argues that there is a shared human consciousness of a common moral law. However, he also contends that our consciousness of this universal law is "the fact of reason" and thus that the "moral law is a product of reason."[63] As he states in *The Critique of Practical Reason*, "pure reason is practical of itself alone and gives (to man) a universal law which we call the *moral law*."[64] For Kant, our common awareness of morality itself implies an indispensable moral law (the "categorical imperative") and the faculty of reason (which all human subjects share) gives us this law and allows us to derive other "specific moral duties" from it.[65] For Deleuze and Guattari, the autonomy of Kantian morality underpins the modern state, as within it "everything revolves around the legislator and the subject," and "the more you obey, the more you will be master, for you will only be obeying pure reason, in other words yourself."[66] In *Respiración artificial*, however, Tardewski suggests that Descartes provides the basis for the modern fascistic state. Nonetheless, while discussing *The Discourse on Method* as a detective novel, Tardewski argues that "el cogito es el asesino" (the cogito is the murderer), later describes it as "ese huevo infernal" (this infernal egg), and argues that "esa razón produce monstruos" (that reason produces monsters).[67] I propose that the cogito established by Descartes and developed by Kant constitutes the microfascism that sustains the modern state in *Respiración artificial*, much as it does for Deleuze.

While Tardewski is correct in tracing the origins of the cogito to *The Discourse on Method*, it is significant that Kant directly addresses Descartes twice in the *Critique of Pure Reason* (1781). In the first instance, Kant argues that the cogito "is the vehicle of all concepts" as the "I" within the proposition "I think" "serves to express the identity of the subject that thinks a variety of thoughts about objects of perceptual experience and commits himself to the consistency of his thoughts about those objects."[68] It is this subject, endowed with the faculty of reason, that gives itself the moral law within Kantian philosophy. For Deleuze and Guattari, this "moral common sense" is "the State consensus raised to the absolute" because the illusion of unified subjectivity allows us to believe that we are applying pure reason when in fact we unwittingly obey "order words" disseminated by the state, where the "order-word" is "a function immanent to language that compels obedience": for example, a "judge's sentence that transforms the accused into a convict."[69] When Deleuze and Guattari explicitly state that the illusion of morality generated by the commonsense application of pure reason masked the function of order words in Nazi Germany and "provides a profound explanation for the Nazis' feeling of innocence" following the war, they closely parallel Tardewski's argument that *Mein Kampf* is the logical conclusion of the theories expounded in *The Discourse on Method*.[70] Given these arguments, a certain irony emerges from Piglia's text when Renzi relates that psychoanalysis has supplanted linguistics within Argentine literary criticism. Where Menton suggests that "Renzi seems happy to report" this development, I would suggest that, given the linguistic nature of order words and that Deleuze argues that "today, psychoanalysis lays claim to the role of *Cogitatio universalis* as the thought of the Law," each option in fact sustains the fascistic state; hence one could not be happy with either development.[71]

While in *The Critique of Practical Reason*, Kant defends human autonomy by arguing that the faculty of reason "gives itself the moral law," in the *Critique of Pure Reason*, he contends that the faculty of "human understanding is the source of the general laws of nature that structure all our experience."[72] As we shall see, this faculty is again centered on the cogito and will have important implications for my interpretation of *Respiración artificial*. Kant's fundamental argument is that the sensible world "is constructed by the human mind from a combination of sensory matter that we receive passively and a priori forms that are supplied by our cognitive faculties." In turn, this means that "a priori knowledge is possible only if and to the extent that the sensible world itself depends on the way the human mind structures its experience."[73] From this basis, Kant reaches the conclusion that "our *a priori* knowledge of reason . . . has to do only with appearances, and must leave the thing in itself as indeed real *per se*, but as not known by us."[74] The vital point is that Kant posits "a metaphysical thesis that distinguishes between two classes of objects: appearances and things in themselves," where the latter is the inaccessible, *transcendental* form of the object.[75] This thesis immediately brings Kant into conflict with Deleuze's fully immanent philosophy. As previously discussed, the principal objective of Deleuzian philosophy is to reject transcendentalism and "to think immanence not as immanent to something else, but as immanent only to itself" and thus to overturn the entire system of representation.[76] Crucially, as Kant contends that a priori forms inherent to the human subject structure the sensible world, he also posits that "it must be possible for the 'I think' to accompany all my representations," thus placing the cogito at the center of the system of representation.[77] For precisely this reason, Deleuze states that "the 'I think' is the most general principle of representation—in other words, the source of these elements and of the unity of all these faculties: I conceive, I judge, I imagine, I remember and I perceive—as though these were the four branches of the Cogito."[78] Deleuze therefore argues that "on precisely these branches, difference is crucified."[79] The significance of this philosophical dispute to my interpretation of *Respiración artificial* is twofold. First, Piglia's novel is profoundly connected with Deleuzian difference and repetition. Second, Deleuze specifically opposes the process of becoming to the Kantian conception of the law. As he writes, repetition "affirms itself against the law," and to think in terms of difference and repetition is to "oppose repetition to moral law, to the point where it becomes the suspension of ethics, a thought beyond good and evil."[80]

Menton argues that Piglia is influenced by such Borges stories as "Tema del traidor y del héroe" and "Historia del guerrero y de la cautiva," as *Respiración artificial* suggests that "history repeats itself."[81] This is clearly seen in the repetition of violent repression that Piglia cites within the text. For example, in one of the letters that constitute Enrique Ossorio's utopic novel, the imagined Inés Angélica Echevarne envisions the Nazi murder of the Jews before also foreseeing the events repeated "en Belén, provincia de Catamarca" (in Belén, province of Catamarca). That Echevarne mentions "Belén, Palestina" (Bethlehem, Palestine), and states that "los pájaros vuelan sobre las cenizas" (the birds fly over the ashes) is evocative of the falcon in W. B. Yeats's "The Second Coming," "turning and turning in the widening gyre" and announcing that "surely some revelation is at hand; / surely the Second Coming is at hand."[82] Notably, the mention of Bethlehem in connection with birds cycling in flight arguably invokes the poem's concluding lines:

> The darkness drops again; but now I know
> That twenty centuries of stony sleep

Were vexed to nightmare by a rocking cradle,
And what rough beast, its hour come round at last,
Slouches towards Bethlehem to be born?[83]

In Yeats's poem esoteric and occult imagery blends with the Christian and apocalyptic, and the flight of the bird reflects the cycles of history. In *Respiración artificial* it could be argued that the avian imagery in Echevarne's letter performs this same function. This idea is strengthened when Enrique states that one of the prostitutes that he frequents in New York "sabe leer el porvenir en el vuelo de los pájaros marinos" (knows how to read the future in the flight of marine birds) and when Luciano describes himself as an albatross.[84] Luciano's image of the albatross links metaphorically to the weight of the past with which he is burdened in the present: given the infinite and unpayable debt of which he feels himself to be the recipient, the image of the albatross immediately calls to mind Coleridge's "The Rime of the Ancient Mariner" in which the eponymous character laments the burden and the debt that he feels he carries for shooting the albatross that followed his ship by stating that "Instead of the Cross the Albatross / About my neck was hung."[85]

This repetitive understanding of history is reinforced when Renzi states that the history of the Americas since their discovery is merely a series of births, deaths, and military parades. Moreover, his suggestion that no one has more than two or three experiences in their life evokes the kind of wearied exhaustion from the cycles of history perceptible in Ecclesiastes as discussed in chapter 3. In each case, however, "repetition would in principle conform to the model of a material, bare and brute repetition, understood as the repetition of the same."[86] This brute repetition is epitomized by another letter sent by Enrique in which the fictitious author relates that a series of events he sees in films and reads in books are reproduced exactly in his own life. While this brute repetition is the simplest form that Deleuze describes, it is problematic. As he explains, this conception of repetition conflates elements that are actually distinct by overlooking their essential difference and relating them to one another through the principle of the "sameness of representation."[87] A clear example would be the seemingly "brute" repetitions of nature, where "the revolving cycles are only abstractions" that mask "evolutionary cycles" consisting of and producing distinct elements.[88] I contend that *Respiración artificial* too contains these deeper repetitions, which produce the new and the absolutely different. Unexpectedly, these can be discerned by considering another aspect of Deleuzian philosophy that he adopts directly from Kant yet extends far beyond its original remit. The element in question is Deleuze's philosophy of time, as articulated in *Difference and Repetition*.

One of Kant's most controversial claims in the *Critique of Pure Reason* is "that space and time are only subjective forms of human intuition" and that "if the subject, or even only the subjective constitution of the senses in general, be removed, the whole constitution and all the relations of objects in space and time, *nay space and time themselves*, would vanish."[89] For Kant space and time themselves are examples of the a priori principles that "structure all possible human experience" and upon which the sensible world itself depends.[90] For this reason Kant posits that "all objects have to be given or imagined in one space and one time," *including the cogito itself*.[91] This argument marks a significant development of Descartes's cogito. As Deleuze explains, Descartes's philosophy relied upon "reducing the Cogito to an instant and entrusting time to the operation of continuous creation carried out by God."[92] In contrast, "Kant's decisive break with Descartes's *cogito* consists in showing that the undetermined existence of the 'I am' can only be determined within time," as Keith Ansell-Pearson explains.[93] Deleuze argues that the introduction of time into thought was Kant's greatest innovation and constructs a philosophy of time from this original principle, which paradoxically undermines both the unified subject constituted by the Kantian cogito and the entire philosophical system of representation that it supports.[94]

Deleuze describes Kant's development of the Cartesian cogito by explaining that in Kant's philosophy "time moves into the subject, in order to distinguish the Ego from the I" and that the Ego is "a passive, or rather receptive, Ego, which experiences changes in time," but "the I is an act which constantly carries out a synthesis of time . . . by dividing up the present, the past and the future at every instant."[95] While Kant gives primacy to the I over the Ego, Deleuze essentially reverses this hierarchy. To achieve this, Deleuze postulates that Kant specifically introduced a "pure and empty form of time" into the cogito.[96] Importantly, this time is "pure because it is free of any imperial designs of an active, foundational subject," and empty "because it involves the movement of difference and repetition."[97] Deleuze thus describes three passive syntheses of time that are independent of the subject and that in fact fracture the I "from one end to the other."[98] Ultimately, Deleuze argues that "time can never originate with a subject . . . because the subject is made and fractured by [these] passive syntheses of time," as James Williams explains.[99] I describe each synthesis of time in greater detail in the following paragraphs because as the characters in *Respiración artificial* struggle to comprehend the brute repetitions of history, they unwittingly reveal that Deleuze's syntheses are operative in the novel.

It is important to note that throughout his diaries Piglia demonstrates a particular preoccupation with the concept of time. Beginning in 1960, when he took an introductory course on philosophy, Piglia muses on conceptions of time as developed by the Greeks, Kant, Heidegger, Nietzsche, and Freud, and most importantly, he also reflects on time in the work of Spinoza, Bergson, and Leibniz, three philosophers who directly influenced Deleuze's conception of time.[100] Similarly, Piglia also reflects on the function of time in literary texts by such diverse authors as Borges, Faulkner, Joyce, Fitzgerald, and Echeverría.[101] Throughout *Respiración artificial* too, several characters attempt to understand the events occurring in the novel by hypothesizing on the nature of time. In three particular instances, these hypotheses are suggestive of Deleuze's three syntheses of time.

The first instance is implied when Luciano proposes that "nada es ya recuerdo para mí: todo es presente, todo está aquí" (nothing is remembrance for me anymore: everything is present, everything is here).[102] In this instance Luciano reflects Piglia's very early assertion (in 1970) that the novel that will become *Respiración artificial* will be "una novela del puro presente" (a novel purely present).[103] Moreover, this seemingly simple statement provides the first connection with Deleuze's first synthesis of time, which is based upon the contraction of "successive independent instants into one another, thereby constituting the lived, or living, present."[104] Luciano's statement is evocative of this synthesis of time because, within it, "the present alone exists" as its very functioning "constitutes time as a living present, and the past and future as dimensions of this present."[105] Deleuze elaborates this synthesis by developing David Hume's conception of habit and argues that within it the past and the future are contracted into the present during any specific repetition.[106] As he explains, the past and future are absorbed in the living present, "the past in so far as the preceding instants are retained in the contraction; the future because its expectation is anticipated in the same contraction."[107] Luciano's actions in *Respiración artificial* also reflect a similar process. When Luciano tells Renzi that he and Arocena receive letters from the past, he explains that they both attempt to "descifrar el mensaje secreto de la historia" (decipher the secret message of history). He then discloses his belief in "una sola frase que, expresada, abriría para todos la verdad de este país" (a single phrase that, when expressed, would open for everyone the truth of this country) and thus "explica este desorden que tiene más de cien años" (explain this disorder that has existed for more than one hundred years).[108] This process can be readily understood in Deleuzian terminology. In attempting to decipher the secret of history, Luciano contracts the past into the living present through his search for this single cryptic phrase from one hundred years prior that will unlock the truth of Argentine history. The anticipation of success also forms a contraction of the future into the present. Similarly, the search itself implies a repeated action whereby each individual and unsuccessful search is retained in every subsequent attempt. Coupled with Luciano's assertion that "todo es presente" (everything is present), this suggests that Luciano's actions can be understood as an example of Deleuze's first synthesis of time.[109] However, Luciano's conception of contraction and the living present ultimately falls short of Deleuze's model. It is essential to note that while Deleuze develops his concept of habit from the work of Hume, he also attacks "the illusions of psychology that would interpret the operations of habit from the perspective of action" as in Hume's model.[110] Deleuze's problem is that within this conception of habit, "we act only on the condition that there is a little Self within us which contemplates: it is this which extracts the new . . . from the pseudo-repetition of particular cases."[111] In contrast, Deleuze argues that his own concept of the first synthesis of time "concerns not only the sensory-motor habits that we have (psychologically), but also, before these, the primary habits that we are; the thousands of passive syntheses of which we are organically composed."[112] While both versions of habit are necessarily related, the key difference is that Hume's model is a subjective and *active* process, while Deleuze's variant is a *passive* process that fractures the subject.[113] Luciano's first failure is thus readily identifiable: he conveys a conception of contraction that fails to transcend the initial subjective and active process. Luciano's contraction of the past (his search) and anticipation of the future centers on his own subjectivity and does not recognize the "passive syntheses of which we are organically composed."[114]

While relating his belief in the single phrase that will explain Argentine history, Luciano postulates that the decisive expression could be: "el movimiento infinito, el punto que todo lo excede, el momento de reposo: infinito sin cantidad, indivisible e infinito" (the infinite movement, the point that exceeds everything, the moment of repose: infinite without quantity, indivisible and infinite).[115] This infinite movement may initially appear to suggest Deleuze's "living present." Luciano's statement appears suggestive of the fact that within the living present, the present moment absorbs all past and future as its own dimensions and becomes seemingly infinite. This simple statement, however, ultimately demonstrates Luciano's second failure. The fundamental problem is that Deleuze's first synthesis of time does not "invoke the illusion of a perpetual present."[116] As Ansell-Pearson explains, "the time of the present is fundamentally paradoxical since in order to be 'present' it must not be self-present, that is, it must pass, and it is the passing of time that prevents the present from ever being coextensive with time."[117] Deleuze's living present can never be infinite, as Luciano suggests, because it necessarily invokes a past that can be contracted into the living present and into which the present moment can pass. This is to say, Deleuze's first synthesis implies another reciprocally dependent synthesis of time through which the present moment can pass in order to become past. It thus appears that although Luciano insists that it is "preciso aprender a resistir" (essential to learn how to resist), the conception of time that he invokes to do so is insufficient to overcome the tyranny of the cogito and the logic of the fascistic state.[118] Nonetheless, Deleuze's second synthesis of time is also discernible in Piglia's novel.

As many critics note, when Maggi comments that "la historia es el único lugar donde consigo aliviarme de esta pesadilla de la que trato de despertar" (history is the only place where I manage to alleviate myself of this nightmare from which I am trying to awaken), his words reformulate those of Stephen Dedalus in *Ulysses*, who famously comments that "history . . . is a nightmare from which I am trying to awake."[119] For Jorge Fornet this reconceptualization of the Joycean phrase alludes to the possibility of writing about and thus living through the horrors of the dictatorship's systematic oppression and resituates the horrors of the past in the present.[120] In contrast, Page argues that Maggi's phrase suggests that history "is a source of hope in the form of alternative visions that would revitalize the present and open up the possibility of thinking about the future."[121] Certain comments made by Piglia support Page's argument. Although Piglia, in line with Fornet, recognizes that "la pesadilla, sin duda, está en el presente, en 1976" (the nightmare is, undoubtedly, in the present, in 1976) he also suggests that for Maggi it is in history that "las cosas pueden cambiar y transformarse" (things can change and transform themselves) and states that "los rastros del futuro están en el pasado" (the traces of the future are found in the past), supporting Page's thesis.[122] The conception of the past as a source of possible freedom in the future also suggests another aspect of Deleuze's philosophy of time.

For Deleuze the first synthesis of time is grounded in a living present constructed from a series of "successive independent instants."[123] Thus it not only posits "time as a present, but [as] a present which passes." As Deleuze observes, "this is the paradox of the present: to constitute time while passing in the time constituted," an observation from which he deduces *"that there must be another time in which the first synthesis of time can occur."*[124] Thus he argues that there must be another time that "causes the present to pass" and that "must be considered the ground of time." Deleuze then categorically states that it "is memory that grounds time," where memory should be understood as "a pure memory identical to the totality of the past."[125] The process by which the former present becomes past is the second synthesis of time. As Deleuze explains, "the passive synthesis of memory constitutes the pure past in time, and makes the former and the present present."[126] Deleuze derives the second synthesis from Henri Bergson's conception of time, within which "the past coexists with the new present," "preserves itself in itself (while the present passes)," and "is the whole, integral past; it is *all* our past, which coexists with each present."[127] Furthermore, Deleuze argues that it is from this total past that differences can be extracted and repeated in the future. For this reason, he asserts that the second synthesis of time harbors the possibility of "freedom and destiny" in the future. This apparent contradiction can be understood by considering the essential Deleuzian proposition that "only difference returns and never the same."[128] Objects in the pure past are destined to be repeated in the future; however, as they will return as pure difference (the absolutely new), this repetition expresses a fundamental freedom.

Maggi's reconceptualization of the aforementioned Joycean aphorism is the first suggestion of Deleuze's second synthesis of time, which is echoed throughout his words and actions. Piglia's suggestion that for Maggi "los rastros del futuro están en el pasado" (the traces of the future are found in the past) and that it is in history that "las cosas pueden cambiar y transformarse" (things can change and transform themselves) is consistent with Deleuze's second synthesis, in which the past is the field of pure differences that can be repeated in the future to produce the new.[129] This argument is reinforced when Luciano reveals that Maggi only ever talked about the past and the future and never of the present and when Maggi states that he reads Enrique's papers "como el reverso de la historia" (as the reverse of history).[130] Moreover, Maggi's statement that "estoy convencido de que nunca nos sucede nada que no hayamos previsto" (I am convinced that nothing happens to us that we have not foreseen), suggests that in his conception of history as in Deleuze's conception of the second synthesis of time, the past contains every future possibility.[131] Thus in his words and actions (in attempting to write the history of the future mediated by Enrique's papers), Maggi can be seen to reflect Deleuze's assertion that the "past itself is repetition by default," as it contains the field of pure differences that can be reactualized in the future.[132] Like Luciano, however, Maggi's experiments with time ultimately fail.

Maggi's failure is exposed when Piglia comments that for Maggi history "prueba que hubo otras situaciones iguales . . . en las que se terminó por encontrar una salida" (proves that there were other similar situations . . . in which they ended up finding a solution).[133] The problem assumes a familiar form in that Deleuze makes a distinction between "memory as the [active] synthesis of representation and as a [passive] synthesis that involves the 'pure past,' that is, a productive unconscious of the past that exceeds the calculations of present needs and habits."[134] The problem is that Maggi actively seeks "empirical correspondences between the present and the past" without realizing that "this network of historical correspondences involves repetition only by analogy or similitude." Maggi's project is fundamentally flawed and can neither lead him beyond the brute repetition of the same nor engage repetition as "the historical condition under which something new is effectively produced."[135]

We have now seen that Deleuze's first two syntheses of time are discernible within *Respiración artificial*. However, while the first synthesis "is originary in the sense of giving rise to time," as "time is made by contraction," and the second establishes the *possibility* of the repetition of pure difference, the production of the new is the function of Deleuze's third synthesis of time.[136] As Deleuze argues, the third synthesis of time makes "repetition the category of the future," as it consists of the repetition of pure difference, the absolutely new, in the future.[137] As in the case of the first and second syntheses of time, Deleuze's third synthesis is related most clearly through a particular character in Piglia's novel, namely, Enrique Ossorio. Unlike Maggi, Enrique articulates that his objective is to become a historian who works with "documentos del porvenir" (documents of the future), and by projecting his letters (the component parts of his utopic novel) from the past into the future, he rejects the search for analogy in preference for the production of the new.[138] As Enrique summarizes his literary process, "Releo mis papeles del pasado para escribir mi romance del porvenir" (I re-read my papers from the past in order to write my novel of the future), reflecting that there is "nada entre el pasado y el futuro" (nothing between the past and the future) and thus that "este presente (este vacío, esta tierra incógnita) es también la utopía" (this present [this void, this terra incognita] is also utopia).[139] Enrique essentially recognizes that the present exists only as a process through which the pure past can be projected into the future to produce the new and thus utopia. It is within Enrique's letters that "the present and past are in turn no more than dimensions of the future: the past as condition, the present as agent," and it is through them that Piglia suggests the possibility of unlocking "the royal repetition" that generates the new.[140] Furthermore, the projection of Enrique's letters from the past to the future closely resembles Deleuze's primary example of the third synthesis of time and provides a model that can structure and explain the events contained in *Respiración artificial*.

In describing Deleuze's third synthesis of time, Williams explains that in effectuating the return of the different and the new, it constitutes both a "break" in time, understood as "a process changing the actual past and the possible future," and a caesura "where series—history if you like—are cut asymmetrically into before and after, yet also set into a new assembly."[141] This means that the caesura formed by the third synthesis of time "creates the possibility of a temporal series" as "every event on the line of time has an ordering of before and after in relation to it."[142] I contend that in *Respiración artificial* the event that accomplishes this ordering of time into before and after is the arrival of Enrique's letters from the past in the present. Deleuze explicates the third synthesis of time with reference to Shakespeare's *Hamlet*, and this analysis is particularly relevant to my discussion of *Respiración artificial*. Specifically, Deleuze focuses on Hamlet's utterance that "time is out of joint" to argue that the ghost of Hamlet's father "carries forth the past into a present that it tears apart."[143] As Williams explains: "For Hamlet, once his father's ghost has spoken, the numbering and legitimacy of kings is out of joint and his time becomes empty (there is no next numbered ruler) and pure (there is no legitimate ruler). Hamlet's task is then to revenge his father by killing his uncle, thereby re-establishing order and legitimacy based upon it."[144] I propose that the arrival of Enrique's letters in *Respiración artificial* is consonant with the appearance of the ghost of Hamlet's father. As discussed, Enrique's letters include the most precise description of Deleuze's brute repetition of the same found in the novel and emphasize the repetition of political violence in Argentina by resituating the horrors of the Nazi holocaust "en Belén, provincia de Catamarca" (in Belén, province of Catamarca).[145] Additionally, I argued that as a historical figure, Enrique undermines the foundational discourse of civilization and barbarism and that Piglia retains yet denounces the Hegelian conception of historical progress in *Respiración artificial* by including Maggi's attempts to write Enrique's personal history within the novel. Thus the arrival of Enrique's letters challenges the legitimacy of the Argentine dictatorship (by condemning its violence) and undermines the sequential ordering of different rulers (by questioning the validity of the Hegelian dialectic, which Piglia suggests underpins the selection of rulers throughout Argentine history). Moreover, much as Hamlet's task is to reconstruct the correct ordering of time following his spectral visitation, so too Maggi, Luciano, and the government censor Arocena all realize that Enrique's letters contain the fundamental explanation for what is happening in the novel. Indeed, Deleuze's reflection on Hamlet provides a possible explanation for the fate of these three characters in Piglia's novel.

In discussing the third synthesis of time, Deleuze also reflects on Marx's *Eighteenth Brumaire* to elucidate part of his argument. Notably, Deleuze relates Marx's assertion that "all the great events and characters of world history occur twice, . . . the first time as high tragedy, the second time as low farce" to his discussion of *Hamlet*.[146] While Deleuze largely accepts this argument, he contests Marx's assertion that the "comic or grotesque repetition necessarily comes *after* the tragic" and argues that the inverse is true.[147] Regarding *Hamlet* Deleuze thus contends that Polonius's death in act 3 is comic while Hamlet's in act 5 is tragic. To justify this argument, Deleuze contends that "repetition is comic when it falls short . . . , when instead of leading to metamorphosis and the production of something new, it forms a kind of involution, the opposite of an authentic creation."[148] This description of comic repetition illuminates the nature of Arocena's intervention in *Respiración artificial*. When Luciano introduces Arocena in *Respiración artificial*, he suggests that Arocena studies the letters he intercepts in order to decipher the secret of history.[149] Luciano's analysis is, however, incorrect. As Arocena later divulges, he examines the letters precisely because "son las cartas *del porvenir*" (they are the letters *of the future*), demonstrating that he understands that the letters contain "verdades secretas y subversivas" (secret and subversive truths) from the *future*.[150] Balderston argues that as Arocena receives and attempts to decipher letters composed by Enrique in the nineteenth century, his actions are inherently paranoid. However, this assertion is somewhat undermined by the fact that, as Balderston himself notes, Arocena's analysis of one particular letter reveals that it refers to the return of Perón in 1973.[151] This specific episode does, however, demonstrate that Arocena's intervention constitutes a comic failure in the Deleuzian sense: his examination of Enrique's letter only uncovers an event that took place six years before the arrival of the same letter. His analysis does not produce the new but only "the opposite of an authentic creation."[152]

In explaining the tragic element of Deleuze's analysis of *Hamlet*, Williams argues that Hamlet is a fundamentally tragic figure because he draws "all the action and all of time on to" his own "activity and identity."[153] This brief comment also explains why Luciano and Maggi are tragic figures. As we have seen, Luciano and Maggi ultimately fail in their respective attempts to comprehend Enrique's letters, as they remain beholden to the logic of representation and identity throughout their investigations. That this is Maggi's tragic flaw is evidenced by one of the few mentions of Kant in *Respiración artificial*. In the novel's second section, Tardewski delivers a long anecdote concerning Kant on his deathbed that he argues demonstrates Kant's continued dedication to "los principios de justicia y verdad" (the principles of justice and truth), even when confronting his own mortality.[154] Tardewski then argues that Maggi is "un hombre moral" (a moral man) and "un hombre de principios" (a man of principles) in the specifically Kantian sense.[155] Like Tardewski's Kant or Deleuze's Hamlet, Maggi remains committed to the system of representation centered on unified subjectivity until his tragic end. Similarly, Luciano only engages an active and subjective synthesis of time in attempting to understand Enrique's letters. His tragic fate is demonstrated by the fact that he has been confined to a wheelchair since 1931 after an act of political violence. Given this interpretation, Luciano's comments that "estoy paralítico, igual que este país" (I am paralytic, just the same as this country) and that "yo soy la Argentina" (I am Argentina) strike a particularly pessimistic note.[156] For Deleuze, however, the third synthesis of time also includes a "third moment beyond the comic and the tragic" and "the production of something new entails a dramatic repetition which excludes even the hero."[157] It remains to be seen whether this third moment is also perceptible in Piglia's novel.

I contend that *Respiración artificial* contains three particular instances that suggest the repetition of pure difference that constitutes the "third moment" of the third synthesis of time. The first is suggested by Patricia Rei in *El cuento de nunca acabar, o, El Pierre Menard de Ricardo Piglia*. Rei's thesis is that the "narrador de *Respiración artificial* parece dialogar con el narrador de *Pierre Menard*" (narrator of *Respiración artificial* seems to dialogue with the narrator of *Pierre Menard*) and that Borges's story provides the model to follow, imitate, copy, and reproduce in the novel's structure.[158] In developing the argument, Rei highlights that in *Respiración artificial* Piglia utilizes "plagio, juego de doble, [y] transformación de los textos" (plagiarism, games with doubles, [and] transformation of the texts) as literary techniques throughout the novel to the extent that it constitutes "una reproducción del trabajo literario del cuento de Menard" (a reproduction of the literary work of the story of Menard).[159] Ultimately, Rei argues that as Borges's story destroys the idea of originality and suggests that every text is a rewriting of other texts, Piglia's use of similar strategies to realize an analogous goal signifies that "Piglia no hace más que reproducir a Menard" (Piglia does nothing more than reproduce Menard).[160] Crucially, in the preface to *Difference and Repetition*, Deleuze "cites Menard . . . as a supreme justification to his philosophy of difference and repetition."[161] Thus Rei highlights that Piglia's novel imitates a Borges story that is exemplary of Deleuze's theory of difference and repetition. It seems that through the use of plagiarism as a creative endeavor, Piglia, like Borges and Deleuze, discovers the potential of the "royal repetition" to produce the new as pure difference.

The second instance that suggests that Piglia's text may contain Deleuze's royal repetition can be discerned through the text's engagement with the work of Witold Gombrowicz. While numerous critics note the relationship between Tardewski and Gombrowicz, Marta Grzegorczyk develops these connections particularly thoroughly. Grzegorczyk argues that "el concepto de la Forma" (the concept of Form) is fundamental to Gombrowicz's work.[162] As she explains, for Gombrowicz, form is essentially the superior part of any given dichotomy, and he advocates "una inversión de la dicotomía superioridad/inferioridad" (an inversion of the dichotomy superiority/inferiority) in order to unleash "el poder transformador" (the transformational power) it contains.[163] The connection between Gombrowicz's resistance to "la dictadura del 'General Forma'" (the dictatorship of "General Form") and Deleuze's conception of becoming-other (as detailed in chapter 2) is immediately apparent.[164] In each case a binary opposition is established and a movement toward the inferior (or minor) part conducted to unlock a "poder transformador" (a transformational power). Regarding *Respiración artificial*, Grzegorczyk argues that Piglia's praise of Arlt's "mala escritura" (bad literature) as "el inicio de la literatura argentina moderna" (the beginning of modern literature in Argentina) follows Gombrowicz in transforming weakness into strength and difference into creative potential.[165] Thus Piglia's valorization of the work of Arlt in itself could be understood as an instance of Deleuzian becoming-other: Piglia attempts to disturb and overcome the traditional hierarchies of Argentine literature by praising the minor partner in a traditional binary opposition between Arlt and Borges (or Arlt and Lugones). When we remember that becoming-other is the political variant of becoming (which can be understood as the continual and unending production of difference through repetition), the connection between this literary repetition and Deleuze's theory is clear.

As a brief aside, it is also notable that Grzegorczyk also argues that Maggi's conception of Argentine intellectual tradition creates a binary opposition between European and Argentine culture that echoes arguments made by Gombrowicz. The Polish author suggests that in the opposition between European and Argentine culture, "los europeos, 'los dictadores,' y 'árbitros' culturales— son responsables de haber creado el complejo de inferioridad en la cultura argentina" (the Europeans, the cultural "dictators," and "referees" are responsible for having created the inferiority complex found in Argentine culture). In a further echo of the work of Chakrabarty, Grzegorczyk argues that "como para Gombrowicz la posición extra-europea es la condición necesaria de la revisión de la Forma europea, el profesor argentino [Maggi] necesita a Tardewski para interpretar su propia cultura" (just as the extra-European position is the necessary condition for the revision of European Form for Gombrowicz, the Argentine teacher [Maggi] needs Tardewski in order to interpret his own culture).[166] This argument leads to further self-reflection. As previously stated, it is possible that a similar dynamic appears to underpin the present volume. While I would not propose that European theory is *necessary* to interpret the Argentine works discussed, it is nonetheless inescapable that the two are reciprocally bound together throughout my analysis. The inclusion of Gombrowicz's theories in *Respiración artificial* thus raise an important point: in the present volume too, it could be argued that the European theory deployed goes through a process of becoming-minor and that the Argentine literary works revise and advance the theories in question.

In arguing that Piglia is influenced by Borges in suggesting that history repeats itself, Menton notes that this implies that "everything is predictable" and thus at odds with the importance of chance in Borges's fiction.[167] However,

Menton also notes that chance is the "key factor" in Tardewski's discovery of the meeting between Kafka and Hitler, as he stumbles upon it when he is brought the wrong book in the reading room of the British Museum. Similarly, Menton highlights that while "the Borgesian leitmotif of the chess game" symbolizes the "predictability of the future," in *Respiración artificial* "Tardewski proposes a change in the rules to allow for random moves by each of the pieces so as to make the outcome more unpredictable."[168] Tardewski's reimagining of the game of chess, in which the position and function of the pieces are subject to continual modification, is the third instance that suggests that Piglia's text may contain the production of the new as pure difference, as it is reminiscent of Deleuze's description of the "divine game." The Deleuzian divine game involves dice throws, where "different throws . . . invent their own rules."[169] Deleuze argues that as the game has "no pre-existing rule" but only continual modification, each "throw of the dice affirms all of chance in one throw."[170] Deleuze suggests that this is the game of difference and repetition itself, as "instead of having the different, or different combinations, result from the Same" (which is to say, limiting the possible outcomes through predetermined rules), the player "has the same, or the repetition, result from the Different" (in that the only repetition is that of the continual modification of the rules).[171] When it is remembered that for Deleuze the divine game is the "system of the future," it would seem that Tardewski describes a theoretical game that involves the royal repetition, as by affirming chance, "divergence itself is the object of affirmation" and the new is produced as the absolutely different.[172] Furthermore, insofar as Deleuze argues that "ontology is the dice throw, the chaosmos from which the cosmos emerges," Tardewski's life story itself corresponds to the divine game of difference and repetition.[173] As Menton indicates, chance has governed the events of Tardewski's life and is the central element in his greatest discovery, namely, the meeting of Kafka and Hitler. However, while Tardewski's discovery certainly confirms the importance of chance, for the reader of Piglia's novel, it leads to the conflation of historical events (the Nazi genocide and the dictatorship's systematic plan of state terrorism) and thus invokes a further brute repetition governed by the logic of the same.

It is now clear that in *Respiración artificial* Piglia employs a similar strategy to Aira in *Ema, la cautiva* to criticize the military government, to condemn its self-styled "Dirty War", and in an abstract philosophical sense, to connect both processes with the development of capitalism in Argentina. However, it is also evident that Piglia constructs a critique of the philosophical system that has inadvertently sustained the military government. Piglia contests the Kantian conception of the law that, through a discussion of Kafka, he equates with the logic underpinning the dictatorship's extreme violence. Moreover, Piglia engages Deleuze's philosophy of time in order to undermine the system of representation, sustained by the cogito, that underpins this same conception of the law. Ultimately, however, for the characters in Piglia's novel, this philosophical engagement fails to produce the new or to liberate them from the repression they suffer. Luciano and Maggi remain committed to the logic of representation in their attempts to decipher the meaning of Enrique's letters, and their fate in the novel is demonstrative of this tragic failure. In contrast, Arocena's attempts to interpret Enrique's letters result in a comic failure that only uncovers events that have already passed. However, the fact that a representative of the violent and terrorist state recognizes the transformative potential of these letters from the future, the possible threat to the regime they contain, and reinstates brute repetition by using them as a tool to instigate further repression articulates a particular problem. Arocena's actions reveal that the violent interventions of the military in Argentine politics are the brute repetitions of history but that these same interventions mask the liberatory potential of the more profound repetitions that would produce the different and the new.

The novel is not, however, entirely without hope. As we have seen, Piglia includes at least three elements in the novel that are suggestive of the unending production of the new through the process of becoming: Tardewski's proposed modifications to the game of chess closely reflect Deleuze's divine game; Renzi's application of Gombrowicz's conception of form to his discussion of Arlt is closely linked with Deleuze's concept of becoming-other; and Piglia's engagement with and rewriting of Borges's "Pierre Menard, autor del *Quijote*" demonstrates that "the most exact, the most strict repetition has as its correlate the maximum of difference."[174] This final example suggests that it is the structure of *Respiración artificial* itself that best reflects the process of becoming, and this is also implied by the characters within the novel. At the conclusion of the text, following Maggi's disappearance, Tardewski entrusts Maggi and Enrique's papers to Renzi. The insinuation is that *Respiración artificial* is the text that Renzi has produced from these papers. Ultimately, this suggests that it is Piglia/Renzi's book as an object, in and of itself, that realizes the potential suggested by Enrique's letters. As I discuss in chapter 6, Piglia conducts a more profound investigation of this potential for literature to realize the production of the new in the future through its own formal devices in his later novel *La ciudad ausente*.

CHAPTER 6

TO BECOME WORTHY OF WHAT HAPPENS TO US

As I argue in chapter 5, in *Respiración artificial* Piglia adopts a remarkably similar strategy to Aira in *Ema, la cautiva* to explore the philosophical structures that sustained the Junta through the most recent period of Argentine military rule. As in Aira's text, there are only oblique references to the so-called Dirty War throughout Piglia's novel, and he traces the origins of both capitalism and the political violence perpetrated by the military government to the consolidation of the nation in 1880. In another parallel with *Ema, la cautiva*, it is revealed that the movement of inheritance in *Respiración artificial* can be philosophically linked to capitalism and shown to be the hidden motor of both Piglia's narrative and Argentine history. Unlike Aira, however, Piglia expands his critique and explores the nature of the philosophical formations that supported the military government. Piglia finds that the cogito, established by Descartes and developed by Kant, and the Kantian conception of the law that it sustains are the microfascisms that inadvertently sustained the military government. Finally, Piglia attempts to overcome this philosophical system by engaging a Deleuzian conception of time radically opposed to Kantian law. Such attempts are, however, ultimately frustrated. In this way, Piglia's text can be considered a continuation of Aira's critique that more fully accounts for the nature of the dictatorship's systematic repression. In the present chapter, we see that in *La ciudad ausente* Piglia projects this critique forward and ultimately becomes an important precursor to the work of Cohen. In particular, I demonstrate that *La ciudad ausente* can be understood as a forerunner to Cohen's depiction of the Deleuzian society of control sustained through the mass media's proliferation of Baudrillardian simulacra. I also argue that Piglia, like Cohen, advocates the cultivation of paranoia as an act of resistance. Ultimately, however, I again demonstrate that Piglia uses a series of intertextual links to create a radically different conception of time, rendering the text itself a timeless act of resistance that overcomes the system of representation that became a barrier to dissension in *Respiración artificial*.

Unlike *Respiración artificial* Piglia's *La ciudad ausente* is a science fiction novel set fifteen years after the fall of the Berlin Wall. Within this world Buenos Aires is under the control of a mysterious and repressive regime, and the text is centered on a machine (ostensibly created by the Argentine author Macedonio Fernández) that generates fictional texts by reinterpreting and reconstructing previous literary works.[1] The authorities in Buenos Aires attempt to control the machine by placing it in a guarded museum and restricting access to the texts it produces. Ultimately, they desire to deactivate the machine. Nonetheless, the machine's texts circulate by clandestine means and become an obsession among the population. The protagonist, Junior, works for a newspaper and the main narrative follows him through the city as he attempts to decipher the machine's stories to discover both the story of its origin and the identity of those attempting to resist the authorities in the city. As the text progresses the possibility is raised that in an attempt to preserve the life of his late wife, Elena Obieta, beyond her untimely death, Fernández has incorporated her memory into the writing machine. Indeed, the novel concludes with Elena's internal monologue as she is trapped alone in the museum. Over the course of the novel, several of the machine's stories are incorporated into the text, each story assimilating elements of Argentine history into recreations of various texts from literary history. Internally, these texts provide clues for Junior to follow. For example, the story "La isla" (The Island), a rewriting of Joyce's *Finnegans Wake*, leads Junior to one of the creators of the machine, who explicates its history. The stories, however, also have the potential to undermine the foundations of the novel's main narrative. For example, "Los nudos blancos" (The White Nodes) suggests that Elena is in fact a patient in a psychiatric hospital who believes herself to be a machine trapped in a museum. Ultimately, the text resists linear narrative progression and generates multiple compossible or logically incompatible readings.

Several superficial connections between Piglia's novel and the work of Cohen are immediately apparent. In the first instance, each author describes a similar vision of the dystopian future: the informal economic structure sustained by petty criminality and various pornoshops that Cohen describes in *Insomnio* is equally discernible in Piglia's description of the ad-hoc society and economy organized in the tunnels that connect underground stations in his version of the future Buenos Aires. In addition, where Cohen describes the situation of a female tango singer reproduced as a hologram in order to extend her career beyond her death in the novel *Inolvidables veladas* (1996), so too Piglia describes a writing machine imbued with the memory of Elena Obieta in order to preserve her life. Similarly, where Cohen's texts feature robots and bodies surgically redesigned as imitations of famous figures, *La ciudad ausente* features an ex-anarchist destroyed by a bomb and reconfigured in metal.[2] Beyond these superficial connections, however, there are more substantial thematic, political, and philosophical links between *La ciudad ausente* and Cohen's literature. As in the case of the Cohen texts previously discussed, as several critics note, *La ciudad ausente* is concerned with analyzing the nature of the "posdictadura que había comenzado en 1983" (postdictatorship that had begun in 1983).[3] Moreover, the text is situated in the context of neoliberal capitalist reform and the opening of the Argentine economy. This is evidenced, for example, by the inclusion of a Korean character in the novel, Tanka Fuyita, who "vino con la segunda generación de inmigrantes" (came with the second generation of immigrants) and specialized in the sale of contraband watches. Piglia suggests that the business has been ruined "por el mercado libre" (by the free market) and "el liberalismo" (liberalism) before stating that "las tasas libres liquidaron el negocio" (tax exemptions wiped out the business).[4] Importantly, however, Piglia's critique can now be understood as a philosophical antecedent to Cohen's analysis. Thus, where in "La ilusión monarca" Cohen explores the limited freedom gained through the transition to democracy by depicting the violence, corruption, and abuses of the contemporary criminal justice system as a continuation of that experienced during the so-called Dirty War, Piglia works backward in *La ciudad ausente* to expose the continuum of political violence that led to and endured beyond the dictatorship. Hence during Elena's final monologue she describes the actions of Leopoldo Lugones Jr., who, following General Uriburu's coup of 1930 that ousted Radical president Hipólito Yrigoyen, founded the Sección Especial (Special Section), which in turn established a far-reaching surveillance network, greatly increased the use of torture in police precincts, and introduced the use of the "picana eléctrica" (electric cattle prod) to extract information from their victims.[5] Additionally, Elena references the case of "el estudiante Bravo torturado por Amoresano y Lombilla" (the student, Bravo, tortured by Amoresano and Lombilla).[6] In this instance, Piglia refers to the case of Ernesto Mario Bravo, a student tortured by Cipriano Lombilla and José Faustino Amoresano during the first Peronist administration. Although identified, Lombilla and Amoresano were not imprisoned for this crime due to the intervention of the Peronist government. Crucially, Lombilla and Amoresano first worked under the command of Lugones Jr. yet continued operating in much the same fashion under Perón in the 1950s.[7] By including these details in Elena's monologue, Piglia highlights that a continuum of political violence instigated in the early twentieth century under military rule continued through the Peronist regime of the 1940s and 1950s and ultimately led to the dictatorship's systematic repression, where the electric cattle prod was a favored instrument of torture.[8] Thus Piglia clearly links the political violence of the past to that he perceives in postdictatorship Argentine society, an assessment that at least in part is shared with Laura Kalmanowiecki. In 2000 she argued that "events in Argentina (now under a democratic regime) demonstrate that the police continue to resort to illegal procedures and, more important, still enjoy virtual impunity from any type of legal and civil mechanism of control."[9] In this way Piglia shares a common objective with Cohen and can be considered to provide the historical groundwork for my analysis of "La ilusión monarca." Moreover, this contextual information also connects my analysis of *La ciudad ausente* with my discussion of *Respiración artificial* in chapter 5: Piglia's earlier novel suggests that the establishment of a national state was coextensive with the use of political violence and torture. Similarly, the novel highlights the importance of Leopoldo Lugones in instituting a national literature and language to consolidate the newly formed state. In *La ciudad ausente* Piglia highlights the role of Lugones's son in promoting a particularly virulent form of political violence. As Piglia writes in the later novel, "El comisario Lugones dirigió la inteligencia del Estado y realizó y llevó a su culminación la obra de su padre" (Commissioner Lugones managed State intelligence and realized and brought to its culmination the work of his father).[10]

As *La ciudad ausente* prepares the critical foundation for Cohen's analysis of the abuses of the contemporary criminal justice system in a historical sense, so too Piglia's dystopian vision of Buenos Aires anticipates the theoretical examination we have already observed in the work of Cohen. Specifically, Piglia's representation of power relations in *La ciudad ausente* can now be understood as a precursor to Cohen's description and investigation of the Deleuzian society of control. As in the case of Cohen's texts, the repressive regime that Piglia illustrates demonstrates a strong correlation with Foucauldian panopticism. For example, information is tightly controlled in the city, and the narrator notes that the population is under permanent video surveillance. Elena is similarly monitored by a camera within the museum. However, the society Piglia describes does not correspond precisely to the description of Foucauldian disciplinary society but rather portrays a new form of power relations. Although the repressive society that Piglia describes does not display all of the features of the control society we have observed in the work of Cohen, he nonetheless states that in his dystopian future "los controles eran continuos" (the controls were continuous), an almost perfect reflection of Deleuze's description of the control society.[11] In addition, when Junior encounters Russo, a Hungarian engineer who later reveals that he helped Macedonio construct the machine, Russo argues that society has entered into "una nueva etapa en la historia de las instituciones" (a new era in the history of institutions), which he defines as "el Estado mental" (the mental State).[12] Undoubtedly, this description is suggestive of both the redundancy of Foucauldian disciplinary enclosures and the internalization of control (and subsequent self-regulation) essential to the Deleuzian control society.

As the narrative of *La ciudad ausente* advances, it also becomes clear that "el Estado mental" (the mental State) utilizes the mass media as an important technology of power. However, the method by which the mass media contributes to the preservation of control is markedly different to that we observed in chapter 4: where power is maintained through the proliferation of Baudrillardian simulacra in the work of Cohen, in *La ciudad ausente* it is preserved through the use of psycho-power as defined by Bernard Stiegler. For Stiegler as for Deleuze, contemporary capitalist society no longer functions by "disciplining the body or regulating life" but instead conditions "the *psyche* to stimulate consumption."[13] Thus psycho-power is "characteristic of control societies" and involves the "systematic organisation of the capture of attention made possible by the psycho-technologies that have developed with the radio (1920), with television (1950) and with digital technologies (1990)."[14] In particular, the use of television as an instrument of psycho-power is closely reflected in *La ciudad ausente*. Thus in one version of the future, Piglia explains that time has been synchronized throughout the world so that the evening news is broadcast simultaneously to all global citizens. That such techniques are utilized to exercise control is made explicit by Fuyita, who explains that the Argentine state is telepathic and that there is a specific relationship between this telepathy and television broadcasts. As Fuyita explains, "el ojo técnico-miope de la cámara graba y transmite los pensamientos reprimidos y hostiles de las masas convertidos en imágenes" (the techno-myopic eye of the camera records and transmits the repressed and hostile thoughts of the masses in images), and thus to watch television "es leer el pensamiento de millones de personas" (is to read the thoughts of millions of people).[15] Within Stiegler's conception of the psycho-power of television, he argues that as broadcast images exist as a "temporal flux," "when someone watches a movie or a broadcast, his or her consciousness passes into the flux of this temporal object" and "that the temporality of cinematic images will be adopted by the temporality of consciousness." While Stiegler recognizes that every person watching the same broadcast will initially perceive the images in a unique way, he argues "that they synchronize themselves for the duration of the broadcast" and that persistent simultaneous repetition of the same broadcasts will lead to "a hyper-synchronization" of the audience, which will result in "an atomized society in which the 'I' and the *we* will be dissolved into . . . an amorphous *they*" that is more readily manipulated and controlled.[16] This process is readily identifiable in Piglia's description of the function of television in *La ciudad ausente*. As in Stiegler's analysis the hyper-synchronized audience is exposed to a temporal flux of images that represses the audience's initially hostile reaction to the state. In an amplification of Stiegler's theories, Piglia even suggests that through such strategies the state is able to learn the personal histories of all its subjects and translate them into new narratives that are transmitted by the president and that are in turn consumed and internalized by the population to maintain control. This assessment of the use of the mass media as a technology of power can be considered a corollary to Cohen's analysis, which explicates the mechanism through which the citizenry of the control society becomes especially susceptible to the manipulation of Baudrillardian simulacra.

Although Piglia describes the mass media as an instrument of psycho-power within a Deleuzian control society, *La ciudad ausente* also features a proliferation of Baudrillardian simulacra. As Francine Masiello notes, Piglia's "novel is composed through different copying machines: cassettes, walkmen, radios, television monitors, maps, and mirrors—even tattoos—reproduce in miniature the larger representations of life and feeling," thus confirming James Cisneros argument that in *La ciudad ausente* Buenos Aires is "un simulacro, . . . replicada y desdoblada en imágenes" (a simulacrum, . . . replicated and divided into images).[17] The precise nature of these simulated copies, however, remains to be defined. Moreover, it will become clear that although they belong to a different order and serve a different function than they do in Cohen's work, they nonetheless serve as a further historical and theoretical connection between the two authors' work. That the numerous copies and reproductions that abound in Piglia's novel can be understood as Baudrillardian simulacra is suggested particularly clearly when one considers Piglia's description of Russo's personal history. When Piglia describes Russo's past, he reveals that he came to Argentina to escape the Nazis and that while traveling through the pampa had murdered a man and appropriated his victim's life, personal history, and employment. When another character, Ríos, becomes suspicious and scrutinizes

Russo's past, he overlooks the substitution of one man for another, and Piglia subsequently comments that "Ríos hizo la investigación de una vida equivocada; todos los datos eran verdaderos, pero el hombre era otro" (Ríos carried out an investigation of the wrong life; all the information was correct, but the man was another).[18] This line immediately calls to mind the final denouement of Borges's story "Emma Zunz," where Borges argues that the effects of the crime simulated by the eponymous Emma were true, and "sólo eran falsas las circunstancias, la hora y uno o dos nombres propios" (the only falsehoods were the circumstances, the time, and one or two proper names).[19] In each instance, a character simulates a situation so effectively that in a certain sense it becomes true. Thus the cases of Russo and Emma are particularly evocative of Baudrillard's description of the difference between those who *fake* an illness and those who *simulate* an illness: the latter group will actually acquire some of the symptoms of the illness as the simulacrum becomes true.[20] As in Baudrillard's analysis, both Emma and Russo acquire false characteristics but absorb them so effectively that their simulated histories effectively become true. This connection is further strengthened when one considers Junior's father's comments that "había que tener cuidado al enfrentar un delirio de simulación[,] . . . por ejemplo el de los locos furiosos capaces de fingir docilidad o el de los idiotas capaces de simular gran inteligencia" (one had to be careful when confronted with a delirium of simulation[,] . . . for example, that of a furious madman capable of feigning docility or of an idiot capable of simulating great intelligence). Junior's father concludes that "nunca se sabe si una persona es inteligente o si es un imbécil que finge ser inteligente" (one never knows if a person is intelligent or is a moron who pretends to be intelligent), closely echoing Baudrillard's analysis of psychosomatic illnesses and the difficulty (if not impossibility) of discerning the simulator from the mentally ill.[21]

For our present discussion, however, there is another, more pertinent example of Baudrillardian simulation in Piglia's text. This example serves to link the historical and theoretical critiques previously elaborated in relation to *La ciudad ausente* and effectively anticipates Cohen's later analysis. In the first of the machine's stories contained in Piglia's novel, "La grabación" (The Recording), the narrator describes trucks full of hooded people brought to the Argentine pampa where they are unloaded and shot, their bodies discarded in numerous "pozos" (ditches) scattered throughout the landscape. As in the case of the bodies that wash ashore in "La ilusión monarca," this description cannot but call to mind the fate of the disappeared during the so-called Dirty War. Piglia's brutal depiction of state terrorism is, however, evocative of two further interconnected referents. Throughout the story, the narrator consistently describes the landscape as "el mapa del infierno" (the map of hell), and it becomes clear that for the narrator the landscape and its map have become indistinguishable: hell has become visible in the form of a landscape-map of unknown tombs.[22] The coalescence of map and landscape indubitably invokes Borges's story "Del rigor en la ciencia," in which a nation of skilled cartographers create a map so detailed it corresponds exactly to the landscape of the national territory.[23] Piglia, however, reinvents Borges's story with a specific political resonance. As before, this process strongly invokes Baudrillard's conception of simulation, a correlation that is not at all surprising given that Borges's story also serves as the inspiration for Baudrillard's theory as developed in "The Precession of Simulacra."[24] Once more, it is by following Borges that Piglia becomes a contemporary with the European theorists deployed in the present text.[25] As in Baudrillard's analysis of Borges's story, Piglia's "mapa del infierno" (map of hell) manifests "the discrete charm of second-order simulacra," which is to say that "it masks and denatures a profound reality."[26] Piglia's tale depicts the Argentine landscape as its own map, a map that masks a profound reality by disavowing the dictatorship's crimes and hiding them in plain sight. This description leads us to the second referent for Piglia's story. As Piglia recounted in interview, in June 1977 the military government replaced bus stops in Buenos Aires with new signs marked "Zona de detención" (Stopping Area).[27] Piglia's analysis is grounded in the double meaning of the word "detención" in Spanish. On the one hand, the word can be understood as the action of "stopping" or on the other, as the privation of an individual's freedom, or "detention." Piglia argues that the new signs installed by the military government disavowed their crimes as the population was aware that the country had been divided into several "zonas" (zones) where "los grupos 'de detención'" (the "detention" groups) could act freely.[28] Piglia thus argues that the new signs perfectly captured the dual nature of this explicit yet invisible threat made by the military government. Hence the city also became a map that masked yet revealed the repression inflicted by the military government. Thus "La grabación" (The Recording) ultimately reveals that the military government manipulated second-order Baudrillardian simulacra in order to mask yet divulge its own crimes and further oppress those who had not been directly affected by the violence. The story therefore provides the historical and theoretical link between the work of Piglia and Cohen: where Piglia demonstrates that the military government manipulated second-order simulacra as a repressive tool, Cohen suggests that once direct military violence had been replaced by the mass media as a coercive tool following the transition to democracy, it is the proliferation of fourth-order simulacra, which have "no relation to any reality whatsoever" and only ever refer to other simulacral images, that maintains control.[29]

In interviews and throughout his critical work, Piglia consistently expresses a preoccupation with the strategies employed to maintain power and exercise control in society. Frequently, this is mediated through reflection on the nature of the discursive structures that sustained the military government. For example, Piglia frequently refers to his belief that "la realidad está tejida de ficciones" (reality is woven of fictions) and that "el discurso militar ha tenido la pretensión de ficcionalizar lo real para borrar la opresión" (the military government's discourse has had the pretention of fictionalizing the real in order to erase its oppression).[30] A good example of one such discursive formation, which Piglia often returns to, is that "se construyó una versión de la realidad" (a version of reality was created) in which "los militares aparecían en ese mito como el reaseguro médico de la sociedad" (the military appeared in the myth as the medical reinsurance for society).[31] As Piglia expands on this premise, he explains that the military government argued that "el país estaba enfermo, un virus lo había corrompido, [y] era necesario realizar una intervención drástica" (the country was sick, a virus had corrupted it, [and] it was necessary to carry out a drastic intervention) to save it. As Piglia explains, the "Estado militar se autodefinía como el único cirujano capaz de operar" (military State defined itself as the only surgeon capable of operating). He concludes, "ese relato venía a encubrir una realidad criminal, de cuerpos mutilados y operaciones sangrientas" (this tale came to cover the criminal reality of mutilated corpses and bloody operations).[32] There is also an echo of this narrative in *La ciudad ausente*: when Junior meets a young female informant who provides him with information that will ultimately lead him to Russo, the police arrive and arrest the girl, claiming that she is "esquizo-anarcoide" (schizo-anarchoid) and that "es un médico al que ella llamaba el Ingeniero" (it's a doctor that she calls the Engineer). In this instance, Junior reflects that "la policía usaba ahora esa jerga lunática, a la vez psiquiátrica y militar" (the police now used this lunatic jargon that was simultaneously psychiatric and military) in order to explain their actions and exert their authority.[33] As in Piglia's historical anecdote, the authorities utilize medical discourse to justify yet mask their true intentions.

More generally, Piglia frequently argues that "el Estado narra" (the State narrates) and that when "se ejerce el poder político se está siempre imponiendo una manera de contar la realidad" (it exercises political power it is always imposing a way of narrating reality). However, Piglia also contends that "no hay una historia única y excluyente circulando en la sociedad" (there is no unique and exclusive story circulating in society) and thus that the creation of alternative narratives can be considered an act of resistance.[34] In *La ciudad ausente* this form of resistance is manifest in the "tensión existente entre dos mundos muy opuestos: el del Estado y el de la novela" (existing tension between two completely opposite worlds: that of the State and that of the novel) and in "los relatos subversivos de la máquina" (the machine's subversive tales), as Neri Francisco Enrique Romero notes.[35] Indeed, as Russo explicitly states, he and Macedonio created the story machine specifically to defend against "las experiencias y los experimentos y las mentiras del Estado" (the experiences and the experiments and the lies of the State).[36] Importantly, this form of defense also highlights a further connection between the work of Piglia and Cohen. As the novel progresses it becomes clear that elements of historical fact and present-day reality are absorbed into the stories produced by the machine. However, the proliferation of innumerable stories throughout the city, some of which are apocryphal imitations, leads to constant speculation as to the veracity of specific elements of the stories. When Junior reflects that "Los nudos blancos" describes "las ramificaciones paranoicas de la vida en la ciudad" (the paranoid ramifications of life in the city), the connection with Cohen becomes explicit.[37] As in the case of El oído absoluto, the unverifiable stories effectively circulate as rumor, which specifically foments paranoia. As in Cohen's novel, "faced with only the signifier, people construct a signified," and the stories, regardless of whether they are "true" productions of the machine or apocryphal copies, encourage the paranoid fantasies of the oppressed population that nevertheless reveal something of the true nature of their own repression.[38] As in the case of rumor in El oído absoluto, each text in La ciudad ausente "is elusive and transitive, anonymous, and without origin" and thus "belongs to no one and is possessed by everyone."[39] That the stories thus become "accessible to insurgency" is evidenced by the actions of Ana Lidia, who deliberately distributes apocryphal stories as a resistance strategy.[40]

As we have seen, Cohen and Piglia share a conception of the paranoiac circulation of rumor as an act of resistance. I would contend that in Insomnio and La ciudad ausente, they also share a common structural device, namely, Joycean metempsychosis. Somewhat paradoxically, however, the two authors' use of this concept marks the point at which my analyses of their respective projects diverge. As related in La ciudad ausente, the writing machine had initially been designed as "una máquina de traducir" (a translation machine), and the first text entered into it was Edgar Allan Poe's "William Wilson." However, the machine expanded and modified the text to such an extent that it effectively produced a new story, entitled "Stephen Stevensen." Thus the inventors created "una máquina transformadora de historias" (a machine that transformed stories).[41] The title of the new story not only invokes Poe's original story but also establishes a connection with Robert Louis Stevenson's The Strange Case of Dr. Jekyll and Mr. Hyde. Indeed, a previous version of the story "Stephen Stevensen" which appeared in Piglia's Prisión perpetua makes this connection explicit by stating that the character Stephen Stevensen wrote a book titled *Jekyl*.[42] More importantly for our own discussion, however, is that Piglia's story subtly suggests two further literary sources and the process of metempsychosis. First, the revitalization of Poe's story establishes a connection to Macedonio Fernández, who states in *Museo de la Novela de la Eterna*, "Yo creo parecerme mucho a Poe, . . . yo creo *ser* Poe otra vez" (I believe that I appear very similar to Poe, . . . I believe myself *to be* Poe again).[43] The "otra vez" (again) is possibly a reference to a draft version of *Tantalia*, in which Macedonio claimed to be "la refiguración humana de Poe" (the human reproduction of Poe).[44] While the connection between Poe and Macedonio implied by Piglia's novel has also been noted by Evelia Romano Thuesen, the title of Piglia's recreated Poe story also conceals a further connection with James Joyce.[45] María Antonieta Pereira has argued persuasively that William Wilson/Stephen Stevensen in Piglia's novel can also be connected with Joyce's literary alter ego Stephen Dedalus.[46] I would augment this analysis by suggesting that it is also important that while composing *Finnegans Wake*, Joyce wrote that should he be unable to complete the text, the task should be entrusted to fellow Irish writer James Stephens. Joyce's motivation for this choice was that the latter writer's name combined his own with that of his literary alter ego and that both men shared a birthday.[47] Thus I would suggest that Piglia's invented story subtly invokes the processes of "metempsicosis, transmigración, [y] reencarnación" (metempsychosis, transmigration, [and] reincarnation), which he has argued form the nucleus of *Ulysses*, and that he utilizes these processes as a structural device in a similar way to Joyce, Fernández, and Cohen.[48]

While investigating the stories generated by the machine, Junior returns to "Stephen Stevensen" several times, arguing that as it was the first text produced, it will reveal the "procedimiento" (process) at work in all the subsequent texts.[49] I would contend that the process engaged in "Stephen Stevensen" is indeed exemplary of that at work in *La ciudad ausente* as a whole. However, as opposed to the metempsychosis demonstrated in our previous example and shared with Cohen, I would suggest that another formal device is illustrative of Piglia's literary process in the novel, namely, Joyce's use of portmanteaux. As we have seen, the two-word title "Stephen Stevensen" invokes texts by Poe, Stevensen, Fernández, and Joyce and could thus be considered an unusual portmanteau combining these other referents. When one considers that *Finnegans Wake* largely consists of complex portmanteaux drawn from sixty-five different languages, a connection can be made to Ruben Borg's assertion that "one may think of Joyce's portmanteaux as temporal junctures holding together a variety of destinies, of plots, [and] of virtual time frames."[50] Because allusive references to "Stephen Stevensen" are not solely linguistic in form, I would suggest that they are in fact unconventional portmanteaux that hold together several Deleuzian "virtual objects." For Deleuze, a virtual object is one that belongs to two different temporal series at once. As such, "virtual objects exist only as fragments of themselves" in any given series, and each one "determines transformations of terms and modifications of imaginary relations within the two real series in which it appears, and therefore between the two presents."[51] As the example "Stephen Stevensen" is a composite of (at least) five different sources, it forms a peculiar virtual object that combines an equal number of temporal series. As we shall now see, it is the transformative potential of such virtual objects that underpins the present analysis.

The most significant virtual object contained in *La ciudad ausente* for my own interpretation of the text is the figure of Elena herself. As previously stated Piglia's writing machine potentially contains the memory of Macedonio Fernández's late wife, Elena Obieta, thus establishing an immediate connection with the latter author. Early in Piglia's novel, one of the first times Elena is mentioned, she is described as "una mujer en una lata" (a woman in a tin), which could also be considered an oblique reference to the fact that the poem Fernández wrote in her honor, "Elena Bellamuerte," was kept in "una lata de galletitas" (a biscuit tin) for some twenty years before it was published.[52] The description could also serve as a further connection to Joyce's *Ulysses*. In this text, Leopold Bloom reads an advertisement for canned meat (Plumtree's Potted Meat) in a newspaper and recalls the ad several hours (and almost one hundred pages) later when he contemplates the recent death of his friend Dignam and describes him as "Dignam's potted meat," remembering too that the ad was situated below his obituary.[53] The link is established in a rather less oblique manner when Piglia invokes Fernández's *Museo de la Novela de la Eterna* by describing Elena as "la Eterna, el río del relato" (the Eternal, the river of the story).[54] This brief description serves as another virtual object connecting Fernández to Joyce when we recall that the central female character of *Finnegans Wake*, Anna Livia Plurabelle, is the embodiment of the River Liffey.[55] Moreover, such statements as "Anna was, Livia is, Plurabelle's to be" not only reflect the Catholic doxology but also strongly invoke the fact that Anna Livia is the incarnation of time itself. In Piglia's machine story "La isla" (The Island), Elena metamorphoses into Anna Livia, space within the titular island is defined in relation to the Liffey, and "el concepto de frontera es temporal" (the concept of the "border" is temporal).[56] When it is remembered that the island in question is "una isla del Tigre" (an island in the Tigre delta), the description also invariably invokes Borges's famous remarks in "Nueva refutación del tiempo" that "el tiempo es un río que me arrebata, pero yo soy el río; es un tigre que me destroza, pero yo soy el tigre; es un fuego que me consume, pero yo soy el fuego" (time is a river that carries me away, but I am the river; it is a tiger that destroys me, but I am the tiger; it is a fire that consumes me, but I am the fire).[57] In his critical work, Piglia himself has drawn various connections between Borges, Fernández and Joyce, a line of argumentation followed by several critics in their interpretation of *La ciudad ausente*.[58] In line with these analyses, I contend that these three authors are of fundamental importance in understanding the philosophical function of Piglia's novel.

As Borg continues his analysis of *Finnegans Wake*, he argues that each Joycean portmanteau constitutes a "part of a whole that does not totalize, of a unity that does not unify," and thus "stands for a fragment of the universe—but a fragment in which the entire universe (the totality of space and time) can be surveyed."[59] As Borg makes clear, "such a whole is for Deleuze the realm of the virtual," and I contend that each of the key authors Piglia engages in *La ciudad ausente* constructs a similar virtual whole within their literature.[60] Seamus Deane's assertion that each portmanteau contained in the *Wake* generates "so many possible meanings that it is safe to assume that not even Joyce could have been aware of all (or even many) that his readers have found" confirms the hypothesis for Joyce's text: while the *Wake* is a single work and thus whole, its method of construction encourages the potentially limitless production of new interpretations, such that it shall never be complete.[61] Additionally, the paradoxical idea that a fragment of the universe could contain the entirety of that same universe cannot but invoke Borges's "infinito Aleph" (infinite Aleph), found in the cellar of a house in Buenos Aires, just as the conception of a "whole that does not totalize" is readily identifiable with his famous library, which is simultaneously total (and therefore limited) and infinite.[62] Similarly, the same images invariably evoke Fernández's *Museo de la Novela de la Eterna*, which he refused to grant a "cierre hermético" (hermetic closure), arguing instead that it should have "la peculiaridad de ser interminable" (the peculiarity of being endless).[63] This strange conception is evidenced by the text's concluding section, ironically titled "Prólogo final" (The Final Prologue), in which Macedonio writes "la dejo libro abierto: será el primer 'libro abierto' en la historia literaria" (I leave it as an open book: it will be the first "open book" in the history of literature).[64] Following these suggestions, Piglia himself describes Fernández's *Museo* as "la novela infinita que incluye todas las variantes y todos los desvíos; la novela que dura lo que dura la vida" (the infinite novel that includes all variations and all diversions; the novel that lasts as long as life).[65] This is certainly suggested by the fact that there are seven different manuscript versions of the text, none of which contain all of the fifty-six prologues that Macedonio composed throughout the 1920s, 1930s, and 1940s.[66] With regard to Piglia's text, James Cisneros argues that "*La ciudad ausente es el espacio virtual*" (*La ciudad ausente is a virtual space*) in a specifically Deleuzian sense and that the stories produced by the machine provide virtual alternatives to the actuality of political repression in the novel's main narrative.[67] In much the same way, Joanna Page suggests that Piglia's story machine defies "authoritarian control" through "its radical reworking of divisions between the real and the virtual" and also argues that due to the "wealth of intertextual references in *La ciudad ausente*" it can be considered "an open system," as defined in biology and physics, which "draws energy from transactions taking place across its borders, feeding on pre-existing texts, which are then subjected to a process of transformation."[68] In this way, Page demonstrates that the same virtual processes that function within the internal structure of the novel also function externally through the intertextual links contained throughout the novel. Building upon this common conception of virtuality within Piglia's novel, I propose that Piglia acquires specific theories from texts written by Joyce, Borges, and Fernández and recombines them into something of a conceptual portmanteau in *La ciudad ausente*. Moreover, this will lead to a new philosophical understanding of the political function of the text that in turn will prove essential in the elaboration of the philosophical connection between Aira, Cohen, and Piglia.

La ciudad ausente and *Finnegans Wake* share several key structural components. For example, Page contends that Piglia utilizes "Scheherazade of the Arabian Nights," who is mentioned in the text, as "a formal device."[69] Similarly, Eric McLuhan notes that the "ten Thunders in *Finnegans Wake*," which he argues form the major rhetorical structure for the text, consist of "100-letter words, except for the tenth which has an extra letter" and thus "may well be an allusion to Scheherazade and *The Thousand and One Nights*."[70] Indeed, references to the Arabian Nights are found throughout *Finnegans Wake*, for example, at one stage Joyce states that "there extand by now one thousand and one stories, all told, of the same."[71] Other less conspicuous examples are, however, more important to the present discussion. For instance, at several points during the *Wake*, Joyce explicitly discusses "the faroscope of television" and demonstrates a particular preoccupation with the material processes involved in televisual broadcasting.[72] For example, Joyce describes in great detail how "the users of television . . . are electrically decomposed by the iconoscope tube in the television camera and are reassembled in the receiver," and he augments "his account of a televised broadcast . . . with a reconstruction of the physics involved in its production."[73] Thus Joyce provides an early literary exploration of the physical reality of the television image, while Piglia investigates its use as a contemporary technology of psycho-power.[74] Moreover, what plot there is in *Finnegans Wake* revolves around a mysterious letter that implies that a crime, "sexual in nature," has been committed by the father of the central Earwicker family and "involves his daughter."[75] Of particular importance is that while the letter in question appears to have multiple authors, the final (and arguably definitive) version of the letter is composed by Anna Livia and is included in the text immediately before her final soliloquy.[76] This plot has a particular resonance with the central narrative in *La ciudad ausente* that involves Junior's investigation into the stories produced by the machine. Undoubtedly these stories also imply that the state has committed many crimes, and as in *Finnegans Wake* they are ostensibly generated by the writing machine but due to the proliferation of apocryphal copies, become somewhat "anonymous" and "possessed by everyone," which is to say that they circulate as rumor.[77] These two Joycean structural elements thus form the foundation of the political analysis I have previously argued that Piglia shares with Cohen. More significant than these connections, however, is that "Joyce is on record as having once affirmed that Time is the real hero of his final masterpiece" and that the text itself constitutes a "collideorscape" of images and linguistic representations of all "ideareal history" and every "probapossible" future.[78] I contend that Piglia appropriates the techniques utilized by Joyce to explore the nature of time, yet transforms them by engaging Borges and Fernández in order to develop the political argument that his novel contains.

Borg's comprehensive analysis of the function of time in *Finnegans Wake* is particularly useful in elaborating the temporal connections between Joyce's novel and *La ciudad ausente*.[79] For example, Borg notes that in *Finnegans Wake* the "periodic re-emergence of a given motif" functions "independently of that sense of historical inevitability, of rational consequence, that is the mark of well-constructed plots."[80] The same process is readily observed in Piglia's novel. For instance, the very name Anna Livia Plurabelle, which Piglia acquires from Joyce, is not only applied to a character in the story "La isla" but emerges in the form of Ana Lidia, the underground distributor of apocryphal stories, and is also connected to and transforms into "Lucía Joyce," the first character Junior encounters during his investigation. In this instance the name also references Joyce's daughter, Lucia, who developed schizophrenia in 1932 while Joyce was working on *Finnegans Wake* and who has been considered the inspiration for the text. As in the *Wake*, such re-emergence functions independently of the novel's central narrative and suggests that something other than the unidirectional flow of historical time is at play in the text. Indeed, as Borg goes on to argue, Joyce's last novel thematically "foregrounds the difficulty of seeking to invent the future by recycling the past," a feature that is also discernible in Piglia's novel.[81] When Borg highlights the fact that Joyce utilizes the "technique of ventriloquism" throughout *Finnegans Wake* and rejects "accepted protocols of citation" to facilitate this process, the connection between the two authors becomes clear.[82] As we have seen, plagiarism and false attribution are also an essential component of Piglia's literary technique and in *La ciudad ausente* (a text largely composed through the reinvention of previous literary texts, including *Finnegans Wake*), he essentially ventriloquizes several historical literary figures in order to recycle the past. Crucially, this particular technique also reintroduces Borges to our present discussion through the story "Pierre Menard, autor del *Quijote*." Moreover, when Borg argues that Joyce's use of this technique implies "that every word in the text, every thinkable notion, is always already employed second-hand," a clear connection can also be made to Macedonio's *Museo* where he reflects that, even before the creation of the world, "todo se ha escrito, todo se ha dicho, todo se ha hecho" (everything has been written, everything has been said, everything has been done).[83]

Given the discussion of Piglian plagiarism in the previous chapter, this technique also returns us to Deleuze's philosophy of time that will once more form the basis of my interpretation. In this instance, however, Piglia's presentation of Deleuzian time is subtly yet radically different to that which we observed in *Respiración artificial*. As elaborated in the previous chapter, Luciano's, Maggi's, and Arocena's attempts to reorder time following the temporal disruption caused by the arrival of Enrique's letters from the past result in either a comic or a tragic failure to produce the new. For Arocena the failure is comic because his intervention blocks "the production of something new" rather than producing metamorphosis.[84] For Luciano and Maggi the failure is tragic because they only engage in active syntheses of time and thus remain committed to a conception of unified subjectivity. In this case the system of representation centered on the Kantian cogito becomes a seemingly insurmountable obstacle to the potential resistance contained in the novel. Piglia's approach to time in *La ciudad ausente* takes a rather different form. In the story "La isla," it becomes clear that Anna Livia Plurabelle is a further reincarnation of Elena, the writing machine, when it is revealed that "siente que le arrancan el cerebro y dice que su cuerpo está hecho de tubos y conexiones eléctricas" (she feels that her brain is pulled out of her, and she says that her body is made of tubes and electrical connections).[85] This description of Elena's/Anna's material reality is immediately evocative of Jacques Derrida's description of *Finnegans Wake* as a "1000th generation computer" that affirms the redundancy of all existing information technologies.[86] When Borg comments that such a computer is simultaneously "both less and more than a live human consciousness" and "marks the possibility of a survival of consciousness, allowing consciousness to exist beyond its projected end," the importance of Derrida's metaphor to our present analysis is evident.[87] As in Borg's interpretation of Derrida's machine, Elena literally embodies the machinic possibility of "a survival of consciousness" and is thus "less and more than a live human consciousness." This transgression of human subjectivity is entirely in keeping with Joyce's own work. As explained in a letter to a close friend, in writing the Penelope episode contained in *Ulysses*, Joyce attempted "to depict the earth which is prehuman and presumably posthuman" and thus transcend the conception of unified subjectivity.[88] Not only is this assault on human subjectivity of central importance to *Finnegans Wake*, but it is also a recurrent theme in *La ciudad ausente*. For example, Elena's subjectivity is further called into question in "Los nudos blancos," when the possibility is raised that the entire text is taking place in the mind of a psychiatric patient. Similarly, Page notes that Junior's own family history "is structurally suspiciously similar" to that of another character depicted later in the text, and she highlights that Piglia himself has suggested that "Junior may be just another of the fictional characters invented by the storytelling machine."[89] It appears that in *La ciudad ausente* the concept of human subjectivity is consistently challenged, a feature that is also pivotal to such Borges stories as "Borges y yo" and "La memoria de Shakespeare."[90] Moreover, Macedonio Fernández also consistently contests notions of human subjectivity and, more importantly, "the self Macedonio challenges is a direct product of Cartesian philosophy."[91] This is particularly clear in *Museo de la Novela de la Eterna*, where Macedonio explicitly states that it is his desire that the reader of his text "por un instante crea él mismo no vivir" (for a moment believes that he himself is not living) and where he specifically advocates the substitution of Descartes' cogito for its antithesis: "yo no existo" (I do not exist).[92] As Todd S. Garth makes clear, "the source of delusion" that Macedonio "hopes to remedy lies in a philosophical and ideological legacy of Descartes and Kant, and Macedonio's mission is to undermine the viability of that legacy."[93] Thus the incorporation of Macedonio Fernández within *La ciudad ausente* serves to reaffirm the philosophical and political critique that has already been discerned in *Respiración artificial*. Therefore, I would suggest that, in the first instance, Piglia mobilizes Joyce in *La ciudad ausente* to undermine the conception of unified human subjectivity and thus evade and supersede the strictures of the active syntheses of time that plagued *Respiración artificial*. Piglia also engages Fernández, however, to add a specifically political dimension to this strategy. As will become clear, Borges adds a further component to this political critique.[94]

Throughout his career, Macedonio opposed Descartes and Kant through his creation of the concept of the "maximum individual."[95] I would suggest that Piglia employs a rather different strategy by evoking the work of Joyce and Borges. In discussing Derrida's machine metaphor for *Finnegans Wake*, Borg notes that it implies "a memory in excess of subjective identity."[96] Such a conception of memory, as related in chapter 5, forms the ground of Deleuze's second synthesis of time. As previously discussed, Deleuze derives his concept of memory from the work of Bergson, and it can be understood as the totality of the past that is real, coexistent, and coextensive with the present. In this memory, objects exist in a field of pure differences and thus have the potential to produce the new as they can undergo repetition in the future. Joyce succinctly and perfectly encapsulates this conception of the past in the *Wake* when he writes that "there is a future in every past that is present."[97] Moreover, Joyce's image of the "wholemole millwheeling vicociclometer," which clearly evokes Giambattista Vico's *Scienza Nuovo*, is also predicated on such a conception of the past and provides a further connection with *La ciudad ausente*. Joyce describes the vicociclometer as "a tetradomational gazebocroticon . . . , autokinatonetically preprovided with a clappercoupling smeltingworks exprogressive process" that "receives through a portal vein the dialytically separated elements of precedent decomposition for the verypetpurpose of subsequent recombination" of "the heroticisms, catastrophes and eccentricities transmitted by the ancient legacy of the past."[98] As Borg deciphers Joyce's machine metaphor, he explains that "if a cyclometer is an instrument that gauges the revolutions of a wheel, the vicociclometer must be a tool by which we count the revolutions" of history.[99] However, Joyce also proposes that the "verypetpurpose" of the machine is the "recombination" of "elements of precedent decomposition" from the past. As Borg explains, the vicociclometer thus "suggests that time is both the driving force behind this operation (the river that runs the millwheel) and its raw material (the previously decomposed and soon to be recombined stuff of history)."[100] This is to say that the functioning of the vicociclometer is predicated upon the passing of the present into the total past for subsequent repetition in the future, which succinctly describes Deleuze's second synthesis of time where the present passes into memory and thus establishes "the historical condition under which something new is effectively produced."[101] When Borg argues that the vicociclometer functions as "a mechanical-mnemonic device that gathers and recycles elements of the past" and that it "is memory understood at once as a process of cultivation and as a work of ingestion, absorption and physical re-elaboration," he reveals a possible connection between Joyce's machine and the story machine in *La ciudad ausente*.[102] Piglia's machine also appears to record the revolutions of history as it absorbs and ingests previous literary texts and events from Argentine and global history and concurrently re-elaborates them in the stories it produces. Thus Piglia's machine also implies a conception of the past as Deleuzian memory, where objects from the pure past are available for subsequent reconstitution in the future. As the writing machine also reconfigures this material to produce new texts, which are far more than simple copies of this previous material (we have already seen, for example, that "Stephen Stevensen" incorporates multiple referents and generates a new text that is inherently different, in the full sense of the word, from its literary precursors), this connection also indicates that Piglia's novel enacts Deleuze's third synthesis of time, which makes "repetition the category of the future" and produces the new as the absolutely different.[103] Indeed, it would appear that the very process instigated by Piglia's writing machine in *La ciudad ausente* implies a metastable form of time caught between Deleuze's second and third syntheses. It is to a closer examination of this metastable time that I now turn.

The machine story "La isla" contained in *La ciudad ausente* takes the form of a report written by an anthropologist, Boas (as Edgardo Berg notes, a reference to the famous anthropologist Franz Boas), on an archipelago of islands that form a strange linguistic utopia.[104] In something of an echo of the actions of General Aramburu during the 1955 Liberating Revolution, which included sending "some 200 . . . high union officials . . . to a prison camp in Tierra del Fuego," the population was founded by militants forcibly moved to the islands as part of an experiment that involved confining exiles on the island in order to contain political rebellions.[105] As becomes immediately clear, within the islands language is unstable and subject to irregular yet periodic transformation: a language can endure for a day or for several weeks before completely changing. Inhabitants immediately grasp the new languages developed while instantly forgetting those that went before. As previously intimated, the story is derived from *Finnegans Wake* and the characters Anna Livia Plurabelle and Nolan appear in both texts. Furthermore, the *Wake* itself is the source of both religion and ideology on the island. For the present discussion, however, the most salient feature of the story is that mutation itself assumes "las formas exteriores de la realidad" (the exterior forms of reality), and governs every aspect of life on the islands: lovers form and break relationships in accordance with the variations in language, the appreciation of literary works transforms with the rhythms of language transformation, and with each alteration "grandes poetas dejan de serlo y se convierten en nada" (great poets cease to be great and become as nothing).[106] These mutable relationships and revolutions in fortune are immediately reminiscent of the shifting social relations that Borges describes in his story "La lotería en Babilonia." As the narrator relates in the opening line of that story, "como todos los hombres de Babilonia, he sido procónsul; como todos, esclavo; también he conocido la omnipotencia, el oprobio, las cárceles" (as with all men in Babylon, I have been proconsul; like everyone, a slave; I have also known omnipotence, disgrace, the prisons).[107] Borges elaborates on the strange societal organization of Babilonia, explaining that every element of life in the nation is governed by the drawing of a lottery: even the consequences of each lottery draw are subject to further draws, so that the lottery engenders "una intensificación del azar, una periódica infusión del caos en el cosmos" (an intensification of randomness, a periodic infusion of chaos into the cosmos).[108] As Borges accounts for the exponential increase in both lottery draws and chance, he explains that "*el número de sorteos es infinito*" (*the number of lottery draws is infinite*) and comments that "los ignorantes suponen que infinitos sorteos requieren un tiempo infinito; en realidad basta que el tiempo sea infinitamente subdivisible" (the ignorant imagine that infinite draws require infinite time; in fact it is sufficient that time is infinitely subdivisible).[109] Although Piglia's story foregoes the necessity of formal lottery draws, it is clear that the constant alterations in language imply a similar conception of time that involves the absorption of chaos into cosmos and that can account for a substantial augmentation in the significance of chance within the islands.

The connection between "La isla" and "La lotería en Babilonia" is of particular importance as Deleuze directly discusses Borges's story in *The Logic of Sense* and argues that the infinitely divisible time that Borges describes "is the Aion."[110] In this text, Deleuze substitutes the terms virtual and actual for Aion and its counterpart Chronos specifically to discuss time. Importantly, where "Chronos is described as the time of the present," Aion "is the substance of both pasts and futures."[111] It would appear that it is the Aion that is invoked through the functioning of Piglia's writing machine. As Deleuze explores the difference between Aion and Chronos, he contends that "Chronos is cyclical," yet the "more radical nature of the Aion means that its shape is a straight line."[112] In this instance Deleuze develops his geometric description. of the Aion through reflection on the "laberinto griego que es una línea única, recta" (Greek labyrinth that is a single straight line) invoked by Borges in "La muerte y la brújula."[113] Importantly, however, Deleuze argues that despite assuming the form of a straight line, Aion also implies a cycle, yet one that is "very different from the circular or monocentered return of Chronos: an eternal return."[114] As Deleuze makes explicitly clear in *Difference and Repetition*, the eternal return "is the becoming-identical of becoming itself"; the eternal return is the very process of pure difference returning as the absolutely new though repetition.[115] It is for this reason that Deleuze states that the third synthesis of time is "the repetition of the future as eternal return."[116] Deleuze goes on to describe the eternal return as the "totality of circles and series" in "a formless *ungrounded* chaos which has no law other than its own repetition, its own reproduction in the development of that which diverges and decentres," which is to say that the eternal return forms "the internal identity of the world and of chaos, the Chaosmos," a concept he draws directly from *Finnegans Wake*, which attempts to depict "every person, place and thing in the chaosmos of Alle."[117] The same vocabulary and concept are, of course, invoked by Borges's description of "una periódica infusión del caos en el cosmos" (a periodic infusion of chaos into the cosmos) in "La lotería en Babilonia."[118] I would suggest that this development justifies Borg's argument that the *Wake* presents an image of the "future considered not from the perspective of the advancing present, or of the instant of imagination, but from a place outside the present—let us say, if that is at all possible, from the future itself."[119] Importantly, it is also now clear that Deleuze derived important elements of his conception of time from the very same sources that Piglia invokes and reworks in *La ciudad ausente*.

It would also appear that Deleuze's conception of time as the chaosmos produced by eternal return on the straight line of Aion is also that invoked by the functioning of Piglia's writing machine. Piglia's novel essentially adopts this form of time as its organizing principle and exists as a metastable mixture of the pure past and possible future.[120] In her discussion of *La ciudad ausente*, Teresa Orecchia Havas argues that the stories produced by Piglia's writing machine contain the "capacidad para construir los recuerdos del futuro" (capacity to construct the remembrances of the future).[121] Page explores this capacity in detail and notes that "the continual transembodiment of narratives in Piglia's fiction . . . leads to a resignification of one of the most sinister tropes of science fiction: memory implantation." She first notes "the common dystopian version of this trope" present in "Los nudos blancos," which echoes the amnesia produced in victims of torture during the dictatorship through the way in which "dissident citizens are reprogrammed with false memories as a method of control."[122] Subsequently, she cites Russo's assertion that the machine's stories are "relatos convertidos en recuerdos invisibles que todos piensan que son propios" (tales converted into invisible memories that everyone believes to be their own) as evidence to support the thesis that the "power of the storytelling-machine in *La ciudad ausente* . . . lies entirely in her ability to insert artificial memories into her listeners/readers."[123] When one considers Piglia's comment that the "teoría del Eterno Retorno puede ser vista como una descripción del efecto de memoria falsa que produce la lectura" (theory of the Eternal Return can be seen as a description of the effect of false memory that reading produces), a tangible connection between *La ciudad ausente* and Deleuze's chaosmos of time begins to materialize.[124] Within the internal logic of Piglia's novel, it appears that the functioning of the machine, which it has been argued can be equated with the functioning of Joyce's vicociclometer, engenders Deleuze's third synthesis of time through the intervention of her audience. Thus in *La ciudad ausente* Piglia "lead[s] us from the sad repetitions of habit to the profound repetitions of memory, and then to the ultimate repetition of death [the repetition of the future as eternal return] in which our freedom is played out" and which Deleuze argues is "the highest object of art."[125] As Page also notes, however, Deleuze additionally argues that "literature's potential to act politically" is derived from this same source, which is to say, from "its expression of what is not yet."[126] I shall now consider the political implications of Piglia's future-oriented literature in greater detail.

In discussing *Museo de la Novela de la Eterna*, Piglia states categorically that in "el mundo inédito de ese museo secreto se arma la otra historia de la ficción argentina: ese libro interminable anuncia la novela futura, la ficción del porvenir" (the unprecedented world of this secret museum the other history of Argentine fiction is assembled: this interminable book announces the future novel, the fiction of the future).[127] In this way, it becomes clear that Piglia's conception of literature as "la utopía del estado futuro" (the utopia of the future state) is also derived from the work of Macedonio Fernández.[128] Given this connection, it is especially important to remember that Fernández "felt his political views to be integral to his artistic and metaphysical ideas."[129] Furthermore, the challenge to notions of selfhood derived from the cogito is the central idea that transverses politics, art, and metaphysics in his work. It is certain that Borges, Joyce, and Fernández each challenge the notion of unified subjectivity in an attempt to depict "an open totality of past and future time," yet it is Fernández who argues that this "radicalization of art is a fundamentally political act" and attempts to construct "a living novel that invades public space."[130] The notion that politics, art, and metaphysics are inseparably intertwined through the destruction of the self is the most significant of Piglia's appropriations from Macedonio Fernández in *La ciudad ausente*. It is essential to remember that the stories that Piglia's machine produces serve a political function. Edgardo Berg provides a useful summary of this political position: "Contra el relato monológico y estereotipado del Estado que quiere imponer el modo de percibir el mundo y el criterio sobre lo real, la máquina provoca el desfasaje narrativo, articula y narra su contrafigura utópica: la ficción de los inventores, hermeneutas o alucinados" (Against the State's mono-logical and stereotyped tale which seeks to impose the way in which the world is perceived and the judgment of the real, the machine causes narrative discordance, it articulates and narrates its utopic counter-representation: the fiction of inventors, of the practitioners of hermeneutics, or of visionaries).[131] In the main narrative of the novel, the production of alternative narratives, time frames, and worlds is an act of resistance that counteracts those disseminated by the repressive regime that governs Junior's world. I have already noted that Cisneros frames this strategy in Deleuzian terms and have been able to more fully account for the philosophical processes at work in the novel. However, it is also imperative to remember that Piglia derives his theory concerning the narrative constructions that justify political violence by reflecting on those that sustained the last military government during their so-called Dirty War. Additionally, *La ciudad ausente* contains several real-world referents: it highlights the limited freedoms obtained through the transition to democracy, draws attention to continued instances of police brutality, and demonstrates the new forms of control that emerge concurrently with the transition to a neoliberal economic model. As in the case of Macedonio, this political critique is integral to the philosophical analysis we have elaborated. In Deleuze's description of the eternal return of the future, he argues that such a return "is no longer that of individuals, persons, and worlds, but only of pure events."[132] In refining his description of the event, Deleuze explains that "there is indeed the present moment of its actualization, the moment in which the event is embodied in a state of affairs, an individual, or a person" but equally that "there is the future and the past of the event considered in itself, sidestepping each present, being free of the limitations of a state of affairs, impersonal and preindividual, neutral, neither general nor particular."[133] It would appear that the representation of the "presubjective and preindividual" aspect of the event is common to each of the authors presently discussed.[134] However, by engaging the work of Macedonio Fernández, Piglia also invokes the ethical dimension of the Deleuzian event, where to act ethically is "to become worthy of what happens to us, and thus to will and release the event, to become the offspring of one's own events, and thereby to be reborn, to have one more birth, and to break with one's carnal birth—to become the offspring of one's events and not of one's actions, for the action is itself produced by the offspring of the event."[135] Constantin V. Boundas explains this idea by writing that "the ethics of the event presupposes a will that seeks in the state of affairs the eternal truth of events," which is to say a will that does not accept "the actual state of affairs" but attempts to engage the event's virtual component in order to affect "the 'counteractualization' of the actual."[136] We have seen that the story machine generates resistance to the fictional state Piglia describes by engendering paranoid rumor. However, as in the work of Fernández, Piglia's political critique is inseparably linked to his philosophical exploration of time, and the proliferation of narratives that transpire in the future-oriented Aion can be understood as counteracting the *actual* states of affairs of Argentine history at the moment Piglia publishes his novel. As previously discussed, the text constitutes a metastable chaosmos permanently between the second and third syntheses of time, yet the moment of actualization of the eternal return is displaced and absent from the text itself, and this is precisely the point. When Piglia asserts that the "teoría del Eterno Retorno puede ser vista como una descripción del efecto de memoria falsa *que produce la lectura*" (theory of the Eternal Return can be seen as a description of the effect of false memory *that reading produces*), he suggests that, far from being a unique property of his writing machine in *La ciudad ausente*, this is the general condition of literature.[137] Page acknowledges much the same argument when she suggests that Piglia's use of memory implantation is derived from the "ability of literature to embed itself into the memory of the reader" and thus suggests that "for Piglia, literature does not ultimately derive from (record or comment on) the past experience of the author *but creates future experiences for the reader*, becoming not so much an archive of the past as a laboratory of the future."[138] This aspect of Piglia's novel can also be traced back to the political component of Fernández's masterwork. As Garth acknowledges, Fernández's last novel is presented as "a Museum" and while "its value lies in its capacity to inspire radical change, . . . it alone cannot effect that change."[139] When we remember that Deleuze also argues that the purpose of literature is to "sow the seeds of, or even engender, the people to come," it would appear that Fernández and Deleuze share this conception of political literature.[140] In addition, Piglia demonstrates a similar preoccupation elsewhere in his critical work.

In interviews Piglia has argued that literature always contains "un fundamento utópico" (a utopic foundation).[141] The statement is potentially unexpected, as his work frequently references repression and suffering, and it is further complicated when he states that for him "utopía" (utopia) is evocative of "revolución" (revolution) and that in Argentina the revolution still has to be realized before one can talk about politics.[142] I would suggest that Jacques Rancière's interpretation of the avant-garde potentially resolves the difficulty. For Rancière "the very idea of a political avant-garde is divided between the strategic conception and the aesthetic conception of the avant-garde," where the former implies "a form of political intelligence that sums up the essential conditions for change" while the latter entails "the invention of sensible forms and material structures for a life to come."[143] In my interpretation of Piglia, the latter appears to be the prior condition of the former. In *La ciudad ausente* Piglia describes "the actual state of affairs" of the new oppressive politics arising from the transition to democracy and the opening of the Argentine economy, and in the main narrative of the novel he demonstrates how literature can become a tool that engenders resistance, but the final act of resistance must take place outside the confines of the text. As in Deleuze's description of political literature, Piglia's "literary machine thus becomes the relay for a revolutionary machine-to-come," which must be constructed by his audience to confront the reality of the neoliberal Argentine state.[144] It is in this way that *La ciudad ausente* can be considered a perpetual act of resistance in itself: it permanently threatens to induce an act of resistance but requires a further intervention to actualize this virtual possibility.

In his exploration of Macedonio Fernández's *Museo de la Novela de la Eterna*, Garth acknowledges that the "very premise" of the text is that it constitutes "La Primera Novela Buena" (The First Good Novel), while "its companion *Adriana Buenos Aires*" forms "La Última Novela Mala" (The Last Bad Novel).[145] Garth further elaborates the contrast between the two texts, explaining that "*Adriana* reveals much of what is wrong with the world, or rather with *Buenos Aires*, in terms accessible to people that Macedonio projects as contemporary readers" but equally reveals that "its own aesthetics are incapable of addressing those ills."[146] I would suggest that the relationship established between *Respiración artificial* and *La ciudad ausente* in the last two chapters conforms to the same model. *Respiración artificial* articulates the origins and nature of "what is wrong with the world," and while it indicates a potential solution to the problems encountered, "its own aesthetics are incapable of addressing those ills." Through the experimental structure of *La ciudad ausente*, however, Piglia overcomes those same problems and wills the Deleuzian event in an attempt "to become worthy" of the reality that surrounds him. Coincidentally, I would also propose that equating *Respiración artificial* with Macedonio's "Última Novela Mala" (Last Bad Novel) suggests a possible means of reconciling my analysis of the text with Aira's assertion that it is "una de las peores novelas de su generación" (one of the worst novels of his generation).[147]

The correspondence between Aira's and Kafka's stories and between Cohen's and Kafka's unfinished novels having been established, we must now connect Piglia's literature with the final component of the Kafka machine Deleuze and Guattari defined: the letters. Not only will this analysis complete the description of the literary machine collectively constructed by the three writers, but as it develops it will become clear that rather than serving as a historical connection between Aira and Cohen, Piglia's work can be considered the twist in the Möbius strip that returns all the authors to a single plane of immanence. For Deleuze and Guattari Kafka's letters "are an integrative part of the writing machine" and help us to understand "why certain literary forms as the novel have naturally made use of the epistolary form."[148] The connection with Piglia's work is immediately apparent, as despite Marcelo Maggi's assertion that "correspondencia, en el fondo, es un género anacrónico" (correspondence is, in essence, an anachronistic genre), *Respiración artificial* also takes the form of an epistolary novel.[149] Moreover, when Maggi asserts that the epistolary novel "necesita la distancia y de la ausencia para prosperar" (requires distance and absence in order to flourish), a connection can also be made with *La ciudad ausente*.[150] As Deleuze and Guattari note, "Kafka distinguishes two series of technical inventions: those that tend to restore natural communication by triumphing over distances and bringing people together (the train, the car, the airplane), and those that represent the vampirish revenge of the phantom where there is reintroduced 'the ghostly element between people' (the post, the telegraph, the telephone, wireless telegraphy)."[151] As in Renzi's analysis, communication for Kafka is predicated upon an essential distance and reciprocal absence between the two correspondents.

La ciudad ausente is based on similar methods of communication. For example, early in the text Renzi comments that Junior's father habitually listened to BBC broadcasts from London, and this reminds him of "los tiempos de la resistencia" (the times of resistance) when his own father listened to "las cintas de Perón" (the tapes from Perón), sent from exile and smuggled into Argentina.[152] As the story progresses, Junior receives anonymous, enigmatic, and secretive phone calls that divulge clues for him to follow in his quest to discover the origin of the machine, and the novel itself is sustained by the stories the machine produces, which constitute another form of communication predicated on distance and absence. The machine's stories, Perón's tapes, and Enrique Ossorio's letters in *Respiración artificial* all suggest a potential political use of an essentially epistolary form of writing, but as in Kafka's letters the first connection between these elements is that they "suponen una distancia no sólo espacial, sino también temporal, entre los personajes" (imply a distance, not only spatial, but also temporal, between the characters), as Roberto Echavarren notes of the letters in *Respiración artificial*.[153] Indeed, as we shall now see, it is in fact the inclusion of this temporal element that explains why Piglia's novels "have naturally made use of the epistolary form" to convey their political content.[154]

As Echavarren continues his discussion of the epistolary form of Piglia's *Respiración artificial*, he argues that it is "la separación misma" (separation itself) and the "no inmediatez entre emisor y receptor" (lack of immediacy between transmitter and receiver) that allow the letters to function as a metaphor for "el exilio y la utopía" (exile and utopia).[155] Indeed, within the text Enrique explains that his own utopic novel utilizes the epistolary form because to send a letter is to "enviar un mensaje al futuro" (send a message to the future) and is thus the utopic form of conversation because it "anula el presente y hace el futuro el único lugar posible del diálogo" (nullifies the present and makes the future the only possible location for dialogue).[156] These comments could also be applied to *La ciudad ausente*, and Piglia's motivation for using communication predicated on distance and absence becomes clear: he exploits the temporal gap introduced by the epistolary form (whether materialized in letters, phone calls, or the circulating texts produced by the machine) in order to construct literature oriented toward the future. This is first attempted in *Respiración artificial* to escape the brute repetitions of political violence but only reaches fruition in *La ciudad ausente* through the willing of the Deleuzian event. When Enrique claims that "el exilio es la utopía" (exile is utopia) and Maggi asserts that "*el exilio es como un largo insomnio*" (exile is like a long bout of insomnia), a crucial connection with Cohen also emerges.[157]

While living in voluntary exile in Spain, Cohen composed a novel titled *Insomnio* that, as established in chapter 3, features characters who endure an *inverted* exile as they are forced to remain in the city of Krámer, which has been encircled by a foreign military.[158] The connection may be coincidental, but it leads to a profound realization: an important component of Cohen's literary project is also found in *Respiración artificial*. Echavarren summarizes Enrique's vision of utopic literature by explaining that "la literariedad sería un resultado del exilio, y la escritura el espacio utópico que puebla el exiliado" (literariness would be a result of exile, and writing the utopic space in which the exile lives).[159] In the work of Cohen, the literary may still be the result of exile, but writing becomes the *dystopic* space that the exile inhabits. Despite the strong correlation previously noted between Cohen's texts and *La ciudad ausente*, it now becomes clear that the epistolary and utopic element of *Respiración artificial* represents, in nascent form, the very method by which Cohen describes the diabolical powers to come of neoliberal capitalism. Thus Piglia's epistolary texts contain an "insufficiently utilized and . . . ineffective" version of a technique that will be employed effectively in Cohen's novels, much as Deleuze and Guattari argue Kafka's letters contain an incipient form of the strategies that will only be adequately developed in his unfinished novels.[160] It would appear that as in Deleuze and Guattari's analysis of Kafka, Piglia's letters "are an indispensable gear, a motor part for the literary machine" that has been elaborated throughout the preceding chapters.[161]

As Deleuze and Guattari continue their discussion of Kafka's letters, they argue that in general letters "maintain a duality of . . . two subjects," namely, "a subject of enunciation as the form of expression that writes the letter, and a subject of the statement that is the form of content that the letter is speaking about (even if *I* speak about *me*)." Subsequently, Deleuze and Guattari contend that Kafka puts this duality "to a perverse or diabolical use," as "instead of the subject of enunciation using the letter to recount his own situation, it is the subject of the statement that will take on a whole movement that has become fictive or no more than superficial. It is the sending of the letter, the trajectory of the letter, the gestures of the postman that will take the place of the subject of enunciation's recounting."[162] For Deleuze and Guattari, this separation of the subject of enunciation from the subject of the statement is another method by which the letters form an "integrative part of the writing machine," as it will develop a political resonance more fully elaborated elsewhere in Kafka's oeuvre.[163] Deleuze and Guattari argue that throughout Kafka's literary output, there "isn't a subject who emits the statement or a subject about which the statement would be emitted" but rather that statements occur "necessarily as a function of a national, political, and social community, even if the objective conditions of this community are not yet given to the moment except in literary enunciation."[164] The point is that, due to their very form, the letters begin to eliminate the subject of enunciation and displace the subject of the statement. According to Deleuze and Guattari this is the first step in a process that disassembles both subjects across Kafka's work and allows subjectless statements to proliferate. It is by this mechanism, they argue, that "the literary machine thus becomes the relay for a revolutionary machine-to-come, not at all for ideological reasons but because the literary machine alone is determined to fill the conditions of a collective enunciation that is lacking elsewhere in this milieu."[165] Thus Kafka can be considered as a "prophet of a future world" in a new way.[166] Not only does Kafka describe the diabolical powers to come of fascism, Stalinism, and capitalism, but beginning with his letters he exploits a temporal gap to construct subjectless statements oriented toward the future that encapsulate "a revolutionary machine-to-come." The connection between Piglia's novels and Kafka's letters is now palpable: both Enrique's letters and Elena's stories are directed toward the future to construct a revolutionary machine-to-come among their audience. Moreover, a new connection with the work of Cohen has also come to light, as he too explores the potential of subjectless statements to foment revolutionary inclinations within the society of control. As discussed in chapter 3, in *Insomnio* Ezequiel comes to embody Foucauldian statements extracted from the text of Ecclesiastes, in which "the position of the subject can be assigned," in order to effectuate his own act of resistance.[167] Similarly, in chapter 4, we have seen that rumors essentially circulate as subjectless statements, which the inhabitants of Lorelei invest with significance in order to resist the oppressive regime that controls the world of *El oído absoluto*. Furthermore, a new explanation for the failure of these attempts is also clear. As in the work of Kafka, the problem is that "the people are what is missing."[168] Indeed, it is precisely "because the people are missing" that Cohen and Piglia are "in a situation of producing utterances which are already collective, which are like the seeds of the people to come, and whose political impact is immediate and inescapable."[169]

There remains one aspect of Kafka's letters that I have yet to discuss in relation to Piglia's oeuvre. I have not hitherto commented on the fact that, for Deleuze and Guattari, Kafka's letters "represent the vampirish revenge of the phantom."[170] As Deleuze and Guattari expand on this claim, they argue that Kafka's "is a perverse, diabolical utilization of the letter," as "there is always a woman behind these letters who is the real addressee" and thus the letters themselves constitute an attempt "to deterritorialize love. To substitute for the feared conjugal contract a pact with the devil." Ultimately, Deleuze and Guattari will argue that the letters "are this pact itself" and thus "pose directly, innocently, the diabolical power of the literary machine."[171] As we shall now see, a more thorough analysis of this vampiric, diabolical, and phantasmagorical contract with the devil will reveal an additional connection between Piglia's literary production and the work of Kafka. Furthermore, this analysis will necessarily introduce desire to the discussion of Piglia's oeuvre, a stratagem that will reciprocally return us to Aira and Cohen and complete the turn I am attempting to realize.

In the first instance it is important to remember that Kafka's diabolical pact is linked to the separation of the subject of the statement from the subject of the enunciation. In addition to our previous discussion, however, this process is intimately connected with desire. Deleuze and Guattari explain this connection by stating that

> Given their generic nature, the desire of the letters thus consists of the following: it transfers movement onto the subject of the statement; it gives the subject of the statement an apparent movement, an unreal movement, that spares the subject of enunciation all need for a real movement.
> . . . This exchange, or this reversal of the duality of the two subjects, the subject of the statement taking on that real movement that is normally the province of the subject of the enunciation, produces a doubling. And it is this doubling that is already diabolical; the devil is this very doubling.[172]

Thus there is a diabolical doubling of the subject; the subject of the statement liberated from the subject of enunciation gains movement through the epistolary form. A similar process can be observed in *La ciudad ausente*. As Teresa Orecchia Havas notes, "la problemática de la creación de autómatas" (the problem of the creation of automata) introduces the theme of the double and of "las maneras del desdoblamiento, con presencia de contenidos fantasmáticos que expresan el temor de que la creación afecte la unidad del yo creador, convirtiéndose en su *otro*, en una imagen idealizada o persecutorio de sí mismo" (the methods of splitting oneself in two, with the presence of phantasmagorical contents that express the fear that this creation will affect the unity of the "I" creator, converting him into his *other*, in an idealized or persecutory image of himself).[173] Although the doubling is related through a different mechanism (which is to say, through the use of automata) it serves a similar purpose as in Kafka's letters: it creates a fantastic double that haunts the original creator. When we remember that "there is always a woman behind" Kafka's letters and thus that the liberated statement is also a fragment of desire, the connection is further strengthened.[174] As Havas writes,

> La necesidad de alegorizar el misterio lingüístico y psicológico de la creación de literatura atrae aquí el motivo del objeto mecánico, dispositivo complejo y en cierta medida incontrolable, pero la *presión* fantasmática en torno a la gestación requiere una justificación ficcional de la parte *femenina* que intervendría en el proceso de la creación artística.[175]

> (The necessity of allegorizing the linguistic and psychological mystery of literary creation draws out the motive of the mechanical object, a complex and to a certain degree uncontrollable machine, but the phantasmagorical *pressure* on the gestation requires a fictional justification for the *feminine* role that would participate in the process of artistic creation.)

As in the case of Kafka's letters, the doubling represented in Piglia's novel through the creation of automata also entails a gendered aspect. This gendered component is, of course, represented most fully through the creation of the central story-producing machine, Elena. As discussed previously, beset by grief and unable to accept Elena Obieta's death, Macedonio Fernández decides to insert her memory into the translating machine to preserve her existence beyond her physical demise. When we remember that for Deleuze and Guattari, Kafka "is Dracula" and that there "is a vampirism in the letters," a further possible connection between *La ciudad ausente*'s spectral machine and Kafka's letters begins to emerge.[176] In the first instance, vampirism, like Piglia's machine, extends life beyond death; however, a more careful consideration of Piglia's decision to gender his writing machine is necessary to fully explicate this relationship.

The exact motivation for or function of the gendering of Piglia's story-producing machine remains contested in existent criticism. For example, Cristina Iglesia reads this gendered aspect in a positive light, arguing that "Elena es *la máquina de defensa femenina contra las experiencias y los experimentos y las mentiras del Estado*" (Elena is *the feminine machine of defense against the experiences and the experiments and the lies of the State*), which can be related to the work of "*las Madres de la Plaza*" (*the Mothers of the Plaza*), who were able publicly to denounce the repression of the military government when others were not.[177] In an equally positive reading, Pampa Olga Arán suggests that Piglia's machine can be considered "un devenir mujer, una máquina de Guerra en el sentido deleuziano cuyos poderes son el secreto y el afecto, la potencia creadora y la metamorfosis continua" (a becoming-woman, a War machine in the Deleuzian sense whose powers are the secret and affect, creative potential and continual metamorphosis).[178] Having discussed becoming-other at length in relation to Aira and Cohen, Arán's reading is particularly appealing, and it is not my intention to undermine or challenge either Arán or Iglesia's interpretations. Indeed, these arguments clearly constitute another fruitful connection to and augmentation of my own discussion of Piglia's texts and their relation to the work of Aira and Cohen. However, several other critics introduce a more negative critical engagement with the feminization of Piglia's literary machine and, for our present discussion, these interpretations are more important. For instance, Neri Francisco Enrique Romero notes that Elena can be understood "como mujer original de la especie, fuente de seducción, transgresión y creación, *construida a partir de un sueño o un deseo masculino (el de un hombre solitario)*" (as the original woman of the species, source of seduction, transgression and creation, *created from a dream, or a masculine desire—that of a lonely man*), and Havas argues that Piglia's novel (at least in part) contains "una meditación sobre la relación entre el creador y su obra *que explora fantasmas masculinos*" (a meditation on the relationship between the creator and his work *that explores masculine specters*).[179] Immediately, a stronger connection with Deleuze and Guattari's Kafka "who drinks the blood of carnivorous humans" is apparent as these readings begin to suggest an interpretation in which male desire comes to the fore and exploits the woman at the heart of the machine.[180]

No one has gone further in pursuing this line of inquiry than Eva-Lynn Alicia Jagoe, in her essay "The Disembodied Machine: Matter, Femininity and Nation in Piglia's *La ciudad ausente*." Jagoe ultimately argues that Elena forms "a specular figure in a technophallic masculinist discourse that mirrors the male subject, allows it to double, and in the process of duplication, recognize itself."[181] Given our previous discussion, the vocabulary Jagoe uses cannot but call to mind the more sinister aspect of Kafka's vampiric desire represented by his letters. While Jagoe recognizes that the "gendered machine's role is powerful, a symbol of possibility, [and] of resistance," she nonetheless argues persuasively that the "metaphor of woman as machine, as storyteller, as deserted one, as object of passion, inheres in this mythmaking that leaves her no real action" and that the stories she produces "all revolve around a fetishized figure of the woman in bondage."[182] Clearly, it is at least possible to read Piglia's novel as founded upon and thoroughly saturated by male desire. Thus, in the case of both Kafka's letters and Piglia's novel, a gendered doubling is arguably enacted by a vampiric male desire. On the one hand, the epistolary form enables Kafka to liberate a fragment of desire for the female addressee through the doubling of the subject and the liberation of the statement. On the other, Piglia's use of automata engenders a process of doubling that reaches its apotheosis in the form of the feminine machine imbued with Fernández's desire for Elena. Following Fernández's death, this desire is liberated from its original subject and grants Elena a vampiric life beyond death while simultaneously feeding upon her.

Just as I have argued that while predominantly related to *La ciudad ausente*, an incipient version of Cohen's literary project can be found in *Respiración artificial*, I now contend that while predominantly related to *Respiración artificial*, Aira's literary project can also be encountered in miniature in *La ciudad ausente*. As we shall now see, in a certain sense Aira *is* Elena. Just as Elena was originally conceived as "una máquina de traducir" (a translation machine) that rapidly becomes "una máquina transformadora de historias" (a machine that transformed stories), which recycles the literary material entered into it and transforms it into new and fantastic stories,[183] Aira also "juega, destrozos y deleites mediante, con las reliquias de la cultura nacional, convirtiéndolas en materia de curiosidad, ensoñación, entretenimiento o despojo" (plays with delight and destruction, with the relics of national culture, converting them into objects of curiosity, fantasy, entertainment or plunder), as Nancy Fernández contends.[184] Aira's historical novels confirm this connection: just as Elena's stories contain numerous oblique references to real historical events, so too *Ema, la cautiva* mentions Adolfo Alsina and his strategy to confront the indigenous population, and in *La liebre* the historical figures Cafulcurá (who is also named in *Ema*), Juan Manuel de Rosas, and his daughter, Manuelita, appear as characters in the text, but their historical veracity is deformed in their representation. As *La ciudad ausente* develops, Piglia also informs the reader that "las historias se reproducían por todos lados, no pudieron pararla, relatos y relatos y relatos" (the stories reproduced everywhere, they couldn't stop it, stories and stories and stories), stressing the hyperproductivity of the machine.[185] This exponential growth in the number of stories circulating in society can be immediately related to Aira's own prolific literary production, an important part of the "huida hacia adelante" (flight forward), which demands that a writer should "seguir escribiendo hasta que no pueda más, hasta cuando empiece a chochear. Escribir hasta reventar y seguir escribiendo" (continue writing until he can't write anymore, until he begins to produce nonsense as a result of his senility. Write until he bursts and continue writing).[186]

Additionally, Fernández's desire to "anular la muerte" (nullify death) can also be found in Aira's writing.[187] Not only can *Ema, la cautiva* be read as an attempt to affect a stay of execution for the indigenous population of the Argentine pampa, but in each instance of the tendency toward destruction throughout Aira's novels, the impasse reached arguably "se deriva del relato como experiencia de supervivencia" (originates in the conception of the story as an experience of survival), as Contreras claims.[188] This idea is reinforced by Aira's own critical assertion that "un cuento sólo puede contarlo un sobreviviente" (a story can only be told by a survivor).[189] In this regard, it should be noted that even *El juego de los mundos* concludes with the resurrection of the idea of God.[190] A key difference emerges when we recall that the male desire that traps Elena in the machine is liberated in Aira and becomes uninhibited and schizophrenic. As we shall now see, however, a trace of this schizophrenic desire can also be found in Piglia's epistolary project.

In one of Enrique Ossorio's utopic letters contained within *Respiración artificial*, a girl identified only as Juana la loca (Juana the mad) writes to her brother, who is studying physics in England. Juana explains that she has been reading Freud and makes the aberrant statement that she will become a psychologist and marry her brother because incest seems "*muy* interesante, moderno, [y] pecaminoso" (*very* interesting, modern, [and] sinful).[191] As Deleuze and Guattari carefully dissect Kafka's oeuvre, they note that women in his texts "are part sister, part maid, part whore" and furthermore that they "are anticonjugal and antifamilial."[192] Deleuze and Guattari continue their investigation by tracing the appearances of such women through Kafka's stories before noting that the novels "multiply these women who in various ways reunite the qualities of sister, maid, and whore" and argue that "three qualities correspond to three components of the line of escape as well as to three degrees of freedom: freedom of movement, freedom of the statement, [and] freedom of desire."[193] However, they also argue that "none of these elements have any value by themselves" and that "all three are needed at the same time, in the same character if possible, in order to form the strange combination that Kafka so dreams about," which is to "take her for a maid, but also for a sister, and also for a whore" simultaneously. Deleuze and Guattari categorize this "combined formula" as "schizo-incest."[194] As Deleuze and Guattari continue their discussion of schizo-incest, they specifically oppose it to Oedipal incest. They argue that the latter is related to the mother, to territoriality, and ultimately to the "paranoiac transcendental law that prohibits it." In sharp contrast, they argue that schizo-incest is related to the sister "who is on the other side of the class struggle." For Deleuze and Guattari, where Oedipal incest "keeps everything within the limits of the family" and thus neutralizes "any sort of social or political field," schizo-incest allied with the sister "uses as an intermediary maids and whores and the place they occupy in the social series" to oppose the Oedipal triangle at a familial level and to connect to a marginalized political constituency with a view to contesting the "paranoiac transcendental law" at the societal level. In this way schizo-incest is related to deterritorialization and corresponds to "the immanent schizo-law," which is to say that it "forms a line of escape" with "a maximum of connection, [and] a polyvocal extension," as it necessarily connects with a far wider and multifaceted community.[195] Thus in one brief statement Piglia introduces an incipient form of the schizophrenic desire of real importance to Aira's oeuvre.

From the analysis detailed above, it now appears that each author under discussion appears to precede the others. Viewed from a historical perspective, Aira's work anticipates both Cohen and Piglia, as it is he who returns to and critiques both the advent of capitalism in the nineteenth century and the revolutionary fervor of the 1960s and 1970s in Argentina. Thus Aira provides the historical foundation for Cohen's and Piglia's respective philosophical critiques of capitalism and resistance. From the viewpoint of Piglia's literature, however, the order is altered. We have seen that Piglia's novels contain both a nascent version of Cohen's literary project and of Aira's literary process. This immediately disturbs the chronological sequence previously described and situates Piglia as antecedent to the other authors. In this regard, Piglia's brief suggestion of schizo-incest is particularly important. Not only does this concept oppose (or rather evade) the paranoiac transcendental law that Piglia has so carefully traced throughout *Respiración artificial*, but the schizophrenic form of desire it liberates is linked to class struggle on "the side of maids and whores." Thus it can be argued that Piglia's epistolary project also contains the first embryonic trace of the completely liberated desire that Aira will transform into a series of schizophrenic becomings-other, embodied most effectively in the socially excluded Mao and Lenin, who rail against the structures of neoliberal capitalism. As we have now seen, when the pursuit of such desire reaches its impasse, it is Cohen, in texts such as *Inolvidables veladas* and *Variedades*, who will then convert it into the capitalist machine that unites the political and libidinal economies. Crucially, as Deleuze and Guattari argue that such schizophrenic desire is immanent to the capitalist system itself, it is apparent that the functioning of Cohen's machine paradoxically results in the liberation of schizophrenic desire in the first instance. Thus Cohen's social assemblage becomes the necessary precursor to both Aira and Piglia's description of schizophrenic desire. It would appear that each of the authors precedes the others and the processes they describe are co-implicated and complementary. It appears that the twist in the Möbius strip is now complete. Yet, as I discuss in the conclusion, a more detailed analysis of the relationship between the three authors challenges this neat conclusion.

THE PLANE OF IMMANENCE

AT THE TURN OF THE NEW MILLENNIUM, PIGLIA PRESENTED A CON-
ference paper addressing "[el] problema del futuro de la literatura y de su
función" (the problem of the future of literature and its function), during
which he argued that "la experiencia del horror puro de la represión clandes-
tina, una experiencia que a menudo parece estar más allá de las palabras, quizá
define nuestro uso del lenguaje y nuestra relación con la memoria y por lo
tanto nuestra relación con el futuro y el sentido" (the experience of the pure
horror of clandestine repression, an experience that often seems to be beyond
words, perhaps defines our use of language and our relationship with memory
and, therefore, our relationship with the future and meaning).[1] I would suggest
that, despite their vastly different literary projects, this statement holds equally
true for Aira, Cohen, and Piglia. Even Cohen's voluntary exile from Argentina
during this period does not diminish its significance in his literature. Indeed,
it is arguably Cohen's lack of firsthand experience of the military dictatorship
or of the early years of the transition to democracy that allows him to describe
expeditiously and precisely the limits of the apparent freedoms gained during
the *primavera de los pueblos* (springtime of the peoples) apparently initiated
in 1983.[2] Living in postdictatorial Spain while news of the horrors taking

place in Argentina gradually reached him through visits and phone calls from friends, Cohen was conceivably able to distinguish more readily the remnants of the previous system still existent following the return to liberal democracy.[3] Regardless, the experience of repression weighs heavily on all three authors. Additionally, that the crimes of the so-called "Dirty War" are never directly addressed in their texts but appear tangentially through allusive fragments and images perfectly reflects an experience that is "más allá de las palabras" (beyond words).

It has also been shown that in his critical work Piglia proposes "un fundamento utópico" (a utopic foundation) for all literature.[4] In chapter 6 I argued that Piglia's unusual conception of utopía, which necessarily invokes revolución, can be considered in conjunction with Rancière's analysis of political and aesthetic avant-gardes.[5] Through this analysis I advanced the thesis that in Piglia's work "the invention of sensible forms and material structures for a life to come" always retains the potential to precipitate "a form of political intelligence that sums up the essential conditions for change."[6] This is to say that Piglia describes the actual nature of oppressive power structures and suggests methods for dismantling them but that the moment of revolutionary intervention itself is absent from his texts and becomes the responsibility of his audience. I would now suggest that this feature is also discernible in the work of each of the three authors discussed. Each examines the nature of society and attempts to define new methods to resist the "totalitarismos" (totalitarianisms) that they discover.[7] Across all the authors' work, political and structural violence is deeply interconnected and entangled with the development of neoliberal capitalism in Argentina and each author conducts further philosophical explorations to explain this connection. In each case, the author subsequently attempts to invent new ways of being that are inherently opposed to the philosophical systems they discover. Thus the revolutionary impetus to which Piglia alludes and the desire to confront radically both political violence and capitalism is exercised by all three authors through "the potentiality inherent in the innovative sensible modes of experience that anticipate a community to come," as in Rancière's analysis.[8]

While I contend that this strategy is common to Aira, Cohen, and Piglia, each utilizes it in a unique way befitting the context in which they write. Furthermore, it is possible to discern a clear chronological development that governs their deployment of this strategy, an imperfect yet sequential evolution of a common critique framed by a triangulation of factors: the experience of state terrorism, the development of neoliberal capitalism, and a conception of writing as resistance. Thus Aira invokes the revolutionary fervor epitomized by the Cordobazo and transforms it into a literary practice that, in texts such as *Ema, la cautiva* and *La prueba*, finds its origin and target in the capitalist development of Argentina. In turn, Piglia analyses the philosophical elements that sustained the military government during this period of exceptional violence and begins to describe the nascent forms of power that emerge during the transition to democracy. Piglia thus attempts to overcome the cogito, the Kantian conception of law, and the incipient control society by engaging a radically different conception of time. Subsequently, Cohen more thoroughly explores the philosophical nature of the transition to democracy and the limited freedoms it provides. Cohen describes the formation of the control society, first suggested by Piglia, examines the emergence of the media as a new technology of power that essentially replaces overt military violence as a method of coercion, and utilizes a proliferation of hyperreal images to obscure the methods of resistance described by Aira and Piglia. Cohen nonetheless attempts to discover new ways of resisting this advanced control society. I would suggest, however, that this neat thesis obscures the most profound yet enigmatic aspect of the investigation. Thus I have not organized my chapters in the order delineated above but have discussed Piglia's work after that of Aira and Cohen. This decision was made because, in *La ciudad ausente* in particular, Piglia describes an alternative philosophical framework through which the relationship between the three authors can be understood. Illustrating and elaborating this philosophical affiliation between the authors shall be the task undertaken in the remainder of the conclusion.

As Deleuze and Guattari summarize the component parts of Kafka's literary machine, they offer a brief description that perfectly captures the relationship I perceive between Aira, Cohen, and Piglia: "Here, then, are the three elements of the machine of writing or of expression insofar as they are defined by internal criteria, and not by publishing project. The letters and the diabolical pact; the stories and the becoming-animal; the novels and the machinic assemblages. Between these three elements, there is constant transversal communication, in one direction and another."[9] The close correspondence between each author and a specific element of the writing machine has now been explored in detail. Of particular importance is that the parts are linked "by internal criteria, and not by publishing project." It cannot be claimed that these three authors consciously share a common publishing or literary project, but I hope to have demonstrated that they can be linked by internal, philosophical, and political criteria. Furthermore, as in the case of Deleuze and Guattari's analysis of Kafka, "there is constant transversal communication" between the three authors. The literary output of each single author contributes to our understanding of the philosophical potential contained in the work of the other two. As in the case of Deleuze and Guattari's Kafka, this combinatory literary machine "moves in the direction of the unlimited rather than the fragmentary," and the resultant "oeuvre is complete yet heterogeneous: it is constructed from components that do not connect but are always in communication with each other." The literary machine constructed from the work of Aira, Cohen, and Piglia, like the "Kafka machine[,] is, paradoxically, one of continuous contiguity."[10] Ultimately, across the three authors' work, a clear description emerges of "the paranoiac transcendental law" that sustains contemporary Argentine capitalism and political violence. Similarly, an equally clear description of "the immanent schizo-law that functions like justice, an antilaw, a 'procedure' that will dismantle all the assemblages of the paranoiac law" also takes form, as ultimately "this is what it is all about—the discovery of assemblages of immanence and their dismantling."[11] By considering these three authors together it is possible to construct such a literary machine, a machine geared toward the immanent destruction of capitalism and political violence as they have manifested themselves in Argentina.

I am now in a position to describe more fully the contribution each individual author makes to the malleable relationship between them and to elucidate how the machine functions as a whole. In the discussion contained in the first two chapters, we have seen that Aira can be read politically. Where critics such as Contreras and Speranza provide a detailed explanation of Aira's literary process and his connection with Argentine literary history, they do not account for the potential political connotations of this same process. It can be argued that Aira's process is inherently political and that it constitutes a sustained critique of capitalism and political violence. This is first seen in *Ema, la cautiva*, which can be read as an indirect critique of the most recent military government, their systematic and extreme violence, and the origins of capitalism and political violence in nineteenth-century Argentina. Subsequently, I have argued that Aira's novel *La prueba* is paradigmatic of the political component of Aira's literary process. Through analysis of this text, I have argued that Aira's "huida hacia adelante" (flight forward) can be considered an exceptional example of a Badiouian truth-procedure in the field of art and that *La prueba* reflects the political correlate of this process: it identifies capitalism as the target of Aira's critique, transposes the revolutionary impetus of the *Cordobazo* to a moment of contemporary crisis, and unleashes the process of Deleuzian becoming-other that can be found throughout Aira's astonishing body of work. In this regard, it is interesting to note that Abraham suggests that Aira's prolific literary production (another essential component of his "huida hacia adelante") is a deliberate reaction against "la ley de los rendimientos decrecientes" (the law of diminishing returns) that he perceives in contemporary literature.[12] The interesting point is that this principle is derived from David Ricardo's analysis of capitalist economics and that in "La nueva escritura" Aira applies it to modernist literature, stating that "mientras Balzac escribió cincuenta novelas, y le sobró tiempo para vivir, Flaubert escribió cinco, desangrándose, Joyce escribió dos, Proust una sola" (while Balzac wrote fifty novels, and had enough time left over to live, Flaubert wrote five, bleeding to death; Joyce wrote two; Proust just one).[13] As discussed in chapter 2, the becomings-other that proliferate in Aira's work are also inherently political and, in the case of *La prueba*, are intimately connected with the process of schizophrenic subject formation which is both the product and limit of capitalism itself.

With regard to the larger literary machine, when the work of the other authors is viewed from the perspective of my analysis of Aira, a certain revolutionary impulse, mainly derived from the work of Badiou and his conception of the truth-procedure, comes to the fore. When we view the other authors' texts from this vantage point, these features are also emphasized, and a certain revolutionary praxis may be noted in their work. Each displays a consistent desire to write literature as a form of resistance. No less than in the work of Aira, these authors search for ways to resist the powerful systems they describe. Considering Piglia's and Cohen's use of the authorless text demonstrates that this inclination to resist can be understood through Badiou's philosophy. Both Cohen and Piglia explore the potential of authorless texts and statements to foment disquiet and unrest and become accessible to insurgency. In the works analyzed, then, Piglia accounts for the importance of the authorless text by asserting that in order to "construir consenso" (create consensus) the state "necesita construir historias, hacer creer cierta visión de los hechos" (needs to create stories, to make others believe a certain view of the facts) and that to counteract this tendency the writer ought to "establecer dónde está la verdad, actuar como un detective, descubrir el secreto que el Estado manipula, revelar esa verdad que está escamoteada" (establish where the truth is, act like a detective, discover the secret that the State manipulates, reveal the truth that is concealed).[14] This argument can easily be reframed in Badiouian terminology. As in the case of the truth-procedure, Piglia suggests that the seemingly absolute state of the situation masks a remainder that cannot be named within it and sees the writer's task as bringing this to light through an event (in this case the event would take the form of a written text). This process can equally be seen in Cohen. Both Cohen and Piglia describe the circulation of essentially authorless texts that come to be incarnated by certain characters who obtain subjectivity as they are led to political action. The texts remain authorless until this moment, perfectly reflecting the fact that within the state of the situation, the remainder cannot be named. With this in mind, it is important to note that as Bosteels argues, Piglia has deployed "the creative use of plagiarism" in his critical reflections on Borges by appropriating concepts that can be traced to Badiou's essay, "The Autonomy of the Aesthetic Process," which Piglia included in a volume he edited.[15] Yet it is ultimately Aira that describes an event that "represents . . . the general characteristics of what it takes to be an event."[16] While Cohen and Piglia concentrate their efforts on creating subjectless statements that will hopefully come to be fulfilled by a revolutionary people who are not yet present, Aira describes the generic process of subject formation through engagement with the unnamed remainder.

As we have seen in chapters 3 and 4, Cohen contributes a rather more sociological critique to the functioning of the literary machine. I have argued that Cohen's early work can be considered as a sociophilosophical reflection on the contemporary situation of Argentine politics and society. Where other critics have suggested that Cohen's literature is paradigmatic of Foucault's panoptic disciplinary society, I have instead argued that it describes the transition from disciplinary to control society, a movement equally perceptible in the Argentine society of the time.[17] I contend that Cohen explores the shifting nature of power relations engendered by the transition to democracy and the opening to the world economy in order to expose the continuing violence, manipulation, and coercion that still underpin the new system. Furthermore, I have argued that Cohen precisely describes the use of the mass media as a technology of power within the control society: it emits a series of hyperreal images and Baudrillardian simulacra that come to define the paradigm of the new social situation.

By viewing the other authors' work with the same critical perspective I applied to Cohen's early novels, the latent sociopolitical analysis contained in each becomes most prominent. Cohen's texts allusively describe the nature of power relations during the military dictatorship, note their development during the transition to democracy, and diagnose the establishment of the society of control and the manipulation of the mass media as a technology of power. Viewed from this perspective, it is the sociopolitical aspect of Aira's writing that is most pronounced. Particularly in *Ema, la cautiva*, Aira returns to and examines the initial establishment of capitalism (and its links to political violence) in Argentina and lays the historical foundation for the sociological argument Cohen presents. It is also under Cohen's influence that those sociological features of Piglia's novels emerge. Viewed from the perspective of Cohen's account of contemporary late capitalism, Piglia continues Aira's analysis of the establishment of a capitalist economy and its connection to political violence and projects it forward, tracing the history of political violence throughout the twentieth century in Argentina and representing it as a continuous development. This process culminates in an analysis of the philosophical processes that sustained the most recent military government and justified their systematic plan of state terrorism. Through this process Piglia identifies Kant's paranoiac transcendental law, sustained by his version of the cogito, as the root of the problem.[18] Moreover, Piglia also suggests a similar sociological development of power relations under military rule in *Respiración artificial* as Cohen does in his novels, and he begins to describe the society of control in *La ciudad ausente* (albeit in a less explicit and total manner than Cohen).[19] Piglia also discusses the importance of the media as a technology of power and lays the foundation for Cohen's analysis of neoliberal capitalism and the new paradigm of control and simulation. Thus Cohen's work is central in developing the historical and chronological critique that I have argued is shared by the three authors. However, it is also Cohen who provides the most complete description of the functioning of neoliberal capitalism, whereby political and libidinal economies are united, precipitating the schizophrenic pursuit of desire in Aira's work.

Finally we come to the case of Piglia. In chapters 5 and 6, I argued that Piglia's work is eminently Deleuzian, that it "is characterized by the total absence of negation," and that it can be considered as "the bearer of an affirmation without reserve."[20] This statement may initially seem more akin to Aira than to Piglia, particularly as Piglia has expressly stated that the "conciencia artística y la conciencia revolucionaria se identifican por su negatividad" (artistic consciousness and revolutionary consciousness are identified by their negativity), and many critics have argued that there is a fundamental opposition between Aira's tendency toward proliferation and Piglia's affirmation of negativity.[21] However, just as Contreras argues that Aira's literature constitutes "una singular transmutación de la negatividad en afirmación" (a singular transmutation of negativity into affirmation), so too I would suggest that in both *Respiración artificial* and *La ciudad ausente* Piglia engages a conception of negativity most closely connected to Deleuze's reading of Nietzsche and the concept of the eternal return.[22] As in the case of Deleuze's philosophy, in Piglia's writing:

> strong reactive forces are subsequently *incorporated* into the eternal return in order to effect the overcoming of negation and the transformation of reactive into active force. Such revaluation takes place because the eternal return brings the nihilistic will to completion: the absolute spirit of negation involves a negation of reactive forces themselves. Within this negation of negation reactive forces deny and suppress themselves in the name of a paradoxical affirmation: by destroying the reactive in themselves, the strongest spirits come to embody the becoming-active of reactive forces.[23]

I contend that in their discussion of Piglian negativity as counterpoint to Aira's literary oeuvre, Contreras and Galiazo overlook the fact that Piglia engages the work of Joyce and Borges in a remarkably similar way to Deleuze in developing his philosophy of the eternal return, which they apply to Aira's literary output. By extension, such critics fail to account for the fact that Piglia's literary technique can also be considered inherently creative and constituted of "la negación de la negación" (the negation of negation), which they correctly identify in the work of Aira.[24] In my own discussion of each author's writing, this can perhaps be most clearly seen by considering my argument that Aira's literary process constitutes a Badiouian truth-procedure in the field of art. As previously stated, the "terrorist commandment" for the militant of a truth-procedure is taken from Beckett's *The Unnamable* and "is summed up in the famous last words of the text: 'You must go on, I can't go on, I'll go on.'"[25] With this in mind it is imperative to remember that Piglia has categorically stated that Beckett is the embodiment of his theory of "negatividad" (negativity).[26] Thus I propose that the series of literary oppositions that have been erected between Piglia and Aira are ultimately overcome when one considers that each author attempts to extend the eternal return to its Deleuzian conclusion: the production of the absolutely different and the new.

Surprisingly, this also bring us to Piglia's unique contribution to the literary machine: his consistent experimentation with different conceptions of time in an attempt to extract a maximum of difference from the strictest of repetition. Piglia, more completely than the other authors, describes the unending process of becoming (the ceaseless production of difference through repetition) and engages it in an attempt to precipitate political action by willing the Deleuzian event. It is this element that comes to the fore when the other authors' writing is viewed from the Piglian perspective. It is from this viewpoint that the schizophrenic becomings-other described by Aira can be more fully understood and his tendency toward hyper-productivity recognized as another manifestation of this process. Similarly, by exploring this Deleuzian process in greater detail, the consistent attempts to reengage the process of becoming that has been almost entirely obscured by the production of Baudrillardian hyperreal images in the work of Cohen can be better perceived. Furthermore, it becomes apparent that such hyperreal images form a particular subset that imitates the very model of the immanent Deleuzian image. Finally, it is important to note that Piglia's work is especially significant: not only does it contain in miniature elements of both Aira's and Cohen's literary projects (insofar as a nascent form of Cohen's exile literature can be found in *Respiración artificial* and Elena can be considered to embody Aira), but it encourages a way of reading that has guided the analysis throughout. Due to the aleph-like structure of *La ciudad ausente*, the fact that it contains elements from seemingly innumerable other texts and histories and can seem to constitute (like *Finnegans Wake* and *Museo de la Novela de la Eterna* before it) an almost total text, as well as Tardewski's assertion in *Respiración artificial* that "para leer . . . hay que saber asociar" (in order to read . . . one must know how to associate), Piglia's work almost demands to be read by free association.[27] Piglia's writing allows and encourages the reader to link it freely with innumerable other texts, whether the author was conscious of the possibility or not. *La ciudad ausente* essentially encourages the Deleuzian and productive method of reading, outlined in the introduction, that has guided the construction of the present study.

I have now delineated many features of the complex web of interconnecting elements between the work of Aira, Cohen, and Piglia within a single literary machine (though there are undoubtedly others yet to be defined). In discussing the work of Kafka, Deleuze and Guattari note that in contrast to the familial Oedipal triangle, "the other triangles that surge up behind it have something malleable, diffuse, a perpetual transformation from one triangle to another, either because one of the terms or points begins to proliferate, or because the sides of the triangle don't stop deforming."[28] I have attempted to mirror this in the construction of the present text and have produced a number (if not a proliferation) of triangles behind the original trio of Aira, Cohen, and Piglia and their corresponding zones of intensity or plateaus. Thus there is the triangulation of the experience of political violence, the development of neoliberal capitalism in Argentina, and the conception of writing as resistance; the structure of Aira's "tres fechas"; the three elements of the Kafka machine and the corresponding three freedoms they produce. In each case, the triangles formed produce relations that are malleable, diffuse, and continually deforming. As Deleuze and Guattari continue this discussion, they state that "by making triangles transform until they become unlimited, by proliferating doubles until they become indefinite, Kafka opens up a field of immanence that will function as a dismantling, an analysis, a prognostics of social forces and currents, of the forces that in his epoch are only beginning to knock on the door (literature has a sense only if the machine of expression precedes and anticipates contents)."[29] So too in the literary machine I have been describing the triangles and doubles multiply, producing something of a fractal proliferation of connections between the three authors that tend toward the unlimited. These connections that conform, contrast, converge, and bifurcate cumulatively provide a prognosis of the "social forces and currents" that permeate Argentine society. John Marks summarizes Deleuze and Guattari's argument by stating that the "tendency of Kafka's work towards proliferation opens up a field of immanence that takes his social and political analysis out of the domain of the actual and into the virtual," perfectly encapsulating the process we have seen function in the work of Aira, Cohen, and Piglia.[30] We can observe this movement from the actual to the virtual in Aira's movement from hyperproductivity to the innumerable animalistic becomings-monstrous that he describes, in the continual attempts to uncover the process of becoming in Cohen, and in the decoupling of the eternal return to produce the absolutely different in Piglia. While this movement may tend toward the abstract and the abstruse, it is important to remember that within the Deleuzian conception of the real, the virtual and the actual are equally real, necessary, and mutually dependent. So too in my own analysis, the more profound connection I have been describing does not in any way undermine or contradict my first linear and chronological analysis. It is rather that my linear analysis conforms to the actual states of affairs within Argentina while the more profound connection complies with the Deleuzian virtual and tends toward a plane of immanence. As Deleuze describes the plane of immanence, he writes that it

> is the movement (the facet of movement) which is established between the parts of each system and between one system and another, which crosses them all, stirs them all up together and subjects them all to the condition which prevents them from being absolutely closed. . . . It is a bloc of space-time, since the time of movement which is at work within it is part of it every time. There is even an infinite series of such blocs or mobile sections which will be, as it were, so many presentations of the plane, corresponding to the succession of movements in the universe. And the plane is not distinct from this presentation of planes. This is not mechanism, it is machinism.[31]

This is to say that it is in the plane of immanence that the polyphony inherent to the univocity of being is revealed. Between these three authors and their textual systems there is continual movement that crosses them, mixes them, and prevents them from being absolutely closed to one another. Thus we can state that all three authors open up a field of immanence similar to that produced by Kafka. Or rather, continuing with the tripartite multiplication previously described, there are *three* interconnected, entangled, and mutually dependent planes of immanence that emerge from the literary machine constructed by Aira, Cohen, and Piglia.

In the first instance, I want to propose that this literary machine seeks to convert the Argentine nation itself into a plane of immanence. In the introduction, I invoked Doreen Massey's description of space "as a simultaneity of stories-so-far" and places as "collections of those stories" in order to account for the continuing usefulness of the idea of the "nation."[32] The relevance of these arguments is immediately apparent given Piglia's overt focus on the destructive effects of the stories related by the state in order to generate consensus and the consistent attempts each author makes to produce counternarratives as a form of resistance. Nonetheless, the applicability of Massey's concept goes much further than this. In defining place in the aforementioned manner, Massey seeks to defend the concept from "essentialising" definitions that would represent "a protective pulling-up of drawbridges," a "denial," and an "attempted withdrawal from invasion/difference."[33] Such conceptions are readily identifiable in the actions of the various military governments that held power during the twentieth century in Argentina. As we have seen in chapter 2, the ultra-conservative dictator Juan Carlos Onganía sought to create an essential idea of the nation and branded all those outside a narrow conception of the healthy citizen as "subversives." Similarly, members of the most recent dictatorship sought "to promote themselves as guarantors of security, order, progress, and national pride" and, imbued with a "restrictive set of values based around a capitalist-Christian worldview," branded supposed subversives as "the descendants of 'Indians and foreigners.'"[34] This is to say that for the military government political radicals and subversives did not belong to the nation at all, and they sustained themselves in power through the dissemination of narratives that, as Piglia notes, posited the dictatorship as the only surgeon capable of intervening and saving the extremely sick body-politic of the nation.[35]

Nonetheless, to counteract this tendency, Aira, Cohen, and Piglia do not seek to impose a new master narrative to overcode the various dictatorships' essentialized conception of the nation. Rather, the stories they tell invariably tend toward proliferation and incorporate innumerable national and international references in order to produce an image of the nation as a series of "temporary constellations where the repercussions of a multiplicity of histories have been woven together."[36] This is to say that the literary machine I am describing is both polyvocal and polyphonic. Moreover, and as is particularly clear in the work of Aira and Piglia, several of these stories are logically incompatible or mutually contradictory. As in Massey's work, then, rather than a privileged site of internal coherence, Argentina itself becomes the focal point for "the meeting and the nonmeeting of the previously unrelated and thus integral to the generation of novelty."[37] Massey's argument that places should be understood as *spatio-temporal events* is also reflected in my proposal that each author engages the Deleuzian event in order to respond to, and transform, the specific historical conditions encountered in Argentina.[38] Moreover, this description returns us once more to Deleuze's description of the plane of immanence as "a bloc of space-time."[39] Ultimately, to borrow a phrase from

Cohen, each of these authors creates an image of Argentina as "un *lugar*, compuesto y autosuficiente . . . pero con un lado abierto al desorden" (a *place*, complex and self-sufficient . . . but with one side open to disorder) in order to create a conception of the nation as a plane of immanence defined by the production of difference and novelty rather than as a closed site of internal division and exclusion.[40]

It should also be recognized, however, that in novels such as Piglia's *Respiración artificial* and Cohen's *El oído absoluto* and *Variedades*, the authors project their vision of Argentina into the future, and the nation undergoes another definitive transformation. In Cohen's work in particular, it is "capitalism [that] appropriates production and becomes 'the new social full body,' characterized by a generalized decoding and becoming-immanent" through the generation of a seemingly infinite series of hyperreal images.[41] As we have seen, in this vision of the future, previous methods of resistance become obscured or, worse still, become the very method of control itself.[42] This is a possibility that Guattari also recognizes, arguing that it is "capitalism itself [that] is now beginning to shatter into animist and machinic polyvocity."[43] This is to say that in the work of Cohen and Piglia, capitalism too is becoming a plane of immanence, and the state plays only a minor role in exercising power and controlling individuals. This development is equally reminiscent of Guattari's description of Integrated World Capitalism (IWC), which "tends increasingly to decentre its sites of power" such that it becomes "delocalized and deterritorilized, both in extension, by extending its influence over the whole social, economic and cultural life of the planet, and in 'intension,' by infiltrating the most unconscious subjective strata."[44] Such a description is readily identified in Cohen's novels, where power and control are exercised globally and those trapped in the system face a terrible destruction of their own subjectivity. Indeed, several of the features that Cohen and Piglia describe in their future societies are also found in Guattari's analysis of Integrated World Capitalism. For example, Guattari proposes that the threat of nuclear terror is found at the heart of IWC, just as I proposed that Cohen's novels, as in the work León Rozitchner, demonstrate that the threat of dictatorial terror is the means by which this new form of capitalism was implemented in Argentina.[45] In addition, Guattari proposes that in its new formation, capitalism has "an increased capacity for the machinic integration of all human activities and faculties," such that "the remaining private sphere family, personal life, free time, and perhaps even fantasy and dreams" are "subjected to the semiotics of capital."[46] So too in Cohen's novels the characters' private and social lives, their desires, and even their remonstrations are always already accounted for in the capitalist system. Moreover, Guattari argues that it was the new forms of subjectivity that emerged following the uprisings of 1968 that produced these alterations in capitalism, just as the capitalist system that Cohen describes is modeled on the immanent process of becoming that provide the primary form of resistance in the work of Aira.[47] Crucially, Guattari also argues that "IWC's most potent weapon for achieving social control without violence is the mass media," just as it is in the work of Cohen and Piglia.[48] For Guattari people are now "mentally manipulated through the production of a collective, mass-media subjectivity" in ways that are particularly resonant with the work of the Argentine authors.[49] As regards Piglia Guattari proposes that the "mass media creates a climate of unquestioning passivity" and that television exercises "an efficiency that goes far beyond old institutions" in homogenizing subjectivity.[50] As I demonstrated in chapter 6, *La ciudad ausente* describes the manipulation of televisual broadcasts to exercise control in a manner akin to Bernard Stiegler's psycho-power. Regarding Cohen, the correspondence is arguably closer still given that Guattari proposes that "capitalistic subjectivity seeks to gain power by controlling and neutralizing the maximum number of existential refrains," understood as those processes that mark "the intersection of heterogeneous modes of subjectivation."[51] As we have seen in *El oído absoluto*, the process of asubjective subjectification that Lotario attempts to engage by becoming-music is essentially blocked by Campomanes's simplistic *boleros*, which become "una máquina de crear complicidad" (a machine for creating complicity).[52] Campomanes's music essentially homogenizes the process of artistic subjectivation by creating solitary fascistic refrains. Given the seemingly inescapable nature of the capitalist plane of immanence, the question (as always) is what becomes of resistance in this new situation. The answer is that the authors produce a further plane of immanence, a polyphonic machine, that ceaselessly resists capitalist control.

As I have argued throughout, the work of each author discussed is singular and complete but open to disorder. The works of Aira, Cohen, and Piglia share innumerable machinic connections that cumulatively construct a virtual chaosmos of continual communication and transformation. Moreover, they produce an immanent critique of capitalism and political violence and trace a line of escape that forms a productive and future-oriented form of resistance. In Guattari's description of Integrated World Capitalism, he argues that it produces decentralized polyphony but that it concurrently limits and homogenizes the processes of subjectivation. For this reason he proposes that in the current situation, the "micropolitical problem is how we reproduce (or don't reproduce) the dominant modes of subjectivation."[53] Given Deleuze and Guattari's continual assault on conceptions of unified subjectivity, however, he somewhat surprisingly goes on to argue that now "machines of revolutionary struggle are themselves obliged to become disposed for producing new social realities and *new subjectivities*."⁵⁴ It would appear that this mode of resistance is incompatible with the literary machine under discussion. Aira, Cohen, and Piglia also consistently seek to undermine subjectivity throughout the novels discussed. Nonetheless, the applicability of Guattari's argument is clear when it is remembered that this form of revolutionary struggle necessitates the development of "collective and/or individual *processes of singularization*" in order to uncover "the creativity proper to subjective mutations."⁵⁵ Each Argentine author negates traditional notions of subjectivity but equally affirms new forms of becoming-singular that are testament to "our legitimate difference both from each other and from a notional "Self,"" a process that Guattari terms "heterogenesis."⁵⁶ By engaging processes of Deleuzian becoming, individual characters in all of the authors' work discover that "subjectivity is plural *polyphonic*," and collectively Aira, Cohen, and Piglia unearth a "polyphony of modes of subjectivation."⁵⁷ Moreover, it is through this internal, spiritual experimentation that the Argentine authors reveal the third plane of immanence in perpetual resistance to the capitalist system.

Within Guattari's analysis of resistance within the constraints of Integrated World Capitalism, he proposes that it "requires the collective production of unpredictable and untamed 'dissident subjectivities' rather than a mass movement of like-minded people."⁵⁸ Such collectives necessarily invoke a multiplicity of singularities and form "a movement with multiple heads and a proliferating organization."⁵⁹ Evidently, Aira, Cohen, and Piglia also produce dissensus in order to convert their experiments with subjectivity into acts of resistance. In *La prueba* Mao and Lenin radically oppose the capitalist system in the most violent way imaginable, and the novel concludes with Marcia joining the group and establishing a new collectivity defined only by its internal differences.⁶⁰ In Cohen's texts, meanwhile, the characters undergo profound processes of becoming that lead them to withdraw their consent in defiant acts of civil disobedience. Moreover, these acts invariably lead the characters to form new communities with those around them. Following his experience of becoming-imperceptible in the sea, Sergio in "La ilusión monarca" returns to the prison and seeks out a fellow prisoner in an act of solidarity. In *Insomnio* it is following his encounter with pure difference that Ezequiel refuses to leave Krámer and constructs a new community with a small band of fellow survivors. Even in *Variedades*, following his various ordeals, the narrator forms a relationship with a young man he treats like a son. In each case, the characters form a "nucleus, however small, of militancy and of subjectivity-in-progress," just as in Guattari's model of resistance.⁶¹ Piglia approaches the task in a different manner. Through Elena, the writing machine in *La ciudad ausente*, the subjective becomes textual, and it is the written work itself that forms a multiplicity, a generative collectivity of innumerable singularities designed to act on the reader. And so too in the wider polyphonic machine I have been describing. Cumulatively, Aira, Piglia, and Cohen oppose the forces of power by constructing texts that form machinic connections to produce a final plane of immanence: that between the works themselves. Forming a new collective of discrete singularities, they describe the situation of contemporary capitalism and reinvent the Argentine nation in order to resist its homogenizing tendencies through the proliferation of difference. Yet the final act of resistance is off the page. They make suggestions, but ultimately it is the reader who must actualize these virtual possibilities. In the end, the polyphonic machine uncovers a plane of immanence that forms a future-oriented and immanent revolutionary potential to be realized by a people yet to come.

NOTES

Introduction: Capitalism, Political Violence, and Resistance in Contemporary Argentine Literature

1. Michel Foucault, "What Is an Author?," in *The Norton Anthology of Theory and Criticism*, ed. Vincent B. Leitch (New York: Norton, 2001).

2. Ricardo Piglia, *Nombre falso* (Buenos Aires: Seix Barral, 1994); Ricardo Piglia, *Crítica y ficción* (Buenos Aires: Siglo Veinte, 1993), 164. This question emerges in Piglia's critical work from the outset as evidenced by the editorial he scribed for the short-lived journal *Literatura y Sociedad* in 1965. As Piglia explains in his diary, only one issue of the journal was ever produced because the coup led by General Juan Carlos Onganía in 1966 prevented publication of further editions. See Ricardo Piglia, "Literatura y sociedad," *Literatura y sociedad* 1 (1965); Ricardo Piglia, *Los diarios de Emilio Renzi: años de formación* (Barcelona: Anagrama, 2015), 256 (hereafter *Años de formación*).

3. References to Foucault are found at several points in Piglia's diaries, the first of which is the most significant. In referring to his political evolution from anarchism to Marxism in 1962, Piglia explains that he was greatly influenced by his studies in the history department at the University of La Plata. In particular, he states that he changed his position after being taught by a Spanish Communist Party member in exile who had escaped from a Francoist prison. In subsequently defending this position, however, Piglia cites Foucault in order to claim that "fatalmente un historiador es llevado a utilizar en sus análisis las categorías marxistas" (a historian is destined to use Marxist categories in their analysis) and that the term "historiador marxista es un pleonasmo" (Marxist historian is a pleonasm) (Piglia, *Años de formación*, 122–23). Additional references to Foucault can be found throughout Piglia's diaries. See Ricardo Piglia, *Los diarios de Emilio Renzi: los años felices* (Barcelona: Anagrama, 2016), 115, 117, 244, 374 (hereafter *Los años felices*); Ricardo Piglia, *Los diarios de Emilio Renzi: un día en la vida* (Barcelona: Anagrama, 2017), 48 (hereafter *Un día en la vida*).

4. Foucault, "What Is an Author?," 1627.

5. Foucault, "What Is an Author?," 1628.

6. Foucault, "What Is an Author?," 1628.

7. Michel Foucault, "The Subject and Power," *Critical Inquiry* 8, no. 4 (1982): 780.

8. Piglia, *Nombre falso*, 89–91.

9. See Edgardo H. Berg, "La búsqueda del archivo familiar: notas de lectura sobre *Respiración artificial* de Ricardo Piglia," in *Itinerarios entre la ficción y la historia: transdiscursividad en la literatura hispanoaméricana y argentina*, ed. Elisa T. Calabrese (Buenos Aires: Grupo Editor Latinoaméricano, 1994), 117; Roberto Ferro, "Homenaje a Ricardo Piglia y/o Max Brod," in *Conjuntos: teorías y enfoques literarios recientes*, ed. Alberto Vital Díaz (México, D.F.: Instituto de Investigaciones Filológicas, Universidad Nacional Autónoma de México, 1996), 364; Jorge Fornet, "'Homenaje a Roberto Arlt' o la literatura como plagio," *Nueva Revista de Filología Hispánica* 42, no. 1 (1994): 116; Ellen McCracken, "Metaplagiarism and the Critic's Role as Detective: Ricardo Piglia's Reinvention of Roberto Arlt," *PMLA* 106, no. 5 (1991): 1074; Bruno Bosteels, "In the Shadow of Mao: Ricardo Piglia's 'Homenaje a Roberto Arlt,'" *Journal of Latin American Cultural Studies* 12, no. 2 (2003): 234; Edgardo H. Berg, "El

relato ausente (sobre la poética de Ricardo Piglia)," in *Supersticiones de linaje: genealogías y reescrituras*, ed. Elisa Calabrese (Rosario: Beatriz Viterbo, 1996), 143.

10. McCracken, "Metaplagiarism," 1072.

11. See Berg, "La búsqueda," 118; John F. Deredita, "¿Es propiedad? Indeterminación genérica, intertextualidad, diseminación en un texto 'de' Ricardo Piglia," in *Texto/contexto en la literatura iberoamericana: memoria del XIX congreso (Pittsburgh, 27 de mayo–1 de junio de 1979)*, ed. Keith McDuffie and Alfredo A. Roggiano (Madrid: Instituto Internacional de Literatura Iberoamericana, 1980), 62; Rita Gnutzmann, "Homenaje a Arlt, Borges y Onetti de Ricardo Piglia," *Revista Iberoamericana* 58, no. 159 (1992): 443–44, 446; Bosteels, "In the Shadow," 229.

12. Bosteels, "In the Shadow," 230.

13. McCracken, "Metaplagiarism," 1077. Piglia, *Crítica y ficción*, 51.

14. Foucault, "What Is an Author?," 1628.

15. See Fornet, "Homenaje a Roberto Arlt," 133; Diana S. Goodrich, *Facundo and the Construction of Argentine Culture* (Austin: University of Texas Press, 1996), 85.

16. See Ricardo Piglia, *Respiración artificial*, 3rd ed. (Barcelona: Anagrama, 2008), 130–31.

17. Willy Thayer, "Crisis categorial de la universidad," *Revista Iberoamericana* 69, no. 202 (2003): 96n2; Idelber Avelar, "Dictatorship and Immanence," *Journal of Latin American Cultural Studies* 7, no. 1 (1998): 75, 80; Idelber Avelar, *The Untimely Present: Postdictatorial Latin American Fiction and the Task of Mourning* (Durham, NC: Duke University Press, 1999), 11.

18. Avelar, "Dictatorship and Immanence," 79–80.

19. León Rozitchner, "Terror and Grace," *Journal of Latin American Cultural Studies* 21, no. 1 (2012): 149, 150.

20. Rozitchner, "Terror and Grace," 148.

21. Avelar, "Dictatorship and Immanence," 79; original emphasis.

22. See Nelly Richard, "The Reconfigurations of Post-dictatorship Critical Thought," *Journal of Latin American Cultural Studies* 9, no. 3 (2000): 273; Idelber Avelar, "Five Theses on Torture," *Journal of Latin American Cultural Studies* 10, no. 3 (2001): 253. In his own critical work, Avelar too focuses on the "irreducible link that binds allegory and mourning" (Avelar, *Untimely Present*, 3).

23. Avelar, "Dictatorship and Immanence," 75. Avelar, *Untimely Present*, 1–21.

24. Avelar, *Untimely Present*, 11.

25. Piglia, "Literatura y sociedad," 9.

26. Piglia, *Crítica y ficción*, 165; Graciela Speranza, *Fuera de campo: literatura y arte argentinos después de Duchamp* (Barcelona: Anagrama, 2006), 259; Bosteels, "In the Shadow," 231.

27. Piglia continually asserted the importance of uniting the work of Arlt and Borges in his critical writing. As he wrote in his diary in 1970, "Todos nosotros nacemos en Roberto Arlt: el primero que consiga engancharlo con Borges habrá triunfado" (All of us are born in Roberto Arlt: the first who manages to couple him with Borges will have triumphed) (Piglia, *Los años felices*, 178). Similarly, in an interview in 1986, Piglia stated that "cruzar a Arlt con Borges . . . es una de las grandes utopías de la literatura argentina" (to cross Arlt with Borges . . . is one of the greatest utopias in Argentine literature) (Marithelma Costa, "Entrevista con Ricardo Piglia," *Hispamérica* 15, no. 44 (1986): 42).

28. Piglia, *Los años felices*, 222–23.

29. Piglia's fascination with plagiarism can also be encountered throughout his literary and critical work and in his diaries. In the short text entitled "En el umbral," which opens the

first volume of his diaries, Piglia notes that the first exercise in "personal" writing one learns at school is in fact copying, before arguing that there are too many pastiches and parodies and that he prefers direct plagiarism (Piglia, *Años de formación*, 20–21, 27). Similarly, in an entry from 1974 Piglia argues that contemporary cinema is the art of "la adaptación como plagio" (adaption as plagiarism) (*Los años felices*, 378). Frequently, however, these references to plagiarism are tied to the work of Borges. For example, in 1969 Piglia proposes attempting to reproduce an already existent biography as if it were his own. Of course, Borges's character Pierre Menard set himself largely the same task in attempting to produce the *Quijote* as if it were his own work. See Piglia, *Los años felices*, 146.

30. Ricardo Piglia, "Roberto Arlt: una crítica de la economía literaria," *Los libros: para una crítica política de la cultura* 29 (1973): 23. See also Ricardo Piglia, "Roberto Arlt: la ficción del dinero," *Hispamérica* 3, no. 7 (1974).

31. In two separate articles from 1975, Piglia asserts that the release of Brecht's previously unpublished writings on literature and art were the most important developments in Marxist criticism since the publication of Gramsci's prison notebooks. See Ricardo Piglia, "Notas sobre Brecht," *Los libros: para una crítica política de la cultura* 40 (1975): 4; Ricardo Piglia, "Brecht, la producción del arte y de la gloria, selección de textos por Ricardo Piglia," *Ideas, letras, artes en la crisis* 22 (1975): 48.

32. For further discussion of *Los libros*, see Fabio Esposito, "La crítica moderna en Argentina: la revista *Los libros* (1969–1975)," *Orbis Tertius* 20, no. 21 (2015); Diego Peller, "Pasiones teóricas en la Revista *Los Libros*," *Afuera: estudios de crítica cultural* 3, no. 4 (2008). Piglia, "Notas sobre Brecht," 5.

33. María Antonieta Pereira, *Ricardo Piglia y sus precursores* (Buenos Aires: Corregidor, 2001), 170.

34. Ricardo Piglia, "Mao Tse-Tung: práctica estética y lucha de clases," *Los libros: para una crítica política de la cultura* 25 (1971): 22, 24. For Piglia's second important essay on the work of Mao, see Ricardo Piglia, "La lucha ideológica en la construcción socialista," *Los libros: para una crítica política de la cultura* 35 (1974).

35. Piglia, "Mao Tse-Tung," 22; Piglia, "Notas sobre Brecht," 7.

36. Aníbal Ford, Luis Gregorich, Josefina Ludmer, Ángel Núñez, and Ricardo Piglia, "Hacia la crítica," *Los libros: para una crítica política de la cultura* 28 (1972): 6–7. Original emphasis.

37. As Raquel Fernández Cobo notes, journals such as *Los Libros* were fundamental in introducing "la antropología estructural, el psicoanálisis lacaniano, el marxismo althusseriano y gramsciano y, sobre todo, la lingüística" (structural anthropology, Lacanian psychoanalysis Althusserian and Gramscian Marxism, and, above all, linguistics) to Argentina. As she goes on to argue, Piglia deployed French structural linguistics in his introduction to the volume *Yo* which he edited. See Raquel Fernández Cobo, "Los diarios de Ricardo Piglia: una lectura en busca de la experiencia perdida," *Castilla. Estudios de literatura* 8 (2017): 82, 87; Ricardo Piglia, "Nota," in *Yo*, ed. Ricardo Piglia (Buenos Aires: Editorial Tiempo Contemporáneo, 1968).

38. See Foucault, "What Is an Author?," 1628; Piglia, *Los años felices*, 412.

39. Foucault, "What Is an Author?," 1628.

40. Foucault, "What Is an Author?," 1636.

41. Ricardo Piglia, "Nueva narrativa norteamericana," *Los libros: un mes de publicaciones en América Latina* 11 (1970): 13.

42. Piglia, *Los años felices*, 290, 299.

43. Jorge Luis Borges, *Obras completas, 1: 1923–1949* (Buenos Aires: Emecé, 1990), 439.

44. Ricardo Piglia, "Notas sobre Macedonio en un Diario," in *Formas breves* (Barcelona: Anagrama, 2000), 22.

45. Piglia, *Los años felices*, 27.

46. Piglia, *Los años felices*, 82–83, 172–73; Piglia, *Un día en la vida*, 98; María Antonieta Pereira, "Entrevista con Ricardo Piglia," in *Ricardo Piglia y sus precursores* (Buenos Aires: Corregidor, 2001 [1996]), 246.

47. Doreen B. Massey, *For Space* (London: SAGE, 2005), 9.

48. Massey, *For Space*, 131.

49. Massey, *For Space*, 131.

50. Massey, *For Space*, 141, 55.

51. Cliff Stagoll, "Becoming," in *The Deleuze Dictionary*, ed. Adrian Parr (Edinburgh: Edinburgh University Press, 2010), 26; James Williams, *Gilles Deleuze's Philosophy of Time: A Critical Introduction and Guide* (Edinburgh: Edinburgh University Press, 2011), 87.

52. Ronald Bogue, *Deleuze on Music, Painting, and the Arts* (New York: Routledge, 2003), 37.

53. Bogue, *Deleuze on Music*, 37.

54. Gilles Deleuze and Félix Guattari, *A Thousand Plateaus: Capitalism and Schizophrenia*, trans. Brian Massumi (London: Continuum, 2010), 4.

55. Deleuze and Guattari, *A Thousand Plateaus*, 4.

56. Joanna Page, *Creativity and Science in Contemporary Argentine Literature: Between Romanticism and Formalism* (Calgary: University of Calgary Press, 2014), 180.

57. Tomás Abraham, *Fricciones* (Buenos Aires: Sudamericana, 2004), 110.

58. Abraham, *Fricciones*, 171.

59. César Aira, *Las tres fechas* (Rosario: Beatriz Viterbo, 2001), 13.

60. Aira, *Las tres fechas*, 13.

61. Deleuze and Guattari, *A Thousand Plateaus*, 24.

62. Brian Massumi, "Translator's Foreword: Pleasures of Philosophy," in Gilles Deleuze and Félix Guattari, *A Thousand Plateaus: Capitalism and Schizophrenia* (London: Continuum, 2010), ix; Deleuze and Guattari, *A Thousand Plateaus*, 24. Tamsin Lorraine, "Plateau," in *The Deleuze Dictionary*, ed. Adrian Parr (Edinburgh: Edinburgh University Press, 2010), 208.

63. Massumi, "Translator's Foreword," xiv.

64. Jorge Mayer, *Argentina en crisis: política e instituciones 1983–2003* (Buenos Aires: Eudeba, 2012), 78.

65. Aira, *Las tres fechas*, 24.

66. Aira, *Las tres fechas*, 59.

67. Ricardo Piglia, "Una propuesta para el próximo milenio," in *Argentinos: retratos de fin de milenio*, ed. Adrián van der Horst and Miguel Wiñazki (Buenos Aires: Clarín, 1999), 127.

68. Deleuze and Guattari, *A Thousand Plateaus*, 25.

69. Réda Bensmaïa, "Foreword: The Kafka Effect," in Gilles Deleuze and Félix Guattari, *Kafka: Toward a Minor Literature* (Minneapolis: University of Minnesota Press, 1986), xiii.

70. See Pereira, *Ricardo Piglia*, 99. In 1965 Piglia also recorded in his diaries that "los mejores animales de la literatura son los de Kafka" (the best animals in literature are Kafka's) (Piglia, *Años de formación*, 181). In later years Piglia would also reflect on Kafka's literary style in connection with that of Borges and Samuel Beckett (Piglia, *Un día en la vida*, 30, 280).

71. Carlos Alfieri and César Aira, *Conversaciones: entrevistas con César Aira, Guillermo Cabrera Infante, Roger Chartier, Antonio Muñoz Molina, Ricardo Piglia, y Fernando Savater* (Madrid: Katz, 2008), 23.

72. Marcelo Cohen, "Pequeñas batallas por la propiedad de la lengua," in *Poéticas de la distancia: adentro y afuera de la literatura argentina*, ed. Sylvia Molloy and Mariano Siskind (Buenos Aires: Grupo Editorial Norma, 2006), 41.

73. Sandra Contreras, *Las vueltas de César Aira* (Rosario: Beatriz Viterbo, 2002), 12.

74. Contreras, *Las vueltas*, 59. In later years Contreras did write a critical prologue for a new edition of *Ema, la cautiva*. See Sandra Contreras, "Prólogo," in César Aira, *Ema, la cautiva* (Buenos Aires: Eudeba, 2011), 7–22.

75. Speranza, *Fuera de campo*, 301; Contreras, *Las vueltas*, 127, 11–12. Aira's refusal to correct his work stands in sharp contrast to Piglia, who continually revises his writing. Indeed, Piglia has even argued that "la corrección de un escrito se parece a la paradoja de Zenón" (correcting a written work is akin to Zeno's paradox) (Piglia, *Los años felices*, 50). To date, Aira has published over fifty novels.

76. Contreras, *Las vueltas*, 14–15.

77. For example, in his diaries, Piglia recounts that his fellow contributors to the journal *Revista de problemas del tercer mundo* criticized an article he had authored on Manuel Puig's *La traición de Rita Hayworth* for its lack of engagement with literary theory. Piglia rejects their approach, stating that "estamos en mundos distintos" (we are in different worlds) (Piglia, *Los años felices*, 51).

78. Abraham, *Fricciones*, 109.

79. Contreras, *Las vueltas*, 25.

80. See Alfieri and Aira, *Conversaciones*, 35.

81. Abraham, *Fricciones*, 112.

82. Contreras, *Las vueltas*, 27.

83. Piglia, *Un día en la vida*, 142.

84. Piglia, *Un día en la vida*, 145.

85. Piglia, *Un día en la vida*, 146, 149. Similarly, Piglia only ever makes one passing reference to Marcelo Cohen in his diaries. See Piglia, *Un día en la vida*, 165.

86. See Alfieri and Aira, *Conversaciones*, 35.

87. As Piglia writes, "Ahora los cambios en la civilización y en el espíritu absoluto se dan cada diez años, nos han hecho una rebaja en el supermercado de la historia. Nunca vi nada más ridículo; por ejemplo, se acusa a alguna persona de ser de los setenta, es decir, de creer en el socialismo, en la revolución" (Now changes in civilisation and in the absolute spirit occur every ten years, they have given us a great discount in the supermarket of history. I've never seen anything more ridiculous; for example, accusing some person of being from the seventies, which is to say, of believing in socialism, in revolution) (Piglia, *Los años felices*, 13–14). Piglia, "Literatura y sociedad," 9.

88. Massey, *For Space*, 71.

89. Contreras, *Las vueltas*, 28–29.

90. Ricardo Piglia and Juan José Saer, *Diálogo* (Santa Fe, Argentina: Centro de Publicaciones, Universidad Nacional del Litoral, 1995), 17–18.

91. As with many Piglian concepts, it is interesting to note that the genesis of negativity can be traced back to his early theoretical writings and its evolution followed through the musings recorded in his diaries. See for example Ricardo Piglia, "Una lectura de *Cosas con-*

cretas," Los libros: un mes de publicaciones en Argentina y el mundo 6 (1969): 3, and the diary entries for 14 December 1965, 5 January 1967, and 13 June 1967 in Piglia, *Años de formación*, 209, 284, 318.

92. Contreras, *Las vueltas*, 29.

93. Evelyn Galiazo, "La creación es el verdadero poder: César Aira y la tenacidad de lo imposible," *La biblioteca: revista fundada por Paul Groussac. La crítica literaria en Argentina* 4–5 (Summer 2006): 300.

94. Galiazo, "La creación," 298–99.

95. Galiazo, "La creación," 300.

96. Contreras, *Las vueltas*, 29. Original emphasis.

97. See Page, *Creativity and Science*, 42–69, 95–115, 63–84.

98. Berg, "La búsqueda," 119.

99. Pampa Olga Arán, "Voces y fantasmas en la narrativa argentina," in *Umbrales y catástrofes: literatura argentina de los '90*, ed. Pampa Olga Arán et al. (Córdoba, Argentina: Epoké, 2003), 120.

100. Alfieri and Aira, *Conversaciones*, 36–37.

101. Jorge Fornet, "Un debate de poéticas: las narraciones de Ricardo Piglia," in *La narración gana la partida*, ed. Elsa Drucaroff (Buenos Aires: Emecé, 2000), 345, 351; Ariel Schettini, "Lectores argentinos de Manuel Puig," *La biblioteca: revista fundada por Paul Groussac. La crítica literaria en Argentina* 4–5 (Summer 2006): 211; Ricardo Piglia, "Clase media: cuerpo y destino," *Revista de problemas del tercer mundo* 2 (1968).

102. César Aira, *Diccionario de autores latinoamericanos* (Buenos Aires: Emecé, Ada Korn, 2001), 49. Alfieri and Aira, *Conversaciones*, 31. Cited in Graciela Speranza, "Ultimos avatares del surrealismo," *Otra parte: revista de letras y artes* 21 (Spring 2010): 22.

103. Alfieri and Aira, *Conversaciones*, 42.

104. See Piglia, *Años de formación*, 66. This story also serves to remind us that "estos diarios . . . no son los diarios de Ricardo Piglia, sino los diarios de Emilio Renzi" (these diaries are not those of Ricardo Piglia but rather of Emilio Renzi) and "han pasado, por tanto, por el filtro de la ficción'" (have passed, therefore, through the filter of fiction), as Raquel Fernández Cobo argues (Fernández Cobo, "Los diarios," 70).

105. Costa, "Entrevista con Ricardo Piglia," 42.

106. See Piglia and Saer, *Diálogo*; Nancy Fernández, *Narraciones viajeras: César Aira y Juan José Saer* (Buenos Aires: Biblos, 2000).

107. Daniel Link, "Rethinking Past Present," *Review: Literature and Arts of the Americas* 40, no. 2 (2007): 226.

108. See for example John Kraniauskas's analysis of *El fiord* and Ben Bollig's interpretation of Lamborghini's early poetry, in John Kraniauskas, "Porno-Revolution: *El fiord* and the Eva-Peronist State," *Angelaki* 6, no. 1 (2001); Ben Bollig, "Now/Here is Everywhere: Exile and Cynicism in the Verse of Osvaldo Lamborghini," *Journal of Latin American Cultural Studies* 15, no. 3 (2006): 371–74.

109. Link, "Rethinking Past Present," 221.

110. Martín Kohan, "De putas," *Mora* 15, no. 2 (2009): 166.

111. For analysis of time and subjectivity in these novels, see Erica Miller Yozell, "Negotiating the Abyss: The Narration of Mourning in Sergio Chejfec's *Los planetas*," *Latin American Literary Review* 35, no. 70 (2007); Jonathan Dettman, "Epic, Novel, and Subjectivity in Sergio Chejfec's *Lenta biografía*," *A Contracorriente: A Journal on Social History and Literature in Latin America* 6, no. 2 (2009).

112. For analysis of capitalism in these novels, see Steve Buttes, "Towards an Art of Landscapes and Loans: Sergio Chejfec and the Politics of Literary Form," *nonsite.org* 13 (2014), accessed 19 October 2017, http://nonsite.org; Sol Peláez, "Thinking from the 'Desamparo' in *Los Incompletos* by Sergio Chejfec," *Journal of Latin American Cultural Studies* 24, no. 3 (2015).

113. Speranza, *Fuera de campo*, 249.

114. Speranza, *Fuera de campo*, 250.

115. Cited in Speranza, "Ultimos avatares," 22. See César Aira, "La nueva escritura," *Boletín del centro de estudios de teoría y crítica literaria* 8 (October 2000); César Aira, "La innovación," *Boletín del grupo de estudios de teoría literaria* 4 (April 1995).

116. Speranza, *Fuera de campo*, 257.

117. Gregg Lambert, *The Non-Philosophy of Gilles Deleuze* (London: Continuum, 2002), 81; Gilles Deleuze, "Preface," in *Difference and Repetition* (London: Continuum, 2001), xxi–xxii.

118. Piglia, "Nueva narrativa norteamericana," 12–13; Aira, "La nueva escritura," 166.

119. Page, *Creativity and Science*, 19. This influence creates a particularly strong connection between the work of Cohen and Piglia given that, in a diary entry from 1969, Piglia would clearly state that, as regards his literary style, "yo soy 'un norteamericano'" (I am a "North American") (Piglia, *Los años felices*, 133).

120. Abraham, *Fricciones*, 160; Piglia, *Los años felices*, 193. Piglia, *Un día en la vida*, 83. For additional references to Deleuze, see Piglia, *Los años felices*, 118, 372; Piglia, *Un día en la vida*, 119, 126. It is interesting to note that in the last of these references Piglia misattributes the phrase "el cine es el diván del pobre" (cinema is the poor man's couch) to Deleuze. The phrase was actually coined by Guattari, demonstrating that Piglia had also read his work. Interestingly, when Piglia later repeats the phrase, he claims not to remember who authored the expression and postulates that it may have been Sartre. See Félix Guattari, "The Poor Man's Couch," trans. Gianna Quach, in *The Continental Philosophy of Film Reader*, ed. Joseph Westfall (London: Bloomsbury Academic, 2018), 341–47; Piglia,*Un día en la vida*, 214.

121. Piglia, *Los años felices*, 206.

122. György Ligeti, Péter Várnai, Josef Häusler, and Claude Samuel, *György Ligeti in Conversation* (London: Eulenburg, 1983), 136.

123. Ligeti, *György Ligeti in Conversation*, 86.

124. Deleuze, *Difference and Repetition*, 304, 35.

125. Piglia, *Nombre falso*, 145.

126. Borges, *Obras completas*, 1, 499–507.

127. Luis Dapelo and César Aira, "César Aira," *Hispamérica* 36, no. 107 (2007): 49; César Aira, *Diario de la hepatitis* (Buenos Aires: Bajo la Luna, 2007), 35–36.

Chapter 1: Ema is by Nature a Political Animal

An earlier version of this chapter was previously published as Niall Geraghty, "Ema Is by Nature a Political Animal: Politics and Capitalism in César Aira's *Ema, la cautiva*," *Journal of Latin American Cultural Studies* 23, no. 1 (2014).

1. Fernández, *Narraciones viajeras*, 175.

2. Leo Pollmann, "Una estética del más allá del ser: *Ema, la cautiva* de César Aira," in *La novela argentina de los años 80*, ed. Roland Spiller (Frankfurt am Main: Vervuert, 1993), 178.

3. César Aira, *Ema, la cautiva* (Buenos Aires: Editorial de Belgrano, 1981), author's note, back cover.

4. Contreras, *Las vueltas*, 47. This focus is also shared by Masiello. See Francine Masiello, *The Art of Transition: Latin American Culture and Neoliberal Crisis* (Durham, NC: Duke University Press, 2001), 94–98.

5. Contreras, *Las vueltas*, 55. Original emphasis. As noted in the introduction, Contreras has since authored a prologue to a later edition of *Ema, la cautiva*, an analysis that shares much in common with her interpretation of *La liebre*. See Contreras, "Prólogo."

6. Contreras also discusses the various literary referants for Aira's novel at length in her critical prologue. See Contreras, "Prólogo," 12–18.

7. These writings are collated as Alfred Ébélot, *Adolfo Alsina y la ocupación del desierto: relatos de la frontera* (Buenos Aires: El Elefante Blanco, 2008). Aira, *Ema*, 15.

8. Lucio Victorio Mansilla, *Una excursión a los indios ranqueles: edición, prólogo y notas de Julio Caillet-Bois*, ed. Julio Caillet-Bois (México: Fondo de Cultura Económica, 1947), 235. Aira, *Ema*, 151.

9. Contreras, *Las vueltas*, 48.

10. See Ruy Díaz de Guzmán, "Women Captives," in *The Argentina Reader: History, Culture, and Society*, ed. Gabriela Nouzeilles and Graciela R. Montaldo (Durham, NC: Duke University Press, 2002).

11. See Goodrich, *Facundo*, 90; Carlos J. Alonso, "Civilización y barbarie," *Hispania* 72, no. 2 (1989): 261; Enrique de Gandía, "Sarmiento y su teoria de 'Civilizacion y Barbarie,'" *Journal of Inter-American Studies* 4, no. 1 (1962): 70.

12. Aira, *Ema*, 155, 29, 23.

13. Domingo Faustino Sarmiento, *Facundo: Civilización y barbarie*, ed. Roberto Yahni (Madrid: Cátedra, 1990), 268; Domingo Faustino Sarmiento, *Facundo: Civilization and Barbarism: The First Complete English Translation*, trans. Kathleen Ross (Berkeley: University of California Press, 2003), 180.

14. Sarmiento, *Facundo: Civilización*, 104; Sarmiento, *Facundo: Civilization*, 77.

15. Roberto González Echevarría, "*Facundo*: An Introduction," in *Facundo: Civilization and Barbarism: The First Complete English Translation*, by Domingo Faustino Sarmiento (Berkeley: University of California Press, 2003), 10.

16. See for example Goodrich, *Facundo*, 126–30; Eva Gillies, "Introduction," in Lucio V. Mansilla, *A Visit to the Ranquel Indians (Una excursión a los indios ranqueles)* (Lincoln: University of Nebraska Press, 1997), xxxvi.

17. Some subsequent campaigns in outlying regions are often included within the term.

18. Aira, *Ema*, 28.

19. Carlos Martínez Sarasola, *Nuestros paisanos los indios: vida, historia y destino de las comunidades indígenas en la Argentina* (Buenos Aires: Emecé, 1992), 275; Ébélot, *Adolfo Alsina*, 21.

20. This incident is recounted in detail by Ébélot, who Alsina contracted to work on the frontier. See Ébélot, *Adolfo Alsina*, 25–60.

21. David Rock, *State Building and Political Movements in Argentina, 1860–1916* (Stanford: Stanford University Press, 2002), 93.

22. Martínez Sarasola, *Nuestros paisanos los indios*, 270; Ébélot, *Adolfo Alsina*, 74.

23. Aira, *Ema*, 151.

24. Alfred Hasbrouck, "The Conquest of the Desert," *Hispanic American Historical Review* 15, no. 2 (1935): 228.

25. Martínez Sarasola, *Nuestros paisanos los indios*, 275.

26. David Viñas, *Indios, ejército y frontera* (Buenos Aires: Siglo Veintiuno, 1983), 11.

27. Aira, *Ema*, 223.

28. Carlos Martínez Sarasola, "The Conquest of the Desert and the Free Indigenous Communities of the Argentine Plains," in *Military Struggle and Identity Formation in Latin America: Race, Nation, and Community During the Liberal Period*, ed. Nicola Foote and René D. Harder Horst (Gainesville: University Press of Florida, 2010), 220.

29. Michael Goebel, *Argentina's Partisan Past: Nationalism and the Politics of History* (Liverpool: Liverpool University Press, 2011), 187; Gabriela Nouzeilles and Graciela R. Montaldo, *The Argentina Reader: History, Culture, and Society* (Durham, NC: Duke University Press, 2002), 157.

30. Silvana Mariel Arena, "*Ema, la cautiva* de César Aira, a un siglo de la conquista del desierto: reflexiones sobre los modos de representación, el lugar del artista y la construcción del espacio, el tiempo y el sujeto," in *Fin(es) del siglo y modernismo (Volumen II): Congreso Internacional Buenos Aires-La Plata*, ed. María Payeras Grau and Luis Miguel Fernández Ripoll (Palma: Universitat de les Illes Balears, 2001), 756; Pollmann, "Una estética," 191; Florencia Garramuño, *Genealogías culturales: Argentina, Brasil y Uruguay en la novela contemporánea (1981–1991)* (Rosario: Beatriz Viterbo, 1997), 89.

31. Garramuño, *Genealogías culturales*, 89.

32. Claudia N. Briones and Walter Delrio, "The 'Conquest of the Desert' as a Trope and Enactment of Argentina's Manifest Destiny," in *Manifest Destinies and Indigenous Peoples*, ed. David Maybury-Lewis, Theodore Macdonald, and Biorn Maybury-Lewis (Cambridge, MA: Harvard University Press, 2009), 53.

33. Garramuño, *Genealogías culturales*, 89.

34. Goebel, *Argentina's Partisan Past*, 193.

35. Goebel, *Argentina's Partisan Past*, 131.

36. Viñas, *Indios, ejército y frontera*, 150.

37. Aira, *Ema*, 31.

38. Pollmann, "Una estética," 178.

39. Aira, *Ema*, 93; Pollmann, "Una estética," 187.

40. Pollmann, "Una estética," 179.

41. Pollmann, "Una estética," 187n11.

42. Aira, *Ema*, 46.

43. David Rock, "Revolt and Repression in Argentina," *The World Today* 33, no. 6 (1977): 216.

44. Aira, *Ema*, 118–19.

45. Aira, *Ema*, 119.

46. For a detailed analysis of Peronist economic policy, see Paul H. Lewis, *The Crisis of Argentine Capitalism* (Chapel Hill: University of North Carolina Press, 1990), 426–28.

47. Lewis, *The Crisis of Argentine Capitalism*, 422.

48. Lewis, *The Crisis of Argentine Capitalism*, 429.

49. Aira, *Ema*, 89, 94.

50. Aira, *Ema*, 205.

51. For a detailed discussion of Martínez de Hoz's attempts to tackle inflation, see Lewis, *Crisis of Argentine Capitalism*, 460–62.

52. For a discussion of the 1980 banking crisis, see Lewis, *Crisis of Argentine Capitalism*, 462–69.

53. Gerardo Della Paolera, Maria Alejandra Irigoin, and Carlos G. Bózzoli, "Passing the Buck: Monetary and Fiscal Policies," in *A New Economic History of Argentina*, ed. Gerardo Della Paolera and Alan M. Taylor (Cambridge: Cambridge University Press, 2003), 73–74.

54. Paolera, Irigoin, and Bózzoli, "Passing the Buck," 74.

55. Lewis, *Crisis of Argentine Capitalism*, 115.

56. Lewis, *Crisis of Argentine Capitalism*, 119, 229, 230.

57. Goebel, *Argentina's Partisan Past*, 234.

58. Goebel, *Argentina's Partisan Past*, 234–35.

59. Goebel, *Argentina's Partisan Past*, 5.

60. See, for example, Arturo Jauretche, *Política nacional y revisionismo histórico* (Buenos Aires: Corregidor, 2011).

61. Goebel, *Argentina's Partisan Past*, 235.

62. See Aira, *Ema*, 223, 227; Vicente Osvaldo Cutolo, *Nuevo diccionario biográfico argentino, 1750–1930*, vol. 5 (Buenos Aires: Elche, 1978), 156.

63. Karl Marx, "The Eighteenth Brumaire of Louis Bonaparte," in *Marx's 'Eighteenth Brumaire': (Post)modern Interpretations*, ed. Mark Cowling and James Martin (London: Pluto, 2002), 19.

64. Aira, *Ema*, 24.

65. Marx, "Eighteenth Brumaire," 19–20.

66. César Aira, "La ciudad y el campo," in *Norte y Sur: la narrativa rioplatense desde México*, ed. Rose Corral, Hugo J. Verani, and Ana María Zubieta (México: El Colegio de México, 2000), 85.

67. Aira, "La ciudad y el campo," 86.

68. Goebel, *Argentina's Partisan Past*, 1; Echevarría, "*Facundo*: An Introduction," 14.

69. Aira, *Ema*, author's note, back cover.

70. James Williams, "Immanence," in *The Deleuze Dictionary*, ed. Adrian Parr (Edinburgh: Edinburgh University Press, 2010), 129.

71. See César Aira, "Exotismo," *Boletín del grupo de estudios de teoría literaria* 3 (September 1993): 74–75.

72. See, for example, Martínez Sarasola, "Conquest of the Desert," 213.

73. Aira, *Ema*, 46.

74. Aira, *Ema*, 47.

75. Aira, *Ema*, 47.

76. Claude Lévi-Strauss, *Structural Anthropology: Volume 1*, trans. Claire Jacobson and Brooke Grundfest Schoepf (Harmondsworth: Penguin, 1977), 61. Original emphasis.

77. Aira, *Ema*, 88.

78. Aira, *Ema*, 89.

79. Aira, *Ema*, 94.

80. Albert O. Hirschman, *The Passions and the Interests: Political Arguments for Capitalism before Its Triumph* (Princeton: Princeton University Press, 1997), 9.

81. Hirschman, *The Passions*, 41. Original emphasis.

82. Aira, *Ema*, 98.

83. Hirschman, *The Passions*, 80, 85, 62.

84. Gilles Deleuze and Félix Guattari, *Anti-Oedipus: Capitalism and Schizophrenia*, trans. Robert Hurley, Mark Seem, and Helen R. Lane (London: Continuum, 2004), 160.

85. Deleuze and Guattari, *Anti-Oedipus*, 215, 210–11. Deleuze and Guattari name this form of societal organization the "barbarian despotic machine" because they believe that, within it, power resides in "the full body of the Despot," which is to say that meaning emanates from the centralized ruler who assumes the position of a god. See Deleuze and Guattari, *Anti-Oedipus*, 160.

86. Aira, *Ema*, 24.

87. Aira, *Ema*, 89; Deleuze and Guattari, *Anti-Oedipus*, 242.

88. Jonathan Roffe, "Capitalism," in *The Deleuze Dictionary*, ed. Adrian Parr (Edinburgh: Edinburgh University Press, 2010), 40.

89. Deleuze and Guattari, *Anti-Oedipus*, 153.

90. Deleuze and Guattari, *Anti-Oedipus*, 153.

91. Roffe, "Capitalism," 41.

92. Roffe, "Capitalism," 41.

93. Aira, *Ema*, 125.

94. Aira, *Ema*, 125.

95. Aira, *Ema*, 125.

96. Aira, *Ema*, 130–31.

97. Roffe, "Capitalism," 41.

98. Vincent B. Leitch, *The Norton Anthology of Theory and Criticism* (New York: Norton, 2001), 1416. Original emphasis.

99. Aira, *Ema*, 166, 171–72.

100. Aira, *Ema*, 175.

101. Aira, *Ema*, 204.

102. Aira, *Ema*, 151.

103. Roffe, "Capitalism," 42.

104. Martínez Sarasola, *Nuestros paisanos los indios*, 437.

105. Mansilla, *Una excursión*, 184, 115; Lucio Victorio Mansilla, *A Visit to the Ranquel Indians: (Una excursión a los indios ranqueles)*, trans. Eva Gillies (Lincoln: University of Nebraska Press, 1997), 178, 112.

106. Mansilla, *Una excursión*, 278–79; Mansilla, *A Visit*, 270–72.

107. Aira, *Ema*, 158–59.

108. See the descriptions of indigenous *toldos* in Martínez Sarasola, "Conquest of the Desert," 205; Hasbrouck, "Conquest of the Desert," 200.

109. Aira, *Ema*, 94.

110. Aira, *Ema*, 169.

111. W. H. Walsh, *An Introduction to Philosophy of History*, 3rd rev. ed. (London: Hutchinson University Library, 1967), 121.

112. Walsh, *Philosophy of History*, 141.

113. Dipesh Chakrabarty, *Provincializing Europe: Postcolonial Thought and Historical Difference* (Princeton: Princeton University Press, 2008), xiii.

114. Chakrabarty, *Provincializing Europe*, 29.

115. Deleuze and Guattari, *Anti-Oedipus*, 154, 153. My emphasis. Interestingly, Deleuze and Guattari reinterpret indigenous marriage exchanges in this way. See Deleuze and Guattari, *Anti-Oedipus*, 156–68.

116. Deleuze and Guattari, *Anti-Oedipus*, 154.

117. Aira, *Ema*, 165.

118. Francis Fukuyama, "The End of History?," *The National Interest* 16 (Summer 1989): 3–4.

119. Deleuze and Guattari, *Anti-Oedipus*, 247, 243.

120. Deleuze and Guattari, *Anti-Oedipus*, 259.

121. Dapelo and Aira, "César Aira," 44.

122. Dapelo and Aira, "César Aira," 44. This episode is confirmed in Pollmann, "Una estética," 179n4. A version of this experience also appears in César Aira, *La trompeta de mimbre* (Rosario: Beatriz Viterbo, 1998), 42–43.

123. Dapelo and Aira, "César Aira," 44.

124. Aira, *Ema*, author's note, back cover.

125. See César Aira, *La prueba* (México, D.F.: Era, 2002).

Chapter 2: Accessing the Real

1. Dierdra Reber, "Cure for the Capitalist Headache: Affect and Fantastic Consumption in César Aira's Argentine 'Baghdad,'" *MLN* 122 no. 2 (2007): 375.

2. Josefina Ludmer, *El cuerpo del delito: un manual* (Buenos Aires: Perfil Libros, 1999), 366, 368.

3. César Barros, "Del 'macrocosmos de la hamburguesa' a 'lo real de la realidad': consumo, sujeto y acción en *La prueba* de César Aira," *Revista Hispánica Moderna* 65, no. 2 (2012): 135. Miguel Teubal, "Rise and Collapse of Neoliberalism in Argentina: The Role of Economic Groups," *Journal of Developing Societies* 20, nos. 3–4 (2004): 174.

4. Miguel de Beistegui, "The Ontological Dispute: Badiou, Heidegger, and Deleuze," in *Alain Badiou: Philosophy and its Conditions*, ed. Gabriel Riera (Albany: State University of New York Press, 2005), 58.

5. Luiz Carlos Bresser Pereira, José María Maravall, and Adam Przeworski, *Economic Reforms in New Democracies: A Social-Democratic Approach* (Cambridge: Cambridge University Press, 1993), 44.

6. Bresser Pereira, Maravall, and Przeworski, *Economic Reforms in New Democracies*, 45–46.

7. Eduardo Silva, *Challenging Neoliberalism in Latin America* (Cambridge: Cambridge University Press, 2009), 57.

8. Bresser Pereira, Maravall, and Przeworski, *Economic Reforms in New Democracies*, 46.

9. Silva, *Challenging Neoliberalism*, 61.

10. See Silva, *Challenging Neoliberalism*, 62.

11. "A Pumper Nic se le comió la *globalización*," *La Nación*, 14 September 1997, accessed 9 May 2018, www.lanacion.com.ar.

12. Ludmer, *El cuerpo del delito*, 366. For a detailed history of the supermarket Disco since its foundation in 1960, see Luis Chiodo, *Hipermercados en América Latina: historia del comercio de alimentos, de los autoservicios hasta el imperio de cinco cadenas multinacionales* (Buenos Aires: Antropofagia, 2010), 188–201.

13. Aira, *La prueba*, 16.

14. Aira, *La prueba*, 17. Original emphasis.

15. Aira, *La prueba*, 60. Original emphasis.

16. Aira, *La prueba*, 35.

17. Joanna Page, *Crisis and Capitalism in Contemporary Argentine Cinema* (Durham, NC: Duke University Press, 2009), 179.

18. Page, *Crisis and Capitalism*, 177.

19. Silvia Sigal, *Intelectuales y poder en la década del sesenta* (Buenos Aires: Puntosur, 1991), 192. Original emphasis.

20. See Oscar Terán, "Ideas e intelectuales en la Argentina, 1880–1980," in *Ideas en el siglo: intelectuales y cultura en el siglo XX latinoamericano*, ed. Oscar Terán and Gerardo Caetano (Buenos Aires: Siglo Veintiuno, 2004), 82–83; María Sonderéguer, "Presentación," in *Revista Crisis (1973–1976): antología, del intelectual comprometido al intelectual revolucionario*, ed. María Sonderéguer (Bernal: Universidad Nacional de Quilmes, 2008), 20.

21. As outlined in the introduction, Piglia was a prominent participant in this intellectual milieu.

22. See Sigal, *Intelectuales y poder*, 194.

23. Terán, "Ideas e intelectuales," 78.

24. Terán, "Ideas e intelectuales," 74.

25. Alfieri and Aira, *Conversaciones*, 29.

26. Aira, "La nueva escritura," 166.

27. Sigal, *Intelectuales y poder*, 210.

28. Laura Kalmanowiecki, "Police, Politics, and Repression in Modern Argentina," in *Reconstructing Criminality in Latin America*, ed. Carlos Aguirre and Robert Buffington (Wilmington, DE: Scholarly Resources, 2000), 209–10.

29. Jill Hedges, *Argentina: A Modern History* (London: I. B. Tauris, 2011), 185.

30. Hedges, *Argentina*, 185; Terán, "Ideas e intelectuales," 76.

31. Terán, "Ideas e intelectuales," 77.

32. Terán, "Ideas e intelectuales," 76.

33. See Terán, "Ideas e intelectuales," 81.

34. Hedges, *Argentina*, 187.

35. Hedges, *Argentina*, 185–86.

36. Pablo Pozzi, "Popular Upheaval and Capitalist Transformation in Argentina," *Latin American Perspectives* 27, no. 5 (2000): 69.

37. Hedges, *Argentina*, 187–88. See Pozzi, "Popular Upheaval," 64.

38. Pozzi, "Popular Upheaval," 68.

39. See Pozzi, "Popular Upheaval," 64, 78, 80.

40. Gabriel Riera, "Introduction: Alain Badiou, The Event of Thinking," in *Alain Badiou: Philosophy and its Conditions*, ed. Gabriel Riera (Albany: State University of New York Press, 2005), 10.

41. Simon Critchley, "On the Ethics of Alain Badiou," in *Alain Badiou: Philosophy and its Conditions*, ed. Gabriel Riera (Albany: State University of New York Press, 2005), 234.

42. Barros, "Del 'macrocosmos,'" 136. Original emphasis.

43. See Barros, "Del 'macrocosmos'"; Riera, "Introduction," 2. Original emphasis.

44. Justin Clemens, "The Conditions," in *Alain Badiou: Key Concepts*, ed. A. J. Bartlett and Justin Clemens (Durham: Acumen, 2010), 32.

45. Aira, *La prueba*, 13–14, 17.

46. Aira, *La prueba*, 29.

47. Aira, *La prueba*, 17–18.

48. Aira, *La prueba*, 29.

49. Patrick J. O'Connor, "Cesar Aira's Simple Lesbians: Passing '*La prueba*,'" *Latin American Literary Review* 27, no. 54 (1999): 31.

50. See Alain Badiou, "Truth: Forcing and the Unnameable," in *Theoretical Writings*, ed. Ray Brassier and Alberto Toscano (London: Continuum, 2004), 123; Peter Hallward, "Translator's Introduction," in *Ethics: An Essay on the Understanding of Evil*, ed. Alain Badiou (London; New York: Verso, 2001), ix.

51. Alain Badiou, *Ethics: An Essay on the Understanding of Evil*, trans. Peter Hallward (London; New York: Verso, 2001), 68; Jean-Jacques Lecercle, *Badiou and Deleuze Read Literature* (Edinburgh: Edinburgh University Press, 2010), 39, 108. As Peter Hallward notes, Badiou "divides the sphere of human action into two overlapping but sharply differentiated sub-spheres: a) the 'ordinary' realm of established interests and differences, of approved *knowledges* that serve to name, recognize and *place* consolidated identities; and b) an 'exceptional' realm of singular innovations or *truths*, which persist only through the militant

proclamation of those rare individuals who constitute themselves *as the subjects* of a truth, as the 'militants' of their cause" (Hallward, "Translator's Introduction," viii). Original emphasis. For further description of the "truth procedure," the "event" and the "subject," see Riera, "Introduction"; Badiou, *Ethics*.

52. Lecercle, *Badiou and Deleuze*, 39–40.
53. Aira, *La prueba*, 23.
54. Aira, *La prueba*, 26.
55. Aira, *La prueba*, 13.
56. Aira, *La prueba*, 27.
57. Aira, *La prueba*, 46.
58. Badiou, *Ethics*, 68. Original emphasis.
59. Badiou, "The Event as Trans-Being," 98.
60. Aira, *La prueba*, 23.
61. Aira, *La prueba*, 52. Original emphasis.
62. Aira, *La prueba*, 50–51.
63. Aira, *La prueba*, 50.
64. Aira, *La prueba*, 47.
65. Aira, *La prueba*, 51.
66. Aira, *La prueba*, 55.
67. Lecercle, *Badiou and Deleuze*, 142. Original emphasis.
68. Lecercle, *Badiou and Deleuze*, 114, 141.
69. O'Connor, "Cesar Aira's Simple Lesbians," 29.
70. Alfieri and Aira, *Conversaciones*, 29.
71. Aira, "La innovación," 29.
72. Alfieri and Aira, *Conversaciones*, 29.
73. César Aira, *El infinito* (Buenos Aires: Vanagloria, 1994), 4.
74. Aira, *El infinito*, 13.
75. Aira, *El infinito*, 15–16.
76. Aira, "La innovación," 28. My emphasis.
77. Aira, "La innovación," 29.
78. Aira, "La innovación," 32. My emphasis.
79. Silvio Mattoni, "César Aira: Una introducción," in *Umbrales y catástrofes: literatura argentina de los '90*, ed. Pampa Olga Arán, et al. (Córdoba, Argentina: Epoké, 2003), 198.
80. Galiazo, "La creación," 303.
81. Aira, *El infinito*, 17. Aira, *La trompeta de mimbre*, 80.
82. Badiou, *Ethics*, 3. Original emphasis.
83. Aira, *La prueba*, 50.
84. Ernesto Laclau, "An Ethics of Militant Engagement," in *Think Again: Alain Badiou and the Future of Philosophy*, ed. Peter Hallward (New York; London: Continuum, 2004), 122. Original emphasis.
85. Laclau, "Ethics of Militant Engagement," 123. Original emphasis.
86. Aira, *La prueba*, 7.
87. Reber, "Cure for the Capitalist Headache," 376.
88. Reber, "Cure for the Capitalist Headache," 378.
89. Deleuze and Guattari, *Anti-Oedipus*, 36.
90. Eugene W. Holland, "From Schizophrenia to Social Control," in *Deleuze and Guattari: New Mappings in Politics, Philosophy, and Culture*, ed. Eleanor Kaufman and Kevin Jon Heller (Minneapolis: University of Minnesota Press, 1998), 65–66.

91. In keeping with my discussion of capitalism in the previous chapter, Deleuze and Guattari argue that capitalism is universal and "retrospective in that the perspective of schizophrenia only becomes available toward the end of history, under capitalism" (Eugene Holland, "Capitalism + Universal History," in *The Deleuze Dictionary*, ed. Adrian Parr [Edinburgh: Edinburgh University Press, 2010], 42). It is important to note that (with the exception of a reference to Lucia Joyce in chapter 6) my use of the term "schizophrenia" (and its variants) throughout this book refers only to the concept described by Deleuze and Guattari and not to the mental illness whose name they have appropriated.

92. See Bernardo Alexander Attias, "To Each Its Own Sexes?: Towards a Rhetorical Understanding of *Molecular Revolution*," in *Deleuze and Guattari: New Mappings in Politics, Philosophy, and Culture*, ed. Eleanor Kaufman and Kevin Jon Heller (Minneapolis: University of Minnesota Press, 1998), 102.

93. Aira, *La prueba*, 69.

94. Aira, *La prueba*, 69–70.

95. Contreras, *Las vueltas*, 152.

96. Abraham, *Fricciones*, 160.

97. Abraham, *Fricciones*, 140.

98. See Deleuze and Guattari, *A Thousand Plateaus*, 256–341.

99. Aira, *La prueba*, 69.

100. Aira, *La prueba*, 70.

101. Deleuze and Guattari, *A Thousand Plateaus*, 308.

102. Ronald Bogue, *Deleuzian Fabulation and the Scars of History* (Edinburgh: Edinburgh University Press, 2010), 8.

103. César Aira, *Dante y Reina* (Buenos Aires: Mansalva, 2009), 7.

104. César Aira, *La abeja* (Buenos Aires: Emecé, 1996), 171. In each of these cases, there is perhaps a trace of the aftermath of the so-called Dirty War. In the former text, that the child of a murdered mother could cause the destruction of civilization potentially contains an echo of the unresolved cases of children stolen from their mothers in clandestine detention and torture centers. In the latter case, military action leads to the resurrection of the dead and, as before, total destruction. This too could be an oblique reference to the fear that the unpunished crimes of the dictatorship could disturb Argentina's fragile democracy and society.

105. Stagoll, "Becoming," 26; Aira, "La nueva escritura," 167.

106. Deleuze and Guattari, *A Thousand Plateaus*, 294.

107. Masiello, *Art of Transition*, 94.

108. Kathrin Thiele, *The Thought of Becoming: Gilles Deleuze's Poetics of Life* (Zürich: Diaphanes, 2008), 34.

109. Clemens, "The Conditions," 31; Riera, "Introduction," 2. Original emphasis.

110. Williams, "Immanence," 129.

111. Constantin V. Boundas, "Virtual/Virtuality," in *The Deleuze Dictionary*, ed. Adrian Parr (Edinburgh: Edinburgh University Press, 2010), 300.

112. For further discussion of the commonalities, debates, and divergences between the work of Badiou and Deleuze, see Alain Badiou, *Deleuze: The Clamor of Being*, trans. Louise Burchill (Minneapolis: University of Minnesota Press, 2000); Beistegui, "The Ontological Dispute"; Clayton Crockett, *Deleuze Beyond Badiou: Ontology, Multiplicity, and Event* (New York: Columbia University Press, 2013); Lecercle, *Badiou and Deleuze*.

113. Lecercle, *Badiou and Deleuze*, 32.

114. See Badiou, *Deleuze*, 11, 45–48; Crockett, *Deleuze Beyond Badiou*, 13.

115. Badiou, *Deleuze*, 46.

116. Alberto Toscano, "Post-Structuralism + Politics," in *The Deleuze Dictionary*, ed. Adrian Parr (Edinburgh: Edinburgh University Press, 2010), 215.

117. Bogue, *Deleuzian Fabulation*, 8.

118. César Aira, *Alejandra Pizarnik* (Rosario: Beatriz Viterbo, 1998), 26.

119. Reinaldo Laddaga, "Una literatura de la clase media: notas sobre César Aira," *Hispamérica* 30, no. 88 (2001): 46.

120. Contreras, *Las vueltas*, 24; César Aira, "El sultan," *América Hispánica* 3, no. 4 (1990): 10.

121. Contreras, *Las vueltas*, 21.

122. César Aira, *Yo era una mujer casada* (Buenos Aires: Blatt and Ríos, 2010), 76–77.

123. Galiazo, "La creación," 294.

124. Aira, *Yo era una mujer casada*, 76; Alain Badiou, *Conditions*, trans. Steven Corcoran (London; New York: Continuum, 2008), 261; Lecercle, *Badiou and Deleuze*, 171.

125. Tom Conley, "Foucault + Fold," in *The Deleuze Dictionary*, ed. Adrian Parr (Edinburgh: Edinburgh University Press, 2010), 115.

126. Nina Power and Alberto Toscano, "Politics," in *Alain Badiou: Key Concepts*, ed. A. J. Bartlett and Justin Clemens (Durham: Acumen, 2010), 95–96.

127. Slavoj Žižek, "From Purification to Subtraction: Badiou and the Real," in *Think Again: Alain Badiou and the Future of Philosophy*, ed. Peter Hallward (New York; London: Continuum, 2004), 177, 179. Original emphasis. Žižek makes a similar point in his book on Deleuze when he responds to the questions "what would the 'multitude in power' (not only as resistance) be?," "How would it *function*?," and "what would the 'multitude in power' look like?." See Slavoj Žižek, *Organs without Bodies: Deleuze and Consequences* (New York: Routledge, 2004), 197–202.

128. See Gilles Deleuze and Félix Guattari, *Kafka: Toward a Minor Literature*, trans. Dana Polan (Minneapolis: University of Minnesota Press, 1986), 35.

129. Deleuze and Guattari, *Kafka*, 22.

130. Deleuze and Guattari, *Kafka*, 13.

131. Deleuze and Guattari, *Kafka*, 35.

132. Deleuze and Guattari, *Kafka*, 13.

133. Deleuze and Guattari, *Kafka*, 34. Original emphasis.

134. See Deleuze and Guattari, *Kafka*, 12.

135. Deleuze and Guattari, *Kafka*, 41. Original emphasis.

136. Deleuze and Guattari, *Kafka*, 36.

137. Deleuze and Guattari, *Kafka*, 36–37.

138. Deleuze and Guattari, *Kafka*, 37.

Chapter 3: "Is There Any Thing whereof It May Be Said, See, This is New?"

Those elements pertaining to Cohen's short story "La ilusión monarca" in chapters 3 and 4 were previously published as Niall Geraghty, "Power in Transition in Marcelo Cohen's 'La ilusión monarca,'" *Bulletin of Latin American Research* 35, no. 4 (2016).

1. Patrick Dove, "Tonalities of Literature in Transition: The World of the End of the World, or Marcelo Cohen's *El oído absoluto*," *CR: The New Centennial Review* 4, no. 2 (2004): 240–41.

2. Jimena Néspolo, "El fantástico en vigilia: apuntes para una reflexión sobre la obra de Marcelo Cohen," in *Aventuras de la crítica: escrituras latinoamericanas en el siglo XXI*, ed.

Noé Jitrik (Córdoba, Argentina: Instituto de Literatura Hispanoamericana and Alción Editora, 2006), 103–4.

3. Dove, "Tonalities of Literature in Transition," 240.

4. Thayer, "Crisis categorial de la universidad," 96n2; Avelar, "Dictatorship and Immanence," 75, 80; Avelar, *Untimely Present*, 11.

5. Avelar, *Untimely Present*; Annelies Oeyen, "Imágenes de la barbarie en 'La ilusión monarca' de Marcelo Cohen," in *Los imaginarios apocalípticos en la literatura hispanoamericana contemporánea*, ed. Geneviève Fabry, Ilse Logie, and Pablo Decock (Oxford: P. Lang, 2010), 265–66.

6. Page, *Creativity and Science*, 219.

7. Page, *Creativity and Science*, 195.

8. Page, *Creativity and Science*, 209. Original emphasis.

9. Page, *Creativity and Science*, 220.

10. Miguel Dalmaroni, "El fin de lo otro y la disolución del fantástico en un relato de Marcelo Cohen," *Cuadernos Angers-La Plata* 4, no. 4 (2001): 86.

11. Marcelo Cohen, *El fin de lo mismo* (Madrid: Anaya and Mario Muchnik, 1992), 120.

12. The name is appropriate given that "barda" means enclosing wall.

13. Cohen, *El fin de lo mismo*, 14.

14. Luis Alberto Romero, *La crisis argentina: una mirada al siglo XX* (Buenos Aires: Siglo Veintiuno, 2003), 93.

15. Oeyen, "Imágenes de la barbarie," 259.

16. See the excerpt from *Clarín* contained in Comisión Nacional Sobre la Desaparición de Personas CONADEP, Argentina, *Nunca más* (Buenos Aires: Editorial Universitaria de Buenos Aires, 1984), 236.

17. See CONADEP, *Nunca más*, 235. See Federico G. Lorenz and Peter Winn, "Las memorias de la violencia política y la dictadura militar en la Argentina: un recorrido en el año del Bicentenario," in *No hay mañana sin ayer: batallas por la memoria histórica en el Cono Sur*, ed. Federico G. Lorenz and Peter Winn (Buenos Aires: Biblos, 2015), 28; Masiello, *Art of Transition*, 5–6.

18. Claudia Kozak, "Ciudades bajo palabra: Literatura y memoria en el fin de siglo," *Boletín del centro de estudios de teoría y crítica literaria* 6 (October 1998): 58–60.

19. In Spanish, the acronym HIJOS also spells out "Sons and Daughters." For further detailed discussion of the "escrache," see James Scorer, *City in Common: Culture and Community in Buenos Aires* (Albany: State University of New York Press, 2016), 57–59; Hijos por la Identidad y la Justicia Contra el Olvido y el Silencio, "Si No Hay Justicia Hay Escrache," in *Memoria en construcción: El debate sobre la ESMA*, ed. Marcelo Brodsky (Buenos Aires: La Marca, 2005).

20. Masiello, *Art of Transition*, 6–7.

21. See Pozzi, "Popular Upheaval," 64–65.

22. Pozzi, "Popular Upheaval," 73.

23. Marcelo Cohen, *Insomnio* (Barcelona: Muchnik, 1986), 100, 112.

24. Oeyen, "Imágenes de la barbarie," 264. Miriam Chiani, "La 'Fiesta seminal de las palabras.' Sobre Marcelo Cohen," in *Fin(es) del siglo y modernismo (volumen II): congreso internacional Buenos Aires-La Plata*, ed. María Payeras Grau and Luis Miguel Fernández Ripoll (Palma: Universitat de les Illes Balears, 2001), 720.

25. Michel Foucault, *Discipline and Punish: The Birth of the Prison*, trans. Alan Sheridan (London: Penguin Books, 1991), 187.

26. Foucault, *Discipline and Punish*, 280.

27. Foucault, *Discipline and Punish*, 280.

28. Pilar Calveiro, *Poder y desaparición: los campos de concentración en Argentina* (Buenos Aires: Colihue, 1998), 46, 143–44.

29. Calveiro, *Poder y desaparición*, 11.

30. Foucault, *Discipline and Punish*, 271; Calveiro, *Poder y desaparición*, 27, 92. Original emphasis.

31. Foucault, *Discipline and Punish*, 128. Thomas Flynn, "Foucault's Mapping of History," in *The Cambridge Companion to Foucault*, ed. Gary Gutting (Cambridge; New York: Cambridge University Press, 1994), 36.

32. Page, *Creativity and Science*, 207.

33. Oeyen, "Imágenes de la barbarie," 260.

34. Cohen, *El fin de lo mismo*, 11.

35. Foucault, *Discipline and Punish*, 236.

36. Foucault, *Discipline and Punish*, 8, 48.

37. Foucault, *Discipline and Punish*, 34.

38. The details of Jolxen's mutilation are particularly abhorrent. It is noteworthy that severed genitals are found in Jolxen's mouth, as this same form of brutal torture is also encountered in Juan José Saer's novel set during the dictatorship, *Lo imborrable*. See Cohen, *El fin de lo mismo*, 100; Juan José Saer, *Lo imborrable* (Buenos Aires; Madrid: Alianza, 1993), 17. For further discussion of *Lo imborrable*, see Scorer, *City in Common*, 41–43.

39. Foucault, *Discipline and Punish*, 44.

40. Page, *Creativity and Science*, 208.

41. Foucault, *Discipline and Punish*, 50, 80.

42. Cohen, *El fin de lo mismo*, 37, 66. My emphasis.

43. Foucault, *Discipline and Punish*, 50.

44. Foucault, *Discipline and Punish*, 80.

45. Romero, *La crisis argentina*, 78; Calveiro, *Poder y desaparición*, 78.

46. Calveiro, *Poder y desaparición*, 45. Original emphasis.

47. Calveiro, *Poder y desaparición*, 58, 70.

48. Romero, *La crisis argentina*, 82.

49. Rozitchner, "Terror and Grace," 149, 150.

50. Rozitchner, "Terror and Grace," 148.

51. See for example the case of Julio Jorge López in 2006, Lorenz and Winn, "Las memorias de la violencia política y la dictadura militar en la Argentina: un recorrido en el año del Bicentenario," 61; of Facundo Rivera Alegre in 2012, Ludmila da Silva Catela, "Staged Memories: Conflicts and Tensions in Argentine Public Memory Sites," *Memory Studies* 8, no. 1 (2015): 14; and the continued uncertainty surrounding the case of Santiago Maldonado in 2017, Uki Goñi, "Argentina Activist Missing after Indigenous People Evicted from Benetton Land," *The Guardian*, 8 August 2017, accessed 11 August 2017, www.theguardian.com; Diego Rojas, "Joven desaparecido en Chubut: los peritajes apuntarían a Gendarmería," *infobae*, 6 August 2017, accessed 11 August 2017, www.infobae.com; Irina Hauser and Raúl Kollmann, "Una respuesta y nuevos interrogantes," *Página 12*, 25 November 2017, accessed 10 May 2018, www.pagina12.com.ar. For other cases of disappearance since the return to democracy in Argentina, see Matías de Rose, "Los desaparecidos de la democracia argentina," *Bifurcaciones: revista de estudios culturales urbanos*, 15 January 2015, accessed 13 August 2017, www.bifurcaciones.cl.

52. Peter Winn, "Las batalla por la memoria histórica en el Cono Sur: conclusiones comparativas," in *No hay mañana sin ayer: batallas por la memoria histórica en el Cono Sur*, ed. Federico G. Lorenz and Peter Winn (Buenos Aires: Biblos, 2015), 355; Kalmanowiecki, "Police, Politics, and Repression," 196.

53. Romero, *La crisis argentina*, 82–83.

54. Romero, *La crisis argentina*, 83.

55. Mayer, *Argentina en crisis*, 258.

56. Foucault, *Discipline and Punish*, 179.

57. Oeyen, "Imágenes de la barbarie," 261–62.

58. Page, *Creativity and Science*, 207.

59. Page, *Creativity and Science*, 207.

60. Deleuze, *Difference and Repetition*, 21.

61. Deleuze, "Preface," xx.

62. Deleuze, "Preface," xx. Original emphasis.

63. Foucault, *Discipline and Punish*, 182–83. Original emphasis.

64. Cohen, *Insomnio*, 18, 65.

65. James Joyce, *Ulysses*, ed. Jeri Johnson (Oxford; New York: Oxford University Press, 1998), 147.

66. Cohen, *Insomnio*, 25. My emphasis.

67. Ricardo Piglia, *El último lector* (Barcelona: Anagrama, 2005), 169–70.

68. Piglia, *El último lector*, 173.

69. Piglia, *El último lector*, 169.

70. Cohen, *Insomnio*, 32.

71. Cohen, *Insomnio*, 33.

72. Cohen, *Insomnio*, 177.

73. To distinguish the biblical prophet from the protagonist of Cohen's novel, the English spelling (Ezekiel) will be used to refer to the biblical character.

74. Cohen, *Insomnio*, 181.

75. Cohen, *Insomnio*, 182.

76. Piglia, *El último lector*, 171.

77. Piglia, *El último lector*, 177.

78. Cohen, *Insomnio*, 76, 182. Original emphasis.

79. Piglia, *El último lector*, 178.

80. Page, *Creativity and Science*, 217.

81. Deleuze, *Difference and Repetition*, 128.

82. Stagoll, "Becoming," 25, 26.

83. Stagoll, "Difference," 75.

84. Ecclesiastes 1:4–5. All biblical citations are from Robert Carroll, ed., *The Bible, Authorized King James Version [with Apocrypha]* (Oxford: Oxford University Press, 1998).

85. Ecclesiastes 1:6–7, 9.

86. Doug Ingram, *Ambiguity in Ecclesiastes* (New York: T and T Clark International, 2006), 44.

87. Norbert Lohfink, *Qoheleth: A Continental Commentary*, trans. Sean McEvenue (Minneapolis: Fortress Press, 2003), 40; Michael V. Fox, *Ecclesiastes = Kohelet: The Traditional Hebrew Text with the New JPS Translation* (Philadelphia: Jewish Publication Society, 2004), 61.

88. Cohen, *Insomnio*, 177.

89. Piglia, *El último lector*, 169–70.

90. Ecclesiastes 9:10.

91. Ecclesiastes 10:4.

92. Doug Ingram, *Ecclesiastes: A Peculiarly Postmodern Piece* (Cambridge: Grove Books, 2004), 5. Original emphasis.

93. Michel Foucault, *The Archaeology of Knowledge*, trans. A. M. Sheridan Smith (London: Tavistock, 1972), 28. My emphasis.

94. Foucault, *The Archaeology of Knowledge*, 95.

95. Gilles Deleuze, *Foucault*, trans. Seán Hand (London: Athlone, 1999), 4.

96. Deleuze, *Difference and Repetition*, xxii.

97. Ecclesiastes 9:14–15.

98. Ecclesiastes 9:17–18.

99. Oeyen, "Imágenes de la barbarie," 262; Page, *Creativity and Science*, 214.

100. Deleuze, *Difference and Repetition*, 23.

101. Cohen, *El fin de lo mismo*, 116.

102. Page, *Creativity and Science*, 214.

103. Deleuze, *Difference and Repetition*, 66. Original emphasis.

104. Cohen, *El fin de lo mismo*, 118.

105. Deleuze and Guattari, *A Thousand Plateaus*, 34.

106. Gilles Deleuze, *Francis Bacon: The Logic of Sensation*, trans. Daniel W. Smith (New York: Continuum, 2004), 44.

107. Deleuze and Guattari, *A Thousand Plateaus*, 173.

108. Deleuze and Guattari, *A Thousand Plateaus*, 309.

109. Cohen, *El fin de lo mismo*, 116.

110. Cohen, *El fin de lo mismo*, 120.

111. Oeyen, "Imágenes de la barbarie," 263; Page, *Creativity and Science*, 215.

112. CONADEP, *Nunca más*, 66.

113. Deleuze and Guattari, *Kafka*, 82.

114. Irma Antognazzi, "La vida adentro de las cárceles durante la dictadura militar del '76," *Razón y revolución* 4 (Autumn 1998): 88.

115. Antognazzi, "La vida adentro de las cárceles," 89.

116. Foucault, "The Subject and Power," 777.

117. Foucault, "The Subject and Power," 781.

118. Deleuze, *Foucault*, 101.

119. Conley, "Foucault + Fold," 115.

120. Deleuze, *Foucault*, 29.; Michel Foucault and Gilles Deleuze, "Intellectuals and Power," in *Language, Counter-Memory, Practice: Selected Essays and Interviews*, ed. Donald F. Bouchard (Oxford: Blackwell, 1977), 212.

Chapter 4: The Transition to Control

1. Dove, "Tonalities of Literature in Transition," 240–41; Thayer, "Crisis categorial de la universidad," 96n2; Avelar, "Dictatorship and Immanence," 75, 80; Avelar, *Untimely Present*, 11; Rozitchner, "Terror and Grace," 148.

2. Avelar, *Untimely Present*, 11.

3. Page, *Creativity and Science*, 19. See Gilles Deleuze, "Control and Becoming," in *Negotiations, 1972–1990* (New York: Columbia University Press, 1995), 174; Deleuze, "Postscript on Control Societies," 178; Gilles Deleuze, "What is a *Dispositif?*," in *Michel Foucault, Philos-*

opher, ed. Timothy J. Armstrong (New York; London: Harvester Wheatsheaf, 1992), 164; Nathan Moore, "Nova Law: William S. Burroughs and the Logic of Control," *Law and Literature* 19, no. 3 (2007).

4. Foucault, *Discipline and Punish*, 128; Gilles Deleuze, "Having an Idea in Cinema (On the Cinema of Straub-Huillet)," in *Deleuze and Guattari: New Mappings in Politics, Philosophy, and Culture*, ed. Eleanor Kaufman and Kevin Jon Heller (Minneapolis: University of Minnesota Press, 1998), 17.

5. Deleuze, "Postscript on Control Societies," 181; Deleuze, "Control and Becoming," 174.

6. See Mayer, *Argentina en crisis*, 28.

7. Pozzi, "Popular Upheaval," 72.

8. Oeyen, "Imágenes de la barbarie," 259.

9. Franz Kafka, *The Penguin Complete Short Stories of Kafka* (London: Allen Lane, 1983), 153, 158.

10. Deleuze, "Postscript on Control Societies," 178.

11. Flynn, "Foucault's Mapping of History," 36; Cohen, *El fin de lo mismo*, 73.

12. Deleuze, "Postscript on Control Societies," 182.

13. Deleuze, "Postscript on Control Societies," 178–79.

14. Deleuze, *Francis Bacon*, 47.

15. Calveiro, *Poder y desaparición*, 73.

16. Mark Poster, "Afterword," in *Deleuze and New Technology*, ed. Mark Poster and David Savat (Edinburgh: Edinburgh University Press, 2009), 260.

17. Pozzi, "Popular Upheaval," 77.

18. Michael Hardt, "The Withering of Civil Society," in *Deleuze and Guattari: New Mappings in Politics, Philosophy, and Culture*, ed. Eleanor Kaufman and Kevin Jon Heller (Minneapolis: University of Minnesota Press, 1998), 32.

19. Ron Silliman, "What do Cyborgs Want? (Paris, Suburb of the Twentieth Century)," in *Jean Baudrillard: The Disappearance of Art and Politics*, ed. William Stearns and William Chaloupka (London: Macmillan, 1992), 31.

20. Gabriel Ignacio Barreneche, "The Dystopic Theme Park: The Role of Lorelei in Marcelo Cohen's *El oído absoluto*," *Romance Quarterly* 55, no. 2 (2008): 130.

21. Barreneche, "Dystopic Theme Park," 129.

22. Saul Newman, "Politics in the Age of Control," in *Deleuze and New Technology*, ed. Mark Poster and David Savat (Edinburgh: Edinburgh University Press, 2009), 104.

23. Deleuze, "Control and Becoming," 175; Hardt, "The Withering of Civil Society," 30. My emphasis.

24. Deleuze, "Postscript on Control Societies," 179.

25. Poster, "Afterword," 260.

26. Barreneche, "Dystopic Theme Park," 131.

27. Jean Baudrillard, "The Precession of Simulacra," in *Simulacra and Simulation* (Ann Arbor: University of Michigan Press, 1994), 30; Jean Baudrillard and Sylvère Lotringer, *Forget Foucault* (New York: Semiotext(e), 1987), 16.

28. Baudrillard, "Precession of Simulacra," 1. To arrive at this conclusion, Baudrillard argues that the image has fundamentally changed over time, stating that "Such would be the successive phases of the image: it is the reflection of a profound reality; it masks and denatures a profound reality; it masks the absence of a profound reality; it has no relation to any reality whatsoever: it is its own pure simulacrum" (Baudrillard, "Precession of Simulacra," 6).

29. Baudrillard, "Precession of Simulacra," 12.

30. Barreneche, "Dystopic Theme Park," 135.

31. Jean Baudrillard, "Disneyworld Company," in *Screened Out* (London: Verso, 2002), 151.

32. Barreneche, "Dystopic Theme Park," 132.

33. Marcelo Cohen, *El oído absoluto* (Barcelona: Grupo Editorial Norma, 1997), 32, 86.

34. Jean Baudrillard, "Implosion of Meaning in the Media," in *Simulacra and Simulation* (Ann Arbor: University of Michigan Press, 1994), 79.

35. Cohen, *El oído absoluto*, 124.

36. Deleuze, "Having an Idea in Cinema," 17.

37. Cohen, *El oído absoluto*, 71.

38. Cohen, *El oído absoluto*, 142.

39. Jean Baudrillard, "The Orders of Simulacra," in *Simulations* (New York: Semiotext(e), 1983), 125.

40. Brian Massumi, "Requiem for Our Prospective Dead (Toward a Participatory Critique of Capitalist Power)," in *Deleuze and Guattari: New Mappings in Politics, Philosophy, and Culture*, ed. Eleanor Kaufman and Kevin Jon Heller (Minneapolis: University of Minnesota Press, 1998), 55. Original emphasis.

41. Baudrillard, "Precession of Simulacra," 12.

42. Baudrillard, "Precession of Simulacra," 6.

43. Cohen, *El oído absoluto*, 78.

44. Cohen, *El oído absoluto*, 88.

45. Dove, "Tonalities of Literature in Transition," 256.

46. Marcel Swiboda, "Becoming + Music," in *The Deleuze Dictionary*, ed. Adrian Parr (Edinburgh: Edinburgh University Press, 2010), 27.

47. Ronald Bogue, "Rhizomusicosmology," *SubStance* 20, no. 3 (1991): 85.

48. Cohen, *El oído absoluto*, 217.

49. For a detailed examination of the refrain, see Deleuze and Guattari, *A Thousand Plateaus*, 342–86.

50. Bogue, "Rhizomusicosmology," 88. In the same passage, Bogue provides several examples which help to eluducidate the unusual conception of the spatialised refrain. Deleuze and Guattari also provide several examples of different refrains and their corresponding territories. See Deleuze and Guattari, *A Thousand Plateaus*, 341–44.

51. Bogue, "Rhizomusicosmology," 90.

52. Cohen, *El oído absoluto*, 229; Bogue, "Rhizomusicosmology," 88.

53. As Andrew Murphie notes, "deterritorialization of refrains—their disconnection from their territory—is what they [Deleuze and Guattari] call music," Andrew Murphie, "Sound at the End of the World as We Know It: Nick Cave, Wim Wenders' *Wings of Desire* and a Deleuze-Guattarian Ecology of Popular Music," *Perfect Beat* 2, no. 4 (1996): 21.

54. Murphie, "Sound at the End," 23, 22.

55. Cohen, *El oído absoluto*, 217; Deleuze and Guattari, *A Thousand Plateaus*, 341.

56. Cohen, *El oído absoluto*, 229; Murphie, "Sound at the End," 25.

57. Cohen, *El oído absoluto*, 229; Murphie, "Sound at the End," 23.

58. Bogue, "Rhizomusicosmology," 91. Original emphasis.

59. Cohen, *El oído absoluto*, 229.

60. Cohen, *El oído absoluto*, 236.

61. Cohen, *El oído absoluto*, 237.

62. Deleuze and Guattari, *A Thousand Plateaus*, 330.

63. As Murphie comments, "a differentiation is needed between such useful formations

of territories which enable what Deleuze and Guattari would call . . . various 'lines of flight' on the one hand and, on the other, the use of the refrain to return us to sovereignty" (Murphie, "Sound at the End," 26).

64. Deleuze and Guattari, *A Thousand Plateaus*, 383.

65. Baudrillard, "Precession of Simulacra," 6.

66. Cohen, *El oído absoluto*, 259.

67. Cohen, *El oído absoluto*, 261.

68. Ruben Borg, "Mirrored Disjunctions: On a Deleuzo-Joycean Theory of the Image," *Journal of Modern Literature* 33, no. 2 (2010): 134.

69. Borg, "Mirrored Disjunctions," 134.

70. Jean Baudrillard, "The Evil Demon of Images," in *The Jean Baudrillard Reader*, ed. Steve Redhead (Edinburgh: Edinburgh University Press, 2008), 95. My emphasis.

71. Jean Baudrillard, "Revolution and the End of Utopia," in *Jean Baudrillard: The Disappearance of Art and Politics*, ed. William Stearns and William Chaloupka (London: Macmillan, 1992), 241.

72. Deleuze, "Postscript on Control Societies," 178.

73. Newman, "Politics in the Age of Control," 115.

74. Dalmaroni, "El fin de lo otro y la disolución del fantástico," 84.

75. Cohen, *El oído absoluto*, 74.

76. Cohen, *El oído absoluto*, 74.

77. Cohen, *El oído absoluto*, 75.

78. Deleuze, "Having an Idea in Cinema," 18.

79. Rosemary J. Coombe, "Postmodernity and the Rumour: Late Capitalism and the Fetishism of the Commodity/Sign," in *Jean Baudrillard: The Disappearance of Art and Politics*, ed. William Stearns and William Chaloupka (London: Macmillan, 1992), 106.

80. Coombe, "Postmodernity and the Rumour," 101.

81. Hardt, "The Withering of Civil Society," 31.

82. Cohen, *El oído absoluto*, 81.

83. Cohen, *El oído absoluto*, 128.

84. Deleuze, "Having an Idea in Cinema," 18.

85. Baudrillard and Lotringer, *Forget Foucault*, 54.

86. Cohen, *El oído absoluto*, 277.

87. Marcelo Cohen, "Variedades," in *Hombres amables: dos incursiones de Georges LaMente* (Buenos Aires: Grupo Editorial Norma, 1998), 59.

88. Deleuze, "Postscript on Control Societies," 181.

89. Kim Toffoletti, "Body," in *The Baudrillard Dictionary*, ed. Richard G. Smith (Edinburgh: Edinburgh University Press, 2010), 27.

90. Baudrillard, "Precession of Simulacra," 6.

91. Jean Baudrillard and Sylvère Lotringer, "Forget Baudrillard: An Interview with Sylvère Lotringer," in *Forget Foucault* (New York: Semiotext(e), 1987), 75.

92. Cohen, "Variedades," 38.

93. Cohen, "Variedades," 63.

94. For a summary of Baudrillard's critique of Deleuze's conception of desire, see Victoria Grace, *Baudrillard's Challenge: A Feminist Reading* (London; New York: Routledge, 2000), 72–76, 154–55. See also Baudrillard and Lotringer, *Forget Foucault*. Daniel W. Smith, "Deleuze and the Question of Desire: Toward an Immanent Theory of Ethics," in *Essays on Deleuze*, ed. Daniel W. Smith (Edinburgh: Edinburgh University Press, 2012), 183. Original emphasis.

95. The unification of political and libidinal economies is found elsewhere in Cohen's work. For example, in *Inolvidables veladas* the central character and his mother sign a contract when he is still a child that binds him to a company until his mother dies and allows the business to govern all aspects of his life. As many critics note, the relationship between mother and son in *Inolvidables veladas* establishes a strong correlation between the Oedipus myth and capitalism. See Adriana Fernández, "El tango y el espacio de las ciberciudades: sobre *Inolvidables veladas*, de Marcelo Cohen," *Espacios de crítica y producción* July-August 21 (1997): 95; Susana Chiani, "'Ese algo tuyo, eso tan tuyo': sobre *Inolvidables veladas* de Marcelo Cohen," *Tramas: para leer la literatura Argentina* 5, no. 9 (1998): 170; Sandra Gasparini, "Control y fuga: sobre *Inolvidables veladas* de Marcelo Cohen," in *Nuevos territorios de la literatura latinoamericana*, ed. Jorge Monteleone and Sylvia Iparraguirre (Buenos Aires: Instituto de Literatura Hispanoamericana, Universidad de Buenos Aires, 1997), 288.

96. Jean Baudrillard, *Seduction*, trans. Brian Singer (Montréal: New World Perspectives, 1990), 6–7; Baudrillard and Lotringer, *Forget Foucault*, 47.

97. For a summary of the most important feminist critiques of Baudrillard's conception of sexuality and seduction see Grace, *Baudrillard's Challenge*, 158–64.

98. Baudrillard, *Seduction*, 7. In the words of Victoria Grace, "Baudrillard is resolutely critical of this structure and its attendant assumptions" (Grace, *Baudrillard's Challenge*, 150). For a detailed feminist reading of Baudrillardian seduction, see Grace, *Baudrillard's Challenge*, 141–71.

99. Baudrillard, *Seduction*, 86.

100. Cohen, "Variedades," 21.

101. Baudrillard, *Seduction*, 88.

102. Cohen, "Variedades," 62; Baudrillard, "The Gulf War," 110; Baudrillard, "Impossible Exchange," 137.

103. Baudrillard, *Seduction*, 11.

104. Marcus A. Doel, "Seduction," in *The Baudrillard Dictionary*, ed. Richard G. Smith (Edinburgh: Edinburgh University Press, 2010), 186.

105. Baudrillard, *Seduction*, 86.

106. Baudrillard, "Pornography of War," 201.

107. Cohen, "Variedades," 111.

108. Deleuze, "Postscript on Control Societies," 179.

109. Baudrillard, *Seduction*, 166.

110. Rex Butler, "Foucault + Dead Power," in *The Baudrillard Dictionary*, ed. Richard G. Smith (Edinburgh: Edinburgh University Press, 2010), 80.

111. Gerry Coulter, "Reversibility," in *The Baudrillard Dictionary*, ed. Richard G. Smith (Edinburgh: Edinburgh University Press, 2010), 182.

112. Baudrillard and Lotringer, *Forget Foucault*, 47; Baudrillard, *Seduction*, 47.

113. A. Keith Goshorn, "Jean Baudrillard and the Radical Enigma: 'The Object's Fulfilment Without Regard for the Subject,'" in *Jean Baudrillard: The Disappearance of Art and Politics*, ed. William Stearns and William Chaloupka (London: Macmillan, 1992), 225.

114. Foucault, "The Subject and Power," 780.

115. Foucault, "The Subject and Power," 794.

116. John Marks, "Kafka, Franz (1883–1924)," in *The Deleuze Dictionary*, ed. Adrian Parr (Edinburgh: Edinburgh University Press, 2010), 137.

117. Deleuze and Guattari, *Kafka*, 38.

118. Deleuze and Guattari, *Kafka*, 8.

119. Deleuze and Guattari, *Kafka*, 39.

120. Deleuze and Guattari, *Kafka*, 38.
121. Deleuze and Guattari, *Kafka*, 81.
122. Deleuze and Guattari, *Kafka*, 82.
123. Deleuze and Guattari, *Kafka*, 57.
124. Deleuze and Guattari, *Kafka*, 39.
125. Page, *Creativity and Science*, 180.

Chapter 5: The Articulation of a Problem

1. See Daniel Balderston, "El significado latente en *Respiración artificial* de Ricardo Piglia y en *El corazon de junio* de Luis Gusman," in *Ficción y política: la narrativa argentina durante el proceso militar*, ed. Daniel Balderston et al. (Buenos Aires: Alianza, 1987), 112; Fornet, "Un debate de poéticas," 357; Marzena Grzegorczyk, "Discursos desde el margen: Gombrowicz, Piglia y la estética del basurero," *Hispamérica* 25, no. 73 (1996): 16.

2. The publication of Piglia's diaries suggests that the genesis for this idea may have come from his own family history. As Piglia relates, his grandfather fought in the First World War but after being injured was ordered to work in "la sección de cartas de los soldados muertos o desaparecidos en combate" (the section for letters from the soldiers who died or disappeared in combat). While Piglia's grandfather was instructed to collect each soldier's personal possessions (including unsent or half-finished letters) and send them with a condolence letter to their relatives, he instead kept the files and brought them back to Argentina. Piglia worked with his grandfather organizing this archive. See Piglia, *Años de formación*, 23–24. The third volume of Piglia's diary largely covers the period of time in which he wrote and published *Respiración artificial* during the miltiary dictatorship. The development of the novel can therefore be followed throughout the volume. See Piglia, *Un día en la vida*, 18–162.

3. Piglia, *Crítica y ficción*, 192; Seymour Menton, *Latin America's New Historical Novel* (Austin: University of Texas Press, 1993), 132.

4. Teresa Orecchia Havas, "Retratos ficcionales en la narrativa de Ricardo Piglia: Variaciones sobre el retrato del (autor en) artista," in *Cahiers de LI.RI.CO: Littératures contemporaines du Río de la Plata* (Saint Denis: Université de Paris 8 Vincennes, 2006), 278; Balderston, "El significado latente," 115; Menton, *Latin America's New Historical Novel*, 125. See also Piglia's diary entry for 28 August 1978, Piglia, *Un día en la vida*, 81.

5. Balderston, "El significado latente," 109; Berg, "La búsqueda," 130; Sonia Mattalia, "La historicidad del significante: *Respiración artificial* de Ricardo Piglia," in *Coloquio Internacional: el texto latinoamericano. Vol. 2* (Madrid: Fundamentos, 1994), 229; Menton, *Latin America's New Historical Novel*, 127, 135; Havas, "Retratos ficcionales," 283.

6. See, for example, Balderston, "El significado latente," 109; Arán, "Voces y fantasmas," 122; Fornet, "Un debate de poéticas," 357; Berg, "El relato ausente," 144.

7. Balderston, "El significado latente," 114.

8. Chakrabarty, *Provincializing Europe*, 29. Once more, it appears that due to its use of European theory to describe the functioning of Argentine novels, a similar dynamic arguably underpins the present book.

9. Menton, *Latin America's New Historical Novel*, 126.

10. Ricardo Piglia, "Ideología y ficción en Borges," in *Ficciones argentinas: antología de lecturas críticas*, ed. Ana María Barrenechea and Grupo de Investigación de Literatura Argentina Universidad de Buenos Aires (Buenos Aires: Grupo Editorial Norma, 2004), 37. In his diaries, Piglia also expresses surprise when some of his students in Princeton question a belief in binary oppositions. See Piglia, *Un día en la vida*, 213.

11. Balderston, "El significado latente," 112.

12. Fernanda Elisa Bravo Herrera, "Conjeturas e indagaciones: el doble movimiento enunciativo de Ricardo Piglia," in *Creación y proyección de los discursos narrativos*, ed. Daniel Altamiranda and Esther Smith (Buenos Aires: Dunken, 2008), 165.

13. Page, *Creativity and Science*, 230–31.

14. Piglia, *Respiración artificial*, 134.

15. See Aira, "La innovación," 29.

16. Piglia, *Crítica y ficción*, 192–93.

17. For a detailed description of the "intelectual comprometido" see María Sonderéguer, ed. *Revista crisis (1973–1976): antología, del intelectual comprometido al intelectual revolucionario* (Bernal: Universidad Nacional de Quilmes, 2008); Joanna Page, "Intellectuals, Revolution and Popular Culture: A New Reading of *El Eternauta*," *Journal of Latin American Cultural Studies* 19, no. 1 (2010); Sigal, *Intelectuales y poder*.

18. Piglia, *Crítica y ficción*, 32–33.

19. See Aira, *Diario de la hepatitis*, 35–36.

20. Piglia, *Nombre falso*, 111.

21. Aira, "La nueva escritura," 166.

22. See Piglia, *Crítica y ficción*, 35–36; Piglia, "Roberto Arlt: la ficción," 25.

23. Piglia, "Roberto Arlt: la ficción," 27.

24. Piglia, *Nombre falso*, 95, 107; Piglia, *Crítica y ficción*, 117; Ricardo Piglia, "Reivindicación de la práctica," in *Asesinos de papel: ensayos sobre narrativa policial*, ed. Jorge Lafforgue and Jorge B. Rivera (Buenos Aires: Colihue 1996), 53.

25. See Piglia, "Reivindicación," 52–53; Piglia, "Roberto Arlt: la ficción"; Piglia, "Roberto Arlt: una crítica"; Piglia, "Nueva narrativa norteamericana."

26. McCracken, "Metaplagiarism," 1077.

27. Deredita, "¿Es propiedad?," 69.

28. In a diary entry from 20 January 1978, Piglia mentions that he has been reading several volumes on the history of capitalism and specifically states that they are linked to the novel that he is writing (*Respiración artificial*). See Piglia, *Un día en la vida*, 68.

29. Piglia, "Ideología y ficción en Borges," 40.

30. Piglia, "Ideología y ficción en Borges," 41. In this way, Speranza argues that Piglia "recupera definitivamente a Borges para la izquierda" (definitively recovers Borges for the left) (Speranza, *Fuera de campo*, 266).

31. Piglia, *Respiración artificial*, 57, 55. Original emphasis.

32. Piglia, *Respiración artificial*, 56. Original emphasis.

33. Baudrillard, "Impossible Exchange," 136–37.

34. Aira has stated that Kafka "fue un amor de mi infancia y lo he releído a lo largo de mi vida muchas veces—en realidad nunca se sale de él" (was a love of my infancy and I have re-read him many times throughout my life—in reality, I never leave him) (Alfieri and Aira, *Conversaciones*, 23). See Aira, *Diario de la hepatitis*, 35–36.

35. Piglia, *Respiración artificial*, 214. The phrase is a quotation from Kafka's diaries.

36. Deleuze and Guattari, *Kafka*, 16.

37. The citation is from a letter sent to Max Brod in June 1921. See Deleuze and Guattari, *Kafka*, 93n1. Deleuze and Guattari, *Kafka*, 16.

38. Deleuze and Guattari, *Kafka*, 17.

39. Deleuze and Guattari, *Kafka*, 17.

40. Piglia, "Nueva narrativa norteamericana," 13.

41. Piglia, *Respiración artificial*, 209. Tardewski uses several variations of the same phrase. Deleuze and Guattari, *Kafka*, 83, 41. Original emphasis.

42. Piglia, *Respiración artificial*, 51–52.

43. Piglia, *Respiración artificial*, 52–53.

44. See Kalmanowiecki, "Police, Politics, and Repression," 198.

45. See Kalmanowiecki, "Police, Politics, and Repression," 197.

46. See Roberto Echavarren, "La literariedad: *Respiración artificial*, de Ricardo Piglia," *Revista Iberoamericana* 125, no. 49 (1983): 1004.

47. See Kalmanowiecki, "Police, Politics, and Repression," 204–5.

48. See Kalmanowiecki, "Police, Politics, and Repression," 204.

49. See Berg, "La búsqueda," 129.

50. Deleuze and Guattari, *Kafka*, 43.

51. Deleuze and Guattari, *Kafka*, 45.

52. Ricardo Piglia and León Rozitchner, *Tres propuestas para el próximo milenio (y cinco dificultades) / Mi Buenos Aires querida* (Mexico; Buenos Aires: Fondo de Cultura Económica, 2001), 17.

53. Later in his career, Deleuze stated that he wrote his book on Kant "as a book on an enemy" and described Kant's work as "a completely stifling philosophy." Cited in Hugh Tomlinson and Barbara Habberjam, "Translator's Introduction," in Gilles Deleuze, *Kant's Critical Philosophy: The Doctrine of the Faculties* (London: Athlone Press, 1984), xv; Gilles Deleuze, "Seminar on Kant: Synthesis and Time," 14 March 1978, *Webdeleuze*, accessed 9 June 2014, www.webdeleuze.com.

54. Deleuze and Guattari, *Kafka*, 43.

55. Piglia, *Crítica y ficción*, 181.

56. Gilles Deleuze, *Kant's Critical Philosophy: The Doctrine of the Faculties*, trans. Hugh Tomlinson and Barbara Habberjam (London: Athlone Press, 1984), 6, 14.

57. Piglia, *Crítica y ficción*, 181.

58. Deleuze and Guattari, *A Thousand Plateaus*, 236.

59. Deleuze and Guattari, *A Thousand Plateaus*, 237.

60. Piglia, *Respiración artificial*, 192.

61. Piglia, *Respiración artificial*, 195, 192.

62. Michael Rohlf, "Immanuel Kant," in *The Stanford Encyclopedia of Philosophy*, ed. Adward N. Zalta, §5.1, accessed 2 November 2014, https://plato.stanford.edu.

63. Immanuel Kant, *The Critique of Pure Reason; The Critique of Practical Reason and other Ethical Treatises; The Critique of Judgement*, ed. Robert Maynard Hutchins, trans. J. M. D. Meiklejohn, et al., vol. 42 (Chicago: Encyclopaedia Britannica, 1963), 303; Rohlf, "Immanuel Kant," §5.1.

64. Kant, *Practical Reason*, 42, 303. Original emphasis.

65. Kant, *Practical Reason*, 42, 298; Rohlf, "Immanuel Kant," §5.1.

66. Deleuze and Guattari, *A Thousand Plateaus*, 414.

67. Piglia, *Respiración artificial*, 194, 196.

68. Immanuel Kant, *Critique of Pure Reason*, trans. Norman Kemp Smith (London: Macmillan, 1929), 328–83; Kant, *Critique of Pure Reason*, 329; Béatrice Longuenesse, "Kant's 'I Think' versus Descartes' 'I am a Thing That Thinks,'" in *Kant and the Early Moderns*, ed. Daniel Garber and Béatrice Longuenesse (Princeton: Princeton University Press, 2008), 17. For a detailed discussion of the different functions of the "I" in Kant and Descartes's formulation of the cogito, see Longuenesse, "Kant's 'I Think,'" 13–17.

69. Deleuze, *Kant's Critical Philosophy*, 35; Deleuze and Guattari, *A Thousand Plateaus*, 415; Verena Conley, "Order-Word," in *The Deleuze Dictionary*, ed. Adrian Parr (Edinburgh: Edinburgh University Press, 2010), 198.

70. Deleuze and Guattari, *A Thousand Plateaus*, 578n17. Deleuze and Guattari's argument could be considered a development of observations made by Hannah Arendt at the trial of the infamous Nazi Adolf Eichmann. Not only did Eichmann express a profound lack of guilt, but he explained his sense of innocence by claiming that he had only ever obeyed Hitler's oral orders, which he believed had the force of the law. In addition, Arendt notes that Eichmann explicitly stated that his morality was grounded in the work of Kant and the categorical imperative. See Hannah Arendt, *Eichmann in Jerusalem: A Report on the Banality of Evil* (New York: Penguin Books, 2006), 108, 135–37, 148.

71. Menton, *Latin America's New Historical Novel*, 131; Deleuze and Guattari, *A Thousand Plateaus*, 415.

72. Rohlf, "Immanuel Kant," introduction.

73. Rohlf, "Immanuel Kant," §2.2.

74. Kant, *Critique of Pure Reason*, 24. Original emphasis.

75. Rohlf, "Immanuel Kant," §3.1.

76. Thiele, *The Thought of Becoming*, 34.

77. Kant, *Critique of Pure Reason*, 152.

78. Deleuze, *Difference and Repetition*, 138.

79. Deleuze, *Difference and Repetition*, 138.

80. Deleuze, *Difference and Repetition*, 2–3, 6.

81. Menton, *Latin America's New Historical Novel*, 128.

82. Piglia, *Respiración artificial*, 81; W. B. Yeats, *The Poems* (London: Macmillan, 1997), 187.

83. Yeats, *Poems*, 187.

84. Piglia, *Respiración artificial*, 61, 63, 70.

85. William Wordsworth and Samuel Taylor Coleridge, *Lyrical Ballads 1798 and 1800* (Peterborough, Ontario: Broadview Press, 2008), 56.

86. Deleuze, *Difference and Repetition*, 103.

87. Deleuze, *Difference and Repetition*, 15.

88. Deleuze, *Difference and Repetition*, 21.

89. Rohlf, "Immanuel Kant," §3; Kant, *Critique of Pure Reason*, 82. My emphasis.

90. Rohlf, "Immanuel Kant," §3.

91. Longuenesse, "Kant's 'I Think,'" 16.

92. Deleuze, *Difference and Repetition*, 86.

93. Keith Ansell-Pearson, *Germinal Life: The Difference and Repetition of Deleuze* (London: Routledge, 1999), 102.

94. Deleuze, *Difference and Repetition*, 87.

95. Gilles Deleuze, "Preface: On Four Poetic Formulas which Might Summarize the Kantian Philosophy," in *Kant's Critical Philosophy: The Doctrine of the Faculties*, ed. Gilles Deleuze (London: Athlone Press, 1984), ix, viii.

96. Deleuze, *Difference and Repetition*, 86.

97. Ansell-Pearson, *Germinal Life*, 103.

98. Deleuze, *Difference and Repetition*, 82.

99. Williams, *Deleuze's Philosophy of Time*, 17.

100. See Piglia, *Años de formación*, 71–73, 75, 80, 130, 192, 247; Piglia, *Un día en la vida*, 153.

101. See Piglia, *Años de formación*, 150, 171–72, 235, 242; Piglia, *Un día en la vida*, 47.

102. Piglia, *Respiración artificial*, 48.

103. Piglia, *Los años felices*, 184.

104. Deleuze, *Difference and Repetition*, 70.

105. Deleuze, *Difference and Repetition*, 76.

106. To explicate this synthesis, Williams provides the example of using an old water pump that injures your hand as you operate it. As the action is repeated, "the body and the brain" absorb "the earlier injuries and later experiments into a trained and automatic action." Crucially, each individual "stroke at the water pump retains all the earlier attempts it has learnt from," and "future events are synthesised by being anticipated, looked forward to or awaited in the living present, for instance, in the way a learning stroke in the present anticipates future strokes and improvements by driving towards them" (Williams, *Deleuze's Philosophy of Time*, 21, 25). It is this retention of the past and anticipation of the future that Deleuze calls "contraction."

107. Deleuze, *Difference and Repetition*, 70–71.

108. Piglia, *Respiración artificial*, 46–47.

109. Piglia, *Respiración artificial*, 48.

110. Ansell-Pearson, *Germinal Life*, 100.

111. Deleuze, *Difference and Repetition*, 7.

112. Deleuze, *Difference and Repetition*, 74.

113. Regarding Williams's example, he acknowledges that it demonstrates that "there may well be [active] reflection in the preparation of habitual movements" but contends that as the action is repeated, "those preparatory movements are finally contracted together into a movement going beyond each instant of reflection." As he explains, each "smooth and self--enclosed gesture pulls together a series of past processes, some deliberate and others unconscious, such that the current motion is a passive synthesis of earlier events" (Williams, *Deleuze's Philosophy of Time*, 21–22).

114. Deleuze, *Difference and Repetition*, 74.

115. Piglia, *Respiración artificial*, 46–47.

116. Ansell-Pearson, *Germinal Life*, 101.

117. Ansell-Pearson, *Germinal Life*, 101–02.

118. Piglia, *Respiración artificial*, 45.

119. Piglia, *Respiración artificial*, 19; Joyce, *Ulysses*, 34.

120. Fornet, "Un debate de poéticas," 357.

121. Page, *Creativity and Science*, 57.

122. Piglia, *Crítica y ficción*, 161.

123. Deleuze, *Difference and Repetition*, 70.

124. Deleuze, *Difference and Repetition*, 79. Original emphasis.

125. Deleuze, *Difference and Repetition*, 79; Gilles Deleuze, *Bergsonism*, trans. Hugh Tomlinson and Barbara Habberjam (New York: Zone Books, 1988), 27.

126. Deleuze, *Difference and Repetition*, 81.

127. While I am, at present, particularly concerned with Deleuze's philosophy of time as articulated in *Difference and Repetition*, his interpretation of Bergson is encountered throughout his oeuvre, and most fully elaborated in *Bergsonism*. Deleuze, *Difference and Repetition*, 81; Deleuze, *Bergsonism*, 59. Original emphasis.

128. See table in James Williams, "Objects in Manifold Times: Deleuze and the Speculative Philosophy of Objects as Processes," *Cosmos and History: The Journal of Natural and Social Philosophy* 7, no. 1 (2011): 64; Williams, *Deleuze's Philosophy of Time*, 16.

129. Piglia, *Crítica y ficción*, 161.

130. Piglia, *Respiración artificial*, 30.
131. Piglia, *Respiración artificial*, 26.
132. Deleuze, *Difference and Repetition*, 90.
133. Piglia, *Crítica y ficción*, 161.
134. Ansell-Pearson, *Germinal Life*, 102.
135. Deleuze, *Difference and Repetition*, 90.
136. Williams, *Deleuze's Philosophy of Time*, 25.
137. Deleuze, *Difference and Repetition*, 94.
138. Piglia, *Respiración artificial*, 83.
139. Piglia, *Respiración artificial*, 80.
140. Deleuze, *Difference and Repetition*, 93, 94.
141. Williams, "Objects in Manifold Times," 74.
142. Deleuze, *Difference and Repetition*, 89; Williams, *Deleuze's Philosophy of Time*, 91.
143. William Shakespeare, *Complete Works of William Shakespeare* (Glasgow: Harper-Collins, 1994), 1091; Deleuze, *Difference and Repetition*, 88; Williams, *Deleuze's Philosophy of Time*, 99.
144. Williams, *Deleuze's Philosophy of Time*, 88–89.
145. Piglia, *Respiración artificial*, 81.
146. Marx, "Eighteenth Brumaire," 19.
147. Deleuze, *Difference and Repetition*, 92. Original emphasis.
148. Deleuze, *Difference and Repetition*, 91.
149. Piglia, *Respiración artificial*, 46.
150. Piglia, *Respiración artificial*, 96; Balderston, "El significado latente," 113. My emphasis.
151. Balderston, "El significado latente," 113.
152. Deleuze, *Difference and Repetition*, 91.
153. Williams, *Deleuze's Philosophy of Time*, 102.
154. Piglia, *Respiración artificial*, 216.
155. Piglia, *Respiración artificial*, 217.
156. Piglia, *Respiración artificial*, 22.
157. Deleuze, *Difference and Repetition*, 92.
158. Patricia Rei, *El cuento de nunca acabar, o, El Pierre Menard de Ricardo Piglia* (Rosario: Ciudad Gótica, 2005), 50–51.
159. Rei, *El cuento de nunca acabar*, 50.
160. Rei, *El cuento de nunca acabar*, 52.
161. Lambert, *Non-Philosophy*, 81; Deleuze, "Preface," xxi–xxii.
162. Grzegorczyk, "Discursos desde el margen," 21.
163. Grzegorczyk, "Discursos desde el margen," 25.
164. Grzegorczyk, "Discursos desde el margen," 24.
165. Grzegorczyk, "Discursos desde el margen," 28.
166. Grzegorczyk, "Discursos desde el margen," 26.
167. Menton, *Latin America's New Historical Novel*, 129.
168. Menton, *Latin America's New Historical Novel*, 129.
169. Deleuze, *Difference and Repetition*, 283.
170. Deleuze, *Difference and Repetition*, 116, 200.
171. Deleuze, *Difference and Repetition*, 200–201.
172. Deleuze, *Difference and Repetition*, 116, 198.
173. Deleuze, *Difference and Repetition*, 199.
174. Deleuze, *Difference and Repetition*, xxii.

Chapter 6: To Become Worthy of What Happens to Us

1. The origins of Piglia's writing machine can now be traced to Piglia's early encounters with scientists working on artificial intelligence at universities in the United States. See Piglia, *Un día en la vida*, 190–92.

2. See the description of Rajzarov in Piglia, *La ciudad ausente*, 152–53; Havas, "Retratos ficcionales," 288.

3. Arán, "Voces y fantasmas," 114.

4. Piglia, *La ciudad ausente*, 166.

5. Piglia, *La ciudad ausente*, 160. Piglia's depiction of the actions of Lugones Jr. is verified in Kalmanowiecki, "Police, Politics, and Repression," 203–4.

6. Piglia, *La ciudad ausente*, 143.

7. See Kalmanowiecki, "Police, Politics, and Repression," 206.

8. Instances of the use of the "picana eléctrica" (electric cattle prod) are cited throughout *Nunca más*. For example, see CONADEP, *Nunca más*, 46, 155. Piglia himself mentions in his diaries that one of his friends was tortured in this way in 1971. He also recounts that his friend's captors threatened to throw him into the Río de la Plata as nobody knew that he was imprisoned. See Piglia, *Los años felices*, 265–66. For a full account of the continual abuses perpetrated by the Argentine police force throughout the twentieth century see Kalmanowiecki, "Police, Politics, and Repression," 203–11.

9. Kalmanowiecki, "Police, Politics, and Repression," 195.

10. Piglia, *La ciudad ausente*, 160.

11. Piglia, *La ciudad ausente*, 87. As argued with regard to Cohen's literature, the applicability of Deleuze's theory to Piglia's work is not at all surprising given that Piglia too has stressed the influence of William Burroughs on his literature.

12. Piglia, *La ciudad ausente*, 145.

13. Nathan Van Camp, "From Biopower to Psychopower: Bernard Stiegler's Pharmacology of Mnemotechnologies," *Ctheory*, 5 September 2012, accessed 6 October 2014, www.ctheory.net; original emphasis.

14. Bernard Stiegler, "Within the Limits of Capitalism, Economizing Means Taking Care," *Ars Industrialis*, 2006, accessed 6 October 2014, http://arsindustrialis.org.

15. Piglia, *La ciudad ausente*, 63.

16. Van Camp, "From Biopower to Psychopower." Original emphasis.

17. Masiello, *Art of Transition*, 166; James Cisneros, "El ocaso del museo del interior: *La ciudad ausente* de Ricardo Piglia," *Cuadernos americanos: nueva época* 2, no. 116 (2006): 112.

18. Piglia, *La ciudad ausente*, 109.

19. Borges, *Obras completas*, 1, 568. On several occasions Piglia appropriates and paraphrases this line of Borges's text within his personal diary. See Piglia, *Años de formación*, 150, 283.

20. Baudrillard, "Precession of Simulacra," 3.

21. Piglia, *La ciudad ausente*, 14–15. See Baudrillard, "Precession of Simulacra," 3–4.

22. Piglia, *La ciudad ausente*, 37.

23. See Jorge Luis Borges, *Obras completas, 2: 1952–1972* (Buenos Aires: Emecé, 1990), 225.

24. See Baudrillard, "Precession of Simulacra," 1.

25. The resonance between Piglia's fiction and the work of Borges and Baudrillard can be found in several instances in his wider oeuvre. For example, the short text "La moneda griega" (included in the first volume of Piglia's diaries) features a character that creates an exact copy of the city of Buenos Aires in his house. The text is undoubtedly a reinvention of

Borges's seminal story "El Aleph." Nonetheless, when Piglia comments that the character "ha alterado las relaciones de representación, de modo que la ciudad real es la que esconde en su casa y la otra es sólo un espejismo o un recuerdo" (has altered the relations of representation in such a way that the real city is the one concealed in his house and the other is merely a mirage or a memory), it invariably echoes Baudrillard's argument that simulacral copies have supplanted reality in contemporary hyperreality (as in his analysis of Disneyland discussed in chapter 4, for example). See Piglia, *Años de formación*, 273–80; Borges, *Obras completas*, 1, 617–28; Baudrillard, "Precession of Simulacra," 12.

26. Baudrillard, "Precession of Simulacra," 1, 6.

27. Piglia, *Crítica y ficción*, 182. See also Piglia, *Un día en la vida*, 14–15, 33.

28. Piglia, *Crítica y ficción*, 183.

29. Baudrillard, "Precession of Simulacra," 6. In an earlier text, Baudrillard also suggests a historical development of the various orders of simulacra. See Baudrillard, "The Orders of Simulacra."

30. Piglia, *Crítica y ficción*, 15. In this regard Piglia's argument shares much in common with Arendt's analysis of the strict "language rules" used by the Nazis to mask the horrific nature of the crimes of the Holocaust. See Arendt, *Eichmann in Jerusalem*, 84–86, 108.

31. Piglia, *Crítica y ficción*, 63.

32. Piglia, *Crítica y ficción*, 180.

33. Piglia, *La ciudad ausente*, 95; Ricardo Piglia, *The Absent City*, trans. Sergio Gabriel Waisman (Durham, NC: Duke University Press, 2000), 79.

34. Piglia, *Crítica y ficción*, 61–62.

35. Neri Francisco Enrique Romero, "*Ciudad ausente* de Ricardo Piglia: el imaginario futurista del 'New Order.' La poética de la ficción paranoica," *Cuadernos de la literatura* 8 (1998): 175.

36. Piglia, *La ciudad ausente*, 143.

37. Piglia, *La ciudad ausente*, 65.

38. Coombe, "Postmodernity and the Rumour," 106.

39. Coombe, "Postmodernity and the Rumour," 101.

40. Coombe, "Postmodernity and the Rumour," 101.

41. Piglia, *La ciudad ausente*, 41–42.

42. See Ricardo Piglia, *Prisión perpetua* (Barcelona: Anagrama, 2007), 85.

43. Macedonio Fernández, *Museo de la Novela de la Eterna: edición crítica* (Nanterre: ALLCA XX, 1993), 35. My emphasis.

44. Cited in Fernández, *Museo*, 256n6.

45. Evelia Romano Thuesen, "Macedonio Fernández: su teoría de la novela en *La ciudad ausente* de Ricardo Piglia," *Alba de América* 12, nos. 22–23 (1994): 222.

46. Pereira, *Ricardo Piglia*, 33. Pereira also notes the connections with Poe and Stevenson.

47. For a full account of this episode see Ruben Borg, *The Measureless Time of Joyce, Deleuze and Derrida* (London: Continuum, 2007), 126–27.

48. Piglia, *El último lector*, 171.

49. Piglia, *La ciudad ausente*, 97.

50. Seamus Deane, "Introduction," in James Joyce, *Finnegans Wake* (London: Penguin Books, 2000), xxviii. For detailed analysis of select Joycean portmanteaux see Umberto Eco, *The Aesthetics of Chaosmos: The Middle Ages of James Joyce*, trans. Ellen Esrock (Cambridge, MA: Harvard University Press, 1989), 65; Borg, *Measureless Time*, 71; Ruben Borg, "Neologizing in *Finnegans Wake*: Beyond a Typology of the Wakean Portmanteau," *Poetics Today* 28, no. 1 (2007): 147.

51. Deleuze, *Difference and Repetition*, 102, 106.

52. Piglia, *La ciudad ausente*, 14. Fernández, *Museo*, 256n8.

53. See Joyce, *Ulysses*, 72, 163.

54. Piglia, *La ciudad ausente*, 46.

55. See A. Nicholas Fargnoli and Michael Patrick Gillespie, *Critical Companion to James Joyce: A Literary Reference to His Life and Work* (New York: Facts on File, 2006), 109.

56. See James Joyce, *Finnegans Wake* (London: Penguin Books, 2000), 215. The text of the doxology reads: "Glory be to the Father, and to the Son, and to the Holy Ghost. *As it was in the beginning, is now and ever shall be,* world without end. Amen." Piglia, *La ciudad ausente*, 122.

57. Piglia, *La ciudad ausente*, 115; Borges, *Obras completas*, 2, 149.

58. See Ricardo Piglia, "Notas sobre Macedonio en un diario," in *Museo de la Novela de la Eterna: edición crítica*, ed. Ana María Camblong and Adolfo de Obieta (Nanterre: ALLCA XX, 1993), 519. See for example Masiello, *Art of Transition*, 166.

59. Borg, "Neologizing in *Finnegans Wake*," 149, 150.

60. Borg, "Neologizing in *Finnegans Wake*," 149.

61. Deane, "Introduction," xlviii.

62. Borges, *Obras completas, 1*, 624. See Borges, *Obras completas, 1*, 465–71. In her cabalistic reading of the text, Pereira notes that the aleph is a paradoxical letter that represents a totality "inclusive creador y criatura" (including creator and creature) but that within it "todo puede convertirse en otra cosa: bajo la unidad se encuentra una infinita diversidad" (everything can be transformed into something else: within unity one encounters infinite diversity) (Pereira, *Ricardo Piglia*, 97).

63. Fernández, *Museo*, 65, 109nA.

64. Fernández, *Museo*, 253.

65. Piglia, "Notas sobre Macedonio," 519.

66. See Ana María Camblong, "Estudio preliminar," in *Museo de la Novela de la Eterna: edición crítica*, ed. Ana María Camblong and Adolfo de Obieta (Nanterre: ALLCA XX, 1993), lxiv–lxviii; Todd S. Garth, *The Self of the City: Macedonio Fernández, the Argentine Avant-Garde, and Modernity in Buenos Aires* (Lewisburg, PA: Bucknell University Press, 2005), 14, 46, 56.

67. Cisneros, "El ocaso del museo del interior," 116, 115. Original emphasis.

68. Page, *Creativity and Science*, 179–80, 170. Pereira reads Piglia's fiction similarly by connecting it with Benoit Mandelbrot's discovery of fractals and with the conception of the hypertext. See Pereira, *Ricardo Piglia*, 35, 89–103.

69. Page, *Creativity and Science*, 171.

70. Eric McLuhan, "The Rhetorical Structure of *Finnegans Wake*," *James Joyce Quarterly* 11, no. 4 (1974): 394.

71. Joyce, *Finnegans Wake*, 5.

72. Joyce, *Finnegans Wake*, 150. Other examples of televisual references can be found at Joyce, *Finnegans Wake*, 52 and 349.

73. Eric McLuhan, *The Role of Thunder in Finnegans Wake* (Toronto: University of Toronto Press, 1997), 216; Borg, "Mirrored Disjunctions," 141; Joyce, *Finnegans Wake*, 349–50.

74. For a detailed discussion of television in *Finnegans Wake*, see McLuhan, *The Role of Thunder*, 213–34. For a detailed Deleuzian analysis of the Joycean image more generally, see Borg, "Mirrored Disjunctions."

75. Deane, "Introduction," xxviii.

76. See Deane, "Introduction," xxxvii; Joyce, *Finnegans Wake*, 615–19. Kimberley Devlin

notes that it is first suggested that Anna Livia is the "hypothetical author of the letter" in part 1, chapter 5. See Kimberly Devlin, "ALP's Final Monologue in *Finnegans Wake*: The Dialectical Logic of Joyce's Dream Text," in *Coping with Joyce: Essays from the Copenhagen Symposium*, ed. Morri Beja and Shari Benstock (Columbus: Ohio State University Press, 1989), 232.

77. Coombe, "Postmodernity and the Rumour," 101. It is interesting to note that Piglia also reflects on the central (and secret) crime in *Finnegans Wake* in his diaries, connecting it with various other examples from literary history. See Piglia, *Un día en la vida*, 168.

78. Borg, *Measureless Time*, 1; Joyce, *Finnegans Wake*, 143, 262.

79. See Borg, *Measureless Time*; Ruben Borg, "Two Ps in a Pod: On Time in 'Finnegans Wake,'" *Journal of Modern Literature* 29, no. 1 (2005); Borg, "Neologizing in *Finnegans Wake*."

80. Borg, *Measureless Time*, 7.

81. Borg, *Measureless Time*, 39.

82. Borg, *Measureless Time*, 41.

83. Borg, *Measureless Time*, 41. This sentiment is also echoed in *Ulysses* by Leopold Bloom, who reflects in his interior monologue that you "never know whose thoughts you're chewing" (Joyce, *Ulysses*, 162). Fernández, *Museo*, 8.

84. Deleuze, *Difference and Repetition*, 91.

85. Piglia, *La ciudad ausente*, 127.

86. Jacques Derrida, "Two Words For Joyce," in *Post-Structuralist Joyce: Essays from the French*, ed. Derek Attridge and Daniel Ferrer (Cambridge: Cambridge University Press, 1984), 147.

87. Borg, *Measureless Time*, 103.

88. James Joyce, *Selected Letters of James Joyce* (London: Faber and Faber, 1992), 289.

89. Page, *Creativity and Science*, 165–66.

90. Borges, *Obras completas*, 2, 186; Jorge Luis Borges, *Obras completas, 3: 1975–1985* (Buenos Aires: Emecé, 1989), 393–99.

91. Garth, *The Self of the City*, 25.

92. Fernández, *Museo*, 37.

93. Garth, *The Self of the City*, 63.

94. It is important to note that the questioning of the self is another preoccupation that Piglia maintained throughout his career. Indeed, in 1968 Piglia produced an edited volume of Argentine texts entitled and centered on the question of the *Yo* (I). This volume features both "Borges y yo" and a text by Macedonio Fernández. In addition, a revised version of Piglia's introduction to the text is also reproduced in his diaries, where again Piglia consistently questions notions of the self, reflecting on the importance of Freud in radically altering our perception of subjectivity, repeating his desire to write in the third person in order to evade the illusion of having an interior life, or stressing the necessity of becoming someone else (Renzi) in order to write. See Ricardo Piglia, ed., *Yo* (Buenos Aires: Editorial Tiempo Contemporáneo, 1968); Piglia, *Años de formación*, 228, 336–37; Piglia, *Los años felices*, 8, 113.

95. For a detailed description of the "maximum individual," see Garth, *The Self of the City*, 27, 194–95.

96. Borg, *Measureless Time*, 103.

97. Joyce, *Finnegans Wake*, 496.

98. Joyce, *Finnegans Wake*, 614–15.

99. Borg, *Measureless Time*, 133–34.

100. Borg, *Measureless Time*, 135.

101. Deleuze, *Difference and Repetition*, 90.

102. Borg, *Measureless Time*, 135.

103. Deleuze, *Difference and Repetition*, 94.

104. See Edgardo H. Berg, "La conspiración literaria (sobre *La ciudad ausente* de Ricardo Piglia)," *Hispamérica* 25, no. 75 (1996): 44.

105. Lewis, *Crisis of Argentine Capitalism*, 229.

106. Piglia, *La ciudad ausente*, 123, 121.

107. Borges, *Obras completas, 1*, 456.

108. Borges, *Obras completas, 1*, 459.

109. Borges, *Obras completas, 1*, 459. Original emphasis.

110. Gilles Deleuze, *The Logic of Sense*, ed. Constantin V. Boundas, trans. Mark Lester and Charles Stivale (London: Athlone Press, 1990), 61.

111. Helen Palmer, *Deleuze and Futurism: A Manifesto for Nonsense* (London: Bloomsbury, 2014), 175.

112. Palmer, *Deleuze and Futurism*, 175.

113. Borges, *Obras completas, 1*, 507.

114. Deleuze, *The Logic of Sense*, 176.

115. Deleuze, *Difference and Repetition*, 41.

116. Deleuze, *Difference and Repetition*, 90.

117. Deleuze, *Difference and Repetition*, 69, 299. Joyce, *Finnegans Wake*, 118. Original emphasis.

118. Borges, *Obras completas, 1*, 459.

119. Borg, *Measureless Time*, 39–40.

120. This account of time in *La ciudad ausente* also seeks to reconcile the markedly different conceptions of time that Deleuze presents in *Difference and Repetition* and the later work *The Logic of Sense*. The most obvious difference between the two texts is that Deleuze's original description of the three syntheses of time in the earlier work is replaced by the two times of Aion and Chronos in the later book. Put simply, within the present analysis Chronos is considered to be broadly similar to Deleuze's first synthesis of time and Aion to be a metastable form of time permanently between the second and third syntheses. Williams accounts for this distinction slightly differently. He suggests that Chronos absorbs "the past and future as dimensions of the present" as in the first synthesis of time, that Aion incorporates "the past and present as dimensions of the future" as in the third synthesis of time, and finally that the second synthesis of time, which assimilates "the present and the future as dimensions of the past," is the "relation between Aiôn and Chronos." I would suggest that this subtly different interpretation of Deleuze's contrasting descriptions of time would not substantially affect the present discussion of Piglia's novel. See Williams, *Deleuze's Philosophy of Time*, 138.

121. Havas, "Retratos ficcionales," 293.

122. Page, *Creativity and Science*, 111.

123. Piglia, *La ciudad ausente*, 154–55; Page, *Creativity and Science*, 112.

124. Piglia, *Crítica y ficción*, 79.

125. Deleuze, *Difference and Repetition*, 293.

126. Page, *Creativity and Science*, 235.

127. Piglia, *Crítica y ficción*, 205.

128. Piglia, *Crítica y ficción*, 205.

129. Garth, *The Self of the City*, 90.

130. Borg, "Neologizing in *Finnegans Wake*," 149; Garth, *The Self of the City*, 87–88.

131. Berg, "El relato ausente," 150.

132. Deleuze, *The Logic of Sense*, 176.

133. Gilles Deleuze, "Ethics and the Event," in *The Deleuze Reader*, ed. Constantin V. Boundas (New York: Columbia University Press, 1993), 81.

134. Constantin V. Boundas, "Editor's Introduction," in *The Deleuze Reader*, ed. Constantin V. Boundas (New York: Columbia University Press, 1993), 9.

135. Deleuze, "Ethics and the Event," 79.

136. Boundas, "Editor's Introduction," 9.

137. Piglia, *Crítica y ficción*, 79. My emphasis.

138. Page, *Creativity and Science*, 111, 95. My emphasis.

139. Garth, *The Self of the City*, 190.

140. Deleuze and Guattari, *A Thousand Plateaus*, 381.

141. Piglia, *Crítica y ficción*, 165.

142. Piglia, *Crítica y ficción*, 165.

143. Jacques Rancière, *The Politics of Aesthetics: The Distribution of the Sensible* (London: Continuum, 2006), 30.

144. Deleuze and Guattari, *Kafka*, 17–18.

145. Garth, *The Self of the City*, 56; Fernández, *Museo*, 7.

146. Garth, *The Self of the City*, 57.

147. Cited in Contreras, *Las vueltas*, 25.

148. Deleuze and Guattari, *Kafka*, 32.

149. Piglia, *Respiración artificial*, 32.

150. Piglia, *Respiración artificial*, 34.

151. Deleuze and Guattari, *Kafka*, 30.

152. Piglia, *La ciudad ausente*, 11.

153. Echavarren, "La literariedad," 998–99.

154. Deleuze and Guattari, *Kafka*, 32.

155. Echavarren, "La literariedad," 1001.

156. Piglia, *Respiración artificial*, 84–85.

157. Piglia, *Respiración artificial*, 78, 31. Original emphasis.

158. Cohen's exile endured until 1996. See Cohen, "Pequeñas batallas," 37.

159. Echavarren, "La literariedad," 1000.

160. Deleuze and Guattari, *Kafka*, 29.

161. Deleuze and Guattari, *Kafka*, 29.

162. Deleuze and Guattari, *Kafka*, 30–31.

163. Deleuze and Guattari, *Kafka*, 32.

164. Deleuze and Guattari, *Kafka*, 83–84.

165. Deleuze and Guattari, *Kafka*, 17–18.

166. Marks, "Kafka, Franz," 137.

167. Foucault, *The Archaeology of Knowledge*, 95.

168. Gilles Deleuze, *Cinema 2: The Time Image*, trans. Hugh Tomlinson and Robert Galeta (London: Athlone, 1989), 217.

169. Deleuze, *Cinema 2*, 221.

170. Deleuze and Guattari, *Kafka*, 30.

171. Deleuze and Guattari, *Kafka*, 29.

172. Deleuze and Guattari, *Kafka*, 31.

173. Havas, "Retratos ficcionales," 285–86. Original emphasis.

174. Deleuze and Guattari, *Kafka*, 29.

175. Havas, "Retratos ficcionales," 286. Original emphasis.

176. Deleuze and Guattari, *Kafka*, 32, 29.

177. Cristina Iglesia, "Crimen y castigo: las reglas del juego. Notas sobre *La ciudad ausente* de Ricardo Piglia," *Filología* 39, nos. 1–2 (1996): 102. Original emphasis.

178. Arán, "Voces y fantasmas," 130.

179. Romero, "'Ciudad ausente' de Ricardo Piglia," 177; Havas, "Retratos ficcionales," 285. My emphasis.

180. Deleuze and Guattari, *Kafka*, 29.

181. Eva-Lynn Alicia Jagoe, "The Disembodied Machine: Matter, Femininity and Nation in Piglia's *La ciudad ausente*," *Latin American Literary Review* 23, no. 45 (1995): 16.

182. Jagoe, "The Disembodied Machine," 7, 8, 10.

183. Piglia, *La ciudad ausente*, 42.

184. Fernández, *Narraciones viajeras*, 175.

185. Piglia, *La ciudad ausente*, 145.

186. Alfieri and Aira, *Conversaciones*, 50.

187. Piglia, *La ciudad ausente*, 60.

188. Contreras, *Las vueltas*, 24.

189. Aira, "El sultan," 10.

190. See César Aira, *El juego de los mundos: novela de ciencia ficción* (La Plata, Buenos Aires: El Broche, 2000), 73–78.

191. Piglia, *Respiración artificial*, 95. Original emphasis.

192. Deleuze and Guattari, *Kafka*, 64.

193. Deleuze and Guattari, *Kafka*, 65.

194. Deleuze and Guattari, *Kafka*, 66.

195. Deleuze and Guattari, *Kafka*, 67.

Conclusion: The Plane of Immanence

1. Piglia and Rozitchner, *Tres propuestas*, 12, 31. The citation is for a version of the text published a year later.

2. Romero, *La crisis argentina*, 101. Original emphasis.

3. Related in Cohen, "Pequeñas batallas," 37–39.

4. Piglia, *Crítica y ficción*, 165.

5. Piglia, *Crítica y ficción*, 165.

6. Rancière, *The Politics of Aesthetics*, 30.

7. Arán, "Voces y fantasmas," 124.

8. Rancière, *The Politics of Aesthetics*, 30.

9. Deleuze and Guattari, *Kafka*, 40.

10. Marks, "Kafka, Franz," 138.

11. Deleuze and Guattari, *Kafka*, 59.

12. See Abraham, *Fricciones*, 146–47.

13. Aira, "La nueva escritura," 165. In this, Aira comes into direct conflict with Piglia, who has commented that "es cierto que los grandes escritores a los que uno admira son autores de un solo libro y el resto de los novelistas producen incesantemente obras que se olvidan de inmediato, pero de las que viven. El autor de una sola obra (aunque haya escrito varias otras) está fuera del circuito económico. Ésa es la diferencia entre los autores del siglo XIX (Balzac, Dickens) y los del siglo XX (Joyce o Musil)" (it is certain that the great writers who one admires are authors of one sole book and the rest of the novelists incessantly produce

works that one forgets immediately, but from which they live. The author of a sole work [even though they have written others] is outside the economic circuit. That is the difference between the authors of the nineteenth century [Balzac, Dickens] and those of the twentieth century [Joyce or Musil] (Piglia, *Los años felices*, 275).

14. Piglia and Rozitchner, *Tres propuestas*, 22, 21.

15. Bosteels, "In the Shadow," 232; Alain Badiou, "La autonomía del proceso estético," in *Literatura y sociedad*, ed. Ricardo Piglia (Buenos Aires: Editorial Tiempo Contemporáneo, 1974).

16. Lecercle, *Badiou and Deleuze*, 142.

17. See, for example, Chiani, "La 'Fiesta seminal de las palabras,'" 720.

18. Deleuze and Guattari, *Kafka*, 59.

19. Again, the relevance of the concept of the control society is suggested by the influence of William Burroughs on Cohen, Piglia, and Deleuze.

20. Bensmaïa, "Foreword," xiii.

21. Piglia, *Crítica y ficción*, 94. See for example Contreras, *Las vueltas*, 29; Galiazo, "La creación," 298–99.

22. Contreras, *Las vueltas*, 16.

23. Lee Spinks, "Eternal Return," in *The Deleuze Dictionary*, ed. Adrian Parr (Edinburgh: Edinburgh University Press, 2010), 87. Original emphasis.

24. Aira, *El infinito*, 14.

25. Badiou, *Conditions*, 261; Lecercle, *Badiou and Deleuze*, 171.

26. Piglia and Saer, *Diálogo*, 17–18.

27. Piglia, *Respiración artificial*, 206.

28. Deleuze and Guattari, *Kafka*, 12.

29. Deleuze and Guattari, *Kafka*, 56.

30. Marks, "Kafka, Franz," 139.

31. Gilles Deleuze, *Cinema 1: The Movement Image*, trans. Hugh Tomlinson and Barbara Habberjam (London: Athlone, 1986), 59.

32. Massey, *For Space*, 9, 131.

33. Massey, *For Space*, 5–6.

34. Scorer, *City in Common*, 37, 32; Goebel, *Argentina's Partisan Past*, 193.

35. Piglia, *Crítica y ficción*, 180.

36. Massey, *For Space*, 145.

37. Massey, *For Space*, 71.

38. Massey, *For Space*, 130.

39. Deleuze, *Cinema 1*, 59.

40. Cohen, "Pequeñas batallas," 50. Original emphasis.

41. Gary Genosko, "Introduction," in *The Guattari Reader*, ed. Gary Genosko (Oxford: Blackwell, 1996), 25.

42. Several other critics have noted and commented on this phenomenon. Brian Massumi has stated that "it seems to me that there's been a certain kind of convergence between the dynamic of capitalist power and the dynamic of resistance" (Brian Massumi, "Navigating Movements," in *Hope: New Philosophies for Change*, ed. Mary Zournazi [New York: Routledge, 2002)] 224). Slavoj Žižek goes further still and proposes that "the thought of Foucault, Deleuze and Guattari, the ultimate philosophers of resistance, of marginal positions crushed by the hegemonic power network, is effectively the ideology of the newly emerging ruling class" (Žižek, *Organs without Bodies*, 193).

43. Félix Guattari, "Regimes, Pathways, Subjects," in *The Guattari Reader*, ed. Gary Genosko (Oxford: Blackwell, 1996), 106.

44. Félix Guattari, *The Three Ecologies*, trans. Ian Pindar and Paul Sutton (London: Athlone, 2000), 47, 50. For a detailed description of Integrated World Capitalism, see Félix Guattari and Toni Negri, *Communists Like Us: New Spaces of Liberty, New Lines of Alliance*, trans. Michael Ryan (New York: Semiotext(e), 1990), 47–56; Genosko, "Introduction," 24–30.

45. Genosko, "Introduction," 28–29.

46. Félix Guattari and Eric Alliez, "Capitalistic Systems, Structures and Processes," in *The Guattari Reader*, ed. Gary Genosko (Oxford: Blackwell, 1996), 244; Guattari and Negri, *Communists Like Us*, 24.

47. See Guattari and Negri, *Communists Like Us*, 51.

48. Ian Pindar and Paul Sutton, "Translators' Introduction," in *The Three Ecologies*, by Félix Guattari (London: Athlone, 2000), 6.

49. Guattari, *The Three Ecologies*, 33.

50. Pindar and Sutton, "Translators' Introduction," 15; Félix Guattari and Suely Rolnik, *Molecular Revolution in Brazil*, trans. Karel Clapshow and Brian Holmes (Los Angeles: Semiotext(e), 2007), 163.

51. Guattari, *The Three Ecologies*, 50; Guattari, "Subjectivities: For Better and for Worse," 199.

52. Cohen, *El oído absoluto*, 237.

53. Guattari and Rolnik, *Molecular Revolution in Brazil*, 187.

54. Guattari and Negri, *Communists Like Us*, 120. My emphasis.

55. Félix Guattari, "The New Spaces of Freedom," in *New Lines of Alliance, New Spaces of Liberty* (Brooklyn, NY: Autonomedia, 2010), 124–25; Guattari, "Regimes, Pathways, Subjects," 97.

56. Pindar and Sutton, "Translators' Introduction," 9. See Guattari, *The Three Ecologies*, 51, 69, 90n49; Guattari, "Subjectivities: For Better and for Worse," 194.

57. Guattari, "Subjectivities: For Better and for Worse," 193, 199. Original emphasis.

58. Pindar and Sutton, "Translators' Introduction," 14.

59. Guattari and Negri, *Communists Like Us*, 81. In their coauthored description of Integrated World Capitalism, Guattari and Antonio Negri conceptualise such movements as a new form of communism. Later, Michael Hardt and Negri explore them through their conception of the multitude. See Guattari and Negri, *Communists Like Us*; Michael Hardt and Antonio Negri, *Empire* (Cambridge, MA: Harvard University Press, 2000); Michael Hardt and Antonio Negri, *Multitude: War and Democracy in the Age of Empire* (London: Hamish Hamilton, 2005). For a detailed examination of the multitude in relation to the city of Buenos Aires, see Scorer, *City in Common*, 12–20.

60. While Guattari developed his conception of IWC in collaboration with Negri, the two authors diverge in that Negri retains a belief that overcoming IWC requires the complete destruction of the capitalist totality. Given the propensity for Aira's novels to conclude in moments of total destruction, it would appear that he maintains a similar belief. See Antonio Negri, "Archeological Letter. October 1984," in *New Lines of Alliance, New Spaces of Liberty* (Brooklyn: Autonomedia, 2010).

61. Toni Negri, "Postscript, 1990," in *Communists Like Us: New Spaces of Liberty, New Lines of Alliance* (New York: Semiotext(e), 1990), 151.

BIBLIOGRAPHY

Abraham, Tomás. *Fricciones*. Buenos Aires: Sudamericana, 2004.

Aguirre, Carlos, and Robert Buffington, eds. *Reconstructing Criminality in Latin America*. Wilmington, DE: Scholarly Resources, 2000.

Aira, César. *Moreira*. Buenos Aires: Achával Solo: Distribuye Amauta, 1975.

Aira, César. *Ema, la cautiva*. Buenos Aires: Editorial de Belgrano, 1981.

Aira, César. "El sultan." *América Hispánica* 3.4 (1990): 9–12.

Aira, César. *Copi*. Rosario: Beatriz Viterbo, 1991.

Aira, César. *La liebre*. Buenos Aires: Emecé, 1991.

Aira, César. "Exotismo." *Boletín del grupo de estudios de teoría literaria* 3 (September 1993): 73–79.

Aira, César. *El infinito*. Buenos Aires: Vanagloria, 1994.

Aira, César. "La innovación." *Boletín del grupo de estudios de teoría literaria* 4 (April 1995): 27–33.

Aira, César. *La abeja*. Buenos Aires: Emecé, 1996.

Aira, César. *Alejandra Pizarnik*. Rosario: Beatriz Viterbo, 1998.

Aira, César. *La trompeta de mimbre*. Rosario: Beatriz Viterbo, 1998.

Aira, César. *El congreso de literatura*. Buenos Aires: Tusquets, 1999.

Aira, César. *El juego de los mundos: novela de ciencia ficción*. La Plata, Buenos Aires: El Broche, 2000.

Aira, César. "La ciudad y el campo." In *Norte y Sur: la narrativa rioplatense desde México*, edited by Rose Corral, Hugo J. Verani, and Ana María Zubieta, 85–91. México: El Colegio de México, 2000.

Aira, César. "La nueva escritura." *Boletín del centro de estudios de teoría y crítica literaria* 8 (October 2000): 165–70.

Aira, César. *Diccionario de autores latinoamericanos*. Buenos Aires: Emecé, Ada Korn, 2001.

Aira, César. *Las tres fechas*. Rosario: Beatriz Viterbo, 2001.

Aira, César. *La prueba*. México, D.F.: Era, 2002.

Aira, César. *Los dos payasos*. Rosario: Beatriz Viterbo, 2003.

Aira, César. *Cómo me hice monja: La costurera y el viento*. Rosario: Beatriz Viterbo, 2004.

Aira, César. *Edward Lear*. Rosario: Beatriz Viterbo, 2004.

Aira, César. *Yo era una chica moderna*. Buenos Aires: Interzona, 2004.

Aira, César. *El cerebro musical*. Buenos Aires: Eloísa Cartonera, 2005.

Aira, César. *Diario de la hepatitis*. Buenos Aires: Bajo la Luna, 2007.

Aira, César. *Dante y Reina*. Buenos Aires: Mansalva, 2009.

Aira, César. "El tiempo y el lugar de la literatura." *Otra parte: revista de letras y artes* 19 (Summer 2009–2010): 1–5.

Aira, César. *Yo era una mujer casada.* Buenos Aires: Blatt and Ríos, 2010.

Alfieri, Carlos, and César Aira. *Conversaciones: entrevistas con César Aira, Guillermo Cabrera Infante, Roger Chartier, Antonio Muñoz Molina, Ricardo Piglia, y Fernando Savater.* Madrid: Katz, 2008.

Alí, Alejandra. "La isla de Finnegans." In *Archivos de la memoria,* edited by Ana María Barrenechea, 27–42. Rosario: Beatriz Viterbo, 2003.

Alí, María Alejandra. *La escritura de la historia en las (micro)novelas de Piglia.* Buenos Aires: Universidad de Buenos Aires: Facultad de Filosofía y Letras, 2007.

Alonso, Carlos J. "Civilización y barbarie." *Hispania* 72, no. 2 (1989): 256–63.

Ansell-Pearson, Keith. *Germinal Life: The Difference and Repetition of Deleuze.* London: Routledge, 1999.

Antognazzi, Irma. "La vida adentro de las cárceles durante la dictadura militar del '76." *Razón y revolución* 4 (Autumn 1998): 80–94.

"A Pumper Nic se la comió la globalización." *La Nación,* 14 September 1997. Accessed 9 May 2018, www.lanacion.com.ar.

Arán, Pampa Olga. "Voces y fantasmas en la narrativa argentina." In *Umbrales y catástrofes: literatura argentina de los '90,* edited by Pampa Olga Arán, Candelaria de Olmos, Silvio Mattoni, Cecilia Pacella, Roxana Patriño and Susana Romano Sued, 113–68. Córdoba, Argentina: Epoké, 2003.

Arán, Pampa Olga, Candelaria de Olmos, Silvio Mattoni, Cecilia Pacella, Roxana Patriño, and Susana Romano Sued, eds. *Umbrales y catástrofes: literatura argentina de los '90.* Córdoba, Argentina: Epoké, 2003.

Arena, Silvana Mariel. "*Ema, la cautiva* de César Aira, a un siglo de la conquista del desierto: reflexiones sobre los modos de representación, el lugar del artista y la construcción del espacio, el tiempo y el sujeto." In *Fin(es) del siglo y modernismo (Volumen II): Congreso Internacional Buenos Aires-La Plata,* edited by María Payeras Grau and Luis Miguel Fernández Ripoll, 755–65. Palma: Universitat de les Illes Balears, 2001.

Arendt, Hannah. *Eichmann in Jerusalem: A Report on the Banality of Evil.* New York: Penguin Books, 2006.

Attias, Bernardo Alexander. "To Each Its Own Sexes?: Towards a Rhetorical Understanding of *Molecular Revolution.*" In *Deleuze and Guattari: New Mappings in Politics, Philosophy, and Culture,* edited by Eleanor Kaufman and Kevin Jon Heller, 96–111. Minneapolis: University of Minnesota Press, 1998.

Avelar, Idelber. "Dictatorship and Immanence." *Journal of Latin American Cultural Studies* 7, no. 1 (1998): 75–94.

Avelar, Idelber. *The Untimely Present: Postdictatorial Latin American Fiction and the Task of Mourning.* Durham, NC: Duke University Press, 1999.

Avelar, Idelber. "Five Theses on Torture." *Journal of Latin American Cultural Studies* 10, no. 3 (2001): 253–71.

Badiou, Alain. "La autonomía del proceso estético." In *Literatura y sociedad*, edited by Ricardo Piglia, 93–117. Buenos Aires: Editorial Tiempo Contemporáneo, 1974.

Badiou, Alain. *Deleuze: The Clamor of Being.* Translated by Louise Burchill. Minneapolis: University of Minnesota Press, 2000.

Badiou, Alain. *Ethics: An Essay on the Understanding of Evil.* Translated by Peter Hallward. London: Verso, 2001.

Badiou, Alain. "The Event as Trans-Being." In *Theoretical Writings*, edited by Ray Brassier and Alberto Toscano, 97–102. London: Continuum, 2004.

Badiou, Alain. *Theoretical Writings.* London: Continuum, 2004.

Badiou, Alain. "Truth: Forcing and the Unnameable." In *Theoretical Writings*, edited by Ray Brassier and Alberto Toscano, 119–33. London: Continuum, 2004.

Badiou, Alain. *Being and Event.* Translated by Oliver Feltham. London: Continuum, 2005.

Badiou, Alain. *Conditions.* Translated by Steven Corcoran. London: Continuum, 2008.

Balderston, Daniel. "El significado latente en *Respiración artificial* de Ricardo Piglia y en *El corazon de junio* de Luis Gusman." Translated by Eduardo Paz Leston. In *Ficción y política: la narrativa argentina durante el proceso militar*, edited by Daniel Balderston, David William Foster, Tulio Halperín Donghi, Francine Masiello, Marta Morello-Frosch, and Beatriz Sarlo, 109–21. Buenos Aires: Alianza, 1987.

Balderston, Daniel, David William Foster, Tulio Halperín Donghi, Francine Masiello, Marta Morello-Frosch, and Beatriz Sarlo, eds. *Ficción y política: la narrativa argentina durante el proceso militar.* Buenos Aires: Alianza, 1987.

Barreneche, Gabriel Ignacio. "The Dystopic Theme Park: The Role of Lorelei in Marcelo Cohen's *El oído absoluto.*" *Romance Quarterly* 55, no. 2 (2008): 128–39.

Barrenechea, Ana María, ed. *Archivos de la memoria.* Rosario: Beatriz Viterbo, 2003.

Barrenechea, Ana María, and Universidad de Buenos Aires Grupo de Investigación de Literatura Argentina. *Ficciones argentinas: antología de lecturas críticas.* Buenos Aires: Grupo Editorial Norma, 2004.

Barros, César. "Del 'macrocosmos de la hamburguesa' a 'lo real de la realidad': consumo, sujeto y acción en *La prueba* de César Aira." *Revista Hispánica Moderna* 65, no. 2 (2012): 135–52.

Bartlett, A. J., and Justin Clemens, eds. *Alain Badiou: Key Concepts.* Durham: Acumen, 2010.

Baudrillard, Jean. "The Orders of Simulacra." Translated by Philip Beitchman. In *Simulations*, 81–159. New York: Semiotext(e), 1983.

Baudrillard, Jean. *Simulations.* Translated by Paul Foss, Paul Patton and Philip Beitchman. New York: Semiotext(e), 1983.

Baudrillard, Jean. *Seduction.* Translated by Brian Singer. Montréal: New World Perspectives, 1990.

Baudrillard, Jean. "Revolution and the End of Utopia." Translated by Michel Valentin. In *Jean Baudrillard: The Disappearance of Art and Politics,* edited by William Stearns and William Chaloupka, 233–42. London: Macmillan, 1992.

Baudrillard, Jean. "Clone Story." Translated by Sheila Faria Glaser. In *Simulacra and Simulation,* 95–103. Ann Arbor: University of Michigan Press, 1994.

Baudrillard, Jean. "Holograms." Translated by Sheila Faria Glaser. In *Simulacra and Simulation,* 105–9. Ann Arbor: University of Michigan Press, 1994.

Baudrillard, Jean. "The Implosion of Meaning in the Media." Translated by Sheila Faria Glaser. In *Simulacra and Simulation,* 79–86. Ann Arbor: University of Michigan Press, 1994.

Baudrillard, Jean. "The Precession of Simulacra." Translated by Sheila Faria Glaser. In *Simulacra and Simulation,* 1–42. Ann Arbor: University of Michigan Press, 1994.

Baudrillard, Jean. *Simulacra and Simulation.* Translated by Sheila Faria Glaser. Ann Arbor: University of Michigan Press, 1994.

Baudrillard, Jean. "Disneyworld Company." Translated by Chris Turner. In *Screened Out,* 150–54. London: Verso, 2002.

Baudrillard, Jean. *Screened Out.* Translated by Chris Turner. London: Verso, 2002.

Baudrillard, Jean. *Passwords.* Translated by Chris Turner. London: Verso, 2003.

Baudrillard, Jean. "The Beaubourg Effect: Implosion and Deterrence." In *The Jean Baudrillard Reader,* edited by Steve Redhead, 58–70. Edinburgh: Edinburgh University Press, 2008.

Baudrillard, Jean. "The Evil Demon of Images." In *The Jean Baudrillard Reader,* edited by Steve Redhead, 84–98. Edinburgh: Edinburgh University Press, 2008.

Baudrillard, Jean. "The Gulf War: Is It Really Taking Place?" In *The Jean Baudrillard Reader,* edited by Steve Redhead, 100–121. Edinburgh: Edinburgh University Press, 2008.

Baudrillard, Jean. "Impossible Exchange." In *The Jean Baudrillard Reader,* edited by Steve Redhead, 133–52. Edinburgh: Edinburgh University Press, 2008.

Baudrillard, Jean. "Mass Media Culture." In *The Jean Baudrillard Reader,* edited by Steve Redhead, 15–32. Edinburgh: Edinburgh University Press, 2008.

Baudrillard, Jean. "Pornography of War." In *The Jean Baudrillard Reader,* edited by Steve Redhead, 199–202. Edinburgh: Edinburgh University Press, 2008.

Baudrillard, Jean, and Sylvère Lotringer. "Forget Baudrillard: An Interview with Sylvère Lotringer." In *Forget Foucault,* 65–137. New York: Semiotext(e), 1987.

Baudrillard, Jean, and Sylvère Lotringer. *Forget Foucault.* New York: Semiotext(e), 1987.

Beistegui, Miguel de. "The Ontological Dispute: Badiou, Heidegger, and Deleuze." Translated by Ray Brassier. In *Alain Badiou: Philosophy and Its Conditions*, edited by Gabriel Riera, 45–58. Albany: State University of New York Press, 2005.

Bensmaïa, Réda. "Foreword: The Kafka Effect." In *Kafka: Toward a Minor Literature*, by Gilles Deleuze and Félix Guattari, ix–xxi. Minneapolis: University of Minnesota Press, 1986.

Berg, Edgardo H. "La búsqueda del archivo familiar: notas de lectura sobre *Respiración artificial* de Ricardo Piglia." In *Itinerarios entre la ficción y la historia: transdiscursividad en la literatura hispanoaméricana y argentina*, edited by Elisa T. Calabrese, 117–35. Buenos Aires: Grupo Editor Latinoaméricano, 1994.

Berg, Edgardo H. "La conspiración literaria (sobre *La ciudad ausente* de Ricardo Piglia)." *Hispamérica* 25, no. 75 (1996): 35–47.

Berg, Edgardo H. "El relato ausente: (sobre la poética de Ricardo Piglia)." In *Supersticiones de linaje: genealogías y reescrituras*, edited by Elisa Calabrese, 139–58. Rosario: Beatriz Viterbo, 1996.

Berlanga, Ángel, and Ricardo Piglia. "Entrevista con Ricardo Piglia." In *La literatura argentina por escritores argentinos: narradores, poetas y dramaturgos*, edited by Sylvia Iparraguirre, 41–45. Buenos Aires: Biblioteca Nacional, 2009.

Binkley, Sam, and Jorge Capetillo Ponce, eds. *A Foucault for the 21st Century: Governmentality, Biopolitics and Discipline in the New Millennium*. Newcastle upon Tyne: Cambridge Scholars, 2009.

Bogue, Ronald. "Rhizomusicosmology." *SubStance* 20, no. 3 (1991): 85–101.

Bogue, Ronald. *Deleuze on Music, Painting, and the Arts*. New York: Routledge, 2003.

Bogue, Ronald. *Deleuzian Fabulation and the Scars of History*. Edinburgh: Edinburgh University Press, 2010.

Bollig, Ben. "Now/Here is Everywhere: Exile and Cynicism in the Verse of Osvaldo Lamborghini." *Journal of Latin American Cultural Studies* 15, no. 3 (2006): 369–83.

Borg, Ruben. "Two Ps in a Pod: On Time in 'Finnegans Wake.'" *Journal of Modern Literature* 29, no. 1 (2005): 76–93.

Borg, Ruben. *The Measureless Time of Joyce, Deleuze and Derrida*. London: Continuum, 2007.

Borg, Ruben. "Neologizing in *Finnegans Wake*: Beyond a Typology of the Wakean Portmanteau." *Poetics Today* 28, no. 1 (2007): 143–64.

Borg, Ruben. "Mirrored Disjunctions: On a Deleuzo-Joycean Theory of the Image." *Journal of Modern Literature* 33, no. 2 (2010): 131–48.

Borges, Jorge Luis. *Obras completas, 1: 1923–1949*. Buenos Aires: Emecé, 1990.

Borges, Jorge Luis. *Obras completas, 2: 1952–1972*. Buenos Aires: Emecé, 1990.

Borges, Jorge Luis. *Obras completas, 3: 1975–1985*. Buenos Aires: Emecé, 1989.

Bosteels, Bruno. "In the Shadow of Mao: Ricardo Piglia's 'Homenaje a Roberto Arlt.'" *Journal of Latin American Cultural Studies* 12, no. 2 (2003): 229–59.

Boundas, Constantin V. "Editor's Introduction." In *The Deleuze Reader*, edited by Constantin V. Boundas, 1–23. New York: Columbia University Press, 1993.

Boundas, Constantin V. "Virtual/Virtuality." In *The Deleuze Dictionary*, edited by Adrian Parr, 300–302. Edinburgh: Edinburgh University Press, 2010.

Bowman, Paul, and Richard Stamp, eds. *Reading Rancière*. London: Continuum, 2011.

Bravo Herrera, Fernanda Elisa. "Conjeturas e indagaciones: el doble movimiento enunciativo de Ricardo Piglia." In *Creación y proyección de los discursos narrativos*, edited by Daniel Altamiranda and Esther Smith, 165–73. Buenos Aires: Dunken, 2008.

Bresser Pereira, Luiz Carlos, José María Maravall, and Adam Przeworski. *Economic Reforms in New Democracies: A Social-Democratic Approach.* Cambridge: Cambridge University Press, 1993.

Briones, Claudia N., and Walter Delrio. "The 'Conquest of the Desert' as a Trope and Enactment of Argentina's Manifest Destiny." In *Manifest Destinies and Indigenous Peoples*, edited by David Maybury-Lewis, Theodore Macdonald, and Biorn Maybury-Lewis, 51–83. Cambridge, MA: Harvard University Press, 2009.

Bryant, Levi R. *Difference and Givenness: Deleuze's Transcendental Empiricism and the Ontology of Immanence.* Evanston: Northwestern University Press, 2008.

Butler, Rex. "Foucault + Dead Power." In *The Baudrillard Dictionary*, edited by Richard G. Smith, 78–80. Edinburgh: Edinburgh University Press, 2010.

Buttes, Steve. "Towards an Art of Landscapes and Loans: Sergio Chejfec and the Politics of Literary Form." *nonsite.org*, 2014. Accessed 19 October 2017, http://nonsite.org.

Calveiro, Pilar. *Poder y desaparición: los campos de concentración en Argentina.* Buenos Aires: Colihue, 1998.

Camblong, Ana María. "Estudio preliminar." In *Museo de la Novela de la Eterna: edición crítica*, edited by Ana María Camblong and Adolfo de Obieta, xxxi–lxxix. Nanterre: ALLCA XX, 1993.

Capano, Daniel A. "La voz de la nueva novela histórica. La estética de la clonación y de la aporía en *La liebre* de César Aira." In *Historia, ficción y metaficción en la novela latinoamericana contemporánea*, edited by Mignon Domínguez, 91–119. Buenos Aires: Corregidor, 1996.

Carroll, Robert, ed. *The Bible, Authorized King James Version [with Apocrypha].* Oxford: Oxford University Press, 1998.

Castellarin, Teresita Mauro. "Dos novelistas argentinos en España: Juan Carlos Martín y Marcelo Cohen." In *Exilios y residencias: escrituras de España y*

América, edited by Juana Martínez Gómez, 183–207. Madrid: Iberoamericana, 2007.

Chakrabarty, Dipesh. *Provincializing Europe: Postcolonial Thought and Historical Difference*. Princeton: Princeton University Press, 2008.

Chiani, Miriam. "Escenas de la vida postindustrial: sobre *El fin de lo mismo* de Marcelo Cohen." *Orbis Tertius* 1 (1996): 117–29.

Chiani, Miriam. "Sociedad posindustrial, memoria e identidad. Sobre Marcelo Cohen." *Cuadernos Angers-La Plata* 3, no. 3 (1999): 77–88.

Chiani, Miriam. "La 'Fiesta seminal de las palabras': sobre Marcelo Cohen." In *Fin(es) del siglo y modernismo (volumen II): congreso internacional Buenos Aires-La Plata*, edited by María Payeras Grau and Luis Miguel Fernández Ripoll, 719–24. Palma: Universitat de les Illes Balears, 2001.

Chiani, Miriam. "Represión, exilio, utopía y contrautopía. Sobre Marcelo Cohen." *Orbis Tertius* 8, no. 4 (2001): 21–32.

Chiani, Susana. "'Ese algo tuyo, eso tan tuyo.' Sobre *Inolvidables veladas* de Marcelo Cohen." *Tramas: para leer la literatura Argentina* 5, no. 9 (1998): 166–72.

Chiodo, Luis. *Hipermercados en América Latina: historia del comercio de alimentos, de los autoservicios hasta el imperio de cinco cadenas multinacionales*. Buenos Aires: Antropofagia, 2010.

Cisneros, James. "El ocaso del museo del interior: *La ciudad ausente* de Ricardo Piglia." *Cuadernos americanos: nueva época* 2, no. 116 (2006): 105–18.

Clemens, Justin. "The Conditions." In *Alain Badiou: Key Concepts*, edited by A. J. Bartlett and Justin Clemens, 25–37. Durham: Acumen, 2010.

Cohen, Marcelo. *Insomnio*. Barcelona: Muchnik, 1986.

Cohen, Marcelo. *El fin de lo mismo*. Madrid: Anaya and Mario Muchnik, 1992.

Cohen, Marcelo. *Inolvidables veladas*. Barcelona: Minotauro, 1996.

Cohen, Marcelo. *El oído absoluto*. Barcelona: Grupo Editorial Norma, 1997.

Cohen, Marcelo. "Variedades." In *Hombres amables: dos incursiones de Georges LaMente*, 7–143. Buenos Aires: Grupo Editorial Norma, 1998.

Cohen, Marcelo. "El fin de la palabrística." *Artefacto: pensamientos sobre la técnica* 3 (1999): 30–45.

Cohen, Marcelo. ¡Realmente fantástico! y otros ensayos. Buenos Aires: Grupo Editorial Norma, 2003.

Cohen, Marcelo. "Pequeñas batallas por la propiedad de la lengua." In *Poéticas de la distancia: adentro y afuera de la literatura argentina*, edited by Sylvia Molloy and Mariano Siskind, 35–55. Buenos Aires: Grupo Editorial Norma, 2006.

Cohen, Marcelo. "Ricardo Piglia. La narración como inminencia del cierre." *Otra parte: revista de letras y artes* 21 (Spring 2010): 60–66.

CONADEP, Comisión Nacional Sobre la Desaparición de Personas, Argentina. *Nunca más*. Buenos Aires: Editorial Universitaria de Buenos Aires, 1984.

Conley, Tom. "Foucault + Fold." In *The Deleuze Dictionary*, edited by Adrian Parr, 114–17. Edinburgh: Edinburgh University Press, 2010.

Conley, Verena. "Order-Word." In *The Deleuze Dictionary*, edited by Adrian Parr, 198–99. Edinburgh: Edinburgh University Press, 2010.

Contreras, Alvaro. "Intelectuales, vanguardia y tradición." In *Territorios intelectuales: pensamiento y cultura en América Latina: homenaje a Rafael Gutiérrez Girardot*, edited by Javier Lasarte Valcárcel, 321–35. Caracas: Fondo Editorial La Nave Va, 2001.

Contreras, Sandra. "César Aira: el movimiento de la idea." *Boletín del grupo de estudios de teoría literaria* 4 (April 1995): 45–64.

Contreras, Sandra. "Literalidad, catástrofe, imagen (sobre *La prueba* de César Aira)." *Boletín del centro de estudios de teoría y crítica literaria* 5 (October 1996): 35–47.

Contreras, Sandra. "Estilo y relato: el juego de las genealogías (sobre *La liebre* de César Aira)." *Boletín del centro de estudios de teoría y crítica literaria* 6 (October 1998): 19–38.

Contreras, Sandra. *Las vueltas de César Aira*. Rosario: Beatriz Viterbo, 2002.

Contreras, Sandra. "César Aira. Vueltas sobre el realismo." In *César Aira, une révolution* edited by Michel Lafon, Cristina Breuil, and Margarita Remón-Raillard. Grenoble: Université Stendhal–Grenoble 3, 2005.

Contreras, Sandra. "Prólogo." In *Ema, la cautiva*, by César Aira, 7–22. Buenos Aires: Eudeba, 2011.

Coombe, Rosemary J. "Postmodernity and the Rumour: Late Capitalism and the Fetishism of the Commodity/Sign." In *Jean Baudrillard: The Disappearance of Art and Politics*, edited by William Stearns and William Chaloupka, 98–108. London: Macmillan, 1992.

Coronil, Fernando. "Beyond Occidentalism: Toward Nonimperial Geohistorical Categories." *Cultural Anthropology* 11, no. 1 (1996): 51–87.

Corral, Rose. "Ricardo Piglia: los 'usos' de Arlt." In *Norte y Sur: la narrativa rioplatense desde México*, edited by Rose Corral, Hugo J. Verani, and Ana María Zubieta, 153–60. México: El Colegio de México, 2000.

Corral, Rose, Hugo J. Verani, and Ana María Zubieta, eds. *Norte y Sur: la narrativa rioplatense desde México*. México: El Colegio de México, 2000.

Costa, Marithelma. "Entrevista con Ricardo Piglia." *Hispamérica* 15, no. 44 (1986): 39–54.

Coulter, Gerry. "Reversibility." In *The Baudrillard Dictionary*, edited by Richard G. Smith, 181–83. Edinburgh: Edinburgh University Press, 2010.

Critchley, Simon. "On the Ethics of Alain Badiou." In *Alain Badiou: Philosophy and its Conditions*, edited by Gabriel Riera, 215–35. Albany: State University of New York Press, 2005.

Crockett, Clayton. *Deleuze beyond Badiou: Ontology, Multiplicity, and Event.* New York: Columbia University Press, 2013.

Cutolo, Vicente Osvaldo. *Nuevo diccionario biográfico argentino, 1750–1930.* Vol. 5. Buenos Aires: Elche, 1978.

Dalmaroni, Miguel. "El deseo, el relato, el juicio. Sobre el 'retorno a los setenta' en el debate crítico argentino, 1996–1998." *Tramas para leer la literatura argentina* 5, no. 9 (1998): 35–42.

Dalmaroni, Miguel. "El fin de lo otro y la disolución del fantástico en un relato de Marcelo Cohen." *Cuadernos Angers-La Plata* 4, no. 4 (2001): 83–96.

Dapelo, Luis, and César Aira. "César Aira." *Hispamérica* 36, no. 107 (2007): 41–53.

da Silva Catela, Ludmila. "Staged Memories: Conflicts and Tensions in Argentine Public Memory Sites." *Memory Studies* 8, no. 1 (2015): 9–21.

Daszuk, Silvana. "Frontera, héroe y diferencia: recorridos por la pampa argentina." In *Fábulas del género: sexo y escrituras en América Latina*, edited by Nora Domínguez and Carmen Perilli, 135–47. Rosario: Beatriz Viterbo, 1998.

Deane, Seamus. "Introduction." In *Finnegans Wake*, by James Joyce, vii–xlix. London: Penguin Books, 2000.

Deleuze, Gilles. *Kant's Critical Philosophy: The Doctrine of the Faculties.* Translated by Hugh Tomlinson and Barbara Habberjam. London: Athlone Press, 1984.

Deleuze, Gilles. "Preface: On Four Poetic Formulas which Might Summarize the Kantian Philosophy." Translated by Hugh Tomlinson and Barbara Habberjam. In *Kant's Critical Philosophy: The Doctrine of the Faculties*, vii–xiii. London: Athlone Press, 1984.

Deleuze, Gilles. *Cinema 1: The Movement Image.* Translated by Hugh Tomlinson and Barbara Habberjam. London: Athlone, 1986.

Deleuze, Gilles. *Bergsonism.* Translated by Hugh Tomlinson and Barbara Habberjam. New York: Zone Books, 1988.

Deleuze, Gilles. *Cinema 2: The Time Image.* Translated by Hugh Tomlinson and Robert Galeta. London: Athlone, 1989.

Deleuze, Gilles. *The Logic of Sense.* Translated by Mark Lester and Charles Stivale. Edited by Constantin V. Boundas. London: Athlone Press, 1990.

Deleuze, Gilles. "What is a *Dispositif?*" Translated by Timothy J. Armstrong. In *Michel Foucault, Philosopher*, edited by Timothy J. Armstrong, 159–66. New York: Harvester Wheatsheaf, 1992.

Deleuze, Gilles. *The Deleuze Reader.* New York: Columbia University Press, 1993.

Deleuze, Gilles. "Ethics and the Event." In *The Deleuze Reader*, edited by Constantin V. Boundas, 78–82. New York: Columbia University Press, 1993.

Deleuze, Gilles. "Control and Becoming." Translated by Martin Joughin. In *Negotiations, 1972–1990*, 169–76. New York: Columbia University Press, 1995.

Deleuze, Gilles. *Negotiations, 1972–1990.* Translated by Martin Joughin. New York: Columbia University Press, 1995.

Deleuze, Gilles. "Postscript on Control Societies." Translated by Martin Joughin. In *Negotiations, 1972–1990*, 177–82. New York: Columbia University Press, 1995.

Deleuze, Gilles. *Essays Critical and Clinical.* London: Verso, 1998.

Deleuze, Gilles. "Having an Idea in Cinema (On the Cinema of Straub-Huillet)." In *Deleuze and Guattari: New Mappings in Politics, Philosophy, and Culture*, edited by Eleanor Kaufman and Kevin Jon Heller, 14–19. Minneapolis: University of Minnesota Press, 1998.

Deleuze, Gilles. *Foucault.* Translated by Seán Hand. London: Athlone, 1999.

Deleuze, Gilles. *Difference and Repetition.* Translated by Paul Patton. London: Continuum, 2001.

Deleuze, Gilles. "Preface." In *Difference and Repetition*, xix–xxii. London: Continuum, 2001.

Deleuze, Gilles. *Francis Bacon: The Logic of Sensation.* Translated by Daniel W. Smith. New York: Continuum, 2004.

Deleuze, Gilles. "Seminar on Kant: Synthesis and Time." *Webdeleuze*, 14 March 1978. Accessed 9 June 2014, www.webdeleuze.com.

Deleuze, Gilles, and Félix Guattari. *Kafka: Toward a Minor Literature.* Translated by Dana Polan. Minneapolis: University of Minnesota Press, 1986.

Deleuze, Gilles, and Félix Guattari. *Anti-Oedipus: Capitalism and Schizophrenia.* Translated by Robert Hurley, Mark Seem, and Helen R. Lane. London: Continuum, 2004.

Deleuze, Gilles, and Félix Guattari. *A Thousand Plateaus: Capitalism and Schizophrenia.* Translated by Brian Massumi. London: Continuum, 2010.

Delgado, Verónica. "'Una nación presumiblemente innecesaria' (a propósito de *La liebre* de César Aira)." *Estudios/Investigaciones* 24 (1995): 91–104.

Della Paolera, Gerardo, and Alan M. Taylor, eds. *A New Economic History of Argentina.* Cambridge: Cambridge University Press, 2003.

Deranty, Jean-Philippe, ed. *Jacques Rancière: Key Concepts.* Durham: Acumen, 2010.

Deredita, John F. "¿Es propiedad?: Indeterminación genérica, intertextualidad, diseminación en un texto 'de' Ricardo Piglia." In *Texto/contexto en la literatura iberoamericana: memoria del XIX congreso (Pittsburgh, 27 de mayo-1 de junio de 1979)*, edited by Keith McDuffie and Alfredo A. Roggiano, 61–69. Madrid: Instituto Internacional de Literatura Iberoamericana, 1980.

de Rose, Matías. "Los desaparecidos de la democracia argentina." *Bifurcaciones: revista de estudios culturales urbanos*, 15 January 2015. Accessed 13 August 2017, www.bifurcaciones.cl.

Derrida, Jacques. "Two Words For Joyce." In *Post-Structuralist Joyce: Essays from the French*, edited by Derek Attridge and Daniel Ferrer, 145–59. Cambridge: Cambridge University Press, 1984.

Dettman, Jonathan. "Epic, Novel, and Subjectivity in Sergio Chejfec's *Lenta biografía.*" *A Contracorriente: A Journal on Social History and Literature in Latin America* 6, no. 2 (2009): 46–63.

Devlin, Kimberly. "ALP's Final Monologue in *Finnegans Wake*: The Dialectical Logic of Joyce's Dream Text." In *Coping with Joyce: Essays from the Copenhagen Symposium*, edited by Morri Beja and Shari Benstock, 232–47. Columbus: Ohio State University Press, 1989.

Doel, Marcus A. "Seduction." In *The Baudrillard Dictionary*, edited by Richard G. Smith, 186–88. Edinburgh: Edinburgh University Press, 2010.

Domínguez, Nora. "Subjetividades en peligro, subjetividades peligrosas." In *Fin(es) del siglo y modernismo (volumen II): Congreso Internacional Buenos Aires-La Plata*, edited by María Payeras Grau and Luis Miguel Fernández Ripoll, 547–52. Palma: Universitat de les Illes Balears, 2001.

Dove, Patrick. "Tonalities of Literature in Transition: The World of the End of the World, or Marcelo Cohen's *El oído absoluto.*" *CR: The New Centennial Review* 4, no. 2 (2004): 239–67.

Ébélot, Alfred. *Adolfo Alsina y la ocupación del desierto: relatos de la frontera.* Buenos Aires: El Elefante Blanco, 2008.

Echavarren, Roberto. "La literariedad: *Respiración artificial*, de Ricardo Piglia." *Revista Iberoamericana* 125, no. 49 (1983): 997–1008.

Echevarría, Roberto González. "*Facundo*: An Introduction." In *Facundo: Civilization and Barbarism: The First Complete English Translation*, by Domingo Faustino Sarmiento, 1–15. Berkeley: University of California Press, 2003.

Eco, Umberto. *The Aesthetics of Chaosmos: The Middle Ages of James Joyce.* Translated by Ellen Esrock. Cambridge, MA: Harvard University Press, 1989.

Esposito, Fabio. "La crítica moderna en Argentina: la revista *Los libros* (1969–1975)." *Orbis Tertius* 20, no. 21 (2015): 1–8.

Fargnoli, A. Nicholas, and Michael Patrick Gillespie. *Critical Companion to James Joyce: A Literary Reference to his Life and Work.* New York: Facts on File, 2006.

Fernández, Adriana. "El tango y el espacio de las ciberciudades: sobre *Inolvidables veladas*, de Marcelo Cohen." *Espacios de crítica y producción* 21 (July–August 1997): 94–95.

Fernández, Macedonio. *Museo de la Novela de la Eterna: edición crítica.* Nanterre: ALLCA XX, 1993.

Fernández, Nancy. *Narraciones viajeras: César Aira y Juan José Saer.* Buenos Aires: Biblos, 2000.

Fernández Cobo, Raquel. "Los diarios de Ricardo Piglia: una lectura en busca de la experiencia perdida." *Castilla: Estudios de literatura* 8 (2017): 62–97.

Ferro, Roberto. "Homenaje a Ricardo Piglia y/o Max Brod." In *Conjuntos: teorías y enfoques literarios recientes*, edited by Alberto Vital Díaz, 363–79. México,

D.F.: Instituto de Investigaciones Filológicas, Universidad Nacional Autónoma de México, 1996.

Flynn, Thomas. "Foucault's Mapping of History." In *The Cambridge Companion to Foucault*, edited by Gary Gutting, 28–46. Cambridge: Cambridge University Press, 1994.

Foote, Nicola, and René D. Harder Horst, eds. *Military Struggle and Identity Formation in Latin America: Race, Nation, and Community During the Liberal Period*. Gainesville: University Press of Florida, 2010.

Ford, Aníbal, Luis Gregorich, Josefina Ludmer, Ángel Núñez, and Ricardo Piglia. "Hacia la crítica." *Los libros: para una crítica política de la cultura* 28 (1972): 3–7.

Fornet, Jorge. "'Homenaje a Roberto Arlt' o la literatura como plagio." *Nueva Revista de Filología Hispánica* 42, no. 1 (1994): 115–41.

Fornet, Jorge. "Un debate de poéticas: las narraciones de Ricardo Piglia." In *La narración gana la partida*, edited by Elsa Drucaroff, 345–60. Buenos Aires: Emecé, 2000.

Foucault, Michel. *The Archaeology of Knowledge*. Translated by A. M. Sheridan Smith. London: Tavistock, 1972.

Foucault, Michel. *Language, Counter-Memory, Practice: Selected Essays and Interviews*. Translated by Donald F. Bouchard and Sherry Simon. Oxford: Blackwell, 1977.

Foucault, Michel, ed. *I, Pierre Rivière, Having Slaughtered my Mother, my Sister, and my Brother: A Case of Parricide in the 19th Century*. Harmondsworth: Penguin, 1978.

Foucault, Michel. *The History of Sexuality. Volume 1: An Introduction*. Translated by Robert Hurley. London: Allen Lane, 1979.

Foucault, Michel. "The Subject and Power." *Critical Inquiry* 8, no. 4 (1982): 777–95.

Foucault, Michel. *The Foucault Reader*. New York: Pantheon Books, 1984.

Foucault, Michel. *The History of Sexuality*. Volume 2: *The Use of Pleasure*. Translated by Robert Hurley. London: Penguin, 1987.

Foucault, Michel. *The History of Sexuality*. Volume 3: *The Care of the Self*. Translated by Robert Hurley. London: Allen Lane/Penguin Press, 1988.

Foucault, Michel. *Discipline and Punish: The Birth of the Prison*. Translated by Alan Sheridan. London: Penguin Books, 1991.

Foucault, Michel. "Is It Useless to Revolt?" Translated by James Bernauer. In *Religion and Culture*, edited by Jeremy R. Carrette, 131–34. Manchester: Manchester University Press, 1999.

Foucault, Michel. "What Is an Author?" In *The Norton Anthology of Theory and Criticism*, edited by Vincent B. Leitch, 1622–36. New York: Norton, 2001.

Foucault, Michel, and Gilles Deleuze. "Intellectuals and Power." Translated by Donald F. Bouchard and Sherry Simon. In *Language, Counter-Memory, Practice: Selected Essays and Interviews*, edited by Donald F. Bouchard, 205–17. Oxford: Blackwell, 1977.

Fox, Michael V. *Ecclesiastes = Kohelet: The Traditional Hebrew Text with the New JPS Translation.* Philadelphia: Jewish Publication Society, 2004.

Fukuyama, Francis. "The End of History?" *The National Interest* 16 (Summer 1989): 3–18.

Fukuyama, Francis. "Reflections on the End of History, Five Years Later." *History and Theory* 34, no. 2 (1995): 27–43.

Galiazo, Evelyn. "La creación es el verdadero poder. César Aira y la tenacidad de lo imposible." *La biblioteca: revista fundada por Paul Groussac. La crítica literaria en Argentina* 4–5 (Summer 2006): 290–305.

Gandía, Enrique de. "Sarmiento y su teoria de 'Civilización y Barbarie.'" *Journal of Inter-American Studies* 4, no. 1 (1962): 67–87.

García, Mariano. *Degeneraciones textuales: los géneros en la obra de César Aira.* Rosario: Beatriz Viterbo, 2006.

Garramuño, Florencia. *Genealogías culturales: Argentina, Brasil y Uruguay en la novela contemporánea (1981–1991).* Rosario: Beatriz Viterbo, 1997.

Garth, Todd S. *The Self of the City: Macedonio Fernández, the Argentine Avant-Garde, and Modernity in Buenos Aires.* Lewisburg, PA: Bucknell University Press, 2005.

Gasparini, Sandra. "Control y fuga: sobre *Inolvidables veladas* de Marcelo Cohen." In *Nuevos territorios de la literatura latinoamericana*, edited by Jorge Monteleone and Sylvia Iparraguirre, 281–88. Buenos Aires: Instituto de Literatura Hispanoamericana, Universidad de Buenos Aires, 1997.

Genosko, Gary. "Introduction." In *The Guattari Reader*, edited by Gary Genosko, 1–34. Oxford: Blackwell, 1996.

Geraghty, Niall. "Ema Is by Nature a Political Animal: Politics and Capitalism in César Aira's *Ema, la cautiva.*" *Journal of Latin American Cultural Studies* 23, no. 1 (2014): 1–18.

Geraghty, Niall. "Power in Transition in Marcelo Cohen's 'La ilusión monarca.'" *Bulletin of Latin American Research* 35, no. 4 (2016): 496–509.

Gillies, Eva. "Introduction." In *A Visit to the Ranquel Indians: (Una excursión a los indios ranqueles)*, by Lucio V. Mansilla, xix–xxxviii. Lincoln: University of Nebraska Press, 1997.

Gilloch, Graeme. "Double." In *The Baudrillard Dictionary*, edited by Richard G. Smith, 54–57. Edinburgh: Edinburgh University Press, 2010.

Gnutzmann, Rita. "Homenaje a Arlt, Borges y Onetti de Ricardo Piglia." *Revista Iberoamericana* 58, no. 159 (1992): 437–48.

Gnutzmann, Rita. "Ricardo Piglia o la crítica literaria como relato detectivesco." In *Literatura como intertextualidad: IX Simposio Internacional de Literatura: reunión, Universidad del Norte, Asunción, Paraguay, 22 al 27 de julio de 1991*, edited by Juana Alcira Arancibia, 524–30. Buenos Aires: Vinciguerra, 1993.

Goebel, Michael. *Argentina's Partisan Past: Nationalism and the Politics of History.* Liverpool: Liverpool University Press, 2011.

Goñi, Uki. "Argentina Activist Missing after Indigenous People Evicted from Benetton Land." *The Guardian*, 8 August 2017. Accessed 11 August 2017, www .theguardian.com.

Goodrich, Diana S. *Facundo and the Construction of Argentine Culture.* Austin: University of Texas Press, 1996.

Goshorn, A. Keith. "Jean Baudrillard and the Radical Enigma: 'The Object's Fulfilment Without Regard for the Subject.'" In *Jean Baudrillard: The Disappearance of Art and Politics*, edited by William Stearns and William Chaloupka, 209–29. London: Macmillan, 1992.

Grace, Victoria. *Baudrillard's Challenge: A Feminist Reading.* London: Routledge, 2000.

Grandis, Rita de. *Polémica y estrategias narrativas en América Latina: José María Arguedas, Mario Vargas Llosa, Rodolfo Walsh, Ricardo Piglia.* Rosario: Beatriz Viterbo, 1993.

Grzegorczyk, Marzena. "Discursos desde el margen: Gombrowicz, Piglia y la estética del basurero." *Hispamérica* 25, no. 73 (1996): 15–33.

Guattari, Félix. "Regimes, Pathways, Subjects." Translated by Brian Massumi. In *The Guattari Reader*, edited by Gary Genosko, 95–108. Oxford: Blackwell, 1996.

Guattari, Félix. "Subjectivities: For Better and for Worse." Translated by Sophie Thomas. In *The Guattari Reader*, edited by Gary Genosko, 193–203. Oxford: Blackwell, 1996.

Guattari, Félix. *The Three Ecologies.* Translated by Ian Pindar and Paul Sutton. London: Athlone, 2000.

Guattari, Félix. "The New Spaces of Freedom." Translated by Mitch Verter, Arianna Bove, and Matteo Mandarini. In *New Lines of Alliance, New Spaces of Liberty*, 116–27. Brooklyn: Autonomedia, 2010.

Guattari, Félix. "The Poor Man's Couch." Translated by Gianna Quach. In *The Continental Philosophy of Film Reader*, edited by Joseph Westfall, 341–47. London: Bloomsbury Academic, 2018.

Guattari, Félix, and Eric Alliez. "Capitalistic Systems, Structures and Processes." Translated by Brian Darling. In *The Guattari Reader*, edited by Gary Genosko, 233–47. Oxford: Blackwell, 1996.

Guattari, Félix, and Antonio Negri. *New Lines of Alliance, New Spaces of Liberty.* Translated by Mitch Verter, Arianna Bove, and Matteo Mandarini. Brooklyn: Autonomedia, 2010.

Guattari, Félix, and Toni Negri. *Communists Like Us: New Spaces of Liberty, New Lines of Alliance.* Translated by Michael Ryan. New York: Semiotext(e), 1990.

Guattari, Félix, and Suely Rolnik. *Molecular Revolution in Brazil.* Translated by Karel Clapshow and Brian Holmes. Los Angeles: Semiotext(e), 2007.

Guattari, Pierre-Felix, and Gary Genosko. *The Guattari Reader.* Oxford: Blackwell, 1996.

Gutting, Gary, ed. *The Cambridge Companion to Foucault.* Cambridge: Cambridge University Press, 1994.

Guy, Donna J. "Women, Peonage, and Industrialization: Argentina, 1810–1914." *Latin American Research Review* 16, no. 3 (1981): 65–89.

Guzmán, Ruy Díaz de. "Women Captives." In *The Argentina Reader: History, Culture, and Society*, edited by Gabriela Nouzeilles and Graciela R. Montaldo, 30–33. Durham, NC: Duke University Press, 2002.

Hallward, Peter, ed. *Think Again: Alain Badiou and the Future of Philosophy.* New York: Continuum, 2004.

Hallward, Peter. "Translator's Introduction." In *Ethics: An Essay on the Understanding of Evil*, by Alain Badiou, vii–xlvii. London: Verso, 2001.

Hardt, Michael. "The Withering of Civil Society." In *Deleuze and Guattari: New Mappings in Politics, Philosophy, and Culture*, edited by Eleanor Kaufman and Kevin Jon Heller, 23–39. Minneapolis: University of Minnesota Press, 1998.

Hardt, Michael, and Antonio Negri. *Empire.* Cambridge, MA: Harvard University Press, 2000.

Hardt, Michael, and Antonio Negri. *Multitude: War and Democracy in the Age of Empire.* London: Hamish Hamilton, 2005.

Hasbrouck, Alfred. "The Conquest of the Desert." *The Hispanic American Historical Review* 15, no. 2 (1935): 195–228.

Hauser, Irina, and Raúl Kollmann. "Una respuesta y nuevos interrogantes." *Página 12*, 25 November 2017. Accessed 10 May 2018, www.pagina12.com.ar.

Havas, Teresa Orecchia. "Retratos ficcionales en la narrativa de Ricardo Piglia. Variaciones sobre el retrato del (autor en) artista." In *Cahiers de LI.RI.CO: Littératures contemporaines du Río de la Plata*, 277–95. Saint Denis: Université de Paris 8 Vincennes, 2006.

Hedges, Jill. *Argentina: A Modern History.* London: I.B. Tauris, 2011.

Hijos por la Identidad y la Justicia Contra el Olvido y el Silencio. "Si No Hay Justicia Hay Escrache." In *Memoria en construcción: el debate sobre la ESMA*, edited by Marcelo Brodsky, 175. Buenos Aires: La Marca, 2005.

Hirschman, Albert O. *The Passions and the Interests: Political Arguments for Capitalism Before its Triumph.* Princeton: Princeton University Press, 1997.

Hodge, John E. "The Role of the Telegraph in the Consolidation and Expansion of the Argentine Republic." *The Americas* 41, no. 1 (1984): 59–80.

Holland, Eugene W. "From Schizophrenia to Social Control." In *Deleuze and Guat-*

tari: New Mappings in Politics, Philosophy, and Culture, edited by Eleanor Kaufman and Kevin Jon Heller, 65–73. Minneapolis: University of Minnesota Press, 1998.

Holland, Eugene W. "Capitalism + Universal History." In *The Deleuze Dictionary*, edited by Adrian Parr, 42–43. Endiburgh: Edinburgh University Press, 2010.

Iglesia, Cristina. "Crimen y castigo: las reglas del juego. Notas sobre *La ciudad ausente* de Ricardo Piglia." *Filología* 39, nos. 1–2 (1996): 95–103.

Iglesia, Cristina. *La violencia del azar*. Buenos Aires: Fondo de Cultura Económica, 2003.

Ingram, Doug. *Ecclesiastes: A Peculiarly Postmodern Piece*. Cambridge: Grove Books, 2004.

Ingram, Doug. *Ambiguity in Ecclesiastes*. New York: T and T Clark International, 2006.

Jagoe, Eva-Lynn Alicia. "The Disembodied Machine: Matter, Femininity and Nation in Piglia's *La ciudad ausente*." *Latin American Literary Review* 23, no. 45 (1995): 5–17.

Jauretche, Arturo. *Política nacional y revisionismo histórico*. Buenos Aires: Corregidor, 2011.

Johns, Michael. "Industrial Capital and Economic Development in Turn of the Century Argentina." *Economic Geography* 68, no. 2 (1992): 188–204.

Joyce, James. *Selected Letters of James Joyce*. London: Faber and Faber, 1992.

Joyce, James. *Ulysses*. Edited by Jeri Johnson. Oxford: Oxford University Press, 1998.

Joyce, James. *Finnegans Wake*. London: Penguin Books, 2000.

Jurovietsky, Silvia. "La perseverancia de los cuerpos. Los relatos de Marcelo Cohen." *Zama* 2, no. 2 (2010): 69–80.

Kafka, Franz. *The Penguin Complete Short Stories of Kafka*. London: Allen Lane, 1983.

Kalmanowiecki, Laura. "Police, Politics, and Repression in Modern Argentina." In *Reconstructing Criminality in Latin America*, edited by Carlos Aguirre and Robert Buffington, 195–218. Wilmington, DE: Scholarly Resources, 2000.

Kant, Immanuel. *Critique of Pure Reason*. Translated by Norman Kemp Smith. London: Macmillan, 1929.

Kant, Immanuel. *The Critique of Pure Reason; The Critique of Practical Reason and other Ethical Treatises; The Critique of Judgement*. Translated by J. M. D. Meiklejohn, Thomas Kingsmill Abbott, W. Hastie, and J. C. Meredith. Edited by Robert Maynard Hutchins. Chicago: Encyclopaedia Britannica, 1963.

Kaufman, Eleanor, and Kevin Jon Heller, eds. *Deleuze and Guattari: New Mappings in Politics, Philosophy, and Culture*. Minneapolis: University of Minnesota Press, 1998.

Keizman, Betina. "*El testamento de O'Jaral* de Marcelo Cohen: conciencia, complot y sociedad en fragmentos." In *Cahiers de LI.RI.CO: Littératures contemporaines du Río de la Plata*, edited by Julio Premat, 297–308. Saint Denis: Université de Paris 8 Vincennes, 2006.

Kohan, Martín. "De putas." *Mora* 15, no. 2 (2009): 157–66.

Kohan, Martín. "Lo otro de las palabras: 'El fin de la palabrística' de Marcelo Cohen." In *Escenas interrumpidas II: imágenes del fracaso, utopías y mitos de origen en la literatura nacional*, edited by María Coira, Rosalía Baltar and Carola Hermida, 67–72. Buenos Aires: Katatay, 2012.

Kozak, Claudia. "Ciudades bajo palabra. Literatura y memoria en el fin de siglo." *Boletín del centro de estudios de teoría y crítica literaria* 6 (October 1998): 49–61.

Kraniauskas, John. "PORNO-REVOLUTION: *El fiord* and the Eva-Peronist State." *Angelaki* 6, no. 1 (2001): 145–53.

Laclau, Ernesto. "An Ethics of Militant Engagement." In *Think Again: Alain Badiou and the Future of Philosophy*, edited by Peter Hallward, 120–37. New York: Continuum, 2004.

Laddaga, Reinaldo. "Una literatura de la clase media: notas sobre César Aira." *Hispamérica* 30, no. 88 (2001): 37–48.

Lambert, Gregg. *The Non-Philosophy of Gilles Deleuze*. London: Continuum, 2002.

Lecercle, Jean-Jacques. *Badiou and Deleuze Read Literature*. Edinburgh: Edinburgh University Press, 2010.

Legg, Stephen. "Assemblage/Apparatus: Using Deleuze and Foucault." *Area* 43, no. 2 (2011): 128–33.

Leitch, Vincent B. *The Norton Anthology of Theory and Criticism*. New York: Norton, 2001.

Levinson, Brett. "Trans(re)lations: Dictatorship, Disaster and the 'Literary Politics' of Piglia's *Respiración artificial*." *Latin American Literary Review* 25, no. 49 (1997): 91–120.

Lévi-Strauss, Claude. *Structural Anthropology*, Volume 1. Translated by Claire Jacobson and Brooke Grundfest Schoepf. Harmondsworth: Penguin, 1977.

Lewis, Paul H. *The Crisis of Argentine Capitalism*. Chapel Hill: University of North Carolina Press, 1990.

Ligeti, György, Péter Várnai, Josef Häusler, and Claude Samuel. *György Ligeti in Conversation*. London: Eulenburg, 1983.

Link, Daniel. "Rethinking Past Present." *Review: Literature and Arts of the Americas* 40, no. 2 (2007): 218–30.

Lohfink, Norbert. *Qoheleth: A Continental Commentary*. Translated by Sean McEvenue. Minneapolis: Fortress Press, 2003.

Longuenesse, Béatrice. "Kant's 'I Think' versus Descartes' 'I am a Thing That

Thinks.'" In *Kant and the Early Moderns*, edited by Daniel Garber and Béatrice Longuenesse, 9–31. Princeton; Oxford: Princeton University Press, 2008.

Lorenz, Federico G., and Peter Winn. "Las memorias de la violencia política y la dictadura militar en la Argentina: un recorrido en el año del Bicentenario." In *No hay mañana sin ayer: batallas por la memoria histórica en el Cono Sur*, edited by Federico G. Lorenz and Peter Winn, 19–120. Buenos Aires: Biblos, 2015.

Lorraine, Tamsin. "Plateau." In *The Deleuze Dictionary*, edited by Adrian Parr, 208–9. Edinburgh: Edinburgh University Press, 2010.

Ludmer, Josefina. *El cuerpo del delito: un manual*. Buenos Aires: Perfil Libros, 1999.

Mandarini, Matteo. "Organising Communism." Translated by Mitch Verter, Arianna Bove, and Matteo Mandarini. In *New Lines of Alliance, New Spaces of Liberty*, by Félix Guattari and Antonio Negri, 7–25. Brooklyn: Autonomedia, 2010.

Mansilla, Lucio Victorio. *Una excursión a los indios ranqueles: edición, prólogo y notas de Julio Caillet-Bois*. Edited by Julio Caillet-Bois. México; Buenos Aires: Fondo de Cultura Económica, 1947.

Mansilla, Lucio Victorio. *A Visit to the Ranquel Indians: (Una excursión a los indios ranqueles)*. Translated by Eva Gillies. Lincoln: University of Nebraska Press, 1997.

Marks, John. "Foucault, Michel (1926–84)." In *The Deleuze Dictionary*, edited by Adrian Parr, 112–14. Edinburgh: Edinburgh University Press, 2010.

Marks, John. "Kafka, Franz (1883–1924)." In *The Deleuze Dictionary*, edited by Adrian Parr, 137–39. Edinburgh: Edinburgh University Press, 2010.

Martínez Sarasola, Carlos. *Nuestros paisanos los indios: vida, historia y destino de las comunidades indígenas en la Argentina*. Buenos Aires: Emecé, 1992.

Martínez Sarasola, Carlos. "The Conquest of the Desert and the Free Indigenous Communities of the Argentine Plains." In *Military Struggle and Identity Formation in Latin America: Race, Nation, and Community During the Liberal Period*, edited by Nicola Foote and René D. Harder Horst, 204–23. Gainesville: University Press of Florida, 2010.

Marx, Karl. "The Eighteenth Brumaire of Louis Bonaparte." Translated by Terrell Carver. In *Marx's 'Eighteenth Brumaire': (Post)modern Interpretations*, edited by Mark Cowling and James Martin, 19–109. London: Pluto, 2002.

Masiello, Francine. *The Art of Transition: Latin American Culture and Neoliberal Crisis*. Durham, NC: Duke University Press, 2001.

Massey, Doreen B. *For Space*. London: SAGE, 2005.

Massumi, Brian. *A User's Guide to Capitalism and Schizophrenia: Deviations from Deleuze and Guatarri*. Cambridge, MA: MIT Press, 1992.

Massumi, Brian. "Requiem for Our Prospective Dead (Toward a Participatory Critique of Capitalist Power)." In *Deleuze and Guattari: New Mappings in Politics, Philosophy, and Culture*, edited by Eleanor Kaufman and Kevin Jon Heller, 40–64. Minneapolis: University of Minnesota Press, 1998.

Massumi, Brian. "Navigating Movements." In *Hope: New Philosophies for Change*, edited by Mary Zournazi, 210–42. New York: Routledge, 2002.

Massumi, Brian. "Translator's Foreword: Pleasures of Philosophy." In *A Thousand Plateaus: Capitalism and Schizophrenia*, by Gilles Deleuze and Félix Guattari, ix–xvi. London: Continuum, 2010.

Mattalia, Sonia. "La historicidad del significante: *Respiración artificial* de Ricardo Piglia." In *Coloquio Internacional: el texto latinoamericano*, Vol. 2, 221–30. Madrid: Fundamentos, 1994.

Mattoni, Silvio. "César Aira: una introducción." In *Umbrales y catástrofes: literatura argentina de los '90*, edited by Pampa Olga Arán, Candelaria de Olmos, Silvio Mattoni, Cecilia Pacella, Roxana Patriño, and Susana Romano Sued, 193–220. Córdoba, Argentina: Epoké, 2003.

Maybury-Lewis, David, Theodore Macdonald, and Biorn Maybury-Lewis, eds. *Manifest Destinies and Indigenous Peoples*. Cambridge, MA: Harvard University Press, 2009.

Mayer, Jorge. *Argentina en crisis: política e instituciones 1983–2003*. Buenos Aires: Eudeba, 2012.

McCracken, Ellen. "Metaplagiarism and the Critic's Role as Detective: Ricardo Piglia's Reinvention of Roberto Arlt." *PMLA* 106, no. 5 (1991): 1071–82.

McLuhan, Eric. "The Rhetorical Structure of *Finnegans Wake*." *James Joyce Quarterly* 11, no. 4 (1974): 394–404.

McLuhan, Eric. *The Role of Thunder in Finnegans Wake*. Toronto: University of Toronto Press, 1997.

McLynn, F. J. "The Argentine Presidential Election of 1868." *Journal of Latin American Studies* 11, no. 2 (1979): 303–23.

Menton, Seymour. *Latin America's New Historical Novel*. Austin: University of Texas Press, 1993.

Merkx, Gilbert W. "Recessions and Rebellions in Argentina, 1870–1970." *Hispanic American Historical Review* 53, no. 2 (1973): 285–95.

Merrin, William. *Baudrillard and the Media: A Critical Introduction*. Cambridge: Polity, 2005.

Montaldo, Graciela. "Un argumento contraborgiano en la literatura argentina de los años '80 (sobre C. Aira, A. Laiseca y Copi)." *Hispamérica* 19, no. 55 (1990): 105–12.

Montaldo, Graciela. "Borges, Aira y la literatura para multitudes." *Boletín del centro de estudios de teoría y crítica literaria* 6 (October 1998): 7–17.

Monteleone, Jorge, and Sylvia Iparraguirre, eds. *Nuevos territorios de la literatura latinoamericana*. Buenos Aires: Instituto de Literatura Hispanoamericana, Universidad de Buenos Aires.

Moore, Nathan. "Nova Law: William S. Burroughs and the Logic of Control." *Law and Literature* 19, no. 3 (2007): 435–70.

Mudrovcic, María Eugenia. "En busca de dos décadas perdidas: la novela latinoamericana de los años 70 y 80." *Revista Iberoamericana* 59, nos. 164–65 (1993): 445–68.

Mukerji, Chandra, and Michael Schudson, eds. *Rethinking Popular Culture: Contemporary Perspectives in Cultural Studies*. Berkeley: University of California Press, 1991.

Murphie, Andrew. "Sound at the End of the World as We Know it: Nick Cave, Wim Wenders' *Wings of Desire* and a Deleuze-Guattarian Ecology of Popular Music." *Perfect Beat* 2, no. 4 (1996): 18–42.

Nealon, Jeffrey T. "Foucault's Deleuze; or, On the Incorporeality of Transformation in Foucault." In *A Foucault for the 21st Century: Governmentality, Biopolitics and Discipline in the New Millennium*, edited by Sam Binkley and Jorge Capetillo Ponce, 139–52. Newcastle upon Tyne: Cambridge Scholars, 2009.

Negri, Antonio. "Archeological Letter, October 1984." Translated by Mitch Verter, Arianna Bove, and Matteo Mandarini. In *New Lines of Alliance, New Spaces of Liberty*, 128–42. Brooklyn: Autonomedia, 2010.

Negri, Toni. "Postscript, 1990." Translated by Michael Ryan. In *Communists Like Us: New Spaces of Liberty, New Lines of Alliance*, 149–73. New York: Semiotext(e), 1990.

Néspolo, Jimena. "El fantástico en vigilia: apuntes para una reflexión sobre la obra de Marcelo Cohen." In *Aventuras de la crítica: escrituras latinoamericanas en el siglo XXI*, edited by Noé Jitrik, 103–7. Córdoba, Argentina: Instituto de Literatura Hispanoamericana and Alción Editora, 2006.

Newman, Saul. "Politics in the Age of Control." In *Deleuze and New Technology*, edited by Mark Poster and David Savat, 104–22. Edinburgh: Edinburgh University Press, 2009.

Norris, Christopher. *Badiou's Being and Event: A Reader's Guide*. London: Continuum, 2009.

Nouzeilles, Gabriela, and Graciela R. Montaldo. *The Argentina Reader: History, Culture, and Society*. Durham, NC: Duke University Press, 2002.

O'Connor, Patrick J. "Cesar Aira's Simple Lesbians: Passing 'La prueba.'" *Latin American Literary Review* 27, no. 54 (1999): 23–38.

O'Connor, Patrick J. "César Aira's Life in Pink: Beyond Gender Games in *Cómo me hice monja*." *Revista Canadiense de Estudios Hispánicos* 25, no. 2 (2001): 259–76.

O'Donnell, Pacho, ed. *La otra historia: el revisionismo nacional, popular y feder-alista*. Buenos Aires: Ariel, 2012.

Oeyen, Annelies. "Imágenes de la barbarie en 'La ilusión monarca' de Marcelo Cohen." In *Los imaginarios apocalípticos en la literatura hispanoamericana contemporánea*, edited by Geneviève Fabry, Ilse Logie, and Pablo Decock, 257–67. Oxford: P. Lang, 2010.

Page, Joanna. "Writing as Resistance in Ricardo Piglia's *La ciudad ausente*." *Bulletin of Spanish Studies* 81, no. 3 (2004): 343–60.

Page, Joanna. *Crisis and Capitalism in Contemporary Argentine Cinema*. Durham, NC: Duke University Press, 2009.

Page, Joanna. "Intellectuals, Revolution and Popular Culture: A New Reading of *El Eternauta*." *Journal of Latin American Cultural Studies* 19, no. 1 (2010): 45–62.

Page, Joanna. *Creativity and Science in Contemporary Argentine Literature: Between Romanticism and Formalism*. Calgary: University of Calgary Press, 2014.

Palmer, Helen. *Deleuze and Futurism: A Manifesto for Nonsense*. London: Bloomsbury, 2014.

Paolera, Gerardo Della, Maria Alejandra Irigoin, and Carlos G. Bózzoli. "Passing the Buck: Monetary and Fiscal Policies." In *A New Economic History of Argentina*, edited by Gerardo Della Paolera and Alan M. Taylor, 46–86. Cambridge: Cambridge University Press, 2003.

Parr, Adrian, ed. *The Deleuze Dictionary*. Rev. ed. Edinburgh: Edinburgh University Press, 2010.

Peláez, Sol. "Thinking from the 'Desamparo' in *Los Incompletos* by Sergio Chejfec." *Journal of Latin American Cultural Studies* 24, no. 3 (2015): 371–86.

Peller, Diego. "Pasiones teóricas en la Revista *Los Libros*." *Afuera: estudios de crítica cultural* 3, no. 4 (2008).

Pellicer, Rosa. "Libros y detectives en la narrativa policial argentina." *Hispamérica* 31, no. 93 (2002): 3–18.

Pereira, María Antonieta. "Entrevista con Ricardo Piglia." In *Ricardo Piglia y sus precursores*, 241–50. Buenos Aires: Corregidor, 2001 [1996].

Pereira, María Antonieta. *Ricardo Piglia y sus precursores*. Buenos Aires: Corregidor, 2001.

Piglia, Ricardo. "Cesare Pavese." *El Escarabajo de Oro* 17 (1963): 2, 18.

Piglia, Ricardo. "Un examen con Vasco Pratolini." *El Escarabajo de Oro* 20 (1963): 6–7, 24.

Piglia, Ricardo. "Literatura y sociedad." *Literatura y sociedad* 1 (1965): 1–12.

Piglia, Ricardo. "Clase media: cuerpo y destino." *Revista de problemas del tercer mundo* 2 (1968): 87–93.

Piglia, Ricardo. "Nota." In *Yo*, edited by Ricardo Piglia, 5–6. Buenos Aires: Editorial Tiempo Contemporáneo, 1968.

Piglia, Ricardo, ed. *Yo*. Buenos Aires: Editorial Tiempo Contemporáneo, 1968.

Piglia, Ricardo. "Heller, la carcajada liberal." *Los libros: un mes de publicaciones en Argentina y el mundo* 1 (1969): 11–12.

Piglia, Ricardo. "Una lectura de *Cosas concretas*." *Los libros: un mes de publicaciones en Argentina y el mundo* 6 (1969): 3.

Piglia, Ricardo. "Nueva narrativa norteamericana." *Los libros: un mes de publicaciones en América Latina* 11 (1970): 11–14.

Piglia, Ricardo. "Mao Tse-Tung: práctica estética y lucha de clases." *Los libros: para una crítica política de la cultura* 25 (1971): 22–25.

Piglia, Ricardo. "Roberto Arlt: una crítica de la economía literaria." *Los libros: para una crítica política de la cultura* 29 (1973): 22–27.

Piglia, Ricardo. "La lucha ideológica en la construcción socialista." *Los libros: para una crítica política de la cultura* 35 (1974): 4–9.

Piglia, Ricardo. "Roberto Arlt: la ficción del dinero." *Hispamérica* 3, no. 7 (1974): 25–28.

Piglia, Ricardo. "A mis compañeros Beatriz Sarlo y Carlos Altamirano." *Los libros: para una crítica política de la cultura* 40 (1975): 3.

Piglia, Ricardo. "Brecht, la producción del arte y de la gloria, selección de textos por Ricardo Piglia." *Ideas, letras, artes en la crisis* 22 (1975): 48–51.

Piglia, Ricardo. "Notas sobre Brecht." *Los libros: para una crítica política de la cultura* 40 (1975): 4–9.

Piglia, Ricardo. "Ficción y política en la literatura argentina." *Hispamérica* 18, no. 52 (1989): 59–62.

Piglia, Ricardo. *Crítica y ficción*. Buenos Aires: Siglo Veinte, 1993.

Piglia, Ricardo. "Notas sobre Macedonio en un diario." In *Museo de la Novela de la Eterna: edición crítica*, edited by Ana María Camblong and Adolfo de Obieta, 516–20. Nanterre: ALLCA XX, 1993.

Piglia, Ricardo. *Nombre falso*. Buenos Aires: Seix Barral, 1994.

Piglia, Ricardo. "Reivindicación de la práctica." In *Asesinos de papel: ensayos sobre narrativa policial*, edited by Jorge Lafforgue and Jorge B. Rivera, 51–53. Buenos Aires: Colihue 1996.

Piglia, Ricardo. "Una propuesta para el próximo milenio." In *Argentinos: retratos de fin de milenio*, edited by Adrián van der Horst and Miguel Wiñazki, 126–27. Buenos Aires: Clarín, 1999.

Piglia, Ricardo. *The Absent City*. Translated by Sergio Gabriel Waisman. Durham, NC: Duke University Press, 2000.

Piglia, Ricardo. "¿Existe la novela argentina?: Borges y Gombrowicz." *University of Pittsburgh Borges Center*, 18 April 2000. Accessed 20 October 2014, www.borges.pitt.edu.

Piglia, Ricardo. "Notas sobre Macedonio en un Diario." In *Formas breves*, 13–28. Barcelona: Anagrama, 2000.

Piglia, Ricardo. "La memoria ajena." In *Fin(es) del siglo y modernismo (Volumen II): Congreso Internacional Buenos Aires-La Plata*, edited by María Payeras Grau and Luis Miguel Fernández Ripoll, 701–3. Palma: Universitat de les Illes Balears, 2001.

Piglia, Ricardo. "Ideología y ficción en Borges." In *Ficciones argentinas: antología de lecturas críticas*, edited by Ana María Barrenechea and Grupo de Investigación de Literatura Argentina Universidad de Buenos Aires, 33–41. Buenos Aires: Grupo Editorial Norma, 2004.

Piglia, Ricardo. *El último lector.* Barcelona: Anagrama, 2005.

Piglia, Ricardo. "Teoría del complot." *Casa de las Américas* 46, no. 245 (2006): 32–41.

Piglia, Ricardo. *Prisión perpetua.* Barcelona: Anagrama, 2007.

Piglia, Ricardo. *Respiración artificial.* 3rd ed. Barcelona: Anagrama, 2008.

Piglia, Ricardo. "Saer o la tradición del escritor argentino." In *La literatura argentina por escritores argentinos: narradores, poetas y dramaturgos*, edited by Sylvia Iparraguirre, 29–40. Buenos Aires: Biblioteca Nacional, 2009.

Piglia, Ricardo. *La ciudad ausente.* 2nd ed. Barcelona: Anagrama, 2010.

Piglia, Ricardo. *Los diarios de Emilio Renzi: años de formación.* Barcelona: Anagrama, 2015.

Piglia, Ricardo. *Los diarios de Emilio Renzi: los años felices.* Barcelona: Anagrama, 2016.

Piglia, Ricardo. *Los diarios de Emilio Renzi: un día en la vida.* Barcelona: Anagrama, 2017.

Piglia, Ricardo, and Juan José Saer. *Diálogo.* Santa Fe, Argentina: Centro de Publicaciones, Universidad Nacional del Litoral, 1995.

Piglia, Ricardo, and León Rozitchner. *Tres propuestas para el próximo milenio (y cinco dificultades) / Mi Buenos Aires querida.* Mexico: Fondo de Cultura Económica, 2001.

Pindar, Ian, and Paul Sutton. "Translators' Introduction." In *The Three Ecologies*, by Félix Guattari, 1–20. London: Athlone, 2000.

Pluth, Ed. *Badiou: A Philosophy of the New.* Cambridge: Polity, 2010.

Pollmann, Leo. "Una estética del más allá del ser. *Ema, la cautiva* de César Aira." In *La novela argentina de los años 80*, edited by Roland Spiller, 177–94. Frankfurt am Main: Vervuert, 1993.

Poster, Mark. "Semiology and Critical Theory: From Marx to Baudrillard." *boundary 2* 8, no. 1 (1979): 275–88.

Poster, Mark. "Afterword." In *Deleuze and New Technology*, edited by Mark Poster and David Savat, 258–62. Edinburgh: Edinburgh University Press, 2009.

Poster, Mark, and David Savat, eds. *Deleuze and New Technology.* Edinburgh: Edinburgh University Press, 2009.

Power, Nina, and Alberto Toscano. "Politics." In *Alain Badiou: Key Concepts*, edited by A. J. Bartlett and Justin Clemens, 94–104. Durham: Acumen, 2010.

Pozzi, Pablo. "Popular Upheaval and Capitalist Transformation in Argentina." *Latin American Perspectives* 27, no. 5 (2000): 63–87.

Premat, Julio, ed. *César Aira, une révolution*. Grenoble: Université Stendhal–Grenoble 3, 2005.

Quintero, Ednodio. "César Aira: una trilogía imaginaria." *Actual: revista de la dirección de cultura de la Universidad de los Andes* 33 (February–May 1996): 81–89.

Rancière, Jacques. *The Politics of Aesthetics: The Distribution of the Sensible*. London: Continuum, 2006.

Reber, Dierdra. "Cure for the Capitalist Headache: Affect and Fantastic Consumption in César Aira's Argentine "Baghdad." *MLN* 122, no. 2 (2007): 371–99.

Redhead, Steve, ed. *The Jean Baudrillard Reader*. Edinburgh: Edinburgh University Press, 2008.

Rei, Patricia. *El cuento de nunca acabar, o, El Pierre Menard de Ricardo Piglia*. Rosario: Ciudad Gótica, 2005.

Richard, Nelly. "The Reconfigurations of Post-dictatorship Critical Thought." *Journal of Latin American Cultural Studies* 9, no. 3 (2000): 273–82.

Riera, Gabriel, ed. *Alain Badiou: Philosophy and its Conditions*. Albany: State University of New York Press, 2005.

Riera, Gabriel. "Introduction: Alain Badiou, The Event of Thinking." In *Alain Badiou: Philosophy and its Conditions*, edited by Gabriel Riera, 1–19. Albany: State University of New York Press, 2005.

Rock, David. "Revolt and Repression in Argentina." *The World Today* 33, no. 6 (1977): 215–22.

Rock, David. "State-Building and Political Systems in Nineteenth-Century Argentina and Uruguay." *Past and Present* 167, no. 1 (May 2000): 176–202.

Rock, David. *State Building and Political Movements in Argentina, 1860–1916*. Stanford: Stanford University Press, 2002.

Rodríguez, Fermín. "Movimientos literarios de fines de siglo. Sobre la literatura de fronteras de César Aira." In *Fin(es) del siglo y modernismo (Volumen II): Congreso Internacional Buenos Aires-La Plata*, edited by María Payeras Grau and Luis Miguel Fernández Ripoll, 773–79. Palma: Universitat de les Illes Balears, 2001.

Roffe, Jonathan. "Capitalism." In *The Deleuze Dictionary*, edited by Adrian Parr, 40–42. Edinburgh: Edinburgh University Press, 2010.

Rohlf, Michael. "Immanuel Kant." In *The Stanford Encyclopedia of Philosophy*, edited by Adward N. Zalta. Accessed 2 November 2014, https://plato.stanford.edu.

Rojas, Diego. "Joven desaparecido en Chubut: los peritajes apuntarían a Gendarmería." *infobae*, 6 August 2017. Accessed 11 August 2017, www.infobae.com.

Romero, Luis Alberto. *La crisis argentina: una mirada al siglo XX*. Buenos Aires: Siglo Veintiuno, 2003.

Romero, Neri Francisco Enrique. "*Ciudad ausente* de Ricardo Piglia: el imaginario futurista del 'New Order'. La poética de la ficción paranoica." *Cuadernos de la literatura* 8 (1998): 161–80.

Rozitchner, León. "Terror and Grace." *Journal of Latin American Cultural Studies* 21, no. 1 (2012): 147–57.

Saer, Juan José. *Lo imborrable*. Buenos Aires: Alianza, 1993.

Sarlo, Beatriz. *Ficciones argentinas: 33 ensayos*. Buenos Aires: Mardulce, 2012.

Sarmiento, Domingo Faustino. *Facundo: civilización y barbarie*. Edited by Roberto Yahni. Madrid: Cátedra, 1990.

Sarmiento, Domingo Faustino. *Facundo: Civilization and Barbarism, The First Complete English Translation*. Translated by Kathleen Ross. Berkeley: University of California Press, 2003.

Sastre, Juana Collado de. "El discurso literario y el discurso histórico en la novela argentina, con especial referencia a *Respiración artificial* de Piglia." In *Relecturas, reescrituras: articulaciones discursivas*, edited by Daniel Altamiranda, 314–19. Buenos Aires: Programa L.A.C., Universidad de Buenos Aires, Facultad de Filosofía y Letras, Instituto de Literatura Argentina "Ricardo Rojas," 1999.

Schettini, Ariel. "Lectores argentinos de Manuel Puig." *La biblioteca: revista fundada por Paul Groussac, La crítica literaria en Argentina* 4–5 (Summer 2006): 210–15.

Scorer, James. *City in Common: Culture and Community in Buenos Aires*. Albany: State University of New York Press, 2016.

Shakespeare, William. *Complete Works of William Shakespeare*. Glasgow: HarperCollins, 1994.

Sigal, Silvia. *Intelectuales y poder en la década del sesenta*. Buenos Aires: Puntosur, 1991.

Silliman, Ron. "What do Cyborgs Want? (Paris, Suburb of the Twentieth Century)." In *Jean Baudrillard: The Disappearance of Art and Politics*, edited by William Stearns and William Chaloupka, 27–37. London: Macmillan, 1992.

Silva, Eduardo. *Challenging Neoliberalism in Latin America*. Cambridge: Cambridge University Press, 2009.

Smith, Daniel W. "Deleuze and the Question of Desire: Toward an Immanent Theory of Ethics." In *Essays on Deleuze*, edited by Daniel W. Smith, 175–88. Edinburgh: Edinburgh University Press, 2012.

Smith, Daniel W. *Essays on Deleuze*. Edinburgh: Edinburgh University Press, 2012.

Smith, Richard G., ed. *The Baudrillard Dictionary*. Edinburgh: Edinburgh University Press, 2010.

Sonderéguer, María. "Presentación." In *Revista crisis (1973–1976): antología, del intelectual comprometido al intelectual revolucionario*, edited by María Sonderéguer, 9–26. Bernal: Universidad Nacional de Quilmes, 2008.

Sonderéguer, María, ed. *Revista crisis (1973–1976): antología, del intelectual comprometido al intelectual revolucionario*. Bernal: Universidad Nacional de Quilmes, 2008.

Speranza, Graciela. "El poder de la ficción: sobre *La ciudad ausente* de Ricardo Piglia." *Espacios de crítica y producción* 1 (June–July 1993): 86–87.

Speranza, Graciela. "César Aira: manual de uso." *Milpalabras: letras y artes en revista* 1 (Spring 2001): 2–13.

Speranza, Graciela. *Fuera de campo: literatura y arte argentinos después de Duchamp*. Barcelona: Anagrama, 2006.

Speranza, Graciela. "Ultimos avatares del surrealismo." *Otra parte: Revista de letras y artes* 21 (Spring 2010): 20–26.

Spinks, Lee. "Eternal Return." In *The Deleuze Dictionary*, edited by Adrian Parr, 85–87. Edinburgh: Edinburgh University Press, 2010.

Spiller, Roland, ed. *La novela argentina de los años 80*. 2nd ed. Frankfurt am Main: Vervuert, 1993.

Stagoll, Cliff. "Becoming." In *The Deleuze Dictionary*, edited by Adrian Parr, 25–27. Edinburgh: Edinburgh University Press, 2010.

Stagoll, Cliff. "Difference." In *The Deleuze Dictionary*, edited by Adrian Parr, 74–76. Edinburgh: Edinburgh University Press, 2010.

Stearns, William, and William Chaloupka, eds. *Jean Baudrillard: The Disappearance of Art and Politics*. London: Macmillan, 1992.

Stiegler, Bernard. "Within the Limits of Capitalism, Economizing Means Taking Care." *Ars Industrialis*, 2006. Accessed 6 October 2014, http://arsindustrialis .org.

Swiboda, Marcel. "Becoming + Music." In *The Deleuze Dictionary*, edited by Adrian Parr, 27–29. Edinburgh: Edinburgh University Press, 2010.

Terán, Oscar. "Ideas e intelectuales en la Argentina, 1880–1980." In *Ideas en el siglo: intelectuales y cultura en el siglo XX latinoamericano*, edited by Oscar Terán and Gerardo Caetano, 13–95. Buenos Aires: Siglo Veintiuno, 2004.

Terán, Oscar, and Gerardo Caetano, eds. *Ideas en el siglo: intelectuales y cultura en el siglo XX latinoamericano*. Buenos Aires: Siglo Veintiuno, 2004.

Teubal, Miguel. "Rise and Collapse of Neoliberalism in Argentina: The Role of Economic Groups." *Journal of Developing Societies* 20, nos. 3–4 (2004): 173–88.

Thayer, Willy. "Crisis categorial de la universidad." *Revista Iberoamericana* 69, no. 202 (2003): 95–102.

Thiele, Kathrin. *The Thought of Becoming: Gilles Deleuze's Poetics of Life*. Zürich: Diaphanes, 2008.

Thuesen, Evelia Romano. "Macedonio Fernández: su teoría de la novela en *La ciudad ausente* de Ricardo Piglia." *Alba de América* 12, nos. 22–23 (1994): 213–26.

Toffoletti, Kim. "Body." In *The Baudrillard Dictionary*, edited by Richard G. Smith, 27–29. Edinburgh: Edinburgh University Press, 2010.

Tomlinson, Hugh, and Barbara Habberjam. "Translator's Introduction." In *Kant's Critical Philosophy: The Doctrine of the Faculties*, by Gilles Deleuze, xv–xvi. London: Athlone Press, 1984.

Toscano, Alberto. "Post-Structuralism + Politics." In *The Deleuze Dictionary*, edited by Adrian Parr, 213–15. Edinburgh: Edinburgh University Press, 2010.

Van Camp, Nathan. "From Biopower to Psychopower: Bernard Stiegler's Pharmacology of Mnemotechnologies." *Ctheory*, 5 September 2012. Accessed 6 October 2014, www.ctheory.net.

Viereck, Roberto. "De la tradición a las formas de la experiencia (entrevista a Ricardo Piglia)." *Revista Chilena de Literatura* 40 (November 1992): 129–38.

Viñas, David. *Indios, ejército y frontera*. Buenos Aires: Siglo Veintiuno, 1983.

Walsh, W. H. *An Introduction to Philosophy of History*. 3rd rev. ed. London: Hutchinson University Library, 1967.

Williams, James. "Immanence." In *The Deleuze Dictionary*, edited by Adrian Parr, 128–30. Edinburgh: Edinburgh University Press, 2010.

Williams, James. *Gilles Deleuze's Philosophy of Time: A Critical Introduction and Guide*. Edinburgh: Edinburgh University Press, 2011.

Williams, James. "Objects in Manifold Times: Deleuze and the Speculative Philosophy of Objects as Processes." *Cosmos and History: The Journal of Natural and Social Philosophy* 7, no. 1 (2011): 62–75.

Winn, Peter. "Las batalla por la memoria histórica en el Cono Sur: conclusiones comparativas." In *No hay mañana sin ayer: batallas por la memoria histórica en el Cono Sur*, edited by Federico G. Lorenz and Peter Winn, 327–58. Buenos Aires: Biblos, 2015.

Wordsworth, William, and Samuel Taylor Coleridge. *Lyrical Ballads 1798 and 1800*. Peterborough, Ontario: Broadview Press, 2008.

Yeats, W. B. *The Poems*. London: Macmillan, 1997.

Yozell, Erica Miller. "Negotiating the Abyss: The Narration of Mourning in Sergio Chejfec's *Los planetas*." *Latin American Literary Review* 35, no. 70 (2007): 88–105.

Žižek, Slavoj. "From Purification to Subtraction: Badiou and the Real." In *Think Again: Alain Badiou and the Future of Philosophy*, edited by Peter Hallward, 165–81. New York: Continuum, 2004.

Žižek, Slavoj. *Organs without Bodies: Deleuze and Consequences*. New York: Routledge, 2004.

INDEX

Baudrillard, Jean (*cont.*): relevance of, 6, 11; and reversibility, 128, 129; seduction, 17, 124, 126–29, 236n97, 236n98. *See also* body; Deleuze, Gilles; hyperreality; images; immanence; mass media; rumor; simulacrum; Stiegler, Bernard

Beckett, Samuel, 57, 75, 205, 216n70

becoming, 71–72, 100; and assemblage, 12–13; and Baudrillard, 129; and Body without Organs, 104; as control, 111, 120, 209, 210; and control society, 16; and divine game, 163; and eternal return, 183; literary becoming in Cohen, 100–4, 131; literary becoming in Piglia, 163, 205; and ontology, 73, 120; opposed to Kantian law, 150; reaching an impasse, 76, 106–7, 108, 131–32, 205; and the subject, 72, 73, 100, 102–4, 111, 106, 211; and time, 12. *See also* Aira, César; becoming-other; Baudrillard, Jean; Cohen, Marcelo; control society; Deleuze, Gilles; Kant, Immanuel; Piglia, Ricardo; resistance; the subject; time

becoming-other, 69–71, 73; and Aira, 70–74, 76–79, 135, 140, 143, 197, 201–2, 205; and Baudrillard, 125; becoming-animal, 70, 76–79, 118, 125, 130, 200; becoming-child, 70, 118; becoming-imperceptible, 70, 103–4, 118, 211; becoming-landscape,103–4, 130, 131; becoming-monstrous in Aira, 70–71, 74, 77–78, 207; becoming-music, 116–19, 120, 130, 131, 210; becoming-sea, 103; becoming-woman, 70, 118, 125, 193–94; and European theory, 161; and Gombrowicz, 160–61, 163; and Piglia, 161, 163, 193; reaching an impasse, 78, 79, 111, 132, 135–36; and schizophrenia, 16, 197. *See also* Aira, César; Baudrillard, Jean; becoming; Cohen, Marcelo; Deleuze, Gilles; Gombrowicz, Witold

Bergson, Henri, 153, 155–56, 180–81, 241n127. *See also* Deleuze, Gilles; memory; time

bildungsroman, 16, 52

Black Panthers, 9, 144. *See also* Brown, Ralph; Cleaver, Eldridge; Malcolm X

body: and becoming, 103–4, 111; and control, 113, 124, 128; and discipline, 89, 92, 93, 110, 168; as image/sign, 120, 125, 166; and machine, 179; and torture, 87, 91, 146, 170. *See also* Baudrillard, Jean; control society; Deleuze, Gilles (Body without Organs);

disciplinary society; hyperreality; images; sovereign society; torture

Borges, Jorge Luis, 25–26, 246n94; and Aira, 22; and anonymous texts, 10, 14; and Arlt (Piglia), 3, 7–8, 22–23, 139, 141, 161, 214n27; appropriated by Piglia, 14, 160, 243n19, 243n25; and Baudrillard, 170, 171, 243n25; and chance and predictability, 162, 182–84; and creative plagiarism (Piglia), 2–3, 160, 163, 202–3, 215; and Deleuze, 24, 160, 163, 183, 205; and ideology (Piglia); 138, 141–42, 238n30; and infinity, 176, 183; influence on Piglia, 150, 160, 161, 176; and Joyce and Macedonio Fernández (Piglia), 176–85, 205; and Kafka (Piglia), 216n70; and Macedonio Fernández (Piglia), 10–11; in Piglia's literary genealogy, 21–22; and the subject, 185; and time, 153, 175, 183. *See also* Aira, César; Baudrillard, Jean; Deleuze, Gilles; Fernández, Macedonio; Joyce, James; Piglia, Ricardo, the subject; time

"Borges y yo" (Borges), 180, 246n94. *See also* Borges, Jorge Luis

Brecht, Bertolt, 7, 8, 9, 141, 215n31

Brown, Ralph, 144. *See also* Black Panthers; Cleaver, Eldridge; Malcolm X

Burroughs, William, 24–25, 109, 243n11, 250n19. *See also* cut-up

Cafulcurá, 43, 77, 195

Cage, John, 57, 71

capitalism: for Baudrillard, 126–28, 142–43; and colonialism, 44, 49–50, 11; and consumption, 54, 55, 60, 115, 125, 130, 168; for Deleuze and Guattari, 44–45, 47, 49–50, 68–69, 77–78, 125–28, 197, 202; early development in Argentina, 5, 15, 41–44, 46, 52, 83, 135, 143, 164, 197, 201, 203; and hyperreal control society, 17, 109–10, 116, 122, 130–32, 135, 190, 203–4; intertwining with violence, 5–6, 15, 40, 136, 138, 164, 199, 201, 203; importance for authors, 199, 206; and Kafka, 129, 145, 191; and literature, 2–3, 8–9, 23–24, 139–42, 187, 201–2; neoliberal reforms in the 1990s, 5–6, 16, 18, 53–54, 65, 68, 88, 166, 186, 197; philosophic roots of, 17, 162; as plane of immanence, 209–10; and sexuality, 125–26, 197, 204; societal effects of neoliberal reforms, 93–94, 111; for Stiegler, 168–69; and transition to democracy, 83–84; under dictatorship, 15, 51, 58–59 208; and universal history, 48–49. *See also* Baudrillard, Jean; colonialism; control society; Deleuze, Gilles; dictatorship (1976–83); freedom; globalization; Guattari, Félix; hyperreality; Kafka, Frantz; market (economics); Marxism; resistance; Stiegler, Bernard; structural adjustment program; the subject

Carri, Albertina, 55

The Castle (Kafka), 130. *See also* Kafka, Frantz

La cautiva (Echeverría), 31. *See also* Echeverría, Esteban

El cerebro musical (Aira), 75. *See also* Aira, César

Chakrabarty, Dipesh, 48–49, 138, 161, 237n8. *See also* colonialism

Chejfec, Sergio, 23, 24, 218n111, 219n112

Chronos. *See* time

Civilization and Barbarism, 30, 31–32, 38, 39–40, 47, 137–38, 158

La ciudad ausente (Piglia), 18, 81, 136, 163, 164–88, 188–95, 200, 204, 206, 210, 211–12, 243n2, 247n120. *See also* Piglia, Ricardo

"La ciudad y el campo" (Aira), 39. *See also* Aira, César

Clandestine Centers for Detention, Torture and Extermination, 89, 111, 227n104. *See also* Dirty War; disappearance; police; torture

class: and discipline, 87, 89; and literature, 8, 141, 196–97; ruling classes, 129, 250n42; working class, 4, 55, 59, 96. *See also* disciplinary society; ideology; Piglia, Ricardo; sovereign society

Cleaver, Eldridge, 144. *See also* Black Panthers; Brown, Ralph; Malcolm X

cogito: and Deleuze, 102, 150; and Descartes, 148–50, 152, 180; Descartes and Kant contrasted, 204, 239n68; and Kant, 17, 149–50, 152, 179, 200, 204; and the law, 155, 163, 164, 200; and Macedonio Fernández, 180, 185; and time, 152, 155, 163. *See also* Deleuze, Gilles; Descartes, René; Fernández, Macedonio; Kant, Immanuel; the law; Piglia, Ricardo; time

Cohen, Marcelo, 83–107; and Aira, 103, 107, 130, 132, 135–36; with Aira and Piglia, 5, 12, 15, 18–20, 24, 25, 177, 188, 192, 197, 198–212; and Arlt, 95; and Badiou, 202; and Baudrillard, 17, 112, 114–29, 135, 165, 168–71,

203, 205; and the Bible, 97–98, 99–103; and capitalism, 5, 6, 11, 14, 18, 23, 83–84, 88, 93–94, 108–10, 115–16, 122, 125–27, 130–32, 135, 197, 203–4, 209; co-functioning of Baudrillard and Deleuze in, 116, 119, 120, 122, 125–26, 129, 135, 165, 168–69, 203, 205; and control society, 108–34, 135–36, 191, 200, 203, 209; and Deleuze, 12,13–14, 17, 25, 95, 100, 102, 103–6, 165, 167–69, 194; and Dirty War, 16, 86–87, 89, 92, 105, 111, 198, 199–200, 203; and fascism, 119; and Foucault, 16–17, 85, 88–92, 94–95, 102–3, 106, 108–9, 114, 129, 167, 202–3; and Guattari, 208–10; influences on, 24–25, 109, 250n19; and Joyce, 96–97, 98–102, 174, 178; and Kafka, 110; and Kafka machine, 14–15, 79, 129–32, 188, 200–212; and mass media, 18, 23, 111–14, 120, 124, 125, 130, 135, 165, 168, 169, 171, 203, 210; and music, 116–19, 120, 130, 131, 210; and Piglia, 18, 96–97, 98, 99, 101, 136, 165–67, 169–71, 173, 174, 178, 210, 190–92, 195, 197, 217n85, 219n119, 243n11, 250n19; and transition to democracy, 5, 16, 24, 83–84, 86–87, 93–94, 108–9, 111–12, 130, 135, 166, 198, 200, 203; and undecidable point, 17, 106, 108, 111, 128, 129

Coleridge, Samuel Taylor, 151

collective enunciation, 144, 191. *See also* Deleuze, Gilles; Piglia, Ricardo

colonialism, 6, 38–39, 42, 49–50. *See also* Chakrabarty, Dipesh

CONADEP, 86, 229n16, 243n8. *See also* Clandestine Centers for Detention, Torture and Extermination; dictatorship; disappearance; Dirty War; death flights; torture

El congreso de la literatura (Aira), 68, 71, 75. *See also* Aira, César

Conquest of the Desert, 15, 32–35, 41, 137. *See also* Roca, Julio Argentino

control society: and becoming, 111–12, 125, 129, 135–36; and biopolitics, 113, 124–25, 128; and disciplinary society, 17, 108–10, 112–13, 120, 122, 167–68, 203; and mass media hyperreality 17, 18, 111–29, 135, 169–71, 191, 200, 203, 209; and psycho-power, 168–69; in postdictatorship Argentina, 109–10, 186; relevance to the study, 250n19. *See also* Deleuze, Gilles; disciplinary society; Foucault, Michel; indiscipline; sovereign society

convertibility, 14

Dirty War: and Conquest of the Desert, 15, 33–34, 37; disciplinary and sovereign power during, 16, 92–93; effect on authors, 198–99; equated with Nazism, 137, 148, 149, 150, 158, 162; following the transition to democracy, 17, 86, 93, 227n104; historical antecedents, 166–67; and landscape, 170–71; philosophical underpinnings, 136, 146–51, 155, 162–63, 164, 172, 185–86, 203–204; and resistance, 6, 105–6. *See also* CONADEP; death flights; Deleuze, Gilles; dictatorship; disappearance; disciplinary society; Foucault, Michel; Kant, Immanuel; Scilingo, Adolfo; sovereign society; torture

disappearance, 4, 36, 89, 92–93, 137, 146, 230n51. *See also* death flights; Dirty War; CONADEP

Discipline and Punish (Foucault), 88, 114. *See also* Foucault, Michel

disciplinary society, 88–90, 94–95; and control society, 17, 108–10, 112–13, 120, 122, 167–68, 203; problematizing the theory, 84–85, 89–90, 103, 105; redundancy of, 114, 135; and sovereign society, 16, 92–94, 110. *See also* control society; Deleuze, Gilles; Foucault, Michel; indiscipline; sovereign society

Disco (supermarket). *See* supermarkets

The Discourse on Method (Descartes), 146, 148, 149. *See also* Descartes, René

"The Disembodied Machine: Matter, Femininity and Nation in Piglia's La ciudad ausente" (Alicia Jagoe), 194

Duchamp, Marcel, 24

Duns Scotus, 72

dystopia, 84–85, 90, 111–12, 114, 135, 166–68, 184. *See also* utopia

Ébélot, Alfred, 30–31, 220n7, 220n20

Ecclesiastes, 100–3, 151, 191

Echeverría, Esteban, 31, 153

economic crash (2001), 24

The Eighteenth Brumaire of Louis Bonaparte (Marx), 39, 158. *See also* Marxism

"Elena Bellamuerte" (Fernández), 175. *See also* Fernández, Macedonio

Ema, la cautiva (Aira), 15, 17, 29–51, 52, 53, 73, 78, 137, 139, 140–41, 145, 162, 164, 195, 200, 201, 203, 217n74, 220n5, 220n6. *See also* Aira, César

"Emma Zunz" (Borges), 170, 243n19. *See also* Borges, Jorge Luis

escraches, 87–88, 229n19

Estrada, Ezequiel Martínez, 22

"An Ethics of Militant Engagement" (Laclau), 67–68

Europe: and capitalist expansion, 44; influence in nineteenth-century 31–32; music, 116; and Nazism, 148; and postcolonialism, 6–11, 48–49, 138, 161, 171, 237n8. *See also* capitalism; Chakrabarty, Dipesh; colonialism; scholarly hierarchization

event: for Badiou, 59–70, 202–203, 225n51; contrast Badiou and Deleuze, 53, 72–76; for Deleuze, 18, 157–58, 186–88, 190, 205; space as, 11, 208. *See also* Badiou, Alain; Deleuze, Gilles; Massey, Doreen

Una excursión a los indios ranqueles (Mansilla), 31, 47. *See also* Mansilla, Lucio V

exile, 98, 136, 182, 189–90, 198, 213n3, 248n158. *See also* Cohen, Marcelo; Piglia, Ricardo; utopia

"Exotismo" (Aira), 40–41. *See also* Aira, César

La experiencia dramática (Chejfec), 24, 219n112. *See also* Chejfec, Sergio

Ezekiel, 98–100

Facundo: civilización y barbarie (Sarmiento), 3, 31–32. *See also* civilization and barbarism; Sarmiento, Domingo Faustino

Falklands-Malvinas conflict, 24

false attribution, 3, 7, 22, 169–70, 178–79

false memory, 184, 186

Fanon, Frantz, 56, 59

fascism: in Kafka, 78, 129, 144, 191; microfascism, 146–49, 155, 164; and music, 119, 210; and *nacionalismo*, 38. *See also* becoming-other (becoming-music); Deleuze, Gilles; Kafka, Frantz; music; Nazism

Faulkner, William, 153

Fernández, Macedonio, 188, 246n94: according to Piglia, 10–11, 21, 22, 178, 185; and Borges (Piglia), 10–11; and Borges and Joyce (Piglia), 174–85, 205; character in *La ciudad ausente*, 165, 168, 173, 193, 195; and Deleuze, 186, 187; and negativity, 20. *See also* Borges, Jorge Luis; Cohen, Marcelo; Deleuze, Gilles; Joyce, James; negativity; Piglia, Ricardo; revolution

Finnegans Wake, 165, 174–82, 183, 206, 244n50, 245n73, 246n77. *See also* Joyce, James

and indigenous society, 44; and order words, 149; and schizophrenia, 69, 78, 197, 201. *See also* Badiou, Alain; Baudrillard, Jean; Deleuze, Gilles (Body without Organs; plane of immanence); hyperreality; images; schizophrenia

"In the Penal Colony" (Kafka), 110, 146, 147. *See also* Kafka, Frantz

Los incompletos (Chejfec), 24, 219n112. *See also* Chejfec, Sergio

indiscipline, 90, 92, 103, 105, 108. *See also* control society; disciplinary society; sovereign society

Indios, ejército y frontera (David Viñas), 35

El infinito (Aira), 66–67, 75. *See also* Aira, César

inflation, 35, 36–37, 58, 86, 115, 221n51. *See also* hyperinflation

"La innovación," (Aira), 65–66. *See also* Aira, César

Inolvidables veladas (Cohen), 166, 197, 236n95. *See also* Cohen, Marcelo

Insomnio (Cohen), 16, 83–107, 108, 112, 129, 130, 131, 166, 173, 190, 191, 211. *See also* Cohen, Marcelo

intensity, 12–14, 77, 104, 117, 206. *See also* Deleuze, Gilles (plateau; plane of immanence)

Jauretche, Arturo, 38, 222n60

Joyce, James, 202, 245n74; and Borges and Macedonio Fernández (Piglia), 176–85, 205; and *Insomnio*, 96–97, 98–102; and *La ciudad ausente*, 165, 173, 174–85, 246n83; and *Respiración artificial*, 155, 156; and Piglia, 153, 205, 249n13. *See also* Borges, Jorge Luis; Cohen, Marcelo; Fernández, Macedonio; Piglia, Ricardo

Joyce, Lucia, 178, 227n91

El juego de los mundos (Aira), 74, 77, 196. *See also* Aira, César

junta. *See* dictatorship

Kafka, Frantz, 15, 110, 216n70, 238n35; as character in *Respiración artificial*, 136, 137, 143–47, 162. *See also* Aira, César; Cohen, Marcelo; Deleuze, Gilles; *Kafka: Toward a Minor Literature*; Piglia, Ricardo

Kafka: Toward a Minor Literature (Deleuze and Guattari), 13, 14–15, 16, 17, 18, 23, 76–79, 129–32, 143–47, 188–97, 200–201,

206–7. *See also* Aira, César; Cohen, Marcelo; Deleuze, Gilles; machine; Piglia, Ricardo

Kant, Immanuel: and Deleuze, 146–49, 151–52, 239n53, 240n70; and Macedonio Fernández 180; and Piglia, 153, 159; teleological view of history, 48. *See also* cogito; Deleuze, Gilles; Descartes, René; Fernández, Macedonio; history; the law; Piglia, Ricardo; time

Lacan, Jacques, 56, 59, 60, 215n37

Laclau, Ernesto, 67–68

Lamborghini, Osvaldo, 15, 19, 22, 23, 57, 218n108

"La larga risa de todos estos años" (Rodolfo Enrique Fogwill), 24

Lautréamont, Comte de, 24

Lavalle, General Juan, 136

the law: and the author function, 2, 3, 141; and disciplinary society, 92; and Kant/Deleuze, 17, 149–50, 162–63, 164, 200, 204, 240n70; and the legacy of dictatorship, 93; of the market, 4, 93; origins in Argentina, 145–46; paranoiac and schizo, 196–97, 201, 204; and the state, 106; under dictatorship, 93, 146. *See also* Deleuze, Gilles; dictatorship; disciplinary society; Foucault, Michel; Full Stop Law; history; Kant, Immanuel; Law of Due Obedience; machine; market; transition to democracy

Law of Due Obedience, 86

Lenta biografía (Chejfec), 24, 218n11. *See also* Chejfec, Sergio

Leibniz, Gottfried Wilhelm, 153

Lévi-Strauss, Claude, 41, 45

Ley de Obediencia Debida. *See* Law of Due Obedience

Ley de Punto Final. *See* Full Stop Law

Liberating Revolution. *See* Aramburu, General Pedro Eugenio

Los Libros (journal), 8, 9, 215n32, 215n37

La liebre, 15, 30, 77, 195. *See also* Aira, César

Ligeti, György, 25

literary genealogies, 21–23

The Logic of Sense (Deleuze), 183, 247n120. *See also* Deleuze, Gilles

Los siete locos (Arlt), 95. *See also* Alrt, Roberto

"La lotería en Babilonia" (Borges), 182–84. *See also* Borges, Jorge Luis

Lugones, Leopoldo, 139, 161, 167

Lugones, Leopoldo Jr., 166–67, 243n5

machines: Kafka-machine, 12–15, 76–79, 129–32, 188–96, 200–212; literary machine in *La ciudad ausente*, 18, 165–66, 168, 170, 171–87, 189, 193–96, 243n1; state machines and assemblages, 44–45, 78, 106, 112, 130–32, 197, 200, 201, 222n85. *See also* Aira, César; Cohen, Marcelo; Deleuze, Gilles; Guattari, Félix; Piglia, Ricardo

Madres de la Plaza, 193

Mahler, Gustav, 92, 99

Malcolm X, 144. *See also* Black Panthers; Brown, Ralph; Cleaver, Eldridge

Mansilla, Lucio V., 31–32, 47, 49

Mao Zedong: and Aira, 52, 55–56, 59, 60, 76, 78, 140; and Piglia, 7, 8, 9, 215n34

market (economics): and control society, 109, 110–11, 115–16; and literature 20, 67, 73; and the state 49; labor market, 46, 53; transition to global market 4, 53, 83–84, 108, 166. *See also* capitalism; control society; globalization; the law; transition to democracy

marketing, 111–12, 115, 124

Martínez de Hoz, José Alfredo, 37, 221n51

Marxism: and Aira, 39, 40, 44, 48, 49, 50, 56, 59; and Cohen, 126; and *Los Libros* 215n37; and Piglia, 7, 142, 158, 213n3, 215n31. *See also The Eighteenth Brumaire of Louis Bonaparte*

Massey, Doreen, 11, 20, 207–8

mass media: between control and psycho-power, 171; and hyperreal control society, 18, 111–14, 120, 130, 135, 165, 203; and Integrated World Capitalism, 210; and psycho-power, 168–69, 204; and Puig, 23; and sexuality, 124–25; substitute for military power, 17, 200. *See also* Baudrillard, Jean; Deleuze, Gilles; Guattari, Félix; hyperreality; images; Puig, Manuel; Stiegler, Bernard; transition to democracy

maximum individual. *See* Fernández, Macedonio

May 1968, 56, 58, 87, 209–10

Mein Kampf (Hitler), 148, 149. *See also* Hitler, Adolf

melancholy. *See* mourning

Melon, Jean-François, 43

"La memoria de Shakespeare" (Borges), 180. *See also* Borges, Jorge Luis

memory: implantation, 165–66, 175, 184, 186–87, 193, 198; and postdictatorship, 5, 55, 184; and time, 12, 155–56, 180–81, 184.

See also Deleuze, Gilles; melancholy; Piglia, Ricardo; postdictatorship; time

Menem, Carlos Saúl: and corruption, 86; and "disguised terror," 4, 93; economic parallels with previous dictatorships, 58–59; and mass media, 111–12; and opening to transnational market, 4, 16, 53–54, 88, 108, 109, 135; and pardons, 86; and presidential powers, 93–94. *See also* capitalism; convertibility; globalization; mass media; structural adjustment program

metamorphosis: and Aira, 16–17, 23, 26, 27, 69–71, 73, 75–77, 143; and Cohen, 106, 125; and Piglia, 140, 158, 179, 193–94. *See also* Aira, César; becoming-other; Deleuze, Gilles; Kafka, Franz

military. See Cohen, Marcelo; Conquest of the Desert; coups; dictatorship; Full Stop Law; Law of Due Obedience; military parades; military uprisings

military parades, 151

military uprisings, 93; in *Insomnio*, 91–92, 99, 101, 106

misunderstanding, 26, 27

Möbius strip, 15, 188, 197

money: in Aira, 35, 36–37, 42–43, 44, 46, 48, 49–50, 67; in Arlt, 7; comparing Aira and Arlt, 140–41; and inheritance, 142. *See also* capitalism

Montoneros. *See* armed militants

mourning, 4, 5, 84, 214

"La muerte y la brújula" (Borges), 26, 183. *See also* Borges, Jorge Luis

multiplicity, 11, 72, 100, 208, 211

Museo de la Novela de la Eterna (Fernández), 174, 175, 176, 179, 180, 185, 188, 206. *See also* Fernández, Macedonio

music, 10–11, 25, 58, 71, 116–19, 120, 130, 131, 210. *See also* becoming-other (becoming-music); Cage, John; Deleuze, Gilles (the refrain); Ligeti, György; Mahler, Gustav

"Music of Changes" (Cage), 71. *See also* Cage, John

nacionalismo, 38. *See also* history (political uses of)

Narraciones viajeras: César Aira y Juan José Saer (Nancy Fernández), 29

nation: consolidation of, 15, 33–34, 145–46, 164, 167; contested conceptions of, 38; and globalization, 11, 18, 24, 113; as plane of im-

police: history of, 34, 37, 57, 93, 145, 146; market as, 49; and torture, 93, 166–67, 186, 243n8

political violence. See armed militants; coup; dictatorship; Dirty War; disappearance; police; structural violence; torture

polyphony, 25, 197, 207–12. *See also* Deleuze, Gilles (plane of immanence; univocity of being); Ligeti, György; Massey, Doreen

postcolonialism. See Chakrabarty, Dipesh

postdictatorship, 4–5, 24, 55, 84, 87–88, 110, 166, 167, 198. *See also* transition to democracy

power. See control society; dictatorship; Dirty War; disciplinary society; sovereign society; transition to democracy

praxis, 6, 20, 21, 53, 72, 202

"The Precession of Simulacra" (Baudrillard), 171, 233n28. *See also* Baudrillard, Jean

Prisión perpetua (Piglia), 173. *See also* Piglia, Ricardo

Process of National Reorganization, 33–34, 137. *See also* dictatorship

property, 2–3, 7, 24, 89, 117, 141–42

Proudhon, Pierre-Joseph, 141

Proust, Marcel, 202

Provincializing Europe: Postcolonial Thought and Historical Difference. See Chakrabarty, Dipesh

La prueba (Aira), 16, 51, 52–76, 77–78, 79, 103, 106, 140, 199–200, 201, 202, 211. *See also* Aira, César

psychoanalysis, 23, 56, 149, 215n37

psycho-power. *See* Stiegler, Bernard

Puig, Manuel, 22, 23, 217n77

Pumper Nic, 51, 54–55

Pynchon, Thomas, 24–25

Rancière, Jacques, 187, 199

ready-made, 24, 57, 66

the real: in Aira, 65–66; in Badiou, 61, 62, 63, 64, 65, 66, 76; critique of Badiou and Deleuze, 76; in Deleuze, 72, 177, 207; and dictatorship, 172. *See also* Aira, César; Badiou, Alain; Deleuze, Gilles; dictatorship; Žižek, Slavoj

repetition. *See* difference and repetition

resistance: in Aira, Cohen and Piglia, 12, 197, 199, 202, 206, 209–12; and becoming, 16, 73–74, 106, 108, 116–19, 135, 160; and civil disobedience, 103; as control, 17, 111, 119–20, 123–25, 128, 132, 200; and

dictatorship, 5–6, 105, 185–6; and event, 18, 186–88; feminine, 193–94; and Integrated World Capitalism, 18, 209–12; and Kafka, 15, 78–79; limits of 79, 105–7, 108, 129, 135, 179, 209; and literature, 20, 139–41, 187, 208; and power, 2, 4, 5, 12, 83–84, 116; and rumor, 121–24, 165, 172–73, 186, 191; and schizophrenia, 68–69; and seduction, 17, 124–29. *See also* Aira, César; Baudrillard, Jean; becoming; becoming-other; Cohen, Marcelo; Deleuze, Gilles; Guattari, Félix; *Kafka: Toward a Minor Literature*; machine; Madres de la Plaza; revolution; rumor; schizophrenia

Respiración artificial (Piglia), 3, 15, 17–18, 19, 135–63, 164, 165, 167, 179, 180, 188–90, 195, 196, 197, 204, 205, 206, 209, 237n2, 238n28. *See also* Piglia, Ricardo

revolution: and artistic vanguard, 18; in Badiou, 16, 60, 66, 75, 202; fervor in the 1960s, 53, 57–58, 59, 83, 135, 197, 201; in *Insomnio*, 91–92, 99, 102, 103, 106, 191; and Integrated World Capitalism, 210, 211; limits of, 76, 105, 106, 120, 131; and negativity, 204; in *El oído absoluto*, 119, 191; revolutionary machine-to-come, 187, 191, 199, 203, 212; and utopia, 187, 199. *See also* Aira, César; Badiou, Alain; Cohen, Marcelo; Cordobazo; Deleuze, Gilles; Guattari, Félix; negativity; utopia

Les Revue de Deux Mondes (magazine), 30

"The Rime of the Ancient Mariner" (Coleridge), 151. *See also* Coleridge, Samuel Taylor

Roca, General Julio Argentino, 15, 32, 33, 34, 41, 47, 145. *See also* Conquest of the Desert

Rosas, General Juan Manuel, 32, 77, 136, 138, 195

Rozitchner, León, 4–5, 93, 209

rumor, 17, 121–24, 128, 173, 178, 186, 191. *See also* Baudrillard, Jean; hyperreality; resistance

Sabattini, Amadeo, 146

Saer, Juan José, 15, 20, 21, 23, 29, 230n38

Sarmiento, Domingo Faustino, 3, 31–32, 38, 39–40, 47, 138. *See also* Civilization and Barbarism

Scienza Nuovo. See Vico, Giambattista

schizophrenia: and becoming, 16, 69–70, 197, 205; criticisms of, 76; and desire, 23, 68–69,

73–74, 196–97, 204; and the law, 197, 201; mental illness, 178, 226n91; and the subject, 72, 78, 202; and universal history, 226n91. *See also* Aira, César; becoming; becoming-other; Deleuze, Gilles; the law; the subject

scholarly hierarchization, 6–11, 161, 237n8. *See also* colonialism

Scilingo, Adolfo, 87. *See also* death flights

"The Second Coming" (Yeats), 150–51. *See also* Yeats, W. B.

Seduction (Baudrillard), 124. *See also* Baudrillard, Jean

Shakespeare, William, 158, 180

simulacrum: in Baudrillard, 112, 113–16, 119–20, 125, 165, 169–71, 203, 233n28, 243n25, 244n29; in Badiou, 67–68; in Deleuze, 100; contrast Baudrillard and Deleuze, 17, 120, 129; and rumor, 123; and seduction, 126–29; and psycho-power, 168. *See also* Badiou, Alain; Baudrillard, Jean; Deleuze, Gilles; hyperreality; rumor; Stiegler, Bernard

simulation. *See* Baudrillard, Jean; hyperreality; mass media; simulacrum

Song of Songs, 97, 100, 101

sovereign society, 90–92; and control society, 110; and dictatorship, 92–93; and disciplinary society, 16, 92–94, 110; and transition, 94, 108. *See also* control society; disciplinary society; Foucault, Michel; indiscipline

space. *See* Massey, Doreen

Spinoza, Baruch, 72, 153

state. *See* the law; machine; nation

statements. *See* Foucault, Michel

state terrorism. *See* Dirty War

Stephens, James, 174

Steuart, Sir James, 44

Stevenson, Robert Louis, 173–74, 244n46

Stiegler, Bernard, 168–69, 210

The Strange Case of Dr. Jekyll and Mr. Hyde (Stevenson), 173. *See also* Stevenson, Robert Louis

structural adjustment program, 5, 14, 53, 84, 86. *See also* capitalism; convertibility; globalization; market (economics); Menem, Carlos Saúl

structural violence, 6, 131

the subject: for Badiou, 16, 60–62, 65, 202–3, 225n51; and Borges, Joyce, and Macedonio Fernández, 180, 185, 186; in Clandestine Centers for Detention, Torture and Exter-

mination, 111; and the cogito and the law, 148–50, 152, 179; for Deleuze, 70, 103, 104, 106, 152, 154; difference between Badiou and Deleuze, 72–76; of enunciation/the statement, 190–93, 194, 196; for Foucault, 75–76, 106; in Foucauldian statements, 102–3; for Guattari, 209–11; in hyperreality, 126–27; and microfascism, 147; and Piglia, 246n94; in postdictatorship, 55; and schizophrenia, 68, 72, 78, 202. *See also* Badiou, Alain; Borges, Jorge Luis; Baudrillard, Jean; Clandestine Centers for Detention, Torture and Extermination; cogito; Deleuze, Gilles; fascism; Foucault, Michel; hyperreality; Joyce, James; Fernández, Macedonio; machine; Piglia, Ricardo; postdictatorship; schizophrenia

supermarkets, 51, 52, 54, 59, 224n12

Tantalia (Fernández), 174. *See also* Fernández, Macedonio

"Tema del traidor y del héroe" (Borges), 150. *See also* Borges, Jorge Luis

time: Aion and Chronos, 12, 18, 183–84, 186, 247n120; and Aira, 74–75; and Bergson, 241n127; and Borges, 175, 183, 185; and disciplinary society, 89–90, 94, 109; in Ecclesiastes, 101; and Joyce, 175, 178, 181, 184, 185; and the Kantian cogito, 152; and Macedonio Fernández, 185; and Piglia, 152–53; and plane of immanence, 207, 208; portmanteaux and virtual objects, 174–75; three syntheses of time, 17, 151–60, 162–65, 179–83, 186, 200, 241n106; 241n113; and space, 11, 207–8. *See also* Bergson, Henri; Borges, Jorge Luis; cogito; Deleuze, Gilles; disciplinary society; difference and repetition; Ecclesiastes; Fernández, Macedonio; history; Joyce, James; Kant, Immanuel; Massey, Doreen; Piglia, Ricardo

A Thousand and One Nights, 31, 177

A Thousand Plateaus (Deleuze and Guattari), 12–14, 68, 69–70, 240n70. *See also* Deleuze, Gilles; Guattari, Félix

"Tlön, Uqbar, Orbis Tertius" (Borges), 10. *See also* Borges, Jorge Luis

torture: during Dirty War, 36, 92–93, 105, 184, 230n38, 243n8; historical instances of, 37, 166–67; and sovereign society, 90–92, 110; continued instances of, 93.